1991



Dear Daddy,

"You are the best Daddy known to man on the face of the earth!!"

Love, Joshua

Mommy, Suzanna, Banana, Duchess + Sadie

# ROGER CARAS'
# TREASURY OF GREAT
# DOG STORIES

# ROGER CARAS'

# TREASURY OF GREAT

# DOG STORIES

Robson Books

First published in Great Britain in 1988 by Robson Books Ltd,
Bolsover House, 5–6 Clipstone Street, London W1P 7EB



**British Library Cataloguing in Publication Data**

Caras, Roger A. (Roger Andrew), *1928–*
Roger Caras' treasury of great dog stories.
I. Title
813'.54[F]

ISBN 0 86051 523 0



Printed in Great Britain by Redwood Burn Limited,
Trowbridge, Wiltshire.

Grateful acknowledgment is made to the following for permission to reprint copyright material:

Sholom Aleichem: "Rabchik, A Jewish Dog." Copyright by the Family of Sholom Aleichem. Reprinted by permission of Rosenman Colin Freund Lewis and Cohen.

Vereen Bell: "Brag Dog." Copyright 1939 by Vereen Bell. Reprinted by permission of Harold Ober Associates, Inc.

Ray Bradbury: "The Emissary." Copyright 1947 by Ray Bradbury; copyright renewed © 1975 by Ray Bradbury. Reprinted by permission of Don Congdon Associates, Inc.

Arthur C. Clarke: "Dog Star." Copyright © 1962 by Galaxy Publishing Corporation. Reprinted by permission of the author and the author's agents, Scott Meredith Literary Agency, Inc., 845 Third Avenue, New York, N.Y. 10022.

Lester del Rey: "The Faithful." Copyright 1938 by Street & Smith Publications, Inc.; copyright renewed © 1966 by Lester del Rey. Reprinted by permission of the author and the author's agents, Scott Meredith Literary Agency, Inc., 845 Third Avenue, New York, N.Y. 10022.

Walter D. Edmonds: "Moses." Copyright 1938 by Walter D. Edmonds; copyright renewed © 1965 by Walter D. Edmonds. Reprinted by permission of Harold Ober Associates, Inc.

Mel Ellis: "Mister Dog." Copyright 1950 by *Field & Stream.* Reprinted by permission of Larry Sternig Literary Agency.

Edward Fenton: "Gun-Shy." From *Us and the Duchess,* copyright 1945, 1946, 1947 by Edward Fenton. Reprinted by permission of Doubleday & Company, Inc.

Corey Ford: "Slipstream." Copyright 1949 by Corey Ford; copyright renewed © 1976 by S. John Stebbins and Hugh Grey. Reprinted by permission of Harold Ober Associates, Inc.

Zane Grey: "Don." Copyright 1928 by Zane Grey; copyright renewed © 1953 by Zane Grey, Inc. Reprinted by permission of Dr. Loren Grey.

Dion Henderson: "Broken Treaty." Copyright 1954 by *Field & Stream.* "The Test." Copyright © 1958 by Curtis Publishing Company. Reprinted by permission of Larry Sternig Literary Agency.

MacKinlay Kantor: "The Voice of Bugle Ann." Copyright 1935 by MacKinlay Kantor. Reprinted by permission of John Hawkins & Associates, Inc., 71 West 23rd Street, New York, N.Y. 10010.

Eric Knight: "Lassie Come-Home." Copyright 1940 by Jere Knight; copyright renewed © 1968 by Jere Knight, Betty Noyes Knight, Winifred Knight Mewborn, and Jennie Knight Moore. Reprinted by permission of Curtis Brown, Ltd.

D. H. Lawrence: "Rex." From *Phoenix: The Posthumous Papers of D. H. Lawrence,* edited and with an introduction by Edward D. McDonald. Copyright 1936 by Frieda Lawrence; copyright renewed © 1964 by the Estate of the late Frieda Lawrence Ravagli. Reprinted by permission of Viking Penguin, Inc.

Don Marquis: "Blood Will Tell." Copyright 1915 by Crowell Publishers from *The Revolt of the Oyster* by Don Marquis. Reprinted by permission of Doubleday & Company, Inc.

R. K. Narayan: "Attila" and "The Blind Dog." From *Malgudi Days* by R. K. Narayan. Copyright © 1975, 1978, 1981, 1982 by R. K. Narayan. Reprinted by permission of Viking Penguin, Inc.

Françoise Sagan: "A Dog's Night," from *Silken Eyes*. Copyright © 1975 by Flammarion. English translation copyright © 1977 by Andre Deutsch Ltd. and Dell Publishing Co., Inc. Reprinted by permission of Georges Borchardt Inc.

Booth Tarkington: "Blue Milk." First published in *The Saturday Evening Post.* Copyright 1934 by The Curtis Publishing Company. Reprinted by permission of Brandt & Brandt Literary Agents, Inc.

Albert Payson Terhune: "The Coming of Lad," from *The Heart of a Dog.* Copyright 1924 by Doubleday & Company, Inc. Reprinted by permission of the publisher. "The Grudge," from *Buff, A Collie and Other Dog Stories.* Copyright 1921 by Doubleday & Company, Inc. Reprinted by permission of the publisher.

# CONTENTS

## *Roger Caras*

# INTRODUCTION

Quite literally I have spent my entire life with dogs. There was a Boston terrier already on deck when I arrived. He was followed by a collie and then a wire fox terrier and an English cocker spaniel, and it has never stopped. My wife and I have ten dogs today, our daughter and her husband have two, and our son and his wife have one. Most of our friends have dogs, many of them more than one. Of the one hundred and fifty letters I receive in an average week, at least half of them are about dogs. Because I do work in television some of America's most familiar faces and names have asked me to help them find the right dog. David Hartman got a Labrador retriever, Harry Reasoner and Morley Safer got goldens, Barbara Walters a toy poodle, Bob Brown a PBGV, a French breed whose full name is Petite Basset Griffon Vendeen. He and his wife Nancy had seen our PBGV and fallen in love.

The point to all this name- and dog dropping is that I have always taken dogs for granted. For some people a home isn't a home unless it has a piano, or a fireplace, or some other natural adjunct. For me a house or an apartment becomes a home when you add one set of four legs, a happy tail, and that indescribable measure of love we call a dog.

But something important for all of us has been happening while I have been taking dogs for granted. The dog has been moving up in station and in its influence on adults. Scientists have been discovering all kinds of special things about dogs they presumably did not know before. The dog is therapeutic. Companion animals lower blood pressure in most people. Those people who have managed to create that bond that can exist between a human being and an animal tend to live longer, have fewer heart attacks, get fewer diseases, and, when they do get sick, suffer less and get well quicker than others. Children growing up with pets they love and care for seem to turn out to be good parents and perhaps more selfless mates.

Perhaps it is true that our move from rural roots to the urban and suburban reality of today have deprived us of something Tolstoy understood particularly well. If the unrelenting urban demands that have wrenched many of us away from the soil and the land have been ameliorated somewhat by companion animals, then the new and vital importance of dogs to our mental and physical well-being becomes very clear.

This anthology captures the human-animal bond, specifically our long and close relationship to the dog, in the words of current and recent writers of special note. Together they underline an important point. Dog stories are no longer largely children's fare as has been assumed by many in the past. Stories about dogs, and people and dogs, are increasingly the stuff of an adults's evening in a comfortable armchair. Since World War II, dogs (and cats) have made cities much more tolerable. They have also softened the sharp edges for the lonely, the bereaved, and the stressed.

In the pages that follow read what Mark Twain knew and felt about dogs ("A Dog's Tale") and, for contrast, the sense of it all as expressed by Arthur C. Clarke ("Dog Star") and Françoise Sagan ("A Dog's Night"). There you have as good a literary spread as anyone could want, three brilliant minds, one a nineteenth-century American humorist and philosopher, one a contemporary Frenchwoman, and the other a timeless British genius who would have invented the solar system if God hadn't already done it for him. That minds of this diversity and with all the obviously inherent variables would stop and contemplate the dog must tell us something very important. We can't remember a time, they are saying, when dogs have not been the raw material of adult dreams as well as those of pre-adults. The very words *companion animals* carry a quality of magic that only the truly best writers in the world could hope to capture. We think we have dealt fairly with that idea here.

My thanks go to Martin Greenberg, the best anthologist alive, for his widom and taste in helping me select and assemble the stories you are about to read.

*July 6, 1986*
*East Hampton, Long Island.*

## *Jack London*

# FOR THE LOVE OF A MAN

It was beautiful spring weather, but neither dogs nor humans were aware of it. Each day the sun rose earlier and set later. It was dawn by three in the morning, and twilight lingered till nine at night. The whole day long was a blaze of sunshine. The ghostly winter silence had given way to the great spring murmur of awakening life. This murmur arose from all the land, fraught with the joy of living. It came from the things that lived and moved again, things which had been as dead and which had not moved during the long months of frost. The sap was rising in the pines. The willows and aspens were bursting out in young buds. Shrubs and vines were putting on fresh garbs of green. Crickets sang in the nights, and in the days all manner of creeping, crawling things rustled forth into the sun. Partridges and woodpeckers were booming and knocking in the forest. Squirrels were chattering, birds singing, and overhead honked the wildfowl driving up from the south in cunning wedges that split the air.

From every hill slope came the trickle of running water, the music of unseen fountains. All things were thawing, bending, snapping. The Yukon was straining to break loose the ice that bound it down. It ate away from beneath; the sun ate from above. Air holes formed, fissures sprang and spread apart, while thin sections of ice fell through bodily into the river. And amid all this bursting, rendering, throbbing of awakening life, under the blazing sun and through the soft-sighing breezes, like wayfarers to death, staggered the two men, the woman, and the huskies.

With the dogs falling, Mercedes weeping and riding, Hal swearing innocuously, and Charles's eyes wistfully watering, they staggered into John Thornton's camp at the mouth of White River. When they halted, the dogs dropped down as though they had all been struck dead. Mercedes dried her eyes and looked at John Thornton. Charles sat down on a log to rest. He sat down very slowly and painstakingly what of his great stiffness. Hal did the talking. John Thornton was whittling the last touches on an ax handle he had made from a stick of birch. He whittled and listened, gave monosyllabic replies, and, when it was asked, terse advice. He knew the breed, and he gave his advice in the certainty that it would not be followed.

"They told us up above that the bottom was dropping out of the trail and that the best thing for us to do was lay over," Hal said, in response to Thornton's warning to take no more chances on the rotten ice. "They told us we couldn't make

White River, and here we are." This last with a sneering ring of triumph in it.

"And they told you true," John Thornton answered. "The bottom's likely to drop out at any moment. Only fools, with the blind luck of fools, could have made it. I tell you straight, I wouldn't risk my carcass on that ice for all the gold in Alaska."

"That's because you're not a fool, I suppose," said Hal. "All the same, we'll go on to Dawson." He uncoiled his whip. "Get up there, Buck! Hi! Get up there! Mush on!"

Thornton went on whittling. It was idle, he knew, to get between a fool and his folly; while two or three fools more or less would not alter the scheme of things.

But the team did not get up at the command. It had been long since passed into the stage where blows were required to rouse it. The whip flashed out, here and there, on its merciless errands. John Thornton compressed his lips. Solleks was the first to crawl to his feet. Teek followed. Joe came next, yelping with pain. Pike made painful efforts. Twice he fell over, when half up, and on the third attempt managed to rise. Buck made no effort. He lay quietly where he had fallen. The lash bit into him again and again, but he neither whined nor struggled. Several times Thornton started, as though to speak, but changed his mind. A moisture came into his eyes, and, as the whipping continued, he arose and walked irresolutely up and down.

This was the first time Buck had failed, in itself a sufficient reason to drive Hal into a rage. He exchanged the whip for the customary club. Buck refused to move under the rain of heavier blows which now fell upon him. Like his mates, he was barely able to get up, but, unlike them, he had made up his mind not to get up. He had a vague feeling of impending doom. This had been strong upon him when he pulled in to the bank, and it had not departed from him. What of the thin and rotten ice he had felt under his feet all day, it seemed that he sensed disaster close at hand, out there ahead on the ice where his master was trying to drive him. He refused to stir. So greatly had he suffered, and so far gone was he, that the blows did not hurt much. And as they continued to fall upon him, the spark of life within flickered and went down. It was nearly out. He felt strangely numb. As though from a great distance, he was aware that he was being beaten. The last sensations of pain left him. He no longer felt anything, though very faintly he could hear the impact of the club upon his body. But it was no longer his body, it seemed so far away.

And then, suddenly, without warning, uttering a cry that was inarticulate and more like the cry of an animal, John Thornton sprang upon the man who wielded the club. Hal was hurled backward, as though struck by a falling tree. Mercedes screamed. Charles looked on wistfully, wiped his watery eyes, but did not get up because of his stiffness.

John Thornton stood over Buck, struggling to control himself, too convulsed with rage to speak.

"If you strike that dog again, I'll kill you," he at last managed to say in a choking voice.

"It's my dog," Hal replied, wiping the blood from his mouth as he came back. "Get out of my way, or I'll fix you. I'm going to Dawson."

Thornton stood between him and Buck, and evinced no intention of getting out of the way. Hal drew his long hunting knife. Mercedes screamed, cried, laughed, and manifested the chaotic abandonment of hysteria. Thornton rapped Hal's knuckles with the ax handle, knocking the knife to the ground. He rapped his knuckles again as he tried to pick it up. Then he stooped, picked it up himself, and with two strokes cut Buck's traces.

Hal had no fight left in him. Besides, his hands were full with his sister, or his arms, rather; while Buck was too near dead to be of further use in hauling the sled. A few minutes later they pulled out from the bank and down the river. Buck heard them go and raised his head to see. Pike was leading, Sol-leks was at the wheel, and between were Joe and Teek. They were limping and staggering. Mercedes was riding the loaded sled. Hal guided at the gee-pole, and Charles stumbled along in the rear.

As Buck watched them, Thornton knelt beside him and with rough, kindly hands searched for broken bones. By the time his search had disclosed nothing more than many bruises and a state of terrible starvation, the sled was a quarter of a mile away. Dog and man watched it crawling along over the ice. Suddenly, they saw its back end drop down, as into a rut, and the gee-pole, with Hal clinging to it, jerk into the air. Mercedes's scream came to their ears. They saw Charles turn and make one step to run back, and then a whole section of ice give way and dogs and humans disappear. A yawning hole was all that was to be seen. The bottom had dropped out of the trail.

John Thornton and Buck looked at each other.

"You poor devil," said John Thornton, and Buck licked his hand.

When John Thornton froze his feet in the previous December, his partners had made him comfortable and left him to get well, going on themselves up the river to get out a raft of sawlogs for Dawson. He was still limping slightly at the time he rescued Buck, but with the continued warm weather even the slight limp left him. And here, lying by the riverbank through the long spring days, watching the running water, listening lazily to the songs of birds and the hum of nature, Buck slowly won back his strength.

A rest comes very good after one has traveled three thousand miles, and it must be confessed that Buck waxed lazy as his wounds healed, his muscles swelled out, and the flesh came back to cover his bones. For that matter, they were all loafing—Buck, John Thornton, and Skeet and Nig—waiting for the raft to come that was to carry them down to Dawson. Skeet was a little Irish setter who early made friends with Buck, who, in a dying condition, was unable to resent her first advances. She had the doctor trait which some dogs possess, and as a mother cat washes her kittens, so she washed and cleansed Buck's wounds. Regularly, each morning after he had finished his breakfast, she performed her self-appointed task, till he came to look for her ministrations as much as he did for Thornton's. Nig, equally friendly, though less demonstrative, was a huge black dog, half bloodhound and half deerhound, with eyes that laughed and a boundless good nature.

To Buck's surprise these dogs manifested no jealousy toward him. They seemed to share the kindliness and largeness of John Thornton. As Buck grew stronger they enticed him into all sorts of ridiculous games, in which Thornton himself could not forbear to join, and in this fashion Buck romped through his convalescence and into a new existence. Love, genuine passionate love, was his for the first time. This he had never experienced at Judge Miller's down in the sun-kissed Santa Clara Valley. With the Judge's sons, hunting and tramping, it had been a working partnership; with the Judge's grandsons, a sort of pompous guardianship; and with the Judge himself, a stately and dignified friendship. But love that was feverish and burning, that was adoration, that was madness, it had taken John Thornton to arouse.

This man had saved his life, which was something; but, further, he was the ideal master. Other men saw to the welfare of their dogs from a sense of duty and business expediency; he saw to the welfare of his as if they were his own children, because he could not help it. And he saw further. He never forgot a kindly greeting or a cheering word, and to sit down for a long talk with them ("gas," he called it) was as much his delight as theirs. He had a way of taking Buck's head roughly between his hands, and resting his own head upon Buck's, of shaking him back and forth, the while calling him ill names that to Buck were loving names. Buck knew no greater joy than that rough embrace and the sound of murmured oaths, and at each jerk back and forth it seemed that his heart would be shaken out of his body, so great was its ecstasy. And when, released, he sprang to his feet, his mouth laughing, his eyes eloquent, his throat vibrant with unuttered sound, and in that fashion remained without movement, John Thornton would reverently exclaim, "God! You can all but speak!"

Buck had a trick of love expression that was akin to hurt. He would often seize Thornton's hand in his mouth and close so fiercely that the flesh bore the impress of his teeth for some time afterward. And as Buck understood the oaths to be love words, so the man understood this feigned bite for a caress.

For the most part, however, Buck's love was expressed in adoration. While he went wild with happiness when Thornton touched him or spoke to him, he did not seek these tokens. Unlike Skeet, who was wont to shove her nose under Thornton's hand and nudge and nudge till petted, or Nig, who would stalk up and rest his great head on Thornton's knee, Buck was content to adore at a distance. He would lie by the hour, eager, alert, at Thornton's feet, looking up into his face, dwelling upon it, studying it, following with keenest interest each fleeting expression, every movement or change of feature. Or, as chance might have it, he would lie farther away, to the side or rear, watching the outlines of the man and the occasional movements of his body. And often, such was the communion in which they lived, the strength of Buck's gaze would draw John Thornton's head around, and he would return the gaze, without speech, his heart shining out of his eyes as Buck's heart shone out.

For a long time after his rescue, Buck did not like Thornton to get out of his sight. From the moment he left the tent to when he entered it again, Buck would follow at his heels.

His transient masters since he had come into the Northland had bred in him a fear that no master could be permanent. He was afraid that Thornton would pass out of his life as Perrault and François and the Scotch half-breed had passed out. Even in the night, in his dreams, he was haunted by this fear. At such times he would shake off sleep and creep through the chill to the flap of the tent, where he would stand and listen to the sound of his master's breathing.

But in spite of this great love he bore John Thornton, which seemed to bespeak the soft civilizing influence, the strain of the primitive, which the Northland had aroused in him, remained alive and active. Faithfulness and devotion, things born of fire and roof, were his; yet he retained his wildness and wiliness. He was a thing of the wild, come in from the wild to sit by John Thornton's fire, rather than a dog of the soft Southland stamped with the marks of generations of civilization. Because of his very great love he could not steal from this man, but from any other man, in any other camp, he did not hesitate an instant; while the cunning with which he stole enabled him to escape detection.

His face and body were scored by the teeth of many dogs, and he fought as fiercely as ever and more shrewdly. Skeet and Nig were too good-natured for quarreling—besides, they belonged to John Thornton; but the strange dog, no matter what the breed or valor, swiftly acknowledged Buck's supremacy or found himself struggling for life with a terrible antagonist. And Buck was merciless. He had learned well the law of club and fang, and he never forewent an advantage or drew back from a foe he had started on the way to death. He had lessoned from Spitz, and from the chief fighting dogs of the police and mail, and knew there was no middle course. He must master or be mastered; while to show mercy was a weakness. Mercy did not exist in the primordial life. It was misunderstood for fear, and such misunderstandings made for death. Kill or be killed, eat or be eaten, was the law; and this mandate, down out of the depths of time, he obeyed.

He was older than the days he had seen and the breaths he had drawn. He linked the past with the present, and the eternity behind him throbbed through him in a mighty rhythm to which he swayed as the tides and seasons swayed. He sat by John Thornton's fire, a broad-breasted dog, white-fanged and long-furred; but behind him were the shades of all manner of dogs, half-wolves and wild wolves, urgent and prompting, tasting the savor of the meat he ate, thirsting for the water he drank, scenting the wind with him, listening with him and telling him the sounds made by the wild life in the forest, dictating his moods, directing his actions, lying down to sleep with him when he lay down, and dreaming with him and beyond him and becoming themselves the stuff of his dreams.

So peremptorily did these shades beckon him, that each day mankind and the claims of mankind slipped further from him. Deep in the forest a call was sounding, and as often as he heard this call, mysteriously thrilling and luring, he felt compelled to turn his back upon the fire and the beaten earth around it, and to plunge into the forest, and on and on, he knew not where or why; nor did he wonder where or why, the call sounding imperiously, deep in the forest. But as often as he gained the soft unbroken earth and the green shade, the love for John Thornton drew him back to the fire again.

Thornton alone held him. The rest of mankind was as nothing. Chance travelers might praise or pet him; but he was cold under it all, and from a too demonstrative man he would get up and walk away. When Thornton's partners, Hans and Pete, arrived on the long-expected raft, Buck refused to notice them till he learned they were close to Thornton; after that he tolerated them in a passive sort of way, accepting favors from them as though he favored them by accepting. They were of the same large type as Thornton, living close to the earth, thinking simply and seeing clearly; and ere they swung the raft into the big eddy by the sawmill at Dawson, they understood Buck and his ways, and did not insist upon an intimacy such as obtained with Skeet and Nig.

For Thornton, however, his love seemed to grow and grow. He, alone among men, could put a pack upon Buck's back in the summer traveling. Nothing was too great for Buck to do, when Thornton commanded. One day (they had grubstaked themselves from the proceeds of the raft and left Dawson for the headwaters of the Tanana) the men and dogs were sitting on the crest of a cliff which fell away, straight down, to naked bedrock three hundred feet below. John Thornton was sitting near the edge, Buck at his shoulder. A thoughtless whim seized Thornton, and he drew the attention of Hans and Pete to the experiment he had in mind. "Jump, Buck!" he commanded, sweeping his arm out and over the chasm. The next instant he was grappling with Buck on the extreme edge, while Hans and Pete were dragging them back into safety.

"It's uncanny," Pete said, after it was over and they had caught their speech.

Thornton shook his head. "No, it is splendid, and it is terrible, too. Do you know, it sometimes makes me afraid."

"I'm not hankering to be the man that lays hands on you while he's around," Pete announced conclusively, nodding his head toward Buck.

"Py Jingo!" was Hans's contribution. "Not mineself either."

It was at Circle City, ere the year was out, that Pete's apprehensions were realized. "Black" Burton, a man evil-tempered and malicious, had been picking a quarrel with a tenderfoot at the bar, when Thornton stepped good-naturedly between. Buck, as was his custom, was lying in a corner, head on paws, watching his master's every action. Burton struck out, without warning, straight from the shoulder. Thornton was sent spinning, and saved himself from falling only by clutching the rail of the bar.

Those who were looking on heard what was neither bark nor yelp, but a something which is best described as a roar, and they saw Buck's body rise up in the air as he left the floor for Burton's throat. The man saved his life by instinctively throwing out his arm, but was hurled backward to the floor with Buck on top of him. Buck loosed his teeth from the flesh of the arm and drove in again for the throat. This time the man succeeded only in partly blocking, and his throat was torn open. Then the crowd was upon Buck, and he was driven off; but while a surgeon checked the bleeding, he prowled up and down, growling furiously, attempting to rush in, and being forced back by an array of hostile clubs. A "miners' meeting," called on the spot, decided that the dog had sufficient provocation, and Buck was discharged. But his reputation was made, and from that day his name spread through every camp in Alaska.

Later on, in the fall of the year, he saved John Thornton's life in quite another fashion. The three partners were lining a long and narrow poling-boat down a bad stretch of rapids on Forty-Mile Creek. Hans and Pete moved along the bank, snubbing with a thin Manila rope from tree to tree, while Thornton remained in the boat, helping its descent by means of a pole, and shouting directions to the shore. Buck, on the bank, worried and anxious, kept abreast of the boat, his eyes never off his master.

At a particularly bad spot, where a ledge of barely submerged rocks jutted out into the river, Hans cast off the rope, and, while Thornton poled the boat out into the stream, ran down the bank with the end in his hand to snub the boat when it had cleared the ledge. This it did, and was flying downstream in a current as swift as a millrace, when Hans checked it with the rope and checked too suddenly. The boat flirted over and snubbed into the bank bottom up, while Thornton, flung sheer out of it, was carried downstream toward the worst part of the rapids, a stretch of wild water in which no swimmer could live.

Buck had sprung in on the instant, and at the end of three hundred yards, amid a mad swirl of water, he overhauled Thornton. When he felt him grasp his tail, Buck headed for the bank, swimming with all his splendid strength. But the progress shoreward was slow; the progress downstream amazingly rapid. From below came the fatal roaring where the wild current went wilder and was rent in shreds and spray by the rocks which thrust through like the teeth of an enormous comb. The suck of the water as it took the beginning of the last steep pitch was frightful, and Thornton knew that the shore was impossible. He scraped furiously over a rock, bruised across a second, and struck a third with crushing force. He clutched its slippery top with both hands, releasing Buck, and above the roar of the churning water shouted: "Go, Buck! Go!"

Buck could not hold his own, and swept on downstream, struggling desperately, but unable to win back. When he heard Thornton's command repeated, he partly reared out of the water, throwing his head high, as though for a last look, then turned obediently toward the bank. He swam powerfully and was dragged ashore by Pete and Hans at the very point where swimming ceased to be possible and destruction began.

They knew that the time a man could cling to a slippery rock in the face of that driving current was a matter of minutes, and they ran as fast as they could up the bank to a point far above where Thornton was hanging on. They attached the line with which they had been snubbing the boat to Buck's neck and shoulders, being careful that it should neither strangle him nor impede his swimming, and launched him into the stream. He struck out boldly, but not straight enough into the stream. He discovered the mistake too late, when Thornton was abreast of him and a bare half-dozen strokes away while he was being carried helplessly past.

Hans promptly snubbed with the rope, as though Buck were a boat. The rope thus tightening on him in the sweep of the current, he was jerked under the surface, and under the surface he remained till his body struck against the bank and he was hauled out. He was half drowned, and Hans and Pete threw themselves upon him, pounding the breath into him and the water out of him. He staggered to his feet and fell down. The faint sound of Thornton's voice came to them, and though they could not make out the words of it, they knew that he was in his extremity. His master's voice acted on Buck like an electric shock. He sprang to his feet and ran up the bank ahead of the men to the point of his previous departure.

Again the rope was attached and he was launched, and again he struck out, but this time straight into the stream. He had miscalculated once, but he would not be guilty of it a second time. Hans paid out the rope, permitting no slack, while Pete kept it clear of coils. Buck held on till he was on a line straight above Thornton; then he turned, and with the speed of an express train headed down upon him. Thornton saw him coming, and, as Buck struck him like a battering ram, with the whole force of the current behind him, he reached up and closed with both arms around the shaggy neck. Hans snubbed the rope around the tree, and Buck and Thornton were jerked under the water. Strangling, suffocating, sometimes one uppermost and sometimes the other, dragging over the jagged bottom, smashing against rocks and snags, they veered in to the bank.

Thornton came to, belly downward and being violently propelled back and forth across a drift log by Hans and Pete. His first glance was for Buck, over whose limp and apparently lifeless body Nig was setting up a howl, while Skeet was licking the wet face and closed eyes. Thornton was himself bruised and battered, and he went carefully over Buck's body, when he had been brought around, finding three broken ribs.

"That settles it," he announced. "We camp right here." And camp they did, till Buck's ribs knitted and he was able to travel.

That winter, at Dawson, Buck performed another exploit, not so heroic, perhaps, but one that put his name many notches higher on the totem pole of Alaskan fame. This exploit was particularly gratifying to the three men; for they stood in need of the outfit which it furnished, and were enabled to make a long-desired trip into the virgin East, where miners had not yet appeared. It was brought about by a conversation in the Eldorado Saloon, in which men waxed boastful of their favorite dogs. Buck, because of his record, was the target for these men, and Thornton was driven stoutly to defend him. At the end of half an hour one man stated that his dog could start a sled with five hundred pounds and walk off with it; a second bragged six hundred for his dog; and a third seven hundred.

"Pooh! Pooh!" said John Thornton. "Buck can start a thousand pounds."

"And break it out? And walk off with it for a hundred yards?" demanded Matthewson, a Bonanza king, he of the seven hundred vaunt.

"And break it out, and walk off with it for a hundred yards," John Thornton said coolly.

"Well," Matthewson said, slowly and deliberately, so that all could hear, "I've got a thousand dollars that says he can't. And there it is." So saying, he slammed a sack of gold dust of the size of a bologna sausage down upon the bar.

Nobody spoke. Thornton's bluff, if bluff it was, had been called. He could feel a flush of warm blood creeping up his face. His tongue had tricked him. He did not know whether Buck could start a thousand pounds. Half a ton! The enormousness of it appalled him. He had great faith in Buck's strength and had often thought him capable of starting such a load; but never, as now, had he faced the possibility of it, the eyes of a dozen men fixed upon him, silent and waiting. Further, he had no thousand dollars; nor had Hans or Pete.

"I've got a sled standing outside now, with twenty fifty-pound sacks of flour on it," Matthewson went on with brutal directness, "so don't let that hinder you."

Thornton did not reply. He did not know what to say. He glanced from face to face in the absent way of a man who has lost the power of thought and is seeking somewhere to find the thing that will start it going again. The face of Jim O'Brien, a Mastodon king and old-time comrade, caught his eyes. It was as a cue to him, seeming to rouse him to do what he would never have dreamed of doing.

"Can you lend me a thousand?" he asked, almost in a whisper.

"Sure," answered O'Brien, thumping down a plethoric sack by the side of Matthewson's. "Though it's little faith I'm having, John, that the beast can do the trick."

The Eldorado emptied its occupants into the street to see the test. The tables were deserted, and the dealers and game-keepers came forth to see the outcome of the wager and to lay odds. Several hundred men, furred and mittened, banked around the sled within easy distance. Matthewson's sled, loaded with a thousand pounds of flour, had been standing for a couple of hours, and in the intense cold (it was sixty below zero) the runners had frozen fast to the hard-packed snow. Men offered odds of two to one that Buck could not budge the sled. A quibble arose concerning the phrase "break out." O'Brien contended it was Thornton's privilege to knock the runners loose, leaving Buck to "break it out" from a dead standstill. Matthewson insisted that the phrase included breaking the runners from the frozen grip of the snow. A majority of the men who had witnessed the making of the bet decided in his favor, whereat the odds went up to three to one against Buck.

There were no takers. Not a man believed him capable of the feat. Thornton had been hurried into the wager, heavy with doubt; and now that he looked at the sled itself, the concrete fact, with the regular team of ten dogs curled up in the snow before it, the more impossible the task appeared. Matthewson waxed jubilant.

"Three to one!" he proclaimed. "I'll lay you another thousand at that figure, Thornton. What d'ye say?"

Thornton's doubt was strong in his face, but his fighting spirit was aroused—the fighting spirit that soars above odds, fails to recognize the impossible, and is deaf to all save the clamor for battle. He called Hans and Pete to him. Their sacks were slim, and with his own the three partners could rake together only two hundred dollars. In the ebb of their fortunes, this sum was their total capital; yet they laid it unhesitatingly against Matthewson's six hundred.

The team of ten dogs was unhitched, and Buck, with his own harness, was put into the sled. He had caught the contagion of the excitement, and he felt that in some way he must do a great thing for John Thornton. Murmurs of admiration at his splendid appearance went up. He was in perfect condition, without an ounce of superfluous flesh, and the 150 pounds that he weighed were so many pounds of grit and virility. His furry coat shone with the sheen of silk. Down the neck and across the shoulders, his mane, in repose as it was, half bristled and seemed to lift with every movement, as though excess of vigor made each particular hair alive and active. The great breast and heavy forelegs were no more than in proportion with the rest of the body, where the muscles showed in tight rolls underneath the skin. Men felt these muscles and proclaimed them hard as iron, and the odds went down to two to one.

"Gad, sir! Gad, sir!" stuttered a member of the latest dynasty, a king of the Skookum Benches. "I offer you eight hundred for him, sir, before the test, sir; eight hundred just as he stands."

Thornton shook his head and stepped to Buck's side.

"You must stand off from him," Matthewson protested. "Free play and plenty of room."

The crowd fell silent; only could be heard the voices of the gamblers vainly offering two to one. Everybody acknowledged Buck a magnificent animal, but twenty fifty-pound sacks of flour bulked too large in their eyes for them to loosen their pouch strings.

Thornton knelt down by Buck's side. He took his head in his two hands and rested cheek on cheek. He did not playfully shake him, as was his wont, or murmur soft love curses; but he whispered in his ear. "As you love me, Buck. As you love me," was what he whispered. Buck whined with suppressed eagerness.

The crowd was watching curiously. The affair was growing mysterious. It seemed like a conjuration. As Thornton got to his feet, Buck seized his mittened hand between his jaws, pressing in with his teeth and releasing slowly, half reluctantly. It was the answer, in terms, not of speech, but of love. Thornton stepped well back.

"Now, Buck," he said.

Buck tightened the traces, then slacked them for a matter of several inches. It was the way he had learned.

"Gee!" Thornton's voice rang out, sharp in the tense silence.

Buck swung to the right, ending the movement in a plunge that took up the slack and with a sudden jerk arrested his 150 pounds. The load quivered, and from under the runners arose a crisp crackling.

"Haw!" Thornton commanded.

Buck duplicated the maneuver, this time to the left. The crackling turned into a snapping, the sled pivoting and the runners slipping and grating several inches to the side. The sled was broken out. Men were holding their breaths, intensely unconscious of the fact.

"Now, MUSH!"

Thornton's command cracked out like a pistol shot. Buck threw himself forward, tightening the traces with a jarring lunge. His whole body was gathered compactly together in the tremendous effort, the muscles writhing and knotting like live things under the silky fur. His great chest was low to the ground, his head forward and down, while his feet were flying like mad, the claws scarring the hard-packed snow in parallel grooves. The sled swayed and trembled, half-started forward. One of his feet slipped, and one man groaned aloud. Then the sled lurched ahead in what appeared a rapid succession of jerks, though it never really came to a dead stop again . . . half an inch . . . an inch . . . two inches. . . . The jerks perceptibly diminished; as the sled gained momentum, he caught them up, till it was moving steadily along.

Men gasped and began to breathe again, unaware that for a moment they had ceased to breathe. Thornton was running behind, encouraging Buck with short, cheery words. The distance had been measured off, and as he neared the pile of firewood which marked the end of the hundred yards, a cheer began to grow and grow, which burst into a roar as he passed the firewood and halted at command. Every man was tearing himself loose, even Matthewson. Hats and mittens were flying in the air. Men were shaking hands, it did not matter with whom, and bubbling over in a general incoherent babel.

But Thornton fell on his knees beside Buck. Head was against head, and he was shaking him back and forth. Those who hurried up heard him cursing Buck, and he cursed him long and fervently, and softly and lovingly.

"Gad, sir! Gad, sir!" spluttered the Skookum Bench king. "I'll give you a thousand for him, sir, a thousand, sir—twelve hundred, sir."

Thornton rose to his feet. His eyes were wet. The tears were streaming frankly down his cheeks. "Sir," he said to the Skookum Bench king, "no, sir. You can go to hell, sir. It's the best I can do for you, sir."

Buck seized Thornton's hand in his teeth. Thornton shook him back and forth. As though animated by a common impulse, the onlookers drew back to a respectful distance; nor were they again indiscreet enough to interrupt.

## *Mark Twain*

# A DOG'S TALE

My father was a Saint Bernard, my mother was a collie, but I am a Presbyterian. This is what my mother told me; I do not know these nice distinctions myself. To me they are only fine large words meaning nothing. My mother had a fondness for such; she liked to say them, and see other dogs look surprised and envious, as wondering how she got so much education. But, indeed, it was not real education; it was only show: she got the words by listening in the dining room and drawing room when there was company, and by going with the children to Sunday school and listening there; and whenever she heard a large word she said it over to herself many times, and so was able to keep it until there was a dogmatic gathering in the neighborhood, then she would get it off, and surprise and distress them all, from pocket-pup to mastiff, which rewarded her for all her trouble. If there was a stranger he was nearly sure to be suspicious, and when he got his breath again he would ask her what it meant. And she always told him. He was never expecting this, but thought he would catch her; so when she told him, he was the one that looked ashamed, whereas he had thought it was going to be she. The others were always waiting for this, and glad of it and proud of her, for they knew what was going to happen, because they had had experience.

When she told the meaning of a big word they were all so taken up with admiration that it never occurred to any dog to doubt if it was the right one; and that was natural, because, for one thing, she answered up so promptly that it seemed like a dictionary speaking, and for another thing, where could they find out whether it was right or not? For she was the only cultivated dog there was.

By and by, when I was older, she brought home the word *unintellectual* one time, and worked it pretty hard all the week at different gatherings, making much unhappiness and despondency; and it was at this time that I noticed that during that week she was asked for the meaning at eight different assemblages, and flashed out a fresh definition every time, which showed me that she had more presence of mind than culture, though I said nothing, of course. She had one word which she always kept on hand, and ready, like a life preserver, a kind of emergency word to strap on when she was likely to get washed overboard in a sudden way—that was the word *synonymous.* When she happened to fetch out a long word which had had its day weeks before and its prepared meanings gone to her dump pile, if there was a stranger there of course it knocked him groggy for a couple of minutes, then he would come to, and by that time she would be away down the wind on another tack, and not expecting anything; so when he'd hail and ask her to cash in, I (the only dog on the inside of her game) could see her canvas flicker a moment—but only just a moment—then it would belly out taut and full, and she would say, as calm as a summer's day, "It's synonymous with supererogation," or some godless long reptile of a word like that, and go placidly about and skim away on the next tack, perfectly comfortable, you know, and leave that stranger looking profane and embarrassed, and the initiated slatting the floor with their tails in unison and their faces transfigured with a holy joy.

And it was the same with phrases. She would drag home a whole phrase, if it had a grand sound, and play it six nights and two matinees, and explain it a new way every time—which she had to, for all she cared for was the phrase; she wasn't interested in what it meant, and knew those dogs hadn't wit enough to catch her, anyway. Yes, she was a daisy! She got so she wasn't afraid of anything, she had such confidence in the ignorance of those creatures. She even brought anecdotes that she had heard the family and the dinner guests laugh and shout over; and as a rule she got the nub of one chestnut hitched onto another chestnut, where, of course, it didn't fit and hadn't any point; and when she delivered the nub she fell over and rolled on the floor and laughed and barked in the most insane way, while I could see that she was wondering to herself why it didn't seem as funny as it did when she first heard it. But no harm was done; the others rolled and barked too, privately ashamed of themselves for not seeing the point, and never suspecting that the fault was not with them and there wasn't any to see.

You can see by these things that she was of a rather vain and frivolous character; still, she had virtues, and enough to make up, I think. She had a kind heart and gentle ways, and never harbored resentments for injuries done her, but put them easily out of her mind and forgot them; and she taught her children her kindly way, and from her we learned also to be brave and prompt in time of danger, and not to run away, but face the peril that threatened friend or stranger, and help him the best we could without stopping to think what the cost might be to us. And she taught us not by words only, but by example, and that is the best way and the surest and the most lasting. Why, the brave things she did, the splendid things! She was just a soldier; and so modest about it—well, you couldn't help admiring her, and you couldn't help imitating her; not even a King Charles spaniel could remain entirely despicable in her society. So, as you see, there was more to her than her education.

## 2

When I was well grown, at last, I was sold and taken away, and I never saw her again. She was brokenhearted, and so was I, and we cried; but she comforted me as well as she could, and said we were sent into this world for a wise and good purpose, and must do our duties without repining, take our life as we might find it, live it for the best good of others, and never mind about the results; they were not our affair. She said men who did like this would have a noble and beautiful reward by and by in another world, and although we animals would not go there, to do well and right without reward would give to our brief lives a worthiness and dignity which in itself would be a reward. She had gathered these things from time to time when she had gone to the Sunday school with the children, and had laid them up in her memory more carefully than she had done with those other words and phrases; and she had studied them deeply, for her good and ours. One may see by this that she had a wise and thoughtful head, for all there was so much lightness and vanity in it.

So we said our farewells, and looked our last upon each other through our tears; and the last thing she said—keeping it for the last to make me remember it the better, I think—was, "In memory of me, when there is a time of danger to another do not think of yourself, think of your mother, and do as she would do."

Do you think I could forget that? No.

## 3

It was such a charming home, my new one! A fine great house, with pictures, and delicate decorations, and rich furniture, and no gloom anywhere, but all the wilderness of dainty colors lit up with flooding sunshine; and the spacious grounds around it, and the great garden—oh, greensward, and noble trees, and flowers, no end! And I was the same as a member of the family; and they loved me, and petted me, and did not give me a new name, but called me by my old one that was dear to me because my mother had given it me—Aileen Mavourneen. She got it out of a song; and the Grays knew that song, and said it was a beautiful name.

Mrs. Gray was thirty, and so sweet and so lovely, you cannot imagine it; and Sadie was ten, and just like her mother, just a darling slender little copy of her, with auburn tails down her back, and short frocks; and the baby was a year old, and plump and dimpled, and fond of me, and never could get enough of hauling on my tail, and hugging me, and laughing out its innocent happiness; and Mr. Gray was thirty-eight, and tall and slender and handsome, a little bald in front, alert, quick in his movements, businesslike, prompt, decided, unsentimental, and with that kind of trim-chiseled face that just seems to glint and sparkle with frosty intellectuality! He was a renowned scientist. I do not know what the word means, but my mother would know how to use it and get effects. She would know how to depress a rat terrier with it and make a lapdog look sorry he came. But that is not the best one; the best one was *laboratory.* My mother could organize a *trust* on that one that would skin the tax-collars off the whole herd. The laboratory was not a book, or a picture, or a place to wash your hands in, as the college president's dog said—no, that is the lavatory; the laboratory is quite different, and is filled with jars, and bottles, and electrics, and wires, and strange machines; and every week other scientists came there and sat in the place, and used the machines, and discussed, and made what they called experiments and discoveries; and often I came, too, and stood around and listened, and tried to learn, for the sake of my mother, and in loving memory of her, although it was a pain to me, as realizing what she was losing out of her life and I gaining nothing at all; for try as I might, I was never able to make anything out of it at all.

Other times I lay on the floor in the mistress's workroom and slept, she gently using me for a footstool, knowing it pleased me, for it was a caress; other times I spent an hour in the nursery, and got well tousled and made happy; other times I watched by the crib there, when the baby was asleep and the nurse out for a few minutes on the baby's affairs; other times I romped and raced through the grounds and the garden with Sadie till we were tired out, then slumbered on the grass in the shade of a tree while she read her book; other times I went visiting among the neighbor dogs—for there were some most pleasant ones not far away, and one very handsome and courteous and graceful one, a curly-haired Irish setter by the name of Robin Adair, who was a Presbyterian like me, and belonged to the Scotch minister.

The servants in our house were all kind to me and were fond of me, and so, as you see, mine was a pleasant life. There could not be a happier dog than I was, nor a gratefuler one. I will say this for myself, for it is only the truth: I tried in all ways to do well and right, and honor my mother's memory and her teachings, and earn the happiness that had come to me, as best I could.

By and by came my little puppy, and then my cup was

full, my happiness was perfect. It was the dearest little waddling thing, and so smooth and soft and velvety, and had such cunning little awkward paws, and such affectionate eyes, and such a sweet and innocent face; and it made me so proud to see how the children and their mother adored it, and fondled it, and exclaimed over every little wonderful thing it did. It did seem to me that life was just too lovely to—

Then came the winter. One day I was standing a watch in the nursery. That is to say, I was asleep on the bed. The baby was asleep in the crib, which was alongside the bed, on the side next the fireplace. It was the kind of crib that has a lofty tent over it made of a gauzy stuff that you can see through. The nurse was out, and we two sleepers were alone. A spark from the wood fire was shot out, and it lit on the slope of the tent. I suppose a quiet interval followed, then a scream from the baby woke me, and there was that tent flaming up toward the ceiling! Before I could think, I sprang to the floor in my fright, and in a second was halfway to the door; but in the next half-second my mother's farewell was sounding in my ears, and I was back on the bed again. I reached my head through the flames and dragged the baby out by the waistband, and tugged it along, and we fell to the floor together in a cloud of smoke; I snatched a new hold, and dragged the screaming little creature along and out at the door and around the bend of the hall, and was still tugging away, all excited and happy and proud, when the master's voice shouted—

"Begone, you cursed beast!" and I jumped to save myself; but he was wonderfully quick, and chased me up, striking furiously at me with his cane, I dodging this way and that, in terror, and at last a strong blow fell upon my left foreleg, which made me shriek and fall, for the moment, helpless; the cane went up for another blow, but never descended, for the nurse's voice rang wildly out, "The nursery's on fire!" and the master rushed away in that direction, and my other bones were saved.

The pain was cruel, but, no matter. I must not lose any time; he might come back at any moment; so I limped on three legs to the other end of the hall, where there was a dark little stairway leading up into a garret where old boxes and such things were kept, as I had heard say, and where people seldom went. I managed to climb up there, then I searched my way through the dark amongst the piles of things, and hid in the secretest place I could find. It was foolish to be afraid there, yet still I was; so afraid that I held in and hardly even whimpered, though it would have been such a comfort to whimper, because that eases the pain, you know. But I could lick my leg, and that did me some good.

For half an hour there was a commotion downstairs, and shoutings, and rushing footsteps, and then there was quiet again. Quiet for some minutes, and that was grateful to my spirit, for then my fears began to go down; and fears are worse than pains—oh, much worse. Then came a sound that froze me! They were calling me—calling me by name—hunting for me!

It was muffled by distance, but that could not take the terror out of it, and it was the most dreadful sound to me that I had ever heard. It went all about, everywhere, down there: along the halls, through all the rooms, in both stories, and in the basement and the cellar; then outside, and farther and farther away—then back, and all about the house again, and I thought it would never, never stop. But at last it did, hours and hours after the vague twilight of the garret had long ago been blotted out by black darkness.

Then in that blessed stillness my terrors fell little by little away, and I was at peace and slept. It was a good rest I had, but I woke before the twilight had come again. I was feeling fairly comfortable, and I could think out a plan now. I made a very good one; which was, to creep down, all the way down the back stairs, and hide behind the cellar door, and slip out and escape when the iceman came at dawn, whilst he was inside filling the refrigerator; then I would hide all day, and start on my journey when night came; my journey to—well, anywhere where they would not know me and betray me to the master. I was feeling almost cheerful now; then suddenly I thought, Why, what would life be without my puppy!

That was despair. There was no plan for me; I saw that; I must stay where I was; stay, and wait, and take what might come—it was not my affair; that was what life is—my mother had said it. Then—well, then the calling began again! All my sorrows came back. I said to myself, the master will never forgive. I did not know what I had done to make him so bitter and so unforgiving, yet I judged it was something a dog could not understand, but which was clear to a man and dreadful.

They called and called—days and nights, it seemed to me. So long that the hunger and thirst near drove me mad, and I recognized that I was getting very weak. When you are this way you sleep a great deal, and I did. Once I woke in an awful fright—it seemed to me that the calling was right there in the garret! And so it was: it was Sadie's voice, and she was crying; my name was falling from her lips all broken, poor thing, and I could not believe my ears for the joy of it when I heard her say,

"Come back to us—oh, come back to us, and forgive—it is all so sad without our—"

I broke in with *such* a grateful little yelp, and the next moment Sadie was plunging and stumbling through the darkness and the lumber and shouting for the family to hear, "She's found, she's found!"

The days that followed—well, they were wonderful. The mother and Sadie and the servants—why, they just seemed to worship me. They couldn't seem to make me a bed that was fine enough; and as for food, they couldn't be satisfied with anything but game and delicacies that were out of season; and every day the friends and neighbors flocked in to hear about my heroism—that was the name they called it by, and it means agriculture. I remember my mother pulling it on a kennel once, and explaining it that way, but didn't say what agriculture was, except that it was synonymous with intramural incandescence; and a dozen times a day Mrs. Gray and Sadie would tell the tale to newcomers, and say I risked my life to save the baby's, and both of us had burns to prove it, and then the company would pass me around and pet me and exclaim about me, and you could see the pride in the eyes of Sadie and her mother; and when the people wanted to know what made me limp, they looked ashamed and changed the subject, and sometimes when people hunted them this way and that way with questions about it, it looked to me as if they were going to cry.

And this was not all the glory; no, the master's friends came, a whole twenty of the most distinguished people, and had me in the laboratory, and discussed me as if I was a kind of discovery; and some of them said it was wonderful in a dumb beast, the finest exhibition of instinct they could call to mind; but the master said, with vehemence, "It's far above instinct; it's *reason,* and many a man, privileged to be saved and go with you and me to a better world by right of its possession, has less of it than this poor silly quadruped that's foreordained to perish"; and then he laughed, and said, "Why, look at me—I'm a sarcasm! bless you, with all my grand intelligence, the only thing I inferred was that the dog had gone mad and was destroying the child, whereas but for the beast's intelligence—it's *reason,* I tell you!—the child would have perished!"

They disputed and disputed, and I was the very center and subject of it all, and I wished my mother could know that this grand honor had come to me; it would have made her proud.

Then they discussed optics, as they called it, and whether a certain injury to the brain would produce blindness or not, but they could not agree about it, and said they must test it by experiment by and by; and next they discussed plants, and that interested me, because in the summer Sadie and I had planted seeds—I helped her dig the holes, you know—and after days and days a little shrub or a flower came up there, and it was a wonder how that could happen; but it did, and I wished I could talk—I would have told those people about it and shown them how much I knew, and been all alive with the subject; but I didn't care for the optics; it was dull, and when they came back to it again it bored me, and I went to sleep.

Pretty soon it was spring, and sunny and pleasant and lovely, and the sweet mother and the children patted me and the puppy good-bye, and went away on a journey and a visit to their kin, and the master wasn't any company for us, but we played together and had good times, and the servants were kind and friendly, so we got along quite happily and counted the days and waited for the family.

And one day those men came again, and said now for the test, and they took the puppy to the laboratory, and I limped three-leggedly along, too, feeling proud, for any attention shown the puppy was a pleasure to me, of course. They discussed and experimented, and then suddenly the puppy shrieked, and they set him on the floor, and he went staggering around, with his head all bloody, and the master clapped his hands and shouted:

"There, I've won—confess it! He's as blind as a bat!"

And they all said,

"It's so—you've proved your theory, and suffering humanity owes you a great debt from henceforth," and they crowded around him, and wrung his hand cordially and thankfully, and praised him.

But I hardly saw or heard these things, for I ran at once

to my little darling, and snuggled close to it where it lay, and licked the blood, and it put its head against mine, whimpering softly, and I knew in my heart it was a comfort to it in its pain and trouble to feel its mother's touch, though it could not see me. Then it drooped down, presently, and its little velvet nose rested upon the floor, and it was still, and did not move any more.

Soon the master stopped discussing a moment, and rang in the footman, and said, "Bury it in the far corner of the garden," and then went on with the discussion, and I trotted after the footman, very happy and grateful, for I knew the puppy was out of its pain now, because it was asleep. We went far down the garden to the farthest end, where the children and the nurse and the puppy and I used to play in the summer in the shade of a great elm, and there the footman dug a hole, and I saw he was going to plant the puppy, and I was glad, because it would grow and come up a fine handsome dog, like Robin Adair, and be a beautiful surprise for the family when they came home; so I tried to help him dig, but my lame leg was no good, being stiff, you know, and you have to have two, or it is no use. When the footman had finished and covered little Robin up, he patted my head, and there were tears in his eyes, and he said, "Poor little doggie, you saved *his* child."

I have watched two whole weeks, and he doesn't come up! This last week a fright has been stealing upon me. I think there is something terrible about this. I do not know what it is, but the fear makes me sick, and I cannot eat, though the servants bring me the best of food; and they pet me so, and even come in the night, and cry, and say, "Poor doggie—do give it up and come home; *don't* break our hearts!" and all this terrifies me the more, and makes me sure something has happened. And I am so weak; since yesterday I cannot stand on my feet anymore. And within this hour the servants, looking toward the sun where it was sinking out of sight and the night chill coming on, said things I could not understand, but they carried something cold to my heart.

"Those poor creatures! They do not suspect. They will come home in the morning, and eagerly ask for the little doggie that did the brave deed, and who of us will be strong enough to say the truth to them: 'The humble little friend is gone where go the beasts that perish.' "

*John Muir*

# AN ADVENTURE WITH A DOG

In the summer of 1880 I set out from Fort Wrangel in a canoe, with the Reverend S. H. Young, my former companion, and a crew of Indians, to continue the exploration of the icy region of southeastern Alaska, begun in the fall of 1879. After the necessary provisions, blankets, etc., had been collected and stowed away, and the Indians were in their places ready to dip their paddles, while a crowd of their friends were looking down from the wharf to bid them good-bye and good luck, Mr. Young, for whom we were waiting, at length came aboard, followed by a little black dog that immediately made himself at home by curling up in a hollow among the baggage. I like dogs, but this one seemed so small, dull, and worthless that I objected to his going, and asked the missionary why he was taking him. "Such a helpless wisp of hair will only be in the way," I said; "you had better pass him up to one of the Indian boys on the wharf, to be taken home to play with the children. This trip is not likely to be a good one for toy dogs. He will be rained on and snowed on for weeks, and will require care like a baby." But the missionary assured me that he would be no trouble at all; that he was a perfect wonder of a dog—could endure cold and hunger like a polar bear, could swim like a seal, and was wondrous wise, etc., making out a list of virtues likely to make him the most interesting of the company.

Nobody could hope to unravel the lines of his ancestry. He was short-legged, bunchy-bodied, and almost featureless—something like a muskrat. Though smooth, his hair was long and silky, so that when the wind was at his back it ruffled, making him look shaggy. At first sight his only noticeable feature was his showy tail, which was about as shady and airy as a squirrel's, and was carried curling forward nearly to his ears. On closer inspection you might see his thin, sensitive ears and his keen dark eyes with cunning tan spots. Mr. Young told me that when the dog was about the size of a wood rat he was presented to his wife by an Irish prospector at Sitka, and that when he arrived at Fort Wrangel he was adopted by the Stickeen Indians as a sort of new good-luck totem, and named "Stickeen" for the tribe, with whom he became a favorite. On our trip he soon proved himself a queer character—odd, concealed, independent, keeping invincibly quiet, and doing many inexplicable things that piqued my curiosity. Sailing week after week through the long, intricate channels and inlets among the innumerable islands and mountains of the coast, he spent the dull days in sluggish ease, motionless, and apparently as unobserving as a hibernating marmot. But I discovered that somehow he always knew what was going forward. When the Indians were about to shoot at ducks or seals, or when anything interesting was to be seen along the shore, he would rest his chin on the edge of the canoe and calmly look out. When he heard us talking about making a landing, he roused himself to see what sort of place we were coming to, and made ready to jump overboard and swim ashore as soon as the canoe neared the beach. Then, with a vigorous shake to get rid of the brine in his hair, he went into the woods to hunt small game. But though always the first out of the canoe, he was always the last to get into it. When we were ready to start he could never be found, and refused to come to our call. We soon found out, however, that though we could not see him at such times, he saw us, and from the cover of the briers and huckleberry bushes in the fringe of the woods was watching the canoe with wary eye. For as soon as we were fairly off, he came trotting down the beach, plunged into the surf, and swam after us, knowing well that we would cease rowing and take him in. When the contrary little vagabond came alongside, he was lifted by the neck, held at arm's length a moment to drip, and dropped aboard. We tried to cure him of this trick by compelling him to swim farther before stopping for him; but this did no good: the longer the swim, the better he seemed to like it.

Though capable of most spacious idleness, he was always ready for excursions or adventures of any sort. When the Indians went into the woods for a deer, Stickeen was sure to be at their heels, provided I had not yet left camp. For though I never carried a gun, he always followed me, forsaking the hunting Indians, and even his master, to share my wanderings. The days that were too stormy for sailing I spent in the woods, or on the mountains or glaciers, wherever I chanced to be; and Stickeen always insisted on following me, gliding through the dripping huckleberry bushes and prickly *Panax* and *Rubus* tangles like a fox, scarce stirring their close-set branches, wading and wallowing through snow, swimming ice-cold streams, jumping logs and rocks and the crusty hummocks and crevasses of glaciers with the patience and endurance of a determined mountaineer, never tiring or getting discouraged. Once he followed me over a glacier the surface of which was so rough that it cut his feet until every step was marked with blood; but he trotted on with Indian fortitude until I noticed his pain and, taking pity on him, made him a set of moccasins out of a handkerchief. But he never asked help or made any complaint, as if, like a philosopher, he had learned that without hard work and suffering there could be no pleasure worth having.

Yet nobody knew what Stickeen was good for. He seemed to meet danger and hardships without reason, insisted on having his own way, never obeyed an order, and the hunters could never set him on anything against his will, or make him fetch anything that was shot. I tried hard to make his acquaintance, guessing there must be something in him; but he was as cold as a glacier, and about as invulnerable to fun, though his master assured me that he played at home, and in some measure conformed to the usages of civilization. His equanimity was so immovable it seemed due to unfeeling ignorance. Let the weather blow and roar, he was as tranquil as a stone; and no matter what advances you made, scarce a glance or a tail wag would you get for your pains. No superannuated mastiff or bulldog grown old in office surpassed this soft midget in stoic dignity. He sometimes reminded me of those plump, squat, unshakable cacti of the Arizona deserts that give no sign of feeling. A true child of the wilderness, holding the even tenor of his hidden life with the silence and serenity of nature, he never displayed a trace of the elfish vivacity and fun of the terriers and collies that we all know, nor of their touching affection and devotion. Like children, most small dogs beg to be loved and allowed to love, but Stickeen seemed a very Diogenes, asking only to be let alone. He seemed neither old nor young. His strength lay in his eyes. They looked as old as the hills, and as young and as wild. I never tired looking into them. It was like looking into a landscape; but they were small and rather deep-set, and had no explaining puckers around them to give out particulars. I was accustomed to look into the faces of plants and animals, and I watched the little sphinx more and more keenly as an interesting study. But there is no estimating the wit and wisdom concealed and latent in our lower fellow-mortals until made manifest by profound experiences; for it is by suffering that dogs as well as saints are developed and made perfect.

After we had explored the glaciers of the Sumdum and Tahkoo inlets, we sailed through Stephen's Passage into Lynn Canal, and thence through Icy Strait into Cross Sound, looking for unexplored inlets leading toward the ice fountains of the Fairweather Range. While the tide was in our favor in Cross Sound we were accompanied by a fleet of icebergs drifting out to the ocean from Glacier Bay. Slowly we crawled around Vancouver's Point, Wimbleton, our frail canoe tossed like a feather on the massive swells coming in past Cape Spenser. For miles the Sound is bounded by precipitous cliffs which looked terribly stern in gloomy weather. Had our canoe been crushed or upset, we could have gained no landing here; for the cliffs, as high as those of Yosemite, sink perfectly sheer into deep water. Eagerly we scanned the immense wall on the north side for the first sign of an opening, all of us anxious except Stickeen, who dozed in peace or gazed dreamily at the tremendous precipices when he heard us talking about them. At length we discovered the entrance of what is now called Taylor Bay, and about five o'clock reached the head of it, and encamped near the front of a large glacier which extends as an abrupt barrier all the way across from wall to wall of the inlet, a distance of three or four miles.

On first observation the glacier presented some unusual features, and that night I planned a grand excursion for the morrow. I awoke early, called not only by the glacier, but also by a storm. Rain, mixed with trailing films of scud and the ragged, drawn-out nether surfaces of gray clouds, filled the inlet, and was sweeping forward in a thick, passionate, horizontal flood, as if it were all passing over the country instead of falling on it. Everything was streaming with life and motion —woods, rocks, waters, and the sky. The main perennial streams were booming, and hundreds of new ones, born of the rain, were descending in gray and white cascades on each side of the inlet, fairly streaking their rocky slopes, and roaring like the sea. I had intended making a cup of coffee before starting, but when I heard the storm I made haste to join it; for in storms nature has always something extra fine to show us, and if we have wit to keep in right relations with them the danger is no more than in home-keeping, and we can go with them rejoicing, sharing their enthusiasm, and chanting with the old Norsemen, "The blast of the tempest aids our oars; the hurricane is our servant, and drives us whither we wish to go." So I took my ice ax, buttoned my coat, put a piece of bread in my pocket, and set out. Mr. Young and the Indians were asleep, and so, I hoped, was Stickeen; but I had not gone a dozen rods before he left his warm bed in the tent, and came boring through the blast after me. That a man should welcome storms for their exhilarating music and motion, and go forth to see God making landscapes, is reasonable enough; but what fascination could there be in dismal weather for this poor, feeble wisp of a dog, so pathetically small? Anyhow, on he came, breakfastless, through the choking blast. I stopped, turned my back to the wind, and gave him a good, dissuasive talk. "Now don't," I said, shouting to make myself heard in the storm—"now don't, Stickeen. What has got into your queer noddle now? You must be daft. This wild day has nothing for you. Go back to camp and keep warm. There is no game abroad—nothing but weather. Not a foot or wing is stirring. Wait and get a good breakfast with your master, and be sensible for once. I can't feed you or carry you, and this storm will kill you." But nature, it seems, was at the bottom of the affair; and she gains her ends with dogs as well as with men, making us do as she likes, driving us on her ways, however rough. So after ordering him back again and again to ease my conscience, I saw that he was not to be shaken off; as well might the earth try to shake off the moon. I had once led his master into trouble, when he fell on one of the topmost jags of a mountain, and dislocated his arms. Now the turn of his humble companion was coming. The dog just stood there in the wind, drenched and blinking, saying doggedly, "Where thou goest I will go." So I told him to come on, if he must, and gave him a piece of the bread I had put in my pocket for breakfast. Then we pushed on in company, and thus began the most memorable of all my wild days.

The level flood, driving straight in our faces, thrashed and washed us wildly until we got into the shelter of the trees and ice cliffs on the east side of the glacier, where we rested and listened and looked on in comfort. The exploration of the glacier was my main object, but the wind was too high to allow excursions over its open surface, where one might be dangerously shoved while balancing for a jump on the brink of a crevasse. In the meantime the storm was a fine study. Here the end of the glacier, descending over an abrupt swell of resisting rock about five hundred feet high, leans forward and falls in majestic ice cascades. And as the storm came down the glacier from the north, Stickeen and I were beneath the main current of the blast, while favorably located to see and hear it. A broad torrent, draining the side of the glacier, now swollen by scores of new streams from the mountains, was rolling boulders along its rocky channel between the glacier and the woods with thudding, bumping, muffled sounds, rushing toward the bay with tremendous energy, as if in haste to get out of the mountains, the waters above and beneath calling to each other, and all to the ocean, their home. Looking southward from our shelter, we had this great torrent on our left, with mossy woods on the mountain slope above it, the glacier on our right, the wild, cascading portion of it forming a multitude of towers, spires, and flat-topped battlements seen through the trees, and smooth gray gloom ahead. I tried to draw the marvelous scene in my notebook, but the rain fell on my page in spite of all that I could do to shelter it, and the sketch seemed miserably defective.

When the wind began to abate I traced the east side of the glacier. All the trees standing on the edge of the woods were barked and bruised, showing high ice-mark in a very telling way, while tens of thousands of those that had stood for centuries on the bank of the glacier farther out lay crushed and being crushed. In many places I could see, down fifty feet or so beneath, the margin of the glacier mill, where trunks from one to two feet in diameter were being ground to pulp against outstanding rock ribs and bosses of the bank. About three miles above the front of the glacier, I climbed to the surface of it by means of ax steps, made easy for Stickeen; and as far as the eye could reach, the level, or nearly level, glacier stretched away indefinitely beneath the gray sky, a seemingly boundless prairie of ice. The rain continued, which I did not mind; but a tendency to fogginess in the drooping clouds made me hesitate about venturing far from land. No trace of the west shore was visible, and in case the misty clouds should settle, or the wind again become violent, I feared getting caught in a tangle of crevasses. Lingering undecided, watching the weather, I sauntered about on the crystal sea. For a mile or two out I found the ice remarkably safe. The marginal crevasses were mostly narrow, while the few wider ones were easily avoided by passing around them, and the clouds began to open here and there. Thus encouraged, I at last pushed out for the other side; for nature can make us do anything she likes, luring us along appointed ways for the fulfillment of her plans. At first we made rapid progress, and the sky was not very threatening, while I took bearings occasionally with a pocket compass, to enable me to retrace my way more surely in case the storm should become blinding; but the structure lines of the ice were my main guide. Toward the west side we came to a closely crevassed section, in which we had to make long, narrow tacks and doublings, tracing the edges of tremendous longitudinal crevasses, many of which were from twenty to thirty feet wide, and perhaps a thousand feet deep, beautiful and awful. In working a way through them I was severely cautious, but Stickeen came on as unhesitatingly as the flying clouds. Any crevasse that I could jump he would leap without so much as halting to examine it. The weather was bright and dark, with quick flashes of summer and winter close together. When the clouds opened and the sun shone, the glacier was seen from shore to shore, with a bright array of encompassing mountains partly revealed, wearing the clouds as garments, black in the middle, burning on the edges, and the whole icy prairie seemed to burst into a bloom of iris colors from myriads of crystals. Then suddenly all the glorious show would be again smothered in gloom. But Stickeen seemed to care for none of these things, bright or dark, nor for the beautiful wells filled to the brim with water so pure that it was nearly invisible, the rumbling, grinding moulins, or the quick-flashing, glinting, swirling streams in frictionless channels of living ice. Nothing seemed novel to him. He showed neither caution nor curiosity. His courage was so unwavering that it seemed due to dullness of perception, as if he were only blindly bold; and I warned him that he might slip or fall short. His bunchy body seemed all one skipping muscle, and his peg legs appeared to be jointed only at the top.

We gained the west shore in about three hours, the width of the glacier here being about seven miles. Then I pushed northward, in order to see as far back as possible into the fountains of the Fairweather Mountains, in case the clouds should rise. The walking was easy along the margin of the forest, which, of course, like that on the other side, had been invaded and crushed by the swollen glacier. In an hour we rounded a massive headland and came suddenly on another outlet of the glacier, which, in the form of a wild ice cascade, was pouring over the rim of the main basin toward the ocean with the volume of a thousand Niagaras. The surface was broken into a multitude of sharp blades and pinnacles leaning forward, something like the updashing waves of a flood of water descending a rugged channel. But these ice waves were many times higher than those of river cataracts, and to all appearance motionless. It was a dazzling white torrent two miles wide, flowing between high banks black with trees. Tracing its left bank three or four miles, I found that it discharged into a freshwater lake, filling it with icebergs.

I would gladly have followed the outlet, but the day was waning, and we had to make haste on the return trip to get off the ice before dark. When we were about two miles from the west shore the clouds dropped misty fringes, and snow soon began to fly. Then I began to feel anxiety as to finding a way in the storm through the intricate network of crevasses which we had entered. Stickeen showed no fear. He was still the same silent, sufficient, uncomplaining Indian philosopher. When the storm darkness fell he kept close behind me. The snow warned us to make haste, but at the same time hid our way. At rare intervals the clouds thinned, and mountains, looming in the gloom, frowned and quickly vanished. I pushed on as best I could, jumping innumerable crevasses, and for every hundred rods or so of direct advance traveling a mile in doubling up and down in the turmoil of chasms and dislocated masses of ice. After an hour or two of this work we came to a series of longitudinal crevasses of appalling width, like immense furrows. These I traced with firm nerve, excited and strengthened by the danger, making wide jumps, poising cautiously on the dizzy edges after cutting hollows for my feet before making the spring, to avoid slipping or any uncertainty on the farther sides, where only one trial is granted—exercise at once frightful and inspiring. Stickeen flirted across every gap I jumped, seemingly without effort. Many a mile we thus traveled, mostly up and down, making but little real headway in crossing, most of the time running instead of walking, as the danger of spending the night on the glacier became threatening. No doubt we could have weathered the storm for one night, and I faced the chance of being compelled to do so; but we were hungry and wet, and the north wind was thick with snow and bitterly cold, and of course that night would have seemed a long one. Stickeen gave me no concern. He was still the wonderful, inscrutable philosopher, ready for anything. I could not see far enough to judge in which direction the best route lay, and had simply to grope my way in the snow-choked air and ice. Again and again I was put to my mettle, but Stickeen followed easily, his nerves growing more unflinching as the dangers thickened; so it always is with mountaineers.

At length our way was barred by a very wide and straight crevasse, which I traced rapidly northward a mile or so without finding a crossing or hope of one, then southward down the glacier about as far, to where it united with another crevasse. In all this distance of perhaps two miles there was only one place where I could possibly jump it; but the width of this jump was nearly the utmost I dared attempt, while the danger of slipping on the farther side was so great that I was loath to try it. Furthermore, the side I was on was about a foot higher than the other, and even with this advantage it seemed dangerously wide. One is liable to underestimate the width of crevasses where the magnitudes in general are great. I therefore measured this one again and again, until satisfied that I could jump it if necessary, but that in case I should be compelled to jump back to the higher side, I might fail. Now a cautious mountaineer seldom takes a step on unknown ground which seems at all dangerous, that he cannot retrace in case he should be stopped by unseen obstacles ahead. This is the rule of mountaineers who live long; and though in haste, I compelled myself to sit down and deliberate before I broke it. Retracing my devious path in imagination, as if it were drawn on a chart, I saw that I was recrossing the glacier a mile or two farther upstream, and was entangled in a section I had not before seen. Should I risk this dangerous jump, or try to regain the woods on the west shore, make a fire, and have only hunger to endure while waiting for a new day? I had already crossed so broad a tangle of dangerous ice that I saw it would be difficult to get back to the woods through the storm; while the ice just beyond the present barrier seemed more promising, and the east shore was now perhaps about as near as the west. I was therefore eager to go on; but this wide jump was a tremendous obstacle. At length, because of the dangers already behind me, I determined to venture against those that might be ahead, jumped, and landed well, but with so little to spare that I more than ever dreaded being compelled to take that jump back from the lower side. Stickeen followed, making nothing of it. But within a distance of a few hundred yards we were stopped again by the widest crevasse yet encountered. Of course I made haste to explore it, hoping all might yet be well. About three-fourths of a mile upstream it united with the one we had just crossed, as I feared it would. Then, tracing it down, I found it joined the other great crevasse at the lower end, maintaining a width of forty to fifty feet. We were on an island about two miles long and from one hundred to three hundred yards wide, with two barely possible ways of escape—one by the way we came, the other by an almost inaccessible sliver-bridge that crossed the larger crevasse from near the middle of the island. After tracing the brink, I ran back to the sliver-bridge and cautiously studied it. Crevasses caused by strains from variations of the rate of motion of different parts of the glacier and by convexities in the channel are mere cracks when they first open—so narrow as hardly to admit the blade of a pocketknife—and widen gradually, according to the extent of the strain. Now some of these cracks are interrupted like the cracks in wood, and, in opening, the strip of ice between overlapping ends is dragged out; and if the flow of the glacier there is such that no strain is made on the sliver, it maintains a continuous connection between the sides, just as the two sides of a slivered crack in wood that is being split are connected. Some crevasses remain open for years, and by the melting of their sides continue to increase in width long after the opening strain has ceased, while the sliver-bridges, level on top at first, and perfectly safe, are at length melted to thin, knife-edged blades, the upper portion being most exposed to the weather; and since the exposure is greatest in the middle, they at length curve downward like the cables of suspension bridges. This one was evidently very old, for it had been wasted until it was the worst bridge I ever saw. The width of the crevasse was here about fifty feet, and the sliver, crossing diagonally, was about seventy feet long, was depressed twenty-five or thirty feet in the middle, and the upcurving ends were attached to the sides eight or ten feet below the surface of the glacier. Getting down the nearly vertical wall to the end of it and up the other side were the main difficulties, and they seemed all but insurmountable. Of the many perils encountered in my years of wandering in mountain altitudes, none seemed so plain and stern and merciless as this. And it was presented when we were wet to the skin and hungry, the sky was dark with snow, and the night near, and we had to fear the snow in our eyes and the disturbing action of the wind in any movement we might make. But we were forced to face it. It was a tremendous necessity.

Beginning not immediately above the sunken end of the bridge, but a little to one side, I cut nice hollows on the brink for my knees to rest in; then, leaning over, with my short-handled ax cut a step sixteen or eighteen inches below, which, on account of the sheerness of the wall, was shallow. That step, however, was well made; its floor sloped slightly inward, and formed a good hold for my heels. Then, slipping cautiously upon it, and crouching as low as possible, with my left side twisted toward the wall, I steadied myself with my left hand in a slight notch, while with the right I cut other steps and notches in succession, guarding against glinting of the ax, for life or death was in every stroke, and in the niceness of finish of every foothold. After the end of the bridge was reached, it was a delicate thing to poise on a little platform which I had chipped on its upcurving end, and, bending over the slippery surface, get astride of it. Crossing was easy, cutting off the sharp edge with careful strokes, and hitching forward a few inches at a time, keeping my balance with my knees pressed against its sides. The tremendous abyss on each side I studiously ignored. The surface of that blue sliver was then all the world. But the most trying part of the adventure was, after working my way across inch by inch, to rise from the safe position astride that slippery strip of ice, and to cut a ladder in the face of the wall—chipping, climbing, holding on with feet and fingers in mere notches. At such times one's whole body is eye, and common skill and fortitude are replaced by power beyond our call or knowledge. Never before had I been so long under deadly strain. How I got up the cliff at the end of the bridge I never could tell. The thing seemed to have been done by somebody else. I never have had contempt of death, though in the course of my explorations I oftentimes felt that to meet one's fate on a mountain, in a grand canyon, or in the heart of a crystal glacier would be blessed as compared with death from disease, a mean accident in a street, or from a sniff of sewer gas. But the sweetest, cleanest death, set thus calmly and glaringly clear before us, is hard enough to face, even though we feel gratefully sure that we have already had happiness enough for a dozen lives.

But poor Stickeen, the wee, silky, sleekit beastie—think

of him! When I had decided to try the bridge, and while I was on my knees cutting away the rounded brow, he came behind me, pushed his head past my shoulder, looked down and across, scanned the sliver and its approaches with his queer eyes, then looked me in the face with a startled air of surprise and concern, and began to mutter and whine, saying as plainly as if speaking with words, "Surely you are not going to try that awful place?" This was the first time I had seen him gaze deliberately into a crevasse or into my face with a speaking look. That he should have recognized and appreciated the danger at the first glance showed wonderful sagacity. Never before had the quick, daring midget seemed to know that ice was slippery, or that there was such a thing as danger anywhere. His looks and the tones of his voice when he began to complain and speak his fears were so human that I unconsciously talked to him as I would to a boy, and in trying to calm his fears perhaps in some measure moderated my own. "Hush your fears, my boy," I said. "We will get across safe, though it is not going to be easy. No right way is easy in this rough world. We must risk our lives to save them. At the worst we can only slip; and then how grand a grave we shall have! And by and by our nice bones will do good in the terminal moraine." But my sermon was far from reassuring him; he began to cry, and after taking another piercing look at the tremendous gulf, ran away in desperate excitement, seeking some other crossing. By the time he got back, baffled, of course, I had made a step or two. I dared not look back, but he made himself heard; and when he saw that I was certainly crossing, he cried aloud in despair. The danger was enough to daunt anybody, but it seems wonderful that he should have been able to weigh and appreciate it so justly. No mountaineer could have seen it more quickly or judged it more wisely, discriminating between real and apparent peril.

After I had gained the other side he howled louder than ever, and after running back and forth in vain search for a way of escape, he would return to the brink of the crevasse above the bridge, moaning and groaning as if in the bitterness of death. Could this be the silent, philosophic Stickeen? I shouted encouragement, telling him the bridge was not so bad as it looked, that I had left it flat for his feet, and he could walk it easily. But he was afraid to try it. Strange that so small an animal should be capable of such big, wise fears! I called again and again in a reassuring tone to come on and fear nothing; that he could come if he would only try. Then he would hush for a moment, look again at the bridge, and shout his unshakable conviction that he could never, never come that way; then lie back in despair, as if howling: "Oh-o-o, what a place! No-o-o, I can never go-o-o down there!" His natural composure and courage had vanished utterly in a tumultuous storm of fear. Had the danger been less, his distress would have seemed ridiculous. But in this gulf—a huge, yawning sepulcher big enough to hold everybody in the territory—lay the shadow of death, and his heartrending cries might well have called Heaven to his help. Perhaps they did. So hidden before, he was transparent now, and one could see the workings of his mind like the movements of a clock out of its case. His voice and gestures were perfectly human, and his hopes and fears unmistakable, while he seemed to understand every word of mine. I was troubled at the thought of leaving him. It seemed impossible to get him to venture. To compel him to try by fear of being left, I started off as if leaving him to his fate, and disappeared back of a hummock; but this did no good, for he only lay down and cried. So after hiding a few minutes, I went back to the brink of the crevasse, and in a severe tone of voice shouted across to him that now I must certainly leave him—I could wait no longer; and that if he would not come, all I could promise was that I would return to seek him next day. I warned him that if he went back to the woods the wolves would kill him, and finished by urging him once more by words and gestures to come on. He knew very well what I meant, and at last, with the courage of despair, hushed and breathless, he lay down on the brink in the hollow I had made for my knees, pressed his body against the ice to get the advantage of the friction, gazed into the first step, put his little feet together, and slid them slowly down into it, bunching all four in it, and almost standing on his head. Then, without lifting them, as well as I could see through the snow, he slowly worked them over the edge of the step, and down into the next and the next in succession in the same way, and gained the bridge. Then lifting his feet with the regularity and slowness of the vibrations of a seconds' pendulum, as if counting and measuring one, two, three, holding himself in dainty poise, and giving separate attention to each little step, he gained the foot of the cliff, at the top of which I was kneeling to give him a lift should he get within reach. Here he halted in dead silence, and it was here I feared he might fail, for dogs are poor climbers. I had no cord. If I had had one, I would have dropped a noose over his head and hauled him up. But while I was thinking whether an available cord might be made out of clothing, he was looking keenly into the series of notched steps and fingerholds of the ice ladder I had made, as if counting them and fixing the position of each one in his mind. Then suddenly up he came, with a nervy, springy rush, hooking his paws into the notches and steps so quickly that I could not see how it was done, and whizzed past my head, safe at last!

And now came a scene! "Well done, well done, little boy! Brave boy!" I cried, trying to catch and caress him; but he would not be caught. Never before or since have I seen anything like so passionate a revulsion from the depths of despair to uncontrollable, exultant, triumphant joy. He flashed and darted hither and thither as if fairly demented, screaming and shouting, swirling round and round in giddy loops and circles like a leaf in a whirlwind, lying down and rolling over and over, sidewise and heels over head, pouring forth a tumultuous flood of hysterical cries and sobs and gasping mutterings. And when I ran up to him to shake him, fearing he might die of joy, he flashed off two or three hundred yards, his feet in a mist of motion; then, turning suddenly, he came back in wild rushes, and launched himself at my face, almost knocking me down, all the time screeching and screaming and shouting as if saying, "Saved! Saved! Saved!" Then away again, dropping suddenly at times with his feet in the air, trembling, and fairly sobbing. Such passionate emotion was enough to kill him. Moses' stately song of triumph after escaping the Egyptians and the Red Sea was nothing to it. Who could have guessed the capacity of the dull, enduring little fellow for all that most stirs this mortal frame? Nobody could have helped crying with him.

But there is nothing like work for toning down either excessive fear or joy. So I ran ahead, calling him, in as gruff a voice as I could command, to come on and stop his nonsense, for we had far to go, and it would soon be dark. Neither of us feared another trial like this. Heaven would surely count one enough for a lifetime. The ice ahead was gashed by thousands of crevasses, but they were common ones. The joy of deliverance burned in us like fire, and we ran without fatigue, every muscle, with immense rebound, glorying in its strength. Stickeen flew across everything in his way, and not till dark did he settle into his normal foxlike, gliding trot. At last the mountains crowned with spruce came in sight, looming faintly in the gloaming, and we soon felt the solid rock beneath our feet, and were safe. Then came weariness. We stumbled down along the lateral moraine in the dark, over rocks and tree trunks, through the bushes and devil-club thickets and mossy logs and boulders of the woods where we had sheltered ourselves in the morning. Then out on the level mud slope of the terminal moraine. Danger had vanished, and so had our strength. We reached camp about ten o'clock, and found a big fire and a big supper. A party of Hoona Indians had visited Mr. Young, bringing a gift of porpoise meat and wild strawberries, and hunter Joe had brought in a wild goat. But we lay down, too tired to eat much, and soon fell into a troubled sleep. The man who said, "The harder the toil the sweeter the rest," never was profoundly tired. Stickeen kept springing up and muttering in his sleep, no doubt dreaming that he was still on the brink of the crevasse; and so did I—that night and many others, long afterward, when I was nervous and overtired.

Thereafter Stickeen was a changed dog. During the rest of the trip, instead of holding aloof, he would come to me at night, when all was quiet about the campfire, and rest his head on my knee, with a look of devotion, as if I were his god. And often, as he caught my eye, he seemed to be trying to say, "Wasn't that an awful time we had together on the glacier?"

None of his old friends know what finally became of him. When my work for the season was done I departed for California, and never saw the dear little fellow again. Mr. Young wrote me that in the summer of 1883 he was stolen by a tourist at Fort Wrangel, and taken away on a steamer. His fate is wrapped in mystery. If alive he is very old. Most likely he has left this world—crossed the last crevasse—and gone to another. But he will not be forgotten. Come what may, to me Stickeen is immortal.

## *Stephen Crane*

# A DARK-BROWN DOG

A child was standing on a streetcorner. He leaned with one shoulder against a high board fence and swayed the other to and fro, the while kicking carelessly at the gravel.

Sunshine beat upon the cobbles, and a lazy summer wind raised yellow dust which trailed in clouds down the avenue. Clattering trucks moved with indistinctness through it. The child stood dreamily gazing.

After a time, a little dark-brown dog came trotting with an intent air down the sidewalk. A short rope was dragging from his neck. Occasionally he trod upon the end of it and stumbled.

He stopped opposite the child, and the two regarded each other. The dog hesitated for a moment, but presently he made some little advances with his tail. The child put out his hand and called him. In an apologetic manner the dog came close, and the two had an interchange of friendly pattings and waggles. The dog became more enthusiastic with each moment of the interview, until with his gleeful caperings he threatened to overturn the child. Whereupon the child lifted his hand and struck the dog a blow upon the head.

This thing seemed to overpower and astonish the little dark-brown dog, and wounded him to the heart. He sank down in despair at the child's feet. When the blow was repeated, together with an admonition in childish sentences, he turned over upon his back, and held his paws in a peculiar manner. At the same time with his ears and his eyes he offered a small prayer to the child.

He looked so comical on his back, and holding his paws peculiarly, that the child was greatly amused and gave him little taps repeatedly, to keep him so. But the little dark-brown dog took this chastisement in the most serious way, and no doubt considered that he had committed some grave crime, for he wriggled contritely and showed his repentance in every way that was in his power. He pleaded with the child and petitioned him, and offered more prayers.

At last the child grew weary of this amusement and turned toward home. The dog was praying at the time. He lay on his back and turned his eyes upon the retreating form.

Presently he struggled to his feet and started after the child. The latter wandered in a perfunctory way toward his home, stopping at times to investigate various matters. During one of these pauses he discovered the little dark-brown dog who was following him with the air of a footpad.

The child beat his pursuer with a small stick he had found. The dog lay down and prayed until the child had finished, and resumed his journey. Then he scrambled erect and took up the pursuit again.

On the way to his home the child turned many times and beat the dog, proclaiming with childish gestures that he held him in contempt as an unimportant dog, with no value save for a moment. For being this quality of animal the dog apologized and eloquently expressed regret, but he continued stealthily to follow the child. His manner grew so very guilty that he slunk like an assassin.

When the child reached his doorstep, the dog was industriously ambling a few yards in the rear. He became so agitated with shame when he again confronted the child that he forgot the dragging rope. He tripped upon it and fell forward.

The child sat down on the step and the two had another interview. During it the dog greatly exerted himself to please the child. He performed a few gambols with such abandon that the child suddenly saw him to be a valuable thing. He made a swift, avaricious charge and seized the rope.

He dragged his captive into a hall and up many long stairways in a dark tenement. The dog made willing efforts, but he could not hobble very skillfully up the stairs because he was very small and soft, and at last the pace of the engrossed child grew so energetic that the dog became panic-stricken. In his mind he was being dragged toward a grim unknown. His eyes grew wild with the terror of it. He began to wiggle his head frantically and to brace his legs.

The child redoubled his exertions. They had a battle on the stairs. The child was victorious because he was completely absorbed in his purpose, and because the dog was very small. He dragged his acquirement to the door of his home, and finally with triumph across the threshold.

No one was in. The child sat down on the floor and made overtures to the dog. These the dog instantly accepted. He beamed with affection upon his new friend. In a short time they were firm and abiding comrades.

When the child's family appeared, they made a great row. The dog was examined and commented upon and called names. Scorn was leveled at him from all eyes, so that he became much embarrassed and drooped like a scorched plant. But the child went sturdily to the center of the floor, and, at the top of his voice, championed the dog. It happened that he was roaring protestations, with his arms clasped about the dog's neck, when the father of the family came in from work.

The parent demanded to know what the blazes they were making the kid howl for. It was explained in many words that the infernal kid wanted to introduce a disreputable dog into the family.

A family council was held. On this depended the dog's fate, but he in no way heeded, being busily engaged in chewing the end of the child's dress.

The affair was quickly ended. The father of the family, it appears, was in a particularly savage temper that evening, and when he perceived that it would amaze and anger everybody if such a dog were allowed to remain, he decided that it should be so. The child, crying softly, took his friend off to a retired part of the room to hobnob with him, while the father quelled a fierce rebellion of his wife. So it came to pass that the dog was a member of the household.

He and the child were associated together at all times save when the child slept. The child became a guardian and a friend. If the large folk kicked the dog and threw things at him, the child made loud and violent objections. Once when the child had run, protesting loudly, with tears raining down his face and his arms outstretched, to protect his friend, he had been struck in the head with a very large saucepan from the hand of his father, enraged at some seeming lack of courtesy in the dog. Ever after, the family were careful how they threw things at the dog. Moreover, the latter grew very skillful in avoiding missiles and feet. In a small room containing a stove, a table, a bureau, and some chairs, he would display strategic ability of a high order, dodging, feinting, and scuttling about among the furniture. He could force three or four people armed with brooms, sticks, and handfuls of coal, to use all their ingenuity to get in a blow. And even when they did it, it was seldom that they could do him a serious injury or leave any imprint.

But when the child was present these scenes did not occur. It came to be recognized that if the dog was molested, the child would burst into sobs, and as the child, when started, was very riotous and practically unquenchable, the dog had therein a safeguard.

However, the child could not always be near. At night, when he was asleep, his dark-brown friend would raise from some black corner a wild, wailful cry, a song of infinite loneliness and despair, that would go shuddering and sobbing among the buildings of the block and cause people to swear. At these times the singer would often be chased all over the kitchen and hit with a great variety of articles.

Sometimes, too, the child himself used to beat the dog, although it is not known that he ever had what truly could be called a just cause. The dog always accepted these thrashings with an air of admitted guilt. He was too much of a dog to try to look to be a martyr or to plot revenge. He received the blows with deep humility, and furthermore he forgave his friend the moment the child had finished, and was ready to caress the child's hand with his little red tongue.

When misfortune came upon the child, and his troubles overwhelmed him, he would often crawl under the table and lay his small distressed head on the dog's back. The dog was ever sympathetic. It is not to be supposed that at such times he took occasion to refer to the unjust beatings his friend, when provoked, had administered to him.

He did not achieve any notable degree of intimacy with

the other members of the family. He had no confidence in them, and the fear that he would express at their casual approach often exasperated them exceedingly. They used to gain a certain satisfaction in underfeeding him, but finally his friend the child grew to watch the matter with some care, and when he forgot it, the dog was often successful in secret for himself.

So the dog prospered. He developed a large bark, which came wondrously from such a small rug of a dog. He ceased to howl persistently at night. Sometimes, indeed, in his sleep, he would utter little yells, as from pain, but that occurred, no doubt, when in his dreams he encountered huge flaming dogs who threatened him direfully.

His devotion to the child grew until it was a sublime thing. He wagged at his approach; he sank down in despair at his departure. He could detect the sound of the child's step among all the noises of the neighborhood. It was like a calling voice to him.

The scene of their companionship was a kingdom governed by this terrible potentate, the child; but neither criticism nor rebellion ever lived for an instant in the heart of the one subject. Down in the mystic, hidden fields of his little dog-soul bloomed flowers of love and fidelity and perfect faith.

The child was in the habit of going on many expeditions to observe strange things in the vicinity. On these occasions his friend usually jogged aimfully along behind. Perhaps, though, he went ahead. This necessitated his turning around every quarter-minute to make sure the child was coming. He was filled with a large idea of the importance of these journeys. He would carry himself with such an air! He was proud to be the retainer of so great a monarch.

One day, however, the father of the family got quite exceptionally drunk. He came home and held carnival with the cooking utensils, the furniture, and his wife. He was in the midst of this recreation when the child, followed by the dark-brown dog, entered the room. They were returning from their voyages.

The child's practiced eye instantly noted his father's state. He dived under the table, where experience had taught him was a rather safe place. The dog, lacking skill in such matters, was, of course, unaware of the true condition of affairs. He looked with interested eyes at his friend's sudden dive. He interpreted it to mean: joyous gambol. He started to patter across the floor to join him. He was the picture of a little dark-brown dog en route to a friend.

The head of the family saw him at this moment. He gave a huge howl of joy, and knocked the dog down with a heavy coffeepot. The dog, yelling in supreme astonishment and fear, writhed to his feet and ran for cover. The man kicked out with a ponderous foot. It caused the dog to swerve as if caught in a tide. A second blow of the coffeepot laid him upon the floor.

Here the child, uttering loud cries, came valiantly forth like a knight. The father of the family paid no attention to these calls of the child, but advanced with glee upon the dog. Upon being knocked down twice in swift succession, the latter apparently gave up all hope of escape. He rolled over on his back and held his paws in a peculiar manner. At the same time with his eyes and his ears he offered up a small prayer.

But the father was in a mood for having fun, and it occurred to him that it would be a fine thing to throw the dog out of the window. So he reached down and, grabbing the animal by a leg, lifted him, squirming, up. He swung him two or three times hilariously about his head, and then flung him with great accuracy through the window.

The soaring dog created a surprise in the block. A woman watering plants in an opposite window gave an involuntary shout and dropped a flowerpot. A man in another window leaned perilously out to watch the flight of the dog. A woman who had been hanging out clothes in a yard began to caper wildly. Her mouth was filled with clothespins, but her arms gave vent to a sort of exclamation. In appearance she was like a gagged prisoner. Children ran whooping.

The dark-brown body crashed in a heap on the roof of a shed five stories below. From thence it rolled to the pavement of an alleyway.

The child in the room far above burst into a long, dirge-like cry, and toddled hastily out of the room. It took him a long time to reach the alley, because his size compelled him to go downstairs backward, one step at a time, and holding with both hands to the step above.

When they came for him later, they found him seated by the body of his dark-brown friend.

## *Ivan Turgenev*

# MUMÚ

In one of the remote streets of Moscow, in a gray house with white pillars, an entresol, and a crooked balcony, dwelt in former days a well-born lady, a widow, surrounded by numerous domestics. Her sons were in the service in Petersburg, her daughters were married; she rarely went out into society, and was living out the last years of a miserly and tedious old age in solitude. Her day, cheerless and stormy, was long since over; but her evening also was blacker than night.

Among the ranks of her menials, the most remarkable person was the yard porter, Gerásim, a man six feet, five inches in height, built like an epic hero, and a deaf-mute from his birth. His mistress had taken him from the village, where he lived alone, in a tiny cottage, apart from his brethren, and was considered the most punctual of the taxable serfs. Endowed with remarkable strength, he did the work of four persons. Matters made progress in his hands, and it was a cheerful sight to watch him when he plowed and, applying his huge hands to the primitive plow, seemed to be carving open the elastic bosom of the earth alone, without the aid of his little nag; or about St. Peter's Day wielding the scythe so shatteringly that he might even have hewn off a young birchwood from its roots; or threshing briskly and unremittingly with a chain seven feet in length, while the firm, oblong muscles on his shoulders rose and fell like levers. His uninterrupted muteness imparted to his indefatigable labor a grave solemnity. He was a splendid peasant, and had it not been for his infirmity, any maiden would willingly have married him. But Gerásim was brought to Moscow, boots were bought for him, a broom and a shovel were put into his hand, and he was appointed to be the yard porter.

At first he felt a violent dislike for his new life. From his childhood he had been accustomed to field labor, to country life. Set apart by his infirmity from communion with his fellow men, he had grown up dumb and mighty, as a tree grows on fruitful soil. Transported to the town, he did not understand what was happening to him; he felt bored and puzzled, as a healthy young bull is puzzled when he has just been taken from the pasture, where the grass grew up to his belly—when he has been taken, and placed in a railway wagon, and, lo, with his robust body enveloped now with smoke and sparks, again with billows of steam, he is drawn headlong onward, drawn with rumble and squeaking, and whither, God only knows. Gerásim's occupations in his new employment seemed to him a mere farce after his onerous labors as a peasant; in half an hour he had finished everything, and he was again standing in the middle of the courtyard and staring, open-mouthed, at all the passersby, as though desirous of obtaining from them the solution of his enigmatic situation; or he would suddenly go off to some corner and, flinging his broom or his shovel far from him, would throw himself on the ground face downward, and lie motionless on his breast for whole hours at a time, like a captured wild beast.

But man grows accustomed to everything, and Gerásim got used, at last, to town life! He had not much to do; his entire duty consisted in keeping the courtyard clean, fetching a cask of water twice a day, hauling and chopping up wood for the kitchen and house, and in not admitting strangers, and keeping watch at night. And it must be said that he discharged his duty with zeal; not a chip was ever strewn about his courtyard, nor any dirt; if in muddy weather the broken-winded nag for hauling water and the barrel entrusted to his care got stranded anywhere, all he had to do was to apply his shoulder, and not only the cask but the horse also would be pried from the spot. If he undertook to chop wood, his ax would ring like glass, and splinters and billets would fly in every direction; and as for strangers—after he had, one night, caught two thieves and had banged their heads together and mauled them so that there was no necessity for taking them to the police station afterward, everyone in the neighborhood began to respect him greatly, and even by day passersby who were not in the least rascals, but simply strangers to him, at the sight of the ominous yard porter would brandish their arms as though in self-defense.

With all the other domestics Gerásim sustained relations that were not exactly friendly—they were afraid of him—but gentle. They expressed their meaning to him by signs, and he understood them, accurately executed all orders but knew his own rights also, and no one dared to take his seat at table. On the whole, Gerásim was of stern and serious disposition, and was fond of orderliness in all things; even the cocks did not venture to fight in his presence—but if they did, woe be to them! If he caught sight of them he would instantly seize them by the legs, whirl them round like a wheel half a dozen times in the air, and hurl them in opposite directions. There were geese also in his mistress's courtyard, but a goose, as everybody knows, is a serious and sensible bird; Gerásim respected them, tended them, and fed them; he himself bore a resemblance to a stately gander.

One evening as he was walking by the river and quietly staring into the water, it suddenly seemed to him as though something were floundering in the ooze close to the bank. He bent down and, behold, a small puppy, white with black spots, which, despite all its endeavors, utterly unable to crawl out of the water, was struggling, slipping, and quivering all over its wet, gaunt little body. Gerásim gazed at the unfortunate puppy, picked it up with one hand, thrust it into his breast, and set out with great strides homeward. He entered his little den, laid the rescued puppy on his bed, covered it with his heavy coat, ran first to the stable for straw, then to the kitchen for a cup of milk. Cautiously throwing back the coat and spreading out the straw, he placed the milk on the bed. The poor little dog was only three weeks old; it had only recently gotten its eyes open, and one eye even appeared to be a little larger than the other; it did not yet know how to drink out of a cup, and merely trembled and blinked. Gerásim grasped it lightly with two fingers by the head, and bent its muzzle down to the milk. The dog suddenly began to drink greedily, snorting, shaking itself, and lapping. Gerásim gazed and gazed, and then suddenly began to laugh. All night he fussed over it, put it to bed, wiped it off, and at last fell asleep himself beside it in a joyous, tranquil slumber.

No mother tends her infant as Gerásim tended his nursling. (The dog proved to be a bitch.) In the beginning she was very weak, puny, and ill-favored, but little by little she improved in health and looks, and at the end of eight months, thanks to the indefatigable care of her rescuer, she had turned into a very fair sort of a dog of Spanish breed, with long ears, a feathery tail in the form of a trumpet, and large, expressive eyes. She attached herself passionately to Gerásim, never left him by a pace, and was always following him, wagging her tail. And he had given her a name, too—the dumb know that their bellowing attracts other people's attention to them—he called her Mumú. All the people in the house took a liking to her, and also called her dear little Mumú. She was extremely intelligent, fawned upon everyone, but loved Gerásim alone. Gerásim himself loved her madly, and it was disagreeable to him when others stroked her—whether he was afraid for her, or jealous of her, God knows! She waked him up in the morning by tugging at his coattails; she led to him by the reins the old water horse, with whom she dwelt in great amity; with importance depicted on her face, she went with him to the river; she stood guard over the brooms and shovels, and allowed no one to enter his room. He cut out an aperture in his door expressly for her, and she seemed to feel that only in Gerásim's little den was she the full mistress, and therefore, on entering it, with a look of satisfaction, she immediately leaped upon the bed. At night she did not sleep at all, but she did not bark without discernment, like a stupid watchdog, which, sitting on its haunches and elevating its muzzle, and shutting its eyes, barks simply out of tedium, at the stars, and usually three times in succession. No! Mumú's shrill voice never resounded without cause! Either a stranger was approaching too close to the fence, or some suspicious noise or rustling had arisen somewhere. In a word, she kept capital watch.

Truth to tell, there was, in addition to her, an old dog in the courtyard, yellow in hue speckled with dark brown, Pegtop by name (*Voltchók*); but that dog was never unchained, even by night, and he himself, owing to his decrepitude, did not demand freedom, but lay there, curled up in his kennel, and only now and then emitted a hoarse, almost soundless bark, which he immediately broke off short, as though himself conscious of its utter futility.

Mumú did not enter the manor house, and when Gerásim carried wood to the rooms she always remained behind and impatiently awaited him, with ears pricked up, and her head turning now to the right, then suddenly to the left, at the slightest noise indoors.

In this manner still another year passed. Gerásim continued to discharge his avocations as yard porter and was very well satisfied with his lot, when suddenly an unexpected incident occurred. Namely, one fine summer day the mistress, with her maids, was walking about the drawing room. She was in good spirits, and was laughing and jesting; the maids were laughing and jesting also, but felt no particular mirth; the people of the household were not very fond of seeing the mistress in merry mood, because, in the first place, at such times she demanded instantaneous and complete sympathy from everyone, and flew into a rage if there was a face that did not beam with satisfaction; and, in the second place, these fits did not last very long, and were generally succeeded by a gloomy and cross-grained frame of mind. On that day, she seemed to have gotten up happily; at cards, she held four knaves: the fulfillment of desire (she always told fortunes with the cards in the morning); and her tea struck her as particularly delicious, in consequence whereof the maid received praise in words and ten kopecks in money. With a sweet smile on her wrinkled lips, the lady of the house strolled about her drawing room and approached the window. A flower garden was laid out in front of the window, and in the very middle of the border, under a rosebush, lay Mumú assiduously gnawing a bone. The mistress caught sight of her.

"My God!" she suddenly exclaimed. "What dog is that?"

The maid whom the mistress addressed floundered, poor creature, with that painful uneasiness that generally takes possession of a dependent person when he does not quite know how he is to understand his superior's exclamation.

"I . . . d—do—on't know, ma'am," she stammered; "I think it belongs to the dumb man."

"My God!" her mistress interrupted her. "Why, it is a very pretty dog! Order it to be brought hither. Has he had it long? How is it that I have not seen it before? Order it to be brought hither."

The maid immediately fluttered out into the anteroom.

"Man, man!" she screamed. "Bring Mumú here at once! She is in the flower garden."

"And so her name is Mumú," said the mistress, "a very nice name."

"Akh, very nice indeed, ma'am!" replied the dependent. "Be quick, Stepán!"

Stepán, a sturdy young fellow, who served as footman, rushed headlong to the garden and tried to seize Mumú; but the latter cleverly slipped out of his fingers and, elevating her tail, set off at full gallop to Gerásim, who was in the kitchen beating out and shaking out the water cask, twirling it about in his hands like a child's drum. Stepán ran after her, and tried to seize her at the very feet of her master; but the agile dog would not surrender herself into the hands of a stranger, and kept leaping and evading him. Gerásim looked on at all this tumult with a grin; at last Stepán rose in wrath, and hastily gave him to understand by signs that the mistress had ordered the dog to be brought to her. Gerásim was somewhat surprised, but he called Mumú, lifted her from the ground, and handed her to Stepán. Stepán carried her into the drawing room, and placed her on the polished wood floor. The mistress began to call the dog to her in a caressing voice. Mumú, who had never in her life been in such magnificent rooms, was extremely frightened, and tried to dart through the door, but, rebuffed by the obsequious Stepán, fell to trembling, and crouched against the wall.

"Mumú, Mumú, come hither to me," said the mistress. "Come, thou stupid creature . . . don't be afraid."

"Come, Mumú, come to the mistress," repeated the maids. "Come!"

But Mumú looked anxiously about and did not stir from the spot.

"Bring her something to eat," said the mistress. "What a stupid thing she is! She won't come to the mistress. What is she afraid of?"

"She feels strange still," remarked one of the maids, in a timid and imploring voice.

Stepán brought a saucer of milk and set it in front of Mumú, but Mumú did not even smell the milk, and kept on trembling and gazing about her, as before.

"Akh, who ever saw such a creature!" said the mistress, as she approached her, bent down, and was on the point of stroking her; but Mumú turned her head and displayed her teeth in a snarl. The mistress hastily drew back her hand.

A momentary silence ensued. Mumú whined faintly, as though complaining and excusing herself. The mistress retreated and frowned. The dog's sudden movement had frightened her.

"Akh!" cried all the maids with one accord. "She didn't bite you, did she? God forbid!" (Mumú had never bitten anyone in her life.) "Akh! akh!"

"Take her away," said the old woman, in an altered voice, "the horrid little dog! What a vicious beast she is!"

And slowly turning, she went toward her boudoir. The maids exchanged timorous glances and started to follow her, but she paused, looked coldly at them, said: "Why do you do that? I have not bidden you," and left the room.

The maids waved their hands in despair at Stepán; the latter picked up Mumú and flung her out into the yard as speedily as possible, straight at Gerásim's feet; and half an hour later a profound stillness reigned in the house, and the old gentlewoman sat on her divan more lowering than a thundercloud.

What trifles, when one comes to think of it, can sometimes put a person out of tune!

The lady was out of sorts until evening, talked with no one, did not play cards, and passed a bad night. She took it into her head that they had not given her the same eau de cologne that they usually gave her, that her pillow smelled of soap, and made the keeper of the linen closet smell all the bed linen twice—in a word, she was upset and extremely incensed. On the following morning she ordered Gavríla to be summoned to her presence an hour earlier than usual.

"Tell me, please," she began, as soon as the latter, not without some inward quaking, had crossed the threshold of her boudoir, "why that dog was barking in our courtyard all night long? It prevented my getting to sleep!"

"A dog, ma'am, which one, ma'am? Perhaps it was the dumb man's dog," he uttered in a voice that was not altogether firm.

"I don't know whether it belongs to the dumb man or to someone else, only it interfered with my sleep. And I am amazed that there is such a horde of dogs! I want to know about it. We have a watchdog, have we not?"

"Yes, ma'am, we have, ma'am, Peg-top, ma'am."

"Well, what need have we for any more dogs? They only create disorder. There's no head to the house, that's what's the matter. And what does the dumb man want of a dog? Who has given him permission to keep a dog in my courtyard? Yesterday I went to the window, and it was lying in the garden; it had brought some nasty thing there, and was gnawing it; and I have roses planted there. . . ."

The lady paused for a while.

"See that it is removed this very day . . . do you hear me?"

"I obey, ma'am."

"This very day. And now, go. I will have you called for your report later."

Gavríla left the room.

As he passed through the drawing room, the majordomo transferred a small bell from one table to another, for show, softly blew his duck's-bill nose in the hall, and went out into the anteroom. In the anteroom, on a locker, Stepán was sleeping in the attitude of a slain warrior in a battalion picture, with his bare legs projecting from his coat, which served him in lieu of a coverlet.

The majordomo nudged him, and imparted to him in an undertone some order, to which Stepán replied with a half-yawn, half-laugh. The majordomo withdrew, and Stepán sprang to his feet, drew on his kaftan and his boots, went out, and came to a standstill on the porch. Five minutes had not elapsed before Gerásim made his appearance with a huge fagot of firewood on his back, accompanied by his inseparable Mumú. (The mistress had issued orders that her bedroom and boudoir were to be heated even in summer.) Gerásim stood sideways to the door, gave it a push with his shoulder, and precipitated himself into the house with his burden. Mumú, according to her wont, remained behind to wait for him. Then Stepán, seizing a favorable moment, made a sudden dash at her, like a hawk pouncing on a chicken, crushed her to the ground with his breast, gathered her up in his arms, and, without stopping to don so much as his cap, ran out into the street with her, jumped into the first droshky that came to hand, and galloped off to the Game Market. There he speedily hunted up a purchaser, to whom he sold her for half a ruble, stipulating only that the latter should keep her tied up for at least a week, and immediately returned home; but before he reached the house, he alighted from the droshky, and, making a circuit of the house, he leaped over the fence into the yard from a back alley; he was afraid to enter by the wicket, lest he should encounter Gerásim.

But his anxiety was wasted; Gerásim was no longer in the courtyard. On coming out of the house he had instantly bethought himself of Mumú; he could not remember that she had ever failed to await his return, and he began to run in every direction to hunt for her, to call her after his own fashion. He dashed into his little chamber, to the hayloft; he darted into the street, hither and thither. She was gone! He appealed to the domestics, with the most despairing signs inquired about her; pointing fourteen inches from the ground, he drew her form with his hands. Some of them really did not know what had become of Mumú, and only shook their heads; others did know and grinned at him in reply, but the majordomo assumed a very pompous mien and began to shout at the coachmen. Then Gerásim fled far away from the courtyard.

Twilight was already falling when he returned. One was justified in assuming, from his exhausted aspect, from his unsteady gait, from his dusty clothing, that he had wandered over half of Moscow. He halted in front of the mistress's windows, swept a glance over the porch on which seven house serfs were gathered, turned away, and bellowed once more: "Mumú!" Mumú did not respond. He went away. All stared after him, but no one smiled, no one uttered a word; and the curious postilion, Antípka, narrated on the following morning in the kitchen that the dumb man had moaned all night long.

All the following day Gerásim did not show himself, so that Potáp the coachman was obliged to go for water in his stead, which greatly displeased coachman Potáp. The mistress asked Gavríla whether her command had been executed. Gavríla replied that it had. The next morning Gerásim emerged from his chamber to do his work. He came to dinner, ate, and went off again, without having exchanged greetings with anyone. His face, which was inanimate at the best of times, as is the case with all deaf-and-dumb persons, now seemed to have become absolutely petrified. After dinner he again quitted the courtyard, but not for long; returned, and immediately directed his steps to the hay barn. Night came, a clear, moonlight night. Sighing heavily and incessantly tossing from side to side, Gerásim was lying there, when he suddenly felt as though something were tugging at the skirts of his garments; he trembled all over, but did not raise his head, nevertheless, and even screwed his eyes up tight; but the tugging was repeated, more energetically than before; he sprang to his feet. Before him, with a fragment of rope about her neck, Mumú was capering about. A prolonged shriek of joy burst from his speechless breast; he seized Mumú and clasped her in a close embrace; in one moment she had licked his nose, his eyes, and his beard. He stood still for a while, pondering, cautiously slipped down from the haymow, cast a glance round him, and having made sure that no one was watching him, he safely regained his little chamber.

Even before this Gerásim had divined that the dog had not disappeared of her own volition, that she must have been carried away by the mistress's command, for the domestics had explained to him by signs how his Mumú had snapped at her—and he decided to take precautions of his own. First he fed Mumú some bread, caressed her, and put her to bed; then he began to consider how he might best conceal her. At last he hit upon the idea of leaving her all day in his room, only looking in now and then to see how she was getting along, and taking her out for exercise at night. He closed the opening in his door compactly by stuffing in an old coat of his, and as soon as it was daylight he was in the courtyard, as though nothing had happened, even preserving (innocent guile!) his former dejection of countenance. It could not enter the head of the poor deaf man that Mumú would betray herself by her whining; as a matter of fact, everyone in the house was speedily aware that the dumb man's dog had come back and was locked up in his room; but out of compassion for him and for her, and partly, perhaps, out of fear of him, they did not give him to understand that his secret had been discovered.

The majordomo alone scratched the back of his head and waved his hand in despair, as much as to say: "Well, I wash my hands of the matter! Perhaps the mistress will not get to know of it!" And never had the dumb man worked so zealously as on that day; he swept and scraped out the entire courtyard, he rooted up all the blades of grass to the very last one, with his own hand pulled up all the props in the garden fence, with a view to making sure that they were sufficiently firm, and then hammered them in again—in a word, he fussed and bustled about so, that even the mistress noticed his zeal.

Twice in the course of the day Gerásim went stealthily to his captive; and when night came, he lay down to sleep in her company, in the little room, not in the hay barn, and only at one o'clock did he go out to take a stroll with her in the fresh air. Having walked quite a long time with her in the courtyard, he was preparing to return, when suddenly a noise resounded outside the fence in the direction of the alley. Mumú pricked up her ears, began to growl, approached the fence, sniffed, and broke forth into a loud and piercing bark. Some drunken man or other had taken it into his head to nestle down there for the night. At that very moment, the mistress had just got to sleep after a prolonged "nervous excitement"; she always had these excited fits after too hearty a supper. The sudden barking woke her; her heart began to beat violently, and to collapse.

"Maids, maids!" she moaned. "Maids!"

The frightened maids flew to her bedroom.

"Okh, okh, I'm dying!" said she, throwing her hands apart in anguish. "There's that dog again, again! Okh, send for the doctor! They want to kill me. The dog, the dog again! Okh!"

And she flung back her head, which was intended to denote a swoon.

They ran for the doctor, that is to say, for the household

medical man, Kharitón. The whole art of this healer consisted in the fact that he wore boots with soft soles, understood how to feel the pulse delicately, slept fourteen hours out of the twenty-four, spent the rest of the time in sighing, and was incessantly treating the mistress to laurel drops. This healer immediately hastened to her, fumigated with burned feathers, and, when the mistress opened her eyes, immediately presented to her on a silver tray a wineglass with the inevitable drops.

The mistress took them, but immediately, with tearful eyes, began to complain of the dog, of Gavríla, of her lot, that she, a poor old woman, had been abandoned by everyone, that no one had any pity on her, and that everyone desired her death. In the meantime the unlucky Mumú continued to bark, while Gerásim strove in vain to call her away from the fence.

"There . . . there . . . it goes again!" stammered the mistress, and again rolled up her eyes. The medical man whispered to one of the maids; she rushed into the anteroom, and explained matters to Stepán; the latter ran to awaken Gavríla, and Gavríla, in a passion, gave orders that the whole household should be roused.

Gerásim turned round, beheld the twinkling lights and shadows in the windows, and, foreboding in his heart a catastrophe, he caught up Mumú under his arm, ran into his room, and locked the door. A few moments later, five men were thumping at his door, but, feeling the resistance of the bolt, desisted. Gavríla ran up in a frightful hurry, ordered them all to remain there until morning and stand guard, while he himself burst into the maids' hall and gave orders through the eldest companion, Liubóff Liubímovna—together with whom he was in the habit of stealing and enjoying tea, sugar, and other groceries—that the mistress was to be informed that the dog, unfortunately, had run home again from somewhere or other, but that it would not be alive on the morrow, and that the mistress must do them the favor not to be angry, and must calm down. The mistress probably would not have calmed down very speedily had not the medical man, in his haste, poured out forty drops instead of twelve. The strength of the laurel took its effect—in a quarter of an hour the mistress was sleeping soundly and peacefully, and Gerásim was lying, all pale, on his bed, tightly compressing Mumú's mouth.

On the following morning the mistress awoke quite late. Gavríla was waiting for her awakening in order to make a decisive attack upon Gerásim's asylum, and was himself prepared to endure a heavy thunderstorm. But the thunderstorm did not come off. As she lay in bed, the mistress ordered the eldest servant to be called to her.

"Liubóff Liubímovna," she began in a soft, weak voice—she sometimes liked to pretend to be a persecuted and defenseless sufferer; it is needless to state that at such times all the people in the house felt very uncomfortable. "Liubóff Liubímovna, you see what my condition is; go, my dear, to Gavríla Andréitch, and have a talk with him; it cannot be possible that some nasty little dog or other is more precious to him than the tranquility, the very life of his mistress! I should not like to believe that," she added, with an expression of profound emotion. "Go, my dear, be so good, go to Gavríla Andréitch."

Liubóff Liubímovna betook herself to Gavríla's room. What conversation took place between them is not known; but a while later a whole throng of domestics marched through the courtyard in the direction of Gerásim's little den; in front walked Gavríla, holding on his cap with his hand, although there was no wind; around him walked footmen and cooks; Uncle Tail gazed out of the window, and issued orders—that is to say, he merely spread his hands apart; in the rear of all, the small urchins leaped and capered, half of them being strangers who had run in. On the narrow stairway leading to the den sat one sentry; at the door stood two others with clubs. They began to ascend the staircase, and occupied it to its full length. Gavríla went to the door, knocked on it with his fist, and shouted:

"Open!"

A suppressed bark made itself audible; but there was no reply.

"Open, I say!" he repeated.

"But Gavríla Andréitch," remarked Stepán from below, "he's deaf, you know—he doesn't hear."

All burst out laughing.

"What is to be done?" retorted Gavríla from the top of the stairs.

"Why, he has a hole in his door," replied Stepán, "so wiggle a stick around in it a bit."

Gavríla bent down.

"He has stuffed it up with some sort of coat, that hole."

"But poke the coat inward."

At this point another dull bark rang out.

"See there, see there, she's giving herself away!" someone remarked in the crowd, and again there was laughter.

Gavríla scratched behind his ear.

"No, brother," he went on at last, "you poke the coat through yourself, if you wish."

"Why, certainly!"

And Stepán scrambled up, took a stick, thrust the coat inside, and began to wiggle the stick about in the opening, saying: "Come forth, come forth!" He was still wiggling the stick when the door of the little chamber flew suddenly and swiftly open—and the whole train of menials rolled head over heels down the stairs, Gavríla in the lead. Uncle Tail shut the window.

"Come, come, come, come!" shouted Gavríla from the courtyard. "Just look out, look out!"

Gerásim stood motionless on the threshold. The crowd assembled at the foot of the staircase. Gerásim stared at all these petty folk in their foreign kaftans from above, with his arms lightly set akimbo; in his scarlet peasant shirt he seemed like a giant in comparison with them. Gavríla advanced a pace.

"See here, brother," said he, "I'll take none of your impudence."

And he began to explain to him by signs: "The mistress insists upon having your dog: hand it over instantly, or 'twill be the worse for you."

Gerásim looked at him, pointed to the dog, made a sign with his hand at his own neck, as though he were drawing up a noose, and cast an inquiring glance at the majordomo.

"Yes, yes," replied the latter, nodding his head, "yes, she insists."

Gerásim dropped his eyes, then suddenly shook himself, again pointed at Mumú, who all this time had been standing by his side, innocently wagging her tail and moving her ears to and fro with curiosity, repeated the sign of strangling over his own neck, and significantly smote himself on the breast, as though declaring that he would take it upon himself to annihilate Mumú.

"But you will deceive," waved Gavríla to him in reply.

Gerásim looked at him, laughed disdainfully, smote himself again on the breast, and slammed the door.

All present exchanged glances in silence.

"Well, and what's the meaning of this?" began Gavríla. "He has locked himself in."

"Let him alone, Gavríla Andréitch," said Stepán. "He'll do it, if he has promised. That's the sort of fellow he is. . . . If he once promises a thing, it's safe. He isn't like us folks in that respect. What is true is true. Yes."

"Yes," repeated all, and wagged their heads. "That's so. Yes."

Uncle Tail opened the window and said yes, also.

"Well, we shall see, I suppose," returned Gavríla, "but

the guard is not to be removed, notwithstanding. Hey, there, Eróshka!" he added, addressing a poor man in a yellow nankeen kazák coat, who was reckoned as the gardener. "What are you doing? Take a stick and sit here, and if anything happens, run for me on the instant."

Eróshka took a stick and sat down on the last step of the staircase. The crowd dispersed, with the exception of a few curious bodies and the small urchins, while Gavríla returned home, and through Liubóff Liubímovna gave orders that the mistress should be informed that everything had been done, and that he himself, in order to make quite sure, had sent the postilion for a policeman. The mistress tied a knot in her handkerchief, poured eau de cologne on it, sniffed at it, wiped her temples, sipped her tea, and, being still under the influence of the laurel drops, fell asleep again.

An hour after all this commotion, the door of the tiny den opened and Gerásim made his appearance. He wore a new holiday kaftan; he was leading Mumú by a string. Eróshka drew aside and let him pass. Gerásim directed his way toward the gate. All the small boys who were in the courtyard followed him with their eyes in silence. He did not even turn round; he did not put on his cap until he reached the street. Gavríla dispatched after him that same Eróshka, in the capacity of observer. Eróshka, perceiving from afar that he had entered an eating house in company with his dog, awaited his reappearance.

In the eating house they knew Gerásim and understood his signs. He ordered cabbage soup with meat, and seated himself, with his arms resting on the table. Mumú stood beside his chair, calmly gazing at him with her intelligent eyes. Her coat was fairly shining with gloss; it was evident that she had recently been brushed. They brought the cabbage soup to Gerásim. He crumbled up bread in it, cut the meat up into small pieces, and set the plate on the floor. Mumú began to eat with her customary politeness, hardly touching her muzzle to the food. Gerásim stared long at her; two heavy tears rolled suddenly from his eyes; one fell on the dog's sloping forehead, the other into the soup. He covered his face with his hand. Mumú ate half a plateful and retired, licking her chops. Gerásim rose, paid for the soup, and set out, accompanied by the somewhat astounded glance of the waiter. Eróshka, on catching sight of Gerásim, sprang round the corner, and, allowing him to pass, again set out on his track.

Gerásim walked on without haste, and did not release Mumú from the cord. On reaching the corner of the street he halted, as though in thought, and suddenly directed his course, with swift strides, straight toward the Crimean Ford. On the way he entered the yard of a house to which a wing was being built, and brought thence two bricks under his arm. From the Crimean Ford he turned along the bank, advanced to a certain spot, where stood two boats with oars, tied to stakes (he had already noted them previously), and sprang into one of them, in company with Mumú. A lame little old man emerged from behind a hut placed in one corner of a vegetable garden, and shouted at him. But Gerásim only nodded his head, and set to rowing so vigorously, although against the current, that in an instant he had darted off to a distance of a hundred fathoms. The old man stood and stood, scratched his back, first with the left hand then with the right, and returned, limping, to his hut.

But Gerásim rowed on and on. And now he had left Moscow behind him. Now, already, meadows, fields, groves stretched along the shores, and peasant cottages made their appearance. It smacked of the country. He flung aside the oars, bent his head down to Mumú, who was sitting in front of him on a dry thwart—the bottom was inundated with water —and remained motionless, with his mighty hands crossed on her back, while the boat drifted a little backward with the current toward the town. At last Gerásim straightened up hastily, with a sort of painful wrath on his face, wound the rope around the bricks he had taken, arranged a noose, put it on Mumú's neck, lifted her over the river, for the last time gazed at her. She gazed back at him confidingly and without alarm, waving her little tail slightly. He turned away, shut his eyes, and opened his hands. Gerásim heard nothing, neither the swift whine of the falling Mumú, nor the loud splash of the water; for him the noisiest day was silent and speechless, as not even the quietest night is to us, and when he opened his eyes again, the little waves were hurrying down the river as before; as before they were plashing about the sides of the boat, and only far astern toward the shore certain broad circles were spreading.

*Translated by I. F. Hapgood*

## O. Henry

# MEMOIRS OF A YELLOW DOG

I don't suppose it will knock any of you people off your perch to read a contribution from an animal. Mr. Kipling and a good many others have demonstrated the fact that animals can express themselves in remunerative English, and no magazine goes to press nowadays without an animal story in it, except the old-style monthlies that are still running pictures of Bryan and the Mont Pelée horror.

But you needn't look for any stuck-up literature in my piece, such as Bearoo, the bear, and Snakoo, the snake, and Tammanoo, the tiger, talk in the jungle books. A yellow dog that's spent most of his life in a cheap New York flat, sleeping in a corner on an old sateen underskirt (the one she spilled port wine on at the Lady Longshoremen's banquet), mustn't be expected to perform any tricks with the art of speech.

I was born a yellow pup; date, locality, pedigree, and weight unknown. The first thing I can recollect, an old woman had me in a basket at Broadway and Twenty-third trying to sell me to a fat lady. Old Mother Hubbard was boosting me to beat the band as a genuine Pomeranian-Hambletonian-Red-Irish-Cochin-China-Stoke-Pogis fox terrier. The fat lady chased a *V* around among the samples of grosgrain flannelette in her shopping bag till she cornered it, and gave up. From that moment on I was a pet—a mamma's own wootsey squidlums. Say, gentle reader, did you ever have a two-hundred-pound woman breathing a flavor of Camembert cheese and Peau d'Espagne pick you up and wallop her nose all over you, remarking all the time in an Emma Eames tone of voice: "Oh, oo's um oodlum, doodlum, woodlum, toodlum, bitsy-witsy skoodlums"?

From a pedigreed yellow pup I grew up to be an anonymous yellow cur looking like a cross between an Angora cat and a box of lemons. But my mistress never tumbled. She thought that the two primeval pups that Noah chased into the ark were but a collateral branch of my ancestors. It took two policemen to keep her from entering me at the Madison Square Garden for the Siberian bloodhound prize.

I'll tell you about that flat. The house was the ordinary thing in New York, paved with Parian marble in the entrance hall and cobblestones above the first floor. Our flat was three fl—well, not flights—climbs up. My mistress rented it unfurnished, and put in the regular things—1903 antique upholstered parlor set, oil chromo of geishas in a Harlem teahouse, rubber plant, and husband.

By Sirius! There was a biped I felt sorry for. He was a little man with sandy hair and whiskers a good deal like mine.

Henpecked? Well, toucans and flamingos and pelicans all had their bills in him. He wiped the dishes and listened to my mistress tell about the cheap, ragged things the lady with the squirrel-skin coat on the second floor hung out on her line to dry. And every evening while she was getting supper she made him take me out on the end of a string for a walk.

If men knew how women pass the time when they are alone they'd never marry. Laura Jean Libbey, peanut brittle, a little almond cream on the neck muscles, dishes unwashed, half an hour's talk with the iceman, reading a package of old letters, a couple of pickles and two bottles of malt extract, one hour peeking through a hole in the window shade into the flat across the air shaft—that's about all there is to it. Twenty minutes before time for him to come home from work she straightens up the house, fixes her rat so it won't show, and gets out a lot of sewing for a ten-minute bluff.

I led a dog's life in that flat. 'Most all day I lay there in my corner watching that fat woman kill time. I slept sometimes and had pipe dreams about being out chasing cats into basements and growling at old ladies with black mittens, as a dog was intended to do. Then she would pounce upon me with a lot of that driveling poodle palaver and kiss me on the nose—but what could I do? A dog can't chew cloves.

I began to feel sorry for Hubby, dog my cats if I didn't. We looked so much alike that people noticed it when we went out; so we shook the streets that Morgan's cab drives down, and took to climbing the piles of last December's snow on the streets where cheap people live.

One evening when we were thus promenading, and I was trying to look like a prize Saint Bernard, and the old man was trying to look like he wouldn't have murdered the first organ-grinder he heard play Mendelssohn's wedding march, I looked up at him and said, in my way:

"What are you looking so sour about, you oakum-trimmed lobster? She don't kiss you. You don't have to sit on her lap and listen to talk that would make the book of a musical comedy sound like the maxims of Epictetus. You ought to be thankful you're not a dog. Brace up, Benedick, and bid the blues begone."

The matrimonial mishap looked down at me with almost canine intelligence on his face.

"Why, doggie," says he, "good doggie. You almost look like you could speak. What is it, doggie—cats?"

Cats! Could speak!

But, of course, he couldn't understand. Humans were denied the speech of animals. The only common ground of communication upon which dogs and men can get together is in fiction.

In the flat across the hall from us lived a lady with a black-and-tan terrier. Her husband strung it and took it out every evening, but he always came home cheerful and whistling. One day I touched noses with the black-and-tan in the hall, and I struck him for an elucidation.

"See here, Wiggle-and-Skip," I says, "you know that it ain't the nature of a real man to play dry nurse to a dog in public. I never saw one leashed to a bowwow yet that didn't look like he'd like to lick every other man that looked at him. But your boss comes in every day as perky and set up as an amateur prestidigitator doing the egg trick. How does he do it? Don't tell me he likes it."

"Him?" says the black-and-tan. "Why, he uses Nature's Own Remedy. He gets spifflicated. At first when we go out he's as shy as the man on the steamer who would rather play pedro when they make 'em all jackpots. By the time we've been in eight saloons he don't care whether the thing on the end of his line is a dog or a catfish. I've lost two inches of my tail trying to sidestep those swinging doors."

The pointer I got from that terrier—vaudeville, please copy—set me to thinking.

One evening about six o'clock my mistress ordered him

to get busy and do the ozone act for Lovey. I have concealed it until now, but that is what she called me. The black-and-tan was called "Tweetness." I consider that I have the bulge on him as far as you could chase a rabbit. Still, "Lovely" is something of a nomenclatural tin can on the tail of one's self-respect.

At a quiet place on a safe street I tightened the line of my custodian in front of an attractive, refined saloon. I made a dead-ahead scramble for the doors, whining like a dog in the press dispatches that lets the family know that little Alice is bogged while gathering lilies in the brook.

"Why, darn my eyes," says the old man, with a grin, "darn my eyes if the saffron-colored son of a seltzer lemonade ain't asking me in to take a drink. Lemme see—how long's it been since I saved shoe leather by keeping one foot on the footrest? I believe I'll—"

I knew I had him. Hot Scotches he took, sitting at a table. For an hour he kept the Campbells coming. I sat by his side rapping for the waiter with my tail, and eating free lunch such as mamma in her flat never equaled with her homemade truck bought at a delicatessen store eight minutes before papa comes home.

When the products of Scotland were all exhausted except the rye bread the old man unwound me from the table leg and played me outside like a fisherman plays a salmon. Out there he took off my collar and threw it into the street.

"Poor doggie," says he, "good doggie. She shan't kiss you any more. 'Sa darned shame. Good doggie, go away and get run over by a streetcar and be happy."

I refused to leave. I leaped and frisked around the old man's legs happy as a pug on a rug.

"You old flea-headed woodchuck-chaser," I said to him, "you moon-baying, rabbit-pointing, egg-stealing old beagle, can't you see that I don't want to leave you? Can't you see that we're both Pups in the Wood and the missus is the cruel uncle after you with the dish towel and me with the flea liniment and a pink bow to tie on my tail. Why not cut that all out and be pards forever more?''

Maybe you'll say he didn't understand—maybe he didn't. But he kind of got a grip on the Hot Scotches, and stood still for a minute, thinking.

''Doggie,'' says he, finally, ''we don't live more than a dozen lives on this earth, and very few of us live to be more than three hundred. If I ever see that flat any more I'm a flat, and if you do you're flatter; and that's no flattery. I'm offering sixty to one that Westward Ho wins out by the length of a dachshund.''

There was no string, but I frolicked along with my master to the Twenty-third Street ferry. And the cats on the route saw reason to give thanks that prehensile claws had been given them.

On the Jersey side my master said to a stranger who stood eating a currant bun:

''Me and my doggie, we are bound for the Rocky Mountains.''

But what pleased me most was when my old man pulled both of my ears until I howled, and said:

''You common, monkey-headed, rat-tailed, sulphur-colored son of a doormat, do you know what I'm going to call you?''

I thought of ''Lovey,'' and I whined dolefully.

''I'm going to call you 'Pete,' '' says my master; and if I'd had five tails I couldn't have done enough wagging to do justice to the occasion.

*Ellis Parker Butler*

# GETTING RID OF FLUFF

So, after that, Murchison decided to get rid of Fluff. He told me that he had never really wanted a dog, anyway, but that when a dog is sent all the way from New York, anonymously, with $2.80 charges paid, it is hard to cast the dog out into the cold world without giving it a trial. And Fluff was such a sweet little thing! Just a little fluffy ball with bright eyes. Brownlee—Brownlee lives on the other side of Murchison—was sure the pup had good blood in him, so Murchison tried the pup for a few years, and at last he decided he would have to get rid of him. He came over and spoke to me about it, because I had just moved in next door.

"Do you like dogs?" he asked; and that was the first word of conversation I ever had with Murchison. I told him frankly that I did not like dogs, and that my wife did not like them, and Murchison seemed more pleased than if I had offered him a thousand dollars.

"Now, I am glad of that," he said, "for Mrs. Murchison and I hate dogs. If you do not like dogs, I will get rid of Fluff. I made up my mind several years ago to get rid of Fluff, but when I heard you were going to move into this house I decided not to get rid of him until I knew whether you liked dogs or not. I told Mrs. Murchison that if we got rid of Fluff before you came, and then found that you loved dogs and owned one, you might take our getting rid of Fluff as a hint that your dog was distasteful to us, and it might hurt your feelings. And Mrs. Murchison said that if you had a dog, your dog might feel lonely in a strange place and might like to have Fluff to play with until your dog got used to the neighborhood. So we did not get rid of him, but if you do not like dogs we will get rid of him right away."

I told Murchison that I saw he was the kind of neighbor a man liked to have, and that it was kind of him to offer to get rid of Fluff, but that he mustn't do so just on our account. I said that if he wanted to keep the dog, he had better do so.

"Now that is kind of you," said Murchison, "but we would really rather get rid of him. I decided several years ago that I would get rid of him, but Brownlee likes dogs, and took an interest in Fluff, and wanted to make a bird dog of him, so we kept Fluff for his sake. But now Brownlee is tired of making a bird dog of him. He says Fluff is too strong to make a good bird dog, and not strong enough to rent out as a horse, and he is willing I should get rid of him. He says he is anxious for me to get rid of him as soon as I can."

When I saw Fluff I agreed with Brownlee. At the very first glance I saw that Fluff was a failure as a dog, and that to make a good camel he needed a shorter neck and more hump, but he had the general appearance of an amateur camel. He looked as if someone who had never seen a dog, but had heard of one, had started out to make a dog, and had got to thinking of a camel every once in a while, and had worked in parts of what he thought a camel was like with what he thought a dog was like, and then—when the job was about done—had decided it was a failure, and had just finished it up any way, sticking on the meanest and cheapest hair he could find, and getting most of it on wrong side to.

But the cheap hair did not matter much. Murchison and Brownlee showed me the place where Fluff had worn most of it off the ridgepole of his back crawling under the porch. He tried to show me Fluff that day, but it was so dark under the porch that I could not tell which was Fluff and which was simply underneathness of porch. But from what Brownlee told me that day I knew that Fluff had suffered a permanent dislocation of the spirits. He told me he had taken Fluff out to make a duck dog of him, and that all the duck Fluff was interested in was to duck when he saw a gun, and that after he had heard a gun fired once or twice he had become sad and dejected, and had acquired a permanently ingrowing tail, and an expression of face like a coyote, but more mournful. He had acquired a habit of carrying his head down and forward, as if he was about to lay it on the headsman's block, and knew he deserved that and more, and the sooner it was over the better. He couldn't even scratch fleas correctly, Brownlee said, but would give a couple of weak-minded little flips at the spot with his hind flipper, and then stop and groan. He had become so meek, Brownlee said, that when he met a flea in the road he would not even go around it, but would stoop down like a camel to let the flea get aboard. He was that kind of a dog. He was the most discouraged dog I ever knew.

The next day I was putting down the carpet in the back bedroom, when in came Murchison.

"I came over to speak to you about Fluff," he said. "I am afraid he must have annoyed you last night. I suppose you heard him howl?"

"Yes, Murchison," I said, "I did hear him. I never knew a dog could howl so loud and long as that. He must have been very ill."

"Oh, no!" said Murchison cheerfully. "That is the way he always howls. That is one of the reasons I have decided to get rid of Fluff. But it is a great deal worse for us than it is for you. The air inlet of our furnace is at the side of the house just where Fluff puts his head when he howls, and the register in our room is right at the head of our bed. So his howl goes in at the inlet and down through the furnace and up the furnace pipes, and is delivered right in our room, just as clear and strong as if he was in the room. That is one reason I have fully decided to get rid of Fluff. It would not be so bad if we had only one register in our house, but we have ten, and when Fluff howls his voice is delivered by all ten registers, so it is just as if we had ten Fluffs in the house at one time. And ten howls like Fluff's are too much. Even Brownlee says so."

I told Murchison that I agreed with Brownlee perfectly. Fluff had a bad howl. It sounded as if Cruel Fate, with spikes in his shoes, had stepped on Fluff's inmost soul, and then joggled up and down on the tenderest spot, and Fluff was trying to reproduce his feelings in vocal exercises. It sounded like a cheap phonograph giving a symphony in the key of woe minor, with a megaphone attachment and bad places in the record. Judging by his voice, the machine needed a new needle. But the megaphone attachment was all right.

Brownlee—who knows all about dogs—said that he knew what was the matter with Fluff. He said Fluff had a very high-grade musical temperament, and that he longed to be the

Caruso of dogs. He said he could see that all through his bright and hopeful puppyhood he had looked forward to being a great singer, with a Wagner repertoire and tremolo stops in his song organ, and that he had early set his aim at perfection. He said Fluff was that kind of a dog, and that when he saw what his voice had turned out to be he was dissatisfied, and became morbid. He said that any dog that had a voice like Fluff's had a right to be dissatisfied with it—he would be dissatisfied himself with that voice. He said he did not wonder that Fluff slunk around all day, feeling that he was no good on earth, and that he could understand that when night came and everything was still, so that Fluff could judge of the purity of his tonal quality better, he would pull out his voice and tune it up and look it over and try it again, hoping it had improved since he tried it last. Brownlee said it never had improved, and that was what made Fluff's howl so mournful. It was full of tears. He said Fluff would try it at G flat and B flat and D flat, and so on until he struck a note he felt he was pretty good at, and then he would cling to that note and weep it full of tears. He asked Murchison if he hadn't noticed that the howl was sort of damp and salty from the tears, but Murchison said he hadn't noticed the dampness. He said it probably got dried out of the howl before it reached him, coming through the furnace. Then Brownlee said that if there was only some way of regulating Fluff, so that he could be turned on and off, Murchison would have a fortune in him; he could turn his howl off when people wanted to be cheerful, and then, when a time of great national woe occurred, Murchison could turn Fluff on and set him going. He said he never heard anything in his life that came so near expressing in sound a great national woe as Fluff's howl did. He said Fluff might lack finish in tonal quality, but that in woe quality he was a master; he was stuffed so full of woe quality that it oozed out of his pores. He said he always thought what a pity it was for dogs like Fluff that people preferred cheerful songs like "Annie

Rooney" and "Waltz Me Around Again, Willie" to the nobler woe operas. He said he had tried to like good music himself, but it was no use; whenever he heard Fluff sing he felt that Murchison ought to get rid of Fluff. Then Murchison said that was just what he was going to do. What he wanted to talk about was how to get rid of Fluff.

But I am getting too far ahead of my story. Whenever I get to talking about the howl of Fluff I find I wander on for hours at a time. It takes hours of talk to explain just what a mean howl Fluff had.

But, as I was saying, Murchison came over while I was putting down the carpet in my back bedroom, and told me he had fully decided to get rid of Fluff.

"I have fully decided to get rid of him," he said, "and the only thing that bothers me is how to get rid of him."

"Give him away," I suggested.

"That's a good idea!" said Murchison gratefully. "That's the very idea that occurred to me when I first thought of getting rid of Fluff. It is an idea that just matches Fluff all over. That is just the kind of dog Fluff is. If ever a dog was made to give away, Fluff was made for it. The more I think about him and look at him and study him, the surer I am that the only thing he is good for is to give away."

Then he shook his head and sighed.

"The only trouble," he said, "is that Fluff *is* the giveaway kind of dog. That is the only kind you can't give away. There is only one time of the year that a person can make presents of things that are good for nothing but to give away, and that is at Christmas. Now, I might—"

"Murchison," I said, laying my tack hammer on the floor and standing up, "you don't mean to keep that infernal, howling beast until Christmas, do you? If you do, I shall stop putting down this carpet. I shall pull out the tacks that are already in and move elsewhere. Why, this is only the first of May, and if I have to sleep—if I have to keep awake every night and listen to that animated foghorn drag his raw soul over the teeth of a rusty harrow, I shall go crazy. Can't you think of someone that is going to have a birthday sooner than that?"

"I wish I could," said Murchison wistfully, "but I can't. I want to get rid of Fluff, and so does Brownlee, and so does Massett, but I can't think of a way to get rid of him, and neither can they."

"Murchison," I said with some asperity, for I hate a man who trifles, "if I really thought you and Brownlee and Massett were as stupid as all that, I would be sorry I moved into this neighborhood, but I don't believe it. I believe you do not mean to get rid of Fluff. I believe you and Brownlee and Massett want to keep him. If you wanted to get rid of him, you could do it the same way you got him."

"That's an excellent idea!" exclaimed Murchison. "That is one of the best ideas I ever heard, and I would go and do it if I hadn't done it so often already. As soon as Brownlee suggested that idea I did it. I sent Fluff by express to a man —to John Smith—at Worcester, Massachusetts, and when Fluff came back I had to pay eight dollars and fifty-five cents charges. But I didn't begrudge the money. The trip did Fluff a world of good—it strengthened his voice, and made him broader-minded. I tell you," he said enthusiastically, "there's nothing like travel for broadening the mind! Look at Fluff! Maybe he don't show it, but that dog's mind is so broadened by travel that if he was turned loose in Alaska he would find his way home. When I found his mind was getting so tremendously broad I stopped sending him places. Brownlee—Brownlee knows all about dogs—said it would not hurt Fluff a bit; he said a dog's mind could not get too broad, and that as far as he was concerned he would just like to see once how broad-minded a dog could become; he would like to have Fluff sent out by express every time he came back. He told me it was an interesting experiment—that, so far as he knew, it had never been tried before—and that the thing I ought to do was to keep Fluff traveling all the time. He said that so far as he knew it was the only way to get rid of Fluff; that sometime while he was traveling around in the express car there might be a wreck, and we would be rid of Fluff; and if there wasn't a wreck it would be interesting to see what effect constant travel would have on a coarse dog. He said I might find after a year or two that I had the most cultured dog in the United States. Brownlee was willing to have me send Fluff anywhere. He suggested a lot of good places to send dogs, but he didn't care enough about dog culture to help pay the express charges."

"I see, Murchison," I said scornfully. "I see! You are the kind of man who would let a little money stand between you and getting rid of a dog like Fluff! If I had a dog like Fluff, nothing in the world could prevent me from getting rid of him. I only wish he was my dog."

"Take him!" said Murchison generously. "I make you a full and free present of him. You can have that dog absolutely and wholly. He is yours."

"I will take the dog," I said haughtily, "not because I really want a dog, nor because I hanker for that particular dog, but because I can see that you and Brownlee and Massett have been trifling with him. Bring him over in my yard, and I will show you in very short measure how to get rid of Fluff."

That afternoon both Brownlee and Massett called on me. They came and sat on my porch steps, and Murchison came and sat with them, and all three sat and looked at Fluff and talked him over. Every few minutes they would—Brownlee and Massett would—get up and shake hands with Murchison and congratulate him on having gotten rid of Fluff, and Murchison would blush modestly and say: "Oh, that is nothing. I always knew I would get rid of him."

And there was the dog not five feet from them, tied to my lawn hydrant. I watched and listened to them until I had

had enough of it, and then I went into the house and got my shotgun. I loaded it with a good BB shell and went out.

Fluff saw me first. I never saw a dog exhibit such intelligence as Fluff exhibited right then. I suppose travel had broadened him, and probably the hydrant was old and rusted out, anyway. When a man moves into a house he ought to have *all* the plumbing attended to the first thing. Any ordinary unbroadened dog would have laid down and pulled, but Fluff didn't. First he jumped six feet straight into the air, and that pulled the four feet of hydrant pipe up by the roots, and then he went away. He took the hydrant and the pipe with him, and that might have surprised me, but I saw that he did not know where he was going nor how long he would stay there when he reached the place, and a dog can never tell what will come handy when he is away from home. A hydrant and a piece of iron pipe might be the very thing he would need. So he took it along.

If I had wanted a fountain in my front yard, I could not have gotten one half as quickly as Fluff furnished that one, and I would never have thought of pulling out the hydrant to make one. Fluff thought of that—at least Brownlee said he thought of it—but I think all Fluff wanted was to get away. And he got away, and the fountain didn't happen to be attached to the hydrant, so he left it behind. If it had been attached to the hydrant, he would have taken it with him. He was a strong dog.

"There!" said Brownlee when he had heard the pipe rattle across the Eighth Street bridge. "There is intelligence for you! You ought to be grateful to that dog all your life. *You* didn't know it was against the law to discharge a gun in the city limits, but Fluff did, and he wouldn't wait to see you get into trouble. He has heard us talking about it, Murchison. I tell you travel has broadened that dog! Look what he has saved you," he said to me, "by going away at just the psychological moment. We should have told you about not firing a gun in the city limits. You can't get rid of Fluff that way. It is against the law."

"Yes," said Massett, "and if you knew Fluff as well as we do, you would know that he is a dog you can't shoot. He is a wonderful dog. He knows all about guns. Brownlee tried to make a duck dog out of him, and took him out where the ducks were—showed him the ducks—shot a gun at the ducks —and what do you think that dog learned?"

"To run," I said, for I had heard about Brownlee teaching Fluff to retrieve. Brownlee blushed.

"Yes," said Massett, "but that wasn't all. It doesn't take intelligence to make a dog run when he sees a gun, but Fluff did not run like an ordinary dog. He saw the gun and he saw the ducks, and he saw that Brownlee only shot at ducks when they were on the wing. And he thought Brownlee meant to shoot him, so what does he do? Stand still? No; he tries to fly. Gets right up and tries to fly. He thought that was what Brownlee was trying to teach him. He couldn't fly, but he did his best. So whenever Fluff sees a gun he is on the wing, so to speak. You noticed he was on the wing, didn't you?"

I told him I had noticed it. I said that as far as I could judge Fluff had a good strong wing. I said I didn't mind losing a little thing like a hydrant and a length or two of pipe, but I was glad I hadn't fastened Fluff to the house—I always like my houses to have a cellar, and it would be just like Fluff to stop flying at some place where there wasn't any cellar.

"Oh," said Massett, "he wouldn't have gone far with the house. A house is a great deal heavier than a hydrant. He would probably have moved the house off the foundation a little, but, judging by the direction Fluff took, the house would have wedged between those two trees, and you would have only lost a piece of the porch, or whatever he was tied to. But the lesson is that you must not try to shoot Fluff unless you are a good wing shot. Unless you can shoot like Davy

Crockett you would be apt to wound Fluff without killing him, and then there *would* be trouble!"

"Yes," said Murchison, "the Prevention of Cruelty to Animals folks. There is only one way in which a dog can be killed according to law in this place, and that is to have the Prevention of Cruelty to Animals folks do it. You send them a letter telling them you have a dog you want killed, and asking them to come and kill it. That is according to law."

"That," I said firmly, "is what I will do."

"It won't do any good," said Murchison sadly. "They never come. This addition to Gallatin is too far from their offices to be handy, and they never come. I have eighteen deaths for Fluff on file at their offices already, and not one of them has killed him. When you have had as much experience with dogs as I have you will know that the Prevention of Cruelty to them in this town does not include killing them when they live in the suburbs. The only way a dog can die in the suburbs of Gallatin is to die of old age."

"How old is Fluff?" I asked.

"Fluff is a young dog," said Brownlee. "If he had an ordinary dog constitution, he would live fifteen years yet, but he hasn't. He has an extra-strong constitution, and I should say he was good for twenty years more. But that isn't what we came over for. We came over to learn how much you mean to get rid of Fluff."

"Brownlee," I said, "I shall think up some way to get rid of Fluff. Getting rid of a dog is no task for a mind like mine. But until he returns and gives me back my hydrant I shall do nothing further. I am not going to bother about getting rid of a dog that is not here to be gotten rid of."

By the time Fluff returned I had thought out a plan. Murchison had never paid the dog tax on Fluff, and that was the same as condemning him to death if he was ever caught outside of the yard, and when he was he could not be caught. He was a hasty mover, and little things such as closed gates never prevented him from entering the yard when in haste. When he did not jump over he could go right through a fence. But to a man of my ability these things are trifles. I knew how to get rid of Fluff. I knew how to have him caught in the street without a license. I chained him there.

Brownlee and Massett and Murchison came and watched me do it. Our street is not much used, and the big stake I drove in the street was not much in the way of passing grocery delivery wagons. I fastened Fluff to the stake with a chain, and then I wrote to the city authorities and complained. I said there was a dog without a license that was continually in front of my house, and I wished it removed; and, a week or so after, the dogcatcher came around and had a look at Fluff. He walked all around him, while Massett and Brownlee and Murchison and I leaned over our gates and looked on. He was not at all what I should have expected a dogcatcher to be, being thin and rather gentlemanly in appearance; and after he had looked Fluff over well he came over and spoke to me. He asked me if Fluff was my dog. I said he was.

"I see!" said the dogcatcher. "And you want to get rid of him. If he was my dog, I would want to get rid of him too. I have seen lots of dogs, but I never saw one that was like this, and I do not blame you for wanting to part with him. I have had my eye on him for several years, but this is the first opportunity I have had to approach him. Now, however, he seems to have broken all the dog laws. He has not secured a license, and he is in the public highway. It will be my duty to take him up and gently chloroform him as soon as I make sure of one thing."

"Tell me what it is," I said, "and I will help you make sure of it."

"Thank you," he said, "but I will attend to it"; and with that he got on his wagon and drove off. He returned in about an hour.

"I came back," he said, "not because my legal duty compels me, but because I knew you would be anxious. If I owned a dog like that, I would be anxious, too. I can't take that dog."

"Why not?" we all asked.

"Because," he said, "I have been down to the city hall, and I have looked up the records, and I find that the streets of this addition to the city have not been accepted by the city. The titles to the property are so made out that until the city legally accepts the streets each property owner owns to the middle of the street fronting his property. If you will step out and look, you will see that the dog is on your own property."

"If that is all," I said, "I will move the stake. I will put him on the other side of the street."

"If you would like him any better there," said the dogcatcher, "you can move him, but it would make no difference to me. Then he would be on the private property of the man who owns the property across the street."

"But, my good man," I said, "how is a man to get rid of a dog he does not want?"

The dogcatcher frowned.

"That," he said, "seems to be one of the things our lawmakers have not thought of. But whatever you do, I advise you to be careful. Do not try any underhand methods, for now that my attention has been called to the dog, I shall have to watch his future and see that he is not badly used. I am an officer of the Prevention of Cruelty to Animals as well as a dogcatcher, and I warn you to be careful what you do with that dog."

Then he got on his wagon again and drove away.

The next morning I was a nervous wreck, for Fluff had howled all night, and Murchison came over soon after breakfast. He was accompanied by Brownlee and Massett.

"Now, I am the last man in the world to do anything that my neighbors would take offense at," he said as soon as they were seated on my porch, "and Brownlee and Massett love dogs as few men ever love them; but something has to be done about Fluff. The time has come when we must sleep with our windows open, and neither Massett nor Brownlee nor I got a minute of sleep last night."

"Neither did I," I said.

"That is different entirely," said Murchison. "Fluff is your dog, and if you want to keep a howling dog, you would be inclined to put up with the howl, but we have no interest in the dog at all. We do not own him, and we consider him a nuisance. We have decided to ask you to get rid of him. It is unjust to your neighbors to keep a howling dog. You will have to get rid of Fluff."

"Exactly!" said Massett. "For ten nights I have not slept a wink, and neither has Murchison, nor has Brownlee—"

"Nor I," I added.

"Exactly," said Massett; "and four men going without sleep for ten nights is equal to one man going without sleep forty nights, which would kill any man. Practically, Fluff has killed a man and is a murderer; and as you are responsible for him, it is the same as if you were a murderer yourself, and as you were one of the four who did not sleep, you may also be said to have committed suicide. But we do not mean to give you into the hands of the law until we have remonstrated with you. But we feel deeply, and the more so because you could easily give us some nights of sleep in which to recuperate."

"If you can tell mc how," I said, "I will gladly do it. I need sleep more at this minute than I ever needed it in my life."

"Very well," said Massett. "Just get out your shotgun and show it to Fluff. When he sees the gun he will run. He will take wing like a duck, and while he is away we can get a few nights' rest. That will be something. And if we are not in good condition by that time, you can show him the shotgun again. Why!" he exclaimed as he grew enthusiastic over his idea, "you can keep Fluff eternally on the wing!"

I felt that I needed a vacation from Fluff. I unchained him

and went in to get my shotgun. Then I showed him the shotgun, and we had two good nights of sleep. After that, whenever we felt that we needed a few nights in peace, I just showed Fluff the shotgun and he went away on one of his flying trips.

But it was Brownlee—Brownlee knew all about dogs—who first called my attention to what he called the periodicity of Fluff.

"Now, you would never have noticed it," he said one day when Murchison and I were sitting on my porch with him, "but I did. That is because I have studied dogs. I know all about dogs, and I know Fluff can run. That is because he has greyhound blood in him. With a little wolf. That is why I studied Fluff, and how I came to notice that every time you show him the shotgun he is gone just forty-eight hours. Now you go and get your shotgun and try it."

So I tried it, and Fluff went away as he always did, and Brownlee sat there bragging about how Fluff could run, and about how wonderful he was himself to have thought of the periodicity of Fluff.

"Did you see how he went?" he asked enthusiastically. "That gait was a thirty-mile-an-hour gait. Why, that dog travels—he travels . . ." He took out a piece of paper and a pencil and figured it out. "In forty-eight hours he travels fourteen hundred and forty miles! He gets seven hundred and twenty miles from home!"

"It doesn't seem possible," said Murchison.

"No," said Brownlee frankly, "it doesn't." He went over his figures again. "But that is figured correctly," he said. "If—but maybe I did not gauge his speed correctly. And I didn't allow for stopping to turn around at the end of the out sprint. What we ought to have on that dog is a pedometer. If I owned a dog like that, the first thing I would get would be a pedometer."

I told Brownlee that if he wished I would give him Fluff,

and he could put a pedometer or anything else on him; but Brownlee remembered he had some work to do and went home.

But he was right about the periodicity of Fluff. Almost on the minute at the end of forty-eight hours Fluff returned, and Brownlee and Murchison, who were there to receive him, were as pleased as if Fluff had been going away instead of returning.

"That dog," said Brownlee, "is a wonderful animal. If Sir Isaac Newton had had that dog, he would have proved something or other of universal value by him. That dog is plumb full of ratios and things, if we only knew how to get them out of him. I bet if Sir Isaac Newton had had Fluff as long as you have had him he would have had a formula all worked out:

$$x + y\ (2 \times z - \text{dog}) = \sqrt{4ab \div 3x}$$

or something of that kind, so that anyone with half a knowledge of algebra could figure out the square root of any dog any time of the day or night. I could get up a Law of Dog myself if I had the time, with a dog like Fluff to work on. 'If one dog travels fourteen hundred and forty miles at the sight of a gun, how far would two dogs travel?' All that sort of thing. Stop!" he ejaculated suddenly. "If one dog travels forty-eight hours at sight of one gun, how far would a dog travel at sight of two guns? Murchison," he cried enthusiastically, "I've got it! I've got the fundamental law of periodicity in dogs! Get out your gun," he said to me, "and I will get mine."

He stopped at the gate long enough to say:

"I tell you, Murchison, we are on the verge of a mighty important discovery—a mighty important discovery! If this thing turns out right, we will be at the root of all dog nature. We will have the great underlying law of scared dogs."

He came back with his shotgun carefully hidden behind him, and then he and I showed Fluff the two guns simultaneously. For one minute Fluff was startled. Then he vanished. All we saw of him as he went was the dust he left in his wake. Massett had come over when Brownlee brought over his gun, and Murchison and I sat and smoked while Massett and Brownlee fought out the periodicity of Fluff. Brownlee said that for two guns Fluff would traverse the same distance as for one, but twice as quickly; but Massett said Brownlee was foolish, and that anyone who knew anything about dogs would know that no dog could go faster than Fluff had gone at the sight of one gun. Massett said Fluff would travel at his regular one-gun speed, but would travel a two-gun distance. He said Fluff would not be back for ninety-six hours. Brownlee said he would be back in forty-eight hours, but both agreed that he would travel twenty-eight hundred and eighty miles. Then Murchison went home and got a map, and showed Brownlee and Massett that if Fluff traveled fourteen hundred miles in the direction he had started he would have to do the last two hundred miles as a swim, because he would strike the Atlantic Ocean at the twelve hundredth mile. But Brownlee just turned up his nose and sneered. He said Fluff was no fool, and that when he reached the coast he would veer to the north and travel along the beach for two hundred miles or so. Then Massett said that he had been thinking about Brownlee's theory, and he *knew* no dog could do what Brownlee said Fluff would do—sixty miles an hour. He said he agreed that a dog like Fluff could do thirty miles an hour if he did not stop to howl, because his howl represented about sixty horsepower, but that no dog could ever do sixty miles an hour. Then Brownlee got mad and said Massett was a born idiot, and that Fluff not only *could* do sixty miles, but he could keep on increasing his speed at the rate of thirty miles per gun indefinitely. Then they went home mad, but they agreed to be on hand when Fluff returned. But they were not. Fluff came home in twenty-four hours, almost to the minute.

When I went over and told Brownlee, he wouldn't believe it at first, but when I showed him Fluff he cheered up and clapped me on the back.

"I tell you," he exclaimed, "we have made a great discovery. We have discovered the law of scared dogs. 'A dog is scared in inverse ratio to the number of guns!' Now it wouldn't be fair to try Fluff again without giving him a breathing spell, but tomorrow I will come over, and we will try him with four guns. We will work this thing out thoroughly," he said, "before we write to the Academy of Science, or whatever a person would write to, so that there will be no mistake. Before we give this secret to the world we want to have it complete. We will try Fluff with any number of guns, and with pistols and rifles, and if we can get one we will try him with a cannon. We will keep at it for years and years. You and I will be famous."

I told Brownlee that if he wanted to experiment for years with Fluff he could have him, but that all I wanted was to get rid of him; but Brownlee wouldn't hear of that. He said he would buy Fluff from me if he was rich enough, but that Fluff was so valuable he couldn't think of buying him. He would let me keep him. He said he would be over the next day to try Fluff again.

So the next day he and Murchison and Massett came over and held a consultation on my porch to decide how many guns they would try on Fluff. They could not agree. Massett wanted to try four guns and have Fluff absent only half a day, but Brownlee wanted to have me break my shotgun in two and try that on Fluff. He said that according to the law of scared dogs a half a gun, working it out by inverse ratio, would keep Fluff away for twice as long as one gun, which would be ninety-six hours; and while they were arguing it out Fluff came around the house unsuspectingly and saw us on the porch. He gave us one startled glance and started north by northeast at what Brownlee said was the most marvelous rate of speed he ever saw. Then he and Massett got down off the porch and looked for guns, but there were none in sight. There wasn't anything that looked the least like a gun. Not even a broomstick. Brownlee said he knew what was the matter—Fluff was having a little practice run to keep in good condition, and would be back in a few hours; but judging by the look he gave us as he went, I thought he would be gone longer than that.

I could see that Brownlee was worried, and as day followed day without any return of Fluff, Murchison and I tried to cheer him up, showing him how much better we all slept while Fluff was away; but it did not cheer up poor Brownlee. He had set his faith on that dog, and the dog had deceived him. We all became anxious about Brownlee's health—he moped around so; and just when we began to be afraid he was going into a decline he cheered up, and came over as bright and happy as a man could be.

"I told you so!" he exclaimed joyfully as soon as he was inside my gate. "And it makes me ashamed of myself that I didn't think of it the moment I saw Fluff start off. You will never see that dog again."

I told Brownlee that that was good news, anyway, even if it did upset his law of scared dogs; but he smiled a superior smile.

"Disprove nothing!" he said. "It proves my law. Didn't I say in the first place that the time a dog would be gone was in inverse ratio to the number of guns? Well, the inverse ratio to no guns is infinite time—that is how long Fluff will be gone; that is how long he will run. Why, that dog will never stop running while there is any dog left in him. He can't help it —it is the law of scared dogs."

"Do you mean to say," I asked him, "that that dog will run on and on forever?"

"Exactly!" said Brownlee proudly. "As long as there is a particle of him left he will keep on running. That is the law."

Maybe Brownlee was right. I don't know. But what I would like to know is the name of someone who would like a dog that looks like Fluff, and is his size, and that howls like him, and that answers to his name. A dog of that kind returned to my house a long time before infinity, and I would like to get rid of him. Brownlee says it isn't Fluff; that his law couldn't be wrong; and that this is merely a dog that resembles Fluff. Maybe Brownlee is right, but I would like to know someone that wants a dog with a richly melodious voice.

*Alfred Ollivant*

# THE TAILLESS TYKE AT BAY

The sun was hiding behind the Pike. Over the lowlands the feathery breath of night hovered still. And the hillside was shivering in the chillness of dawn.

Down on the silvery sward beside the Stony Bottom there lay the ruffled body of a dead sheep. All about the victim the dewy ground was dark and patchy like disheveled velvet; bracken trampled down; stones displaced as though by striving feet; and the whole spotted with the all-pervading red.

A score of yards up the hill, in a writhing confusion of red and gray, two dogs at death grips. While yet higher, a pack of wild-eyed hill sheep watched, fascinated, the bloody drama.

The fight raged. Red and gray, blood-spattered, murderous-eyed; the crimson froth dripping from their jaws; now rearing high with arching crests and wrestling paws; now rolling over in tumbling, tossing, worrying disorder—the two fought out their blood feud.

Above, the close-packed flock huddled and stamped, ever edging nearer to watch the issue. Just so must the women of Rome have craned round the arenas to see two men striving in death struggle.

The first cold flicker of dawn stole across the green. The red eye of the morning peered aghast over the shoulder of the Pike. And from the sleeping dale there arose the yodeling of a man driving his cattle home.

Day was upon them.

James Moore was waked by a little whimpering cry beneath his window. He leapt out of bed and rushed to look; for well he knew 'twas not for nothing that the old dog was calling.

"Lord o' mercy! Whativer's come to yo', Owd Un?" he cried in anguish. And, indeed, his favorite, war-daubed almost past recognition, presented a pitiful spectacle.

In a moment the Master was downstairs and out, examining him.

"Poor old lad, yo' have caught it this time!" he cried. There was a ragged tear on the dog's cheek; a deep gash in his throat from which the blood still welled, staining the white escutcheon on his chest; while head and neck were clotted with the red.

Hastily the Master summoned Maggie. After her, Andrew came hurrying down. And a little later a tiny, night-clad, naked-footed figure appeared in the door, wide-eyed, and then fled, screaming.

They doctored the old warrior on the table in the

kitchen. Maggie tenderly washed his wounds, and dressed them with gentle, pitying fingers; and he stood all the while grateful yet fidgeting, looking up into his master's face as if imploring to be gone.

"He mun a had a rare tussle wi' someone—eh, Dad?" said the girl, as she worked.

"Ay; and wi' whom? 'Twasn't for nowt he got fightin', I war'nt. Nay; he's a tale to tell, has the Owd Un, and—Ah-h-h! I thowt as much. Look 'ee!" For, bathing the bloody jaws, he had come upon a cluster of tawny red hair, hiding in the corners of the lips.

The secret was out. Those few hairs told their own accusing tale. To but one creature in the Daleland could they belong—"Th' Tailless Tyke."

"He mun a bin trespassin'!" cried Andrew.

"Ay, and up to some o' his bloody work, I'll lay my life," the Master answered. "But the Owd Un shall show us."

The old dog's hurts proved less severe than had at first seemed possible. His good gray coat, forest-thick about his throat, had never served him in such good stead. And at length, the wounds washed and sewn up, he jumped down all in a hurry from the table and made for the door.

"Noo, owd lad, yo' may show us," said the Master, and, with Andrew, hurried after him down the hill, along the stream, and over Langholm How. And as they neared the Stony Bottom, the sheep, herding in groups, raised frightened heads to stare.

Of a sudden a cloud of poisonous flies rose, buzzing, up before them; and there in a dimple of the ground lay a murdered sheep. Deserted by its comrades, the glazed eyes staring helplessly upward, the throat horribly worried, it slept its last sleep.

The matter was plain to see. At last the Black Killer had visited Kenmuir.

"I guessed as much," said the Master, standing over the mangled body. "Well, it's the worst night's work ever the Killer done. I reck'n the Owd Un come on him while he was at it; and then they fought. And, ma word *it* mun ha' bin a fight too." For all around were traces of that terrible struggle: the earth torn up and tossed, bracken uprooted, and throughout little dabs of wool and tufts of tawny hair, mingling with dark-stained iron-gray wisps.

James Moore walked slowly over the battlefield, stooping down as though he were gleaning. And gleaning he was.

A long time he bent so, and at length raised himself.

"The Killer has killed his last," he muttered; "Red Wull has run his course." Then, turning to Andrew: "Run yo' home, lad, and fetch the men to carry yon away," pointing to the carcass. "And Bob, lad, yo've done your work for today, and right well too; go yo' home wi' him. I'm off to see to this!"

He turned and crossed the Stony Bottom. His face was set like a rock. At length the proof was in his hand. Once and for all the hill country should be rid of its scourge.

As he stalked up the hill, a dark head appeared at his knee. Two big gray eyes, half doubting, half penitent, wholly wistful, looked up at him, and a silvery brush signaled a mute request.

"Eh, Owd Un, but yo' should ha' gone wi' Andrew," the Master said. "Hooiver, as yo' are here, come along." And he strode away up the hill, gaunt and menacing, with the gray dog at his heels.

As they approached the house, M'Adam was standing in the door, sucking his eternal twig. James Moore eyed him closely as he came, but the sour face framed in the door betrayed nothing. Sarcasm, surprise, challenge, were all writ there, plain to read; but no guilty consciousness of the other's errand, no storm of passion to hide a failing heart. If it was acting it was splendidly done.

As man and dog passed through the gap in the hedge, the

expression on the little man's face changed again. He started forward.

"James Moore, as I live!" he cried, and advanced with both hands extended, as though welcoming a long-lost brother. "'Deed and it's a weary while sin' ye've honored ma puir hoose." And, in fact, it was nigh twenty years. "I tak' it gey kind in ye to look in on a lonely auld man. Come ben and let's ha' a crack. James Moore kens weel hoo welcome he aye is in ma bit biggin'."

The Master ignored the greeting.

"One o' ma sheep been killed back o' t' Dyke," he announced shortly, jerking his thumb over his shoulder.

"The Killer?"

"The Killer."

The cordiality beaming in every wrinkle of the little man's face was absorbed in a wondering interest; and that again gave place to sorrowful sympathy.

"Dear, dear! It's come to that, has it—at last?" he said gently, and his eyes wandered to the gray dog and dwelt mournfully upon him. "Man, I'm sorry—I canna tell ye I'm surprised. Masel', I kent it all alang. But gin Adam M'Adam had tell't ye, ye'd no ha' believed him. Weel, weel, he's lived his life, gin ony dog iver did; and noo he maun gang where he's sent a many before him. Puir mon! Puir tyke!" He heaved a sigh, profoundly melancholy, tenderly sympathetic. Then, brightening up a little: "Ye'll ha' come for the gun?"

James Moore listened to this harangue at first puzzled. Then he caught the other's meaning, and his eyes flashed.

"Ye fool, M'Adam! Did ye hear iver tell o' a sheep dog worryin' his master's sheep?"

The little man was smiling and suave again now, rubbing his hands softly together.

"Ye're right, I never did. But your dog is not as ither dogs—'There's none like him—none,' I've heard ye say so yersel, mony a time. An' I'm wi' ye. There's none like him—

for devilment." His voice began to quiver and his face to blaze. "It's his cursed cunning that's deceived ivery one but me—whelp o' Satan that he is!" He shouldered up to his tall adversary. "If not him, wha else had done it?" he asked, looking up into the other's face as if daring him to speak.

The Master's shaggy eyebrows lowered. He towered above the other like the Muir Pike above its surrounding hills.

"Wha, ye ask?" he replied coldly, "and I answer you. Your Red Wull, M'Adam, your Red Wull. It's your Wull's the Black Killer! It's your Wull's bin the plague o' the land these months past! It's your Wull's killed ma sheep back o' yon!"

At that all the little man's affected good humor fled.

"Ye lee, mon! Ye lee!" he cried in a dreadful scream, dancing up to his antagonist. "I knoo hoo 'twad be. I said so. I see what ye're at. Ye've found at last—blind that ye've been! —that it's yer ain hell's tyke that's the Killer; and noo ye think by yer leein' impitations to throw the blame on ma Wullie. Ye rob me o' ma Cup, ye rob me o' ma son, ye wrang me in ilka thing; there's but ae thing left me—Wullie. And noo ye're set on takin' him awa'. But ye shall not—I'll kill ye first!"

He was all a-shake, bobbing up and down like a stopper in a soda-water bottle, and almost sobbing.

"Ha' ye no wranged me enough wi' oot that? Ye lang-leggit liar, wi' yer skulkin' murderin' tyke!" he cried. "Ye say it's Wullie. Where's yer proof?"—and he snapped his fingers in the other's face.

The Master was now as calm as his foe was passionate. "Where?" he replied sternly. "Why, there!" holding out his right hand. "Yon's proof enough to hang a hunner'd." For lying in his broad palm was a little bundle of that damning red hair.

"Where?"

"There!"

"Let's see it!" The little man bent to look closer.

"There's for yer proof!" he cried, and spat deliberately down into the other's naked palm. Then he stood back, facing his enemy in a manner to have done credit to a nobler deed.

James Moore strode forward. It looked as if he was about to make an end of his miserable adversary, so strongly was he moved. His chest heaved, and the blue eyes blazed. But just as one had thought to see him take his foe in the hollow of his hand and crush him, who should come stalking round the corner of the house but the Tailless Tyke.

A droll spectacle he made, laughable even at that moment. He limped sorely, his head and neck were swathed in bandages, and beneath their ragged fringe the little eyes gleamed out fiery and bloodshot.

Round the corner he came, unaware of strangers; then straightway recognizing his visitors, halted abruptly. His hackles ran up, each individual hair stood on end till his whole body resembled a new-shorn wheat field; and a snarl, like a rusty brake shoved hard down, escaped from between his teeth. Then he trotted heavily forward, his head sinking low and lower as he came.

And Owd Bob, eager to take up the gage of battle, advanced, glad and gallant, to meet him. Daintily he picked his way across the yard, head and tail erect, perfectly self-contained. Only the long gray hair about his neck stood up like the ruff of a lady of the court of Queen Elizabeth.

But the war-worn warriors were not to be allowed their will.

"Wullie, Wullie, wad ye!" cried the little man.

"Bob, lad, coom in!" called the other. Then he turned and looked down at the man beside him, contempt flaunting in every feature.

"Well?" he said shortly.

M'Adam's hands were opening and shutting; his face was quite white beneath the tan; but he spoke calmly.

"I'll tell ye the whole story, and it's the truth," he said

slowly. "I was up there the morn"—pointing to the window above—"and I see Wullie crouchin' down alangside the Stony Bottom. (Ye ken he has the run o' ma land o' neets, the same as your dog.) In a minnit I see anither dog squatterin' alang on your side the Bottom. He creeps up to the sheep on th' hillside, chases 'em, and doons one. The sun was risen by then, and I see the dog clear as I see you noo. It was that dog there—I swear it!" His voice rose as he spoke, and he pointed an accusing finger at Owd Bob.

"Noo, Wullie! thinks I. And afore ye could clap yer hands, Wullie was over the Bottom and on to him as he gorged—the bloody-minded murderer! They fought and fought—I could hear the roarin' o't where I stood. I watched till I could watch nae langer, and, all in a sweat, I rin doon the stairs and oot. When I got there, there was yer tyke makin' fu' split for Kenmuir, and Wullie comin' up the hill to me. It's God's truth, I'm tellin' ye. Tak' him hame, James Moore, and let his dinner be an ounce o' lead. 'Twill be the best day's work iver ye done."

The little man must be lying—lying palpably. Yet he spoke with an earnestness, a seeming belief in his own story, that might have convinced one who knew him less well. But the Master only looked down on him with a great scorn.

"It's Monday today," he said coldly. "I gie yo' till Saturday. If yo've not done your duty by then—and well you know what 'tis—I shall come do it for ye. Ony gate, I shall come and see. I'll remind ye agin o' Thursday—yo'll be at the Manor dinner, I suppose. Noo I've warned yo', and you know best whether I'm in earnest or no. Bob, lad!"

He turned away, but turned again.

"I'm sorry for ye, but I've ma duty to do—so've you. Till Saturday I shall breathe no word to ony soul o' this business, so that if you see good to put him oot o' the way wi'oot bother, no one need iver know as hoo Adam M'Adam's Red Wull was the Black Killer."

He turned away for the second time. But the little man sprang after him, and clutched him by the arm.

"Look ye here, James Moore!" he cried in a thick, shaky, horrible voice. "Ye're big, I'm sma'; ye're strang, I'm weak; ye've ivery one to your back, I've niver a one; you tell your story, and they'll believe ye—for you gae to church; I'll tell mine, and they'll think I lie—for I dinna. But a word in your ear! If iver again I catch ye on ma land, by—!" —he swore a great oath—"I'll no spare ye. You ken best if I'm in earnest or no." And his face was dreadful to see in its hideous determinedness.

Dusk was merging into darkness when the Master and Andrew reached the Dalesman's Daughter. It had been long dark when they emerged from the cozy parlor of the inn and plunged out into the night.

As they crossed the Silver Lea the wind fluttered past them in spasmodic gasps.

"There's trouble in the wind," said the Master.

"Ay," answered his laconic son.

All day there had been no breath of air, and the sky dangerously blue. But now a world of black was surging up from the horizon, smothering the starlit night; and small dark clouds, like puffs of smoke, detaching themselves from the main body, were driving tempestuously forward—the vanguard of the storm.

In the distance was a low tumbling like heavy tumbrils on the floor of heaven. All about, the wind sounded hollow like a mighty scythe on corn. The air was oppressed with a leaden blackness—no glimmer of light on any hand; and as they began the ascent of the Pass they reached out blind hands to feel along the rock face.

A sea fret, cool and wetting, fell. A few big raindrops splashed heavily down. The wind rose with a leap and roared past them up the rocky track. And the water gates of heaven were flung wide.

Wet and weary, they battled on, thinking sometimes of the cozy parlor behind, sometimes of the home in front; wondering whether Maggie, in flat contradiction of her father's orders, would be up to welcome them, or whether only Owd Bob would come out to meet them.

The wind volleyed past them like salvos of artillery. The rain stormed at them from above; spat at them from the rock face; and leapt up at them from their feet.

Once they halted for a moment, finding a miserable shelter in a crevice of the rock.

"It's a Black Killer's night," panted the Master. "I reck'n he's oot."

"Ay," the boy gasped, "reck'n he is."

Up and up they climbed through the blackness, blind and buffeted. The eternal thunder of the rain was all about them; the clamor of the gale above; and far beneath, the roar of angry waters.

Once, in a lull in the storm, the Master turned and looked back into the blackness along the path they had come.

"Did ye hear onythin'?" he roared above the muffled soughing of the wind.

"Nay!" Andrew shouted back.

"I thowt I heard a step!" the Master cried, peering down. But nothing could he see.

Then the wind leaped to life again like a giant from his sleep, drowning all sound with its hurricane voice; and they turned and bent to their task again.

Nearing the summit, the Master turned once more.

"There it was again!" he called; but his words were swept away on the storm; and they buckled to the struggle afresh.

Ever and anon the moon gleamed down through the riot of tossing sky. Then they could see the wet wall above them, with the water tumbling down its sheer face; and far below, in the roaring gutter of the Pass, a brown-stained torrent. Hardly, however, had they time to glance around when a mass of cloud would hurry jealously up, and all again was blackness and noise.

At length, nigh spent, they topped the last and steepest pitch of the Pass, and emerged into the Devil's Bowl. There, overcome with their exertions, they flung themselves onto the soaking ground to draw breath.

Behind them, the wind rushed with a sullen roar up the funnel of the Pass. It screamed above them as though ten million devils were a-horse; and blurted out onto the wild Marches beyond.

As they lay there, still panting, the moon gleamed down in momentary graciousness. In front, through the lashing rain, they could discern the hillocks that squat, haglike, round the Devil's Bowl; and lying in its bosom, its white waters, usually so still, plowed now into a thousand furrows, the Lone Tarn.

The Master raised his head and craned forward at the ghostly scene. Of a sudden he reared himself onto his arms, and stayed motionless awhile. Then he dropped as though dead, forcing down Andrew with an iron hand.

"Lad, did'st see?" he whispered.

"Nay; what was't?" the boy replied, roused by his father's tone.

"There!"

But as the Master pointed forward, a blur of cloud intervened and all was dark. Quickly it passed; and again the lantern of the night shone down. And Andrew, looking with all his eyes, saw indeed.

There, in front, by the fretting waters of the Tarn, packed in a solid phalanx, with every head turned in the same direction, was a flock of sheep. They were motionless, all-intent, staring with horror-bulging eyes. A column of steam rose from their bodies into the rain-pierced air. Panting and palpitating, yet they stood with their backs to the water, as though determined to sell their lives dearly. Beyond them, not fifty yards away, crouched a humpbacked boulder, casting a long, misshapen shadow in the moonlight. And beneath it were two black objects, one still struggling feebly.

"The Killer!" gasped the boy, and, all ablaze with excitement, began forging forward.

"Steady, lad, steady!" urged his father, dropping a restraining hand on the boy's shoulder.

Above them a huddle of clouds flung in furious rout across the night, and the moon was veiled.

"Follow, lad!" ordered the Master, and began to crawl silently forward. As stealthily Andrew pursued. And over the sodden ground they crept, one behind the other, like two nighthawks on some foul errand.

On they crawled, lying prone during the blinks of moon, stealing forward in the dark; till, at length, the swish of the rain on the waters of the Tarn, and the sobbing of the flock in front, warned them they were near.

They skirted the trembling pack, passing so close as to brush against the flanking sheep; and yet unnoticed, for the sheep were soul-absorbed in the tragedy in front. Only, when the moon was in, Andrew could hear them huddling and stamping in the darkness. And again, as it shone out, fearfully they edged closer to watch the bloody play.

Along the Tarn edge the two crept. And still the gracious moon hid their approach, and the drunken wind drowned with its revelry the sound of their coming.

So they stole on, on hands and knees, with hearts aghast and fluttering breath; until, of a sudden, in a lull of wind, they could hear, right before them, the smack and slobber of bloody lips, chewing their bloody meal.

"Say thy prayers, Red Wull. Thy last minute's come!" muttered the Master, rising to his knees. Then, in Andrew's ear: "When I rush, lad, follow!" For he thought, when the moon rose, to jump in on the great dog, and, surprising him as he lay gorged and unsuspicious, to deal him one terrible swashing blow, and end forever the lawless doings of the Tailless Tyke.

The moon flung off its veil of cloud. White and cold, it stared down into the Devil's Bowl, on murderer and murdered.

Within a hand's cast of the avengers of blood humped the black boulder. On the border of its shadow lay a dead sheep; and standing beside the body, his coat all ruffled by the hand of the storm—Owd Bob—Owd Bob o' Kenmuir.

Then the light went in, and darkness covered the land.

It was Owd Bob. There could be no mistaking. In the wide world there was but one Owd Bob o' Kenmuir. The silver moon gleamed down on the dark head and rough gray coat, and lit the white escutcheon on his chest.

And in the darkness James Moore was lying with his face pressed downward that he might not see.

Once he raised himself on his arms; his eyes were shut and face uplifted, like a blind man praying. He passed a weary hand across his brow; his head dropped again; and he moaned and moaned like a man in everlasting pain.

Then the darkness lifted a moment, and he stole a furtive glance, like a murderer's at the gallows tree, at the scene in front.

It was no dream. Clear and cruel in the moonlight the humpbacked boulder; the dead sheep; and that gray figure, beautiful, motionless, damned for all eternity.

The Master turned his face and looked at Andrew, a dumb, pitiful entreaty in his eyes; but in the boy's white, horror-stricken countenance was no comfort. Then his head lolled down again, and the strong man was whimpering.

"He! he! he! 'Scuse ma laffin', Mr. Moore—he! he! he!"

A little man, all wet and shrunk, sat hunching on a mound above them, rocking his shriveled form to and fro in the agony of his merriment.

"Ye raskil—he! he! Ye rogue—he! he!" and he shook his fist waggishly at the unconscious gray dog. "I owe ye anither grudge for this—ye've anteecipated me"—and he leant back and shook this way and that in convulsive mirth.

The man below him rose heavily to his feet, and tumbled toward the mocker, his great figure swaying from side to side as though in blind delirium, moaning still as he went. And there was that on his face which no man can mistake. Boy that he was, Andrew knew it.

"Feyther! Feyther! Do'ee not!" he pleaded, running after his father and laying impotent hands on him.

But the strong man shook him off like a fly, and rolled on, swaying and groaning, with that awful expression plain to see in the moonlight.

In front the little man squatted in the rain, bowed double still; and took no thought to flee.

"Come on, James Moore! Come on!" he laughed, malignant joy in his voice; and something gleamed bright in his right hand, and was hid again. "I've bin waitin' this a weary while noo. Come on!"

There had there been done something worse than sheep murder in the dreadful lonesomeness of the Devil's Bowl upon that night; but, of a sudden, there sounded the splash of a man's foot, falling heavily behind; a hand like a falling tree smote the Master on the shoulder; and a voice roared above the noise of the storm:

"Mr. Moore! Look, man! Look!"

The Master tried to shake off that detaining grasp; but it pinned him where he was, immovable.

"Look, I tell yo'!" cried that great voice again.

A hand pushed past him and pointed; and sullenly he turned, ignoring the figure at his side, and looked.

The wind had dropped suddenly as it had risen; the little man on the mound had ceased to chuckle; Andrew's sobs were hushed; and in the background the huddled flock edged closer. The world hung balanced on the pinpoint of the moment. Every eye was in the one direction.

With dull, uncomprehending gaze James Moore stared as bidden. There was the gray dog naked in the moonlight, heedless still of any witnesses; there the murdered sheep, lying within and without that distorted shade; and there the humpbacked boulder.

He stared into the shadow, and still stared. Then he started as though struck. The shadow of the boulder had moved!

Motionless, with head shot forward and bulging eyes, he gazed.

Ay, ay, ay; he was sure of it—a huge dim outline as of a lion *couchant,* in the very thickest of the blackness.

At that he was seized with such a palsy of trembling that he must have fallen but for the strong arm about his waist.

Clearer every moment grew that crouching figure; till at length they plainly could discern the line of arching loins, the crest, thick as a stallion's, the massive, wagging head. No mistake this time. There he lay in the deepest black, gigantic, reveling in his horrid debauch—the Black Killer!

And they watched him at his feast. Now he burrowed into the spongy flesh; now turned to lap the dark pool which glittered in the moonlight at his side like claret in a silver cup. Now lifting his head, he snapped irritably at the raindrops, and the moon caught his wicked, rolling eye and the red shreds of flesh dripping from his jaw. And again, raising his great muzzle as if about to howl, he let the delicious nectar trickle down his throat and ravish his palate.

So he went on, all unsuspicious, wisely nodding in slow-mouthed gluttony. And in the stillness, between the claps of wind, they could hear the smacking of his lips.

While all the time the gray dog stood before him, motionless, as though carved in stone.

At last, as the murderer rolled his great head from side to side, he saw that still figure. At the sight he leaped back, dismayed. Then with a deep-mouthed roar that shook the waters of the Tarn he was up and across his victim with fangs bared, his coat standing erect in wet, rigid furrows from top-knot to tail.

So the two stood, face to face, with perhaps a yard of rain-pierced air between them.

The wind hushed its sighing to listen. The moon stared down, white and dumb. Away at the back the sheep edged closer. While, save for the everlasting thunder of the rain, there was utter stillness.

An age, it seemed, they waited so. Then a voice, clear yet low and far away, like a bugle in a distant city, broke the silence.

"Eh, Wullie!" it said.

There was no anger in the tones, only an incomparable reproach; the sound of the cracking of a man's heart.

At the call the great dog leapt round, snarling in hideous passion. He saw the small, familiar figure, clear-cut against the tumbling sky; and for the only time in his life Red Wull was afraid.

His blood-foe was forgotten; the dead sheep was forgotten; everything was sunk in the agony of that moment. He cowered upon the ground, and a cry like that of a lost soul was wrung from him; it rose on the still night air and floated, wailing, away; and the white waters of the Tarn thrilled in cold pity, out of the lonely hollow, over the desolate Marches, into the night.

On the mound above stood his master. The little man's white hair was bared to the night wind; the rain trickled down his face; and his hands were folded behind his back. He stood there, looking down into the dell below him, as a man may stand at the tomb of his lately buried wife. And there was such an expression on his face as I cannot describe.

"Wullie, Wullie, to me!" he cried at length; and his voice sounded weak and far, like a distant memory.

At that, the huge brute came crawling toward him on his belly, whimpering as he came, very pitiful in his distress. He knew his fate as every sheepdog knows it. That troubled him not. His pain, insufferable, was that this, his friend and father, who had trusted him, should have found him in his sin.

So he crept up to his master's feet; and the little man never moved.

"Wullie—ma Wullie!" he said very gently. "They've aye bin agin me—and noo you! A man's mither—a man's wife—a man's dog! They're all I've iver had; and noo ain o' they three has turned agin me! Indeed I am alone!"

At that the great dog raised himself, and placing his forepaws on his master's chest tenderly, lest he should hurt him who was already hurt past healing, stood towering above him; while the little man laid his two cold hands on the dog's shoulders.

So they stood, looking at one another, like a man and his love.

At M'Adam's word, Owd Bob looked up, and for the first time saw his master.

He seemed in nowise startled, but trotted over to him. There was nothing fearful in his carriage, no haunting blood-guiltiness in the true gray eyes which never told a lie, which never, doglike, failed to look you in the face. Yet his tail was low, and, as he stopped at his master's feet, he was quivering. For he, too, knew, and was not unmoved.

For weeks he had tracked the Killer; for weeks he had followed him as he crossed Kenmuir, bound on his bloody errands; yet always had lost him on the Marches. Now, at last, he had run him to ground. Yet his heart went out to his enemy in his distress.

"I thowt t'had bin yo', lad," the Master whispered, his

hand on the dark head at his knee. "I thowt t'had bin yo'!"

Rooted to the ground, the three watched the scene between M'Adam and his Wull.

In the end the Master was whimpering; Andrew crying; and David turned his back.

So they marched out of the Devil's Bowl, and left those two alone together.

A little later, as they trampled along, James Moore heard little pattering, staggering footsteps behind.

He stopped, and the other two went on.

"Man," a voice whispered, and a face, white and pitiful, like a mother's pleading for her child, looked into his. "Man, ye'll no tell them a'? I'd no like 'em to ken 'twas ma Wullie. Think an t'had bin yer ain dog."

"You may trust me!" the other answered thickly.

The little man stretched out a palsied hand.

"Gie us yer hand on't. And G-God bless ye, James Moore!"

So these two shook hands in the moonlight, with none to witness it but the God who made them.

On the following morning there was a sheep auction at the Dalesman's Daughter.

Early as many of the farmers arrived, there was one earlier. Tupper, the first man to enter the sand-floored parlor, found M'Adam before him.

He was sitting a little forward in his chair; his thin hands rested on his knees; and on his face was a gentle, dreamy expression such as no man had ever seen there before. All the harsh wrinkles seemed to have fled in the night; and the sour face, stamped deep with the bitterness of life, was softened now, as if at length at peace.

"When I coom doon this mornin'," said Teddy Bolstock in a whisper, "I found 'im sittin' just so. And he's nor moved nor spoke since."

"Where's th' Terror, then?" asked Tupper, awed somehow into like hushed tones.

"In t' paddock at back," Teddy answered, "marchin' hoop and doon, hoop and doon, for a' the world like a sentry soger. And so he was when I looked oot o' window when I wake."

A rare thing it was for M'Adam and Red Wull to be apart. So rare that others besides the men in that little taproom noticed it.

Saunderson's old Shep walked quietly to the back door of the house and looked out.

There on the slope below him he saw what he sought, stalking up and down, gaunt and grim, like a lion at feeding time. And as the old dog watched, his tail was gently swaying as though he were well pleased.

He walked back into the taproom just as Teddy began a tale. Twice he made the round of the room, silent-footed. From dog to dog he went, stopping at each as though urging him on to some great enterprise. Then he made for the door again, looking back to see if any followed.

One by one the others rose and trailed out after him: big blue Rasper, Londesley's Lassie, Ned Hoppin's young dog; Grip and Grapple, the publican's bull terriers; Jim Mason's Gyp, foolish and flirting even now; others there were; and last of all, waddling heavily in the rear, that scarred Amazon, the Venus.

Out of the house they pattered, silent and unseen, with murder in their hearts. At last they had found their enemy alone. And slowly, in a black cloud, like the shadow of death, they dropped down the slope upon him.

And he saw them coming, knew their errand—as who should better than the Terror of the Border?—and was glad. Death it might be, and such an one as he would wish to die—at least distraction from that long-drawn, haunting pain. And he smiled grimly as he looked at the approaching crowd, and saw there was not one there but he had humbled in his time.

He ceased his restless pacing, and awaited them. His great head was high as he scanned them contemptuously, daring them to come on.

And on they came, marching slow and silent like soldiers at a funeral: young and old, bobtailed and bull, terrier and collie, flocking like vultures to the dead. And the Venus, heavy with years, rolled after them on her bandy legs, panting in her hurry lest she should be late. For had she not the blood of her blood to avenge?

So they came about him, slow, certain, murderous, opening out to cut him off on every side. There was no need. He never thought to move. Long odds 'twould be—crushingly heavy; yet he loved them for it, and was trembling already with the glory of the coming fight.

They were up to him now; the sheepdogs walking round him on their toes, stiff and short like cats on coals; their backs a little humped; heads averted; yet eyeing him askance.

And he remained stock-still, nor looked at them. His great chin was cocked, and his muzzle wrinkled in a dreadful grin. As he stood there, shivering a little, his eyes rolling back, his breath grating in his throat to set every bristle on end, he looked a devil indeed.

The Venus ranged alongside him. No preliminary stage for her; she never walked where she could stand, or stood where she could lie. But stand she must now, breathing hard through her nose, never taking her eyes off that pad she had marked for her own. Close beside her were crop-eared Grip and Grapple, looking up at the line above them where hairy neck and shoulder joined. Behind was big Rasper, and close to him Lassie. Of the others, each had marked his place, each taken up his post.

Last of all, old Shep took his stand full in front of his enemy, their shoulders almost rubbing, head past head.

So the two stood a moment, as though they were whispering; each diabolical, each rolling back his eyes to watch the other. While from the little mob there rose a snarling, bubbling snore, like some giant wheezing in his sleep.

Then like lightning each struck. Rearing high, they wrestled with striving paws and the expression of fiends incarnate. Down they went, Shep underneath, and the great dog with a dozen of these wolves of hell upon him. Rasper, devilish, was riding on his back; the Venus—well for him!—had struck and missed; but Grip and Grapple had their hold; and the others, like leaping demoniacs, were plunging into the whirlpool vortex of the fight.

And there, where a fortnight before he had fought and lost the battle of the Cup, Red Wull now battled for his life.

Long odds! But what cared he? The long-drawn agony of the night was drowned in that glorious delirium. The hate of years came bubbling forth. In that supreme moment he would avenge his wrongs. And he went in to fight, reveling like a giant in the red lust of killing.

Long odds! Never before had he faced such a galaxy of foes. His one chance lay in quickness—to prevent the swarming crew getting their hold till at least he had diminished their numbers.

Then it was a sight to see the great brute, huge as a bull calf, strong as a bull, rolling over and over and up again, quick as a kitten; leaping here, striking there; shaking himself free; swinging his quarters; fighting with feet and body and teeth—every inch of him at war. More than once he broke right through the mob, only to turn again and face it. No flight for him; nor thought of it.

Up and down the slope the dark mass tossed, like some hulk the sport of the waves. Black and white, sable and gray, worrying at that great centerpiece. Up and down, roaming wide, leaving everywhere a trail of red.

Gyp he had pinned and hurled over his shoulder. Grip followed; he shook her till she rattled, then flung her afar; and she fell with a horrid thud, not to rise. While Grapple, the death to avenge, hung tighter. In a scarlet, soaking patch on the ground lay Big Bell's lurcher, doubled up in a dreadful ball. And Hoppin's young dog, who three hours before had been the children's tender playmate, now fiendish to look on, dragged after the huddle up the hill. Back the mob rolled on her. When it was passed, she lay quite still, grinning, a handful of tawny hair and flesh in her dead mouth.

So they fought on. And ever and anon a great figure rose up from the heaving inferno all around; rearing to his full height, his head ragged and bleeding, the red foam dripping from his jaws. Thus he would appear momentarily, like some dark rock amid a raging sea; and down he would go again.

Silent now they fought, dumb and determined. Only you might have heard the rend and rip of tearing flesh; a hoarse gurgle as some dog went down; the panting of dry throats; and now and then a sob from that central figure. For he was fighting for his life. The Terror of the Border was at bay.

All who meant it were on him now. The Venus, blinded with blood, had her hold at last, and never but once in a long life of battles had she let go; Rasper, his breath coming in rattles, had him horribly by the loins; while a dozen other devils with red eyes and wrinkled nostrils clung still.

Long odds! And down he went, smothered beneath the weight of numbers, yet struggled up again. His great head was torn and dripping; his eyes a gleam of rolling red and white; the little tail stern and stiff like the gallant stump of a flagstaff shot away. He was desperate, but indomitable; and he sobbed as he fought doggedly on.

Long odds! It could not last. And down he went at length, silent still—never a cry should they wring from him in his agony—the Venus glued to that mangled pad; Rasper beneath him now; three at his throat; two at his ears; a crowd on flanks and body.

The Terror of the Border was down at last!

"Wullie, ma Wullie!" screamed M'Adam, bounding down the slope a crook's length in front of the rest. "Wullie! Wullie! To me!"

At the shrill cry the huddle below was convulsed. It heaved and swayed and dragged to and fro, like the sea lashed into life by some dying leviathan.

A gigantic figure, tawny and red, fought its way to the surface. A great tossing head, bloody past recognition, flung out from the ruck. One quick glance he shot from his ragged eyes at the little flying form in front; then with a roar like a waterfall plunged toward it, shaking off the bloody leeches as he went.

"Wullie! Wullie! I'm wi' ye!" cried that little voice, now so near.

Through—through—through! An incomparable effort, and his last. They hung to his throat, they clung to his muzzle, they were round and about him. And down he went again with a sob and a little suffocating cry, shooting up at his master one quick, beseeching glance as the sea of blood closed over him—worrying, smothering, tearing, like foxhounds at the kill.

They left the dead and pulled away the living. And it was no light task, for the pack were mad for blood.

At the bottom of the wet mess of hair and red and flesh was old Shep, stone-dead. And as Saunderson pulled the body out, his face was working; for no man can lose in a crack the friend of a dozen years, and remain unmoved.

The Venus lay there, her teeth clenched still in death; smiling that her vengeance was achieved. Big Rasper, blue no longer, was gasping out his life. Two more came crawling out to find a quiet spot where they might lay them down to die. Before the night had fallen another had gone to his account. While not a dog who fought upon that day but carried the scars of it with him to his grave.

The Terror o' th' Border, terrible in his life, like Samson, was yet more terrible in his dying.

Down at the bottom lay that which once had been Adam M'Adam's Red Wull.

At the sight the little man neither raved nor swore; it was past that for him. He sat down, heedless of the soaking ground, and took the mangled head in his lap very tenderly.

"They've done ye at last, Wullie—they've done ye at last," he said quietly; unalterably convinced that the attack had been organized while he was detained in the taproom.

On hearing the loved little voice, the dog gave one weary wag of his stump tail. And with that the Tailless Tyke, Adam M'Adam's Red Wull, the Black Killer, went to his long home.

## *Jack London*

# THAT SPOT

I don't think much of Stephen Mackaye anymore, though I used to swear by him. I know that in those days I loved him more than my own brother. If ever I meet Stephen Mackaye again, I shall not be responsible for my actions. It passes beyond me that a man with whom I shared food and blanket, and with whom I mushed over the Chilcoot Trail, should turn out the way he did. I always sized Steve up as a square man, a kindly comrade, without an iota of anything vindictive or malicious in his nature. I shall never trust my judgment in men again. Why, I nursed that man through typhoid fever; we starved together on the headwaters of the Stewart; and he saved my life on the Little Salmon. And now, after the years we were together, all I can say of Stephen Mackaye is that he is the meanest man I ever knew.

We started for the Klondike in the fall rush of 1897, and we started too late to get over Chilcoot Pass before the freeze-up. We packed our outfit on our backs partway over, when the snow began to fly, and then we had to buy dogs in order to sled it the rest of the way. That was how we came to get that Spot. Dogs were high, and we paid $110 for him. He looked worth it. I say *looked,* because he was one of the finest-appearing dogs I ever saw. He weighed sixty pounds, and he had all the lines of a good sled animal. We never could make out his breed. He wasn't husky, nor malamute, nor Hudson Bay; he looked like all of them and he didn't look like any of them; and on top of it all he had some of the white man's dog in him, for on one side, in the thick of the mixed yellow-brown-red-and-dirty-white that was his prevailing color, there was a spot of coal black as big as a water bucket. That was why we called him Spot.

He was a good looker all right. When he was in condition his muscles stood out in bunches all over him. And he was the strongest-looking brute I ever saw in Alaska, also the most intelligent-looking. To run your eyes over him, you'd think he could outpull three dogs of his own weight. Maybe he could, but I never saw it. His intelligence didn't run that way. He could steal and forage to perfection; he had an instinct that was positively gruesome for divining when work was to be done and for making a sneak accordingly; and for getting lost and not staying lost he was nothing short of inspired. But when it came to work, the way that intelligence dribbled out of him and left him a mere clot of wobbling, stupid jelly would make your heart bleed.

There are times when I think it wasn't stupidity. Maybe, like some men I know, he was too wise to work. I shouldn't wonder if he put it all over us with that intelligence of his.

Maybe he figured it all out and decided that a licking now and again and no work was a whole lot better than work all the time and no licking. He was intelligent enough for such a computation. I tell you, I've sat and looked into that dog's eyes till the shivers ran up and down my spine and the marrow crawled like yeast, what of the intelligence I saw shining out. I can't express myself about that intelligence. It is beyond mere words. I saw it, that's all. At times it was like gazing into a human soul, to look into his eyes; and what I saw there frightened me and started all sorts of ideas in my own mind of reincarnation and all the rest. I tell you I sensed something big in that brute's eyes; there was a message there, but I wasn't big enough myself to catch it. Whatever it was (I know I'm making a fool of myself)—whatever it was, it baffled me. I can't give an inkling of what I saw in that brute's eyes; it wasn't light, it wasn't color; it was something that moved, away back, when the eyes themselves weren't moving. And I guess I didn't see it move, either; I only sensed that it moved. It was an expression, that's what it was, and I got an impression of it. No, it was different from a mere expression; it was more than that. I don't know what it was, but it gave me a feeling of kinship just the same. Oh, no, not sentimental kinship. It was, rather, a kinship of equality. Those eyes never pleaded like a deer's eyes. They challenged. No, it wasn't defiance. It was just a calm assumption of equality. And I don't think it was deliberate. My belief is that it was unconscious on his part. It was there because it was there, and it couldn't help shining out. No, I don't mean shine. It didn't shine; it *moved.* I know I'm talking rot, but if you'd looked into that animal's eyes the way I have, you'd understand. Steve was affected the same way I was. Why, I tried to kill that Spot once—he was no good for anything—and I fell down on it. I led him out into the brush, and he came along slow and unwilling. He knew what was going on. I stopped in a likely place, put my foot on the rope, and pulled my big Colt's. And that dog sat down and looked at me. I tell you he didn't plead. He just looked. And I saw all kinds of incomprehensible things moving, yes, *moving,* in those eyes of his. I didn't really see them move; I thought I saw them, for, as I said before, I guess I only sensed them. And I want to tell you right now that it got beyond me. It was like killing a man, a conscious, brave man who looked calmly into your gun as much as to say, "Who's afraid?" Then, too, the message seemed so near that, instead of pulling the trigger quick, I stopped to see if I could catch the message. There it was, right before me, glimmering all around in those eyes of his. And then it was too late. I got scared. I was trembly all over, and my stomach generated a nervous palpitation that made me seasick. I just sat down and looked at that dog, and he looked at me, till I thought I was going crazy. Do you want to know what I did? I threw down the gun and ran back to camp with the fear of God in my heart. Steve laughed at me. But I notice that Steve led Spot into the woods, a week later, for the same purpose, and that Steve came back alone, and a little later Spot drifted back, too.

At any rate, Spot wouldn't work. We paid $110 for him from the bottom of our sack, and he wouldn't work. He wouldn't even tighten the traces. Steve spoke to him the first time we put him in harness, and he sort of shivered, that was all. Not an ounce on the traces. He just stood still and wobbled, like so much jelly. Steve touched him with the whip. He yelped, but not an ounce. Steve touched him again, a bit harder, and he howled—the regular long wolf howl. Then Steve got mad and gave him half a dozen, and I came on the run from the tent.

I told Steve he was brutal with the animal, and we had some words—the first we'd ever had. He threw the whip down in the snow and walked away mad. I picked it up and went to it. That Spot trembled and wobbled and cowered before ever I swung the lash, and with the first bite of it he howled like a lost soul. Next he lay down in the snow. I started the rest of the dogs, and they dragged him along while I threw the whip into him. He rolled over on his back and bumped along, his four legs waving in the air, himself howling as though he was going through a sausage machine. Steve came back and laughed at me, and I apologized for what I'd said.

There was no getting any work out of that Spot; and to make up for it, he was the biggest pig-glutton of a dog I ever saw. On top of that, he was the cleverest thief. There was no circumventing him. Many a breakfast we went without our bacon because Spot had been there first. And it was because of him that we nearly starved to death up the Stewart. He figured out the way to break into our meat cache, and what he didn't eat, the rest of the team did. But he was impartial. He stole from everybody. He was a restless dog, always very busy snooping around or going somewhere. And there was never a camp within five miles that he didn't raid. The worst of it was that they always came back on us to pay his board bill, which was just, being the law of the land; but it was mighty hard on us, especially that first winter on the Chilcoot, when we were busted, paying for whole hams and sides of bacon that we never ate. He could fight, too, that Spot. He could do everything but work. He never pulled a pound, but he was the boss of the whole team. The way he made those dogs stand around was an education. He bullied them, and there was always one or more of them fresh-marked with his fangs. But he was more than a bully. He wasn't afraid of anything that walked on four legs; and I've seen him march, single-handed, into a strange team, without any provocation whatever, and put the kibosh on the whole outfit. Did I say he could eat? I caught him eating the whip once. That's straight. He started in at the lash, and when I caught him he was down to the handle, and still going.

But he was a good looker. At the end of the first week we sold him for seventy-five dollars to the Mounted Police.

They had experienced dog-drivers, and we knew that by the time he'd covered the six hundred miles to Dawson he'd be a good sled dog. I say we *knew,* for we were just getting acquainted with that Spot. A little later we were not brash enough to know anything where he was concerned. A week later we woke up in the morning to the dangdest dogfight we'd ever heard. It was that Spot come back and knocking the team into shape. We ate a pretty depressing breakfast, I can tell you; but cheered up two hours afterward when we sold him to an official courier, bound in to Dawson with government dispatches. That Spot was only three days in coming back, and, as usual, celebrated his arrival with a roughhouse.

We spent the winter and spring, after our own outfit was across the pass, freighting other people's outfits; and we made a fat stake. Also, we made money out of Spot. If we sold him once, we sold him twenty times. He always came back, and no one asked for their money. We didn't want the money. We'd have paid handsomely for anyone to take him off our hands for keeps. We had to get rid of him, and we couldn't give him away, for that would have been suspicious. But he was such a fine looker that we never had any difficulty in selling him. "Unbroke," we'd say, and they'd pay any old price for him. We sold him as low as twenty-five dollars, and once we got 150 for him. That particular party returned him in person, refused to take his money back, and the way he abused us was something awful. He said it was cheap at the price to tell us what he thought of us; and we felt he was so justified that we never talked back. But to this day I've never quite regained all the old self-respect that was mine before that man talked to me.

When the ice cleared out of the lakes and river, we put our outfit in a Lake Bennett boat and started for Dawson. We had a good team of dogs, and of course we piled them on top the outfit. That Spot was along—there was no losing him—and a dozen times, the first day, he knocked one or another of the dogs overboard in the course of fighting with them. It was close quarters, and he didn't like being crowded.

"What that dog needs is space," Steve said the second day. "Let's maroon him."

We did, running the boat in at Caribou Crossing for him to jump ashore. Two of the other dogs, good dogs, followed him; and we lost two whole days trying to find them. We never saw those two dogs again; but the quietness and relief we enjoyed made us decide, like the man who refused his 150, that it was cheap at the price. For the first time in months Steve and I laughed and whistled and sang. We were as happy as clams. The dark days were over. The nightmare had been lifted. That Spot was gone.

Three weeks later, one morning, Steve and I were standing on the riverbank at Dawson. A small boat was just arriving from Lake Bennett. I saw Steve give a start, and heard him say something that was not nice and that was not under his breath. Then I looked; and there, in the bow of the boat, with ears pricked up, sat Spot. Steve and I sneaked immediately, like beaten curs, like cowards, like absconders from justice. It was this last that the lieutenant of police thought when he saw us sneaking. He surmised that there were law officers in the boat who were after us. He didn't wait to find out, but kept us in sight, and in the M. & M. saloon got us in a corner. We had a merry time explaining, for we refused to go back to the boat and meet Spot; and finally he held us under guard of another policeman while he went to the boat. After we got clear of him, we started for the cabin, and when we arrived, there was that Spot sitting on the stoop waiting for us. Now how did he know we lived there? There were forty thousand people in Dawson that summer, and how did he savvy our cabin out of all the cabins? How did he know we were in Dawson, anyway? I leave it to you. But don't forget what I have said about his intelligence and that immortal something I have seen glimmering in his eyes.

There was no getting rid of him anymore. There were too many people in Dawson who had bought him up on Chilcoot, and the story got around. Half a dozen times we put him on board steamboats going down the Yukon; but he merely went ashore at the first landing and trotted back up the bank. We couldn't sell him, we couldn't kill him (both Steve and I had tried), and nobody else was able to kill him. He bore a charmed life. I've seen him go down in a dogfight on the main street with fifty dogs on top of him, and when they were separated, he'd appear on all his four legs, unharmed, while two of the dogs that had been on top of him would be lying dead.

I saw him steal a chunk of moose meat from Major Dinwiddie's cache so heavy that he could just keep one jump ahead of Mrs. Dinwiddie's squaw cook, who was after him with an ax. As he went up the hill, after the squaw gave up, Major Dinwiddie himself came out and pumped his Winchester into the landscape. He emptied his magazine twice, and never touched that Spot. Then a policeman came along and arrested him for discharging firearms inside the city limits. Major Dinwiddie paid his fine, and Steve and I paid him for the moose meat at the rate of a dollar a pound, bones and all. That was what he paid for it. Meat was high that year.

I am only telling what I saw with my own eyes. And now I'll tell you something, also. I saw that Spot fall through a water hole. The ice was three and a half feet thick, and the current sucked him under like a straw. Three hundred yards below was the big water hole used by the hospital. Spot crawled out of the hospital water hole, licked off the water, bit out the ice that had formed between his toes, trotted up the bank, and whipped a big Newfoundland belonging to the Gold Commissioner.

In the fall of 1898, Steve and I poled up the Yukon on the last water, bound for Stewart River. We took the dogs along, all except Spot. We figured we'd been feeding him long enough. He'd cost us more time and trouble and money and grub than we'd got by selling him on the Chilcoot—especially grub. So Steve and I tied him down in the cabin and pulled our freight. We camped that night at the mouth of Indian River, and Steve and I were pretty facetious over having shaken him. Steve was a funny cuss, and I was just sitting up in the blankets and laughing when a tornado hit camp. The way that Spot walked into those dogs and gave them what-for was hair-raising. Now how did he get loose? It's up to you. I haven't any theory. And how did he get across the Klondike River? That's another facer. And anyway, how did he know we had gone up the Yukon? You see, we went by water, and he couldn't smell our tracks. Steve and I began to get superstitious about that dog. He got on our nerves, too; and, between you and me, we were just a mite afraid of him.

The freeze-up came on when we were at the mouth of Henderson Creek, and we traded him off for two sacks of flour to an outfit that was bound up White River after copper. Now that whole outfit was lost. Never trace nor hide nor hair of men, dogs, sleds, or anything was ever found. They dropped clean out of sight. It became one of the mysteries of the country. Steve and I plugged away up the Stewart, and six weeks afterward that Spot crawled into camp. He was a perambulating skeleton, and could just drag along; but he got there. And what I want to know is who told him we were up the Stewart? We could have gone a thousand other places. How did he know? You tell me, and I'll tell you.

No losing him. At the Mayo he started a row with an Indian dog. The buck who owned the dog took a swing at Spot with an ax, missed him, and killed his own dog. Talk about magic and turning bullets aside—I, for one, consider it a blamed sight harder to turn an ax aside with a big buck at the other end of it. And I saw him do it with my own eyes. That buck didn't want to kill his own dog. You've got to show me.

I told you about Spot breaking into our meat cache. It

was nearly the death of us. There wasn't any more meat to be killed, and meat was all we had to live on. The moose had gone back several hundred miles and the Indians with them. There we were. Spring was on, and we had to wait for the river to break. We got pretty thin before we decided to eat the dogs, and we decided to eat Spot first. Do you know what that dog did? He sneaked. Now how did he know our minds were made up to eat him? We sat up nights laying for him, but he never came back, and we ate the other dogs. We ate the whole team.

And now for the sequel. You know what it is when a big river breaks up and a few billion tons of ice go out, jamming and milling and grinding. Just in the thick of it, when the Stewart went out, rumbling and roaring, we sighted Spot out in the middle. He'd got caught as he was trying to cross up above somewhere. Steve and I yelled and shouted and ran up and down the bank, tossing our hats in the air. Sometimes we'd stop and hug each other, we were that boisterous, for we saw Spot's finish. He didn't have a chance in a million. He didn't have any chance at all. After the ice run, we got into a canoe and paddled down to the Yukon, and down the Yukon to Dawson, stopping to feed up for a week at the cabins at the mouth of Henderson Creek. And as we came in to the bank at Dawson, there sat that Spot, waiting for us, his ears pricked up, his tail wagging, his mouth smiling, extending a hearty welcome to us. Now how did he get out of that ice? How did he know we were coming to Dawson, to the very hour and minute, to be out there on the bank waiting for us?

The more I think of that Spot, the more I am convinced that there are things in this world that go beyond science. On no scientific grounds can that Spot be explained. It's psychic phenomena, or mysticism, or something of that sort, I guess, with a lot of Theosophy thrown in. The Klondike is a good country. I might have been there yet, and become a millionaire, if it hadn't been for Spot. He got on my nerves. I stood him for two years altogether, and then I guess my stamina broke. It was the summer of 1899 when I pulled out. I didn't say anything to Steve. I just sneaked. But I fixed it up all right. I wrote Steve a note, and enclosed a package of "rough-on-rats," telling him what to do with it. I was worn down to skin and bone by that Spot, and I was that nervous that I'd jump and look around when there wasn't anybody within hailing distance. But it was astonishing the way I recuperated when I got quit of him. I got back twenty pounds before I arrived in San Francisco, and by the time I'd crossed the ferry to Oakland I was my old self again, so that even my wife looked in vain for any change in me.

Steve wrote to me once, and his letter seemed irritated. He took it kind of hard because I'd left him with Spot. Also, he said he'd used the "rough-on-rats," per directions, and that there was nothing doing. A year went by. I was back in the office and prospering in all ways—even getting a bit fat. And then Steve arrived. He didn't look me up. I read his name in the steamer list, and wondered why. But I didn't wonder long. I got up one morning and found that Spot chained to the gatepost and holding up the milkman. Steve went north to Seattle, I learned, that very morning. I didn't put on any more weight. My wife made me buy him a collar and tag, and within an hour he showed his gratitude by killing her pet Persian cat. There is no getting rid of that Spot. He will be with me until I die, for he'll never die. My appetite is not so good since he arrived, and my wife says I am looking peaked. Last night that Spot got into Mr. Harvey's henhouse (Harvey is my next-door neighbor) and killed nineteen of his fancy-bred chickens. I shall have to pay for them. My neighbors on the other side quarreled with my wife and then moved out. Spot was the cause of it. And that is why I am disappointed in Stephen Mackaye. I had no idea he was so mean a man.

Albert Payson Terhune

# THE COMING OF LAD

In the mile-away village of Hampton, there had been a veritable epidemic of burglaries —ranging from the theft of a brand-new ash can from the steps of the Methodist chapel to the ravaging of Mrs. Blauvelt's whole lineful of clothes, on a washday dusk.

Up the Valley and down it, from Tuxedo to Ridgewood, there had been a half-score robberies of a very different order —depredations wrought, manifestly by professionals; thieves whose motorcars served the twentieth-century purpose of such historic steeds as Dick Turpin's Black Bess and Jack Shepard's Ranter. These thefts were in the line of jewelry and the like; and were as daringly wrought as were the modest local operators' raids on ash can and laundry.

It is the easiest thing in the world to stir humankind's ever-tense burglar-nerves into hysterical jangling. In house after house, for miles of the peaceful North Jersey region, old pistols were cleaned and loaded; window fastenings and door locks were inspected and new hiding places found for portable family treasures.

Across the lake from the village, and down the Valley from a dozen country homes, seeped the tide of precautions. And it swirled at last around the Place—a thirty-acre homestead, isolated and sweet, whose grounds ran from highway to lake; and whose wisteria-clad gray house drowsed among big oaks midway between road and water, a furlong or more distant from either.

The Place's family dog, a pointer, had died, rich in years and honor. And the new peril of burglary made it highly needful to choose a successor for him.

The Master talked of buying a whalebone-and-steel-and-snow bullterrier, or a more formidable if more greedy Great Dane. But the Mistress wanted a collie. So they compromised by getting the collie.

He reached the Place in a crampy and smelly crate, preceded by a long envelope containing an intricate and imposing pedigree. The burglary-preventing problem seemed solved.

But when the crate was opened and its occupant stepped gravely forth, on the Place's veranda, the problem was revived.

All the Master and the Mistress had known about the newcomer—apart from his price and his lofty lineage—was that his breeder had named him "Lad."

From these meager facts they had somehow built up a picture of a huge and grimly ferocious animal that should be a terror to all intruders and that might in time be induced to make friends with the Place's vouched-for occupants. In view of this, they had had a stout kennel made and to it they had affixed with double staples a chain strong enough to restrain a bull.

(It may as well be said here that never in all the sixteen years of his beautiful life did Lad occupy that or any other kennel nor wear that or any other chain.)

Even the crate which brought the new dog to the Place failed somehow to destroy the illusion of size and fierceness. But the moment the crate door was opened, the delusion was wrecked by Lad himself.

Out onto the porch he walked. The ramshackle crate behind him had a ridiculous air of a chrysalis from which some bright thing had departed. For a shaft of sunlight was shimmering athwart the veranda floor. And into the middle of the warm bar of radiance Laddie stepped—and stood.

His fluffy puppy coat of wavy mahogany and white caught a million sunbeams, reflecting them back in tawny-orange glints and in a dazzle as of snow. His forepaws were absurdly small, even for a puppy's. Above them the ridging of the stocky leg bones gave as clear promise of mighty size and strength as did the amazingly deep little chest and square shoulders.

Here one day would stand a giant among dogs, powerful as a timber wolf, lithe as a cat, as dangerous to foes as an angry tiger; a dog without fear or treachery; a dog of uncanny brain and great lovingly loyal heart and, withal, a dancing sense of fun. A dog with a soul.

All this, any canine physiologist might have read from the compact frame, the proud head-carriage, the smolder in the deep-set sorrowful dark eyes. To the casual observer, he was but a beautiful and appealing and wonderfully cuddlable bunch of puppyhood.

Lad's dark eyes swept the porch, the soft swelling green of the lawn, the flash of fire-blue lake among the trees below.

Then he deigned to look at the group of humans at one side of him. Gravely, impersonally, he surveyed them; not at all cowed or strange in his new surroundings; courteously inquisitive as to the twist of luck that had set him down here and as to the people who presumably were to be his future companions.

Perhaps the stout little heart quivered just a bit, if memory went back to his home kennel and to the rowdy throng of brothers and sisters, and most of all, to the soft furry mother against whose side he had nestled every night since he was born. But if so, Lad was too valiant to show homesickness by so much as a whimper. And, assuredly, this House of Peace was infinitely better than the miserable crate wherein he had spent twenty horrible and jouncing and smelly and noisy hours.

From one to another of the group strayed the level, sorrowful gaze. After the swift inspection, Laddie's eyes rested again on the Mistress. For an instant he stood, looking at her, in that mildly polite curiosity which held no hint of personal interest.

Then all at once his plumy tail began to wave. Into his sad eyes sprang a flicker of warm friendliness. Unbidden—oblivious of everyone else—he trotted across to where the Mistress sat. He put one tiny white paw in her lap; and stood thus, looking up lovingly into her face, tail awag, eyes shining.

"There's no question whose dog he's going to be," laughed the Master. "He's elected you, by acclamation."

The Mistress caught up into her arms the half-grown youngster, petting his silken head, running her white fingers through his shining mahogany coat; making crooning little friendly noises to him. Lad forgot he was a dignified and stately pocket edition of a collie. Under this spell, he changed in a second to an excessively loving and nestling and adoring puppy.

"Just the same," interposed the Master, "we've been

stung. I wanted a dog to guard the Place and to be a menace to burglars and all that sort of thing. And they've sent us a teddy bear. I think I'll ship him back and get a grown one. What sort of use is—?"

"He is going to be all those things," eagerly prophesied the Mistress. "And a hundred more. See how he loves to have me pet him! And—look—he's learned, already, to shake hands, and—"

"Fine!" applauded the Master. "So when it comes our turn to be visited by this motor Raffles, the puppy will shake hands with him, and register love of petting; and the burly marauder will be so touched by Lad's friendliness that he'll not only spare our house but lead an upright life ever after. I—"

"Don't send him back!" she pleaded. "He'll grow up soon and—"

"And if only the courteous burglars will wait till he's a couple of years old," suggested the Master, "he—"

Set gently on the floor by the Mistress, Laddie had crossed to where the Master stood. The man, glancing down, met the puppy's gaze. For an instant he scowled at the miniature watchdog, so ludicrously different from the ferocious brute he had expected. Then, for some queer reason, he stooped and ran his hand roughly over the tawny coat, letting it rest at last on the shapely head that did not flinch or wriggle at his touch.

"All right," he decreed. "Let him stay. He'll be an amusing pet for you, anyhow. And his eye has the true thoroughbred expression—'the look of eagles.' He may amount to something after all. Let him stay. We'll take a chance on burglars."

So it was that Lad came to the Place. So it was that he demanded and received due welcome—which was ever Lad's way. The Master had been right about the pup's proving "an amusing pet" for the Mistress. From that first hour, Lad was never willingly out of her sight. He had adopted her. The Master, too—in only a little lesser wholeheartedness—he adopted. Toward the rest of the world, from the first, he was friendly but more or less indifferent.

Almost at once, his owners noted an odd trait in the dog's nature. He would of course get into any or all of the thousand mischief-scrapes which are the heritage of puppies. But a single reproof was enough to cure him forever of the particular form of mischief which had just been chidden. He was one of those rare dogs that learn the law by instinct; and that remember for all time a command or a prohibition once given them.

For example: On his second day at the Place, he made a furious rush at a neurotic mother hen and her golden convoy of chicks. The Mistress, luckily for all concerned, was within call. At her sharp summons the puppy wheeled, midway in his charge, and trotted back to her. Severely, yet trying not to laugh at his worried aspect, she scolded Lad for his misdeed.

An hour later, as Lad was scampering ahead of her, past the stables, they rounded a corner and came flush upon the same nerve-racked hen and her brood. Lad halted in his scamper, with a suddenness that made him skid. Then, walking as though on eggs, he made an idiotically wide circle about the feathered dam and her silly chicks. Never thereafter did he assail any of the Place's fowls.

It was the same, when he sprang up merrily at a line of laundry, flapping an alluring invitation from the drying ground lines. A single word of rebuke—and thenceforth the family wash was safe from him.

And so on with the myriad perplexing don'ts which spatter the career of a fun-loving collie pup. Versed in the patience-fraying ways of pups in general, the Mistress and the Master marveled and bragged and praised.

All day and every day, life was a delight to the little dog. He had friends everywhere willing to romp with him. He had squirrels to chase among the oaks. He had the lake to splash ecstatically in. He had all he wanted to eat; and he had all the petting his hungry little heart could crave.

He was even allowed, with certain restrictions, to come into the mysterious house itself. Nor, after one defiant bark at a leopard-skin rug, did he molest anything therein. In the house, too, he found a genuine cave—a wonderful place to lie and watch the world at large, and to stay cool in and to pretend he was a wolf. The cave was the deep space beneath the piano in the music room. It seemed to have a peculiar charm to Lad. To the end of his days, by the way, this cave was his chosen resting place. Nor, in his lifetime, did any other dog set foot therein.

So much for "all day and every day." But the nights were different.

Lad hated the nights. In the first place, everybody went to bed and left him alone. In the second, his hard-hearted owners made him sleep on a fluffy rug in a corner of the veranda instead of in his delectable piano-cave. Moreover, there was no food at night. And there was nobody to play with or to go for walks with or to listen to. There was nothing but gloom and silence and dullness.

When a puppy takes fifty catnaps in the course of the day, he cannot always be expected to sleep the night through. It is too much to ask. And Lad's waking hours at night were times of desolation and of utter boredom. True, he might have consoled himself, as does many a lesser pup, with voicing his woes in a series of melancholy howls. That, in time, would have drawn plenty of human attention to the lonely youngster, even if the attention were not wholly flattering.

But Lad did not belong to the howling type. When he was unhappy, he waxed silent. And his sorrowful eyes took on a deeper woe. By the way, if there is anything more sorrowful than the eyes of a collie pup that has never known sorrow, I have yet to see it.

No, Lad could not howl. And he could not hunt for squirrels. For these enemies of his were not content with the unsportsmanliness of climbing out of his reach in the daytime, when he chased them; but they added to their sins by joining the rest of the world—except Lad—in sleeping all night. Even the lake that was so friendly by day was a chilly and forbidding playfellow on the cool North Jersey nights.

There was nothing for a poor lonely pup to do but stretch out on his rug and stare in unhappy silence up the driveway, in the impossible hope that someone might happen along through the darkness to play with him.

At such an hour and in such lonesomeness, Lad would gladly have tossed aside all prejudices of caste, and all his natural dislikes, and would have frolicked in mad joy with the veriest stranger. Anything was better than this drear solitude throughout the million hours before the first of the maids should be stirring or the first of the farmhands report for work. Yes, night was a disgusting time; and it had not one single redeeming trait for the puppy.

Lad was not even consoled by the knowledge that he was guarding the slumbrous house. He was not guarding it. He had not the very remotest idea what it meant to be a watchdog. In all his five months he had never learned that there is unfriendliness in the world; or that there is anything to guard a house against.

True, it was instinctive with him to bark when people came down the drive, or appeared at the gates without warning. But more than once the Master had bidden him be silent when a rackety puppy salvo of barking had broken in on the arrival of some guest. And Lad was still in perplexed doubt as to whether barking was something forbidden or merely limited.

One night—a solemn, black, breathless August night, when half-visible heat lightning turned the murk of the western horizon to pulses of dirty sulphur—Lad awoke from a fitful dream of chasing squirrels which had never learned to climb.

He sat up on his rug, blinking around through the gloom in the half hope that some of those nonclimbing squirrels might still be in sight. As they were not, he sighed unhappily and prepared to lay his classic young head back again on the rug for another spell of night-shortening sleep.

But before his head could touch the rug, he reared it and half of his small body from the floor and focused his near-sighted eyes on the driveway. At the same time, his tail began to wag a thumping welcome.

Now, by day, a dog cannot see so far nor so clearly as can a human. But at night, for comparatively short distances, he can see much better than can his master. By day or by darkness, his keen hearing and keener scent make up for all defects of eyesight.

And now three of Lad's senses told him he was no longer alone in his tedious vigil. Down the drive, moving with amusing slowness and silence, a man was coming. He was on foot. And he was fairly well dressed. Dogs, the foremost snobs in creation, are quick to note the difference between a well-clad and a disreputable stranger.

Here unquestionably was a visitor—some such man as so often came to the Place and paid such flattering attention to the puppy. No longer need Lad be bored by the solitude of this particular night. Someone was coming toward the house and carrying a small bag under his arm. Someone to make friends with. Lad was very happy.

Deep in his throat a welcoming bark was born. But he stilled it. Once, when he had barked at the approach of a stranger, the stranger had gone away. If this stranger were to go away, all the night's fun would go with him. Also, no later than yesterday, the Master had scolded Lad for barking at a man who had called. Wherefore the dog held his peace.

Getting to his feet and stretching himself, fore and aft,

in true collie fashion, the pup gamboled up the drive to meet the visitor.

The man was feeling his way through the pitch darkness, groping cautiously, halting once or twice for a smolder of lightning to silhouette the house he was nearing. In a wooded lane, a quarter mile away, his lightless motorcar waited.

Lad trotted up to him, the tiny white feet noiseless in the soft dust of the drive. The man did not see him, but passed so close to the dog's hospitably upthrust nose that he all but touched it.

Only slightly rebuffed at such chill lack of cordiality, Lad fell in behind him, tail awag, and followed him to the porch. When the guest should ring the bell, the Master or one of the maids would come to the door. There would be lights and talk; and perhaps Laddie himself might be allowed to slip in to his beloved cave.

But the man did not ring. He did not stop at the door at all. On tiptoe he skirted the veranda to the old-fashioned bay windows at the south side of the living room—windows with catches as old-fashioned and as simple to open as themselves.

Lad padded along, a pace or so to the rear, still hopeful of being petted or perhaps even romped with. The man gave a faint but promising sign of intent to romp, by swinging his small and very shiny brown bag to and fro as he walked. Thus ever did the Master swing Lad's precious canton flannel doll before throwing it for him to retrieve. Lad made a tentative snap at the bag, his tail wagging harder than ever. But he missed it. And in another moment the man stopped swinging the bag and tucked it under his arm again as he began to fumble with a bit of steel.

There was the very faintest of clicks. Then, noiselessly, the window slid upward. A second fumbling sent the wooden inside shutters ajar. The man worked with no uncertainty. Ever since his visit to the Place, a week earlier, behind the aegis of a big and bright and newly forged telephone-inspector badge, he had carried in his trained memory the location of windows and of obstructing furniture and of the primitive small safe in the living-room wall, with its pitifully pickable lock—the safe wherein the Place's few bits of valuable jewelry and other compact treasures reposed at night.

Lad was tempted to follow the creeping body and the fascinatingly swinging bag indoors. But his one effort to enter the house—with muddy paws—by way of an open window, had been rebuked by the Lawgivers. He had been led to understand that really well-bred little dogs come in by way of the door; and then only on permission.

So he waited, doubtfully, at the veranda edge; in the hope that his new friend might reappear or that the Master might perhaps want to show off his pup to the caller, as so often the Master was wont to do.

Head cocked to one side, tulip ears alert, Laddie stood listening. To the keenest human ears the thief's soft progress across the wide living room to the wall safe would have been all but inaudible. But Lad could follow every phase of it—the cautious skirting of each chair; the hesitant pause as a bit of ancient furniture creaked; the halt in front of the safe; the queer grinding noise, muffled but persevering, at the lock; then the faint creak of the swinging iron door, and the deft groping of fingers.

Soon the man started back toward the paler oblong of gloom which marked the window's outlines from the surrounding black. Lad's tail began to wag again. Apparently, this eccentric person was coming out, after all, to keep him company. Now the man was kneeling on the window seat. Now, in gingerly fashion, he reached forward and set the small bag down on the veranda, before negotiating the climb across the broad seat—a climb that might well call for the use of both his hands.

Lad was entranced. Here was a game he understood.

Thus, more than once, had the Mistress tossed out to him his flannel doll, as he had stood in pathetic invitation on the porch, looking in at her as she read or talked. She had laughed at his wild tossings and other maltreatments of the limp doll. He had felt he was scoring a real hit. And this hit he decided to repeat.

Snatching up the swollen little satchel, almost before it left the intruder's hand, Lad shook it joyously, reveling in the faint clink and jingle of the contents. He backed playfully away, the bag handle swinging in his jaws. Crouching low, he wagged his tail in ardent invitation to the stranger to chase him and to get back the satchel. Thus did the Master romp with Lad when the flannel doll was the prize of their game. And Lad loved such races.

Yes, the stranger was accepting the invitation. The moment he had crawled out on the veranda he reached down for the bag. As it was not where he thought he had left it, he swung his groping hand forward in a half-circle, his finger sweeping the floor.

Make that enticing motion, directly in front of a playful collie pup—especially if he has something he doesn't want you to take from him—and watch the effect.

Instantly, Lad was athrill with the spirit of the game. In one scurrying backward jump, he was off the veranda and on the lawn, tail vibrating, eyes dancing; satchel held tantalizingly toward its would-be possessor.

The light sound of his body touching ground reached the man. Reasoning that the sweep of his own arm had somehow knocked the bag off the porch, he ventured off the edge of the veranda and flashed a swathed ray of his pocket light along the ground in search of it.

The flashlight's lens was cleverly muffled, in a way to give forth but a single subdued finger of illumination. That one brief glimmer was enough to show the thief a right impossible sight. The glow struck answering lights from the polished sides of the brown bag. The bag was hanging in air some six inches above the grass and perhaps five feet away from him. Then he saw it swing frivolously to one side and vanish in the night.

The astonished man had seen more. Feeble was the flashlight's shrouded ray—too feeble to outline against the night the small dark body behind the shining brown bag. But that same ray caught and reflected back to the incredulous beholder two splashes of pale fire—glints from a pair of deep-set collie eyes.

As the bag disappeared, the eerie fire-points were gone. The thief all but dropped his flashlight. He gaped in nervous dread; and sought vainly to account for the witch work he had witnessed.

He had plenty of nerve. He had plenty of experience along his chosen line of endeavor. But while a crook may control his nerve, he cannot make it phlegmatic or steady. Always, he must be conscious of holding it in check, as a clever driver checks and steadies and keeps in subjection a plunging horse. Let the vigilance slacken, and there is a runaway.

Now this particular marauder had long ago keyed his nerve to the chance of interruption from some gun-brandishing householder; and to the possible pursuit of police; and to the need of fighting or of fleeing. But all his preparations had not taken into account this newest emergency. He had not steeled himself to watch unmoved the gliding away of a treasure satchel, apparently moving of its own will; nor the shimmer of two greenish sparks in the air just above it. And, for an instant, the man had to battle against a craven desire to bolt.

Lad, meanwhile, was having a beautiful time. Sincerely, he appreciated the playful grab his nocturnal friend had made in his direction. Lad had countered this by frisking away for another five or six feet, and then wheeling about to face once more his playfellow and to await the next move in the blithe gambol. The pup could see tolerably well, in the darkness—quite well enough to play the game his guest had devised. And, of course, he had no way of knowing that the man could not see equally well.

Shaking off his momentary terror, the thief once more pressed the button of his flashlight, swinging the torch in a swift semicircle and extinguishing it at once, lest the dim glow be seen by any wakeful member of the family.

That one quick sweep revealed to his gaze the shiny brown bag a half-dozen feet ahead of him, still swinging several inches above ground. He flung himself forward at it, refusing to believe he also saw that queer double glow of pale light just above. He dived for the satchel with the speed and the accuracy of a football tackle. And that was all the good it did him.

Perhaps there is something in nature more agile and dismayingly elusive than a romping young collie. But that something is not a mortal man. As the thief sprang, Lad sprang in unison with him; darting to the left and a yard or so backward. He came to an expectant standstill once more; his tail wildly vibrating, his entire furry body tingling with the glad excitement of the game. This sportive visitor of his was a veritable godsend. If only he could be coaxed into coming to play with him every night!

But presently he noted that the other seemed to have wearied of the game. After plunging through the air and landing on all fours with his grasping hands closing on nothingness, the man had remained thus, as if dazed, for a second or so. Then he had felt the ground all about him. Then, bewildered, he had scrambled to his feet. Now he was standing, moveless, his lips working.

Yes, he seemed to be tired of the lovely game—and just when Laddie was beginning to enter into the full spirit of it. Once in a while, the Mistress or the Master stopped playing, during the romps with the flannel doll. And Laddie had long since hit on a trick for reviving their interest. He employed this ruse now.

As the man stood, puzzled and scared, something brushed very lightly, even coquettishly, against his knuckles. He started in nervous fright. An instant later, the same thing brushed his knuckles again, this time more insistently. The man, in a spurt of fear-driven rage, grabbed at the invisible object. His fingers slipped along the smooth sides of the bewitched bag that Lad was shoving invitingly at him.

Brief as was the contact, it was long enough for the thief's sensitive fingertips to recognize what they touched. And both hands were brought suddenly into play, in a mad snatch for the prize. The ten avid fingers missed the bag, and came together with clawing force. But before they met, the fingertips of the left hand telegraphed to the man's brain that they had had momentary light experience with something hairy and warm—something that had slipped, eel-like, past them into the night; something that most assuredly was no satchel, but *alive!*

The man's throat contracted, in gagging fright. And, as before, fear scourged him to feverish rage.

Recklessly he pressed the flashlight's button, and swung the muffled bar of light in every direction. In his other hand he leveled the pistol he had drawn. This time the shaded ray revealed to him not only his bag but, vaguely, the Thing that held it.

He could not make out what manner of creature it was which gripped the satchel's handle and whose eyes pulsed back greenish flares into the torch's dim glow. But it was an animal of some kind—distorted and formless in the wavering finger of blunted light, but still an animal. Not a ghost.

And fear departed. The intruder feared nothing mortal. The mystery in part explained, he did not bother to puzzle out the remainder of it. Impossible as it seemed, his bag was carried by some living thing. All that remained for him was to capture the thing and recover his bag. The weak light still turned on, he gave chase.

Lad's spirits arose with a bound. His ruse had succeeded. He had reawakened in this easily discouraged chum a new interest in the game. And he gamboled across the lawn, fairly wriggling with delight. He did not wish to make his friend lose interest again. So instead of dashing off at full speed, he frisked daintily, just out of reach of the clawing hand.

And in this pleasant fashion the two playfellows covered a hundred yards of ground. More than once, the man came within an inch of his quarry. But always, by the most imperceptible spurt of speed, Laddie arranged to keep himself and his dear satchel from capture.

Then, in no time at all, the game ended; and with it ended Lad's baby faith in the friendliness and trustworthiness of all human nature.

Realizing that the sound of his own stumbling running feet and the intermittent flashes of his torch might well awaken some light sleeper in the house, the thief resolved on a daring move. This creature in front of him—dog or bear or goat, or whatever it was—was uncatchable. But by sending a bullet through it, he could bring the animal to a sudden and permanent stop.

Then, snatching up his bag and running at top speed, he himself could easily win clear of the Place before any one of the household should appear. And his car would be a mile away before the neighborhood could be aroused. Fury at the weird beast and the wrenching strain on his own nerves lent eagerness to his acceptance of the idea.

He reached back again for his pistol, whipped it out, and, coming to a standstill, aimed at the pup. Lad, waiting only to bound over an obstruction in his path, came to a corresponding pause, not ten feet ahead of his playmate.

It was an easy shot. Yet the bullet went several inches

above the obligingly waiting dog's back. Nine men out of ten, shooting by moonlight or by flashlight, aim too high. The thief had heard this old marksman maxim fifty times. But, like most hearers of maxims, he had forgotten it at the one time in his speckled career when it might have been of any use to him.

He had fired. He had missed. In another second, every sleeper in the house and in the gate lodge would be out of bed. His night's work was a blank, unless—

With a bull rush he hurled himself forward at the interestedly waiting Lad. And, as he sprang, he fired again. Then several things happened.

Everyone, except movie actors and newly appointed policemen, knows that a man on foot cannot shoot straight, unless he is standing stock-still. Yet, as luck would have it, this second shot found a mark where the first and better aimed bullet had gone wild.

Lad had leaped the narrow and deep ditch left along the lawn edge by workers who were putting in a new water main for the Place. On the far side of this obstacle he had stopped, and had waited for his friend to follow. But the friend had not followed. Instead, he had been somehow responsible for a spurt of red flame and for a most thrilling racket. Lad was more impressed than ever by the man's wondrous possibilities as a midnight entertainer. He waited, gaily expectant, for more. He got it.

There was a second rackety explosion and a second puff of lightning from the man's outflung hand. But, this time, something like a red-hot whiplash smote Lad with horribly agonizing force athwart the right hip.

The man had done this—the man whom Laddie had thought so friendly and playful!

He had not done it by accident. For his hand had been outflung directly at the pup, just as once had been the arm of the kennelman, back at Lad's birthplace, in beating a disobedient mongrel. It was the only beating Lad had ever seen. And it had stuck, shudderingly, in his uncannily sensitive memory. Yet now, he himself had just had a like experience.

In an instant, the pup's trustful friendliness was gone. The man had come on the Place, at dead of night, and had struck him. That must be paid for! Never would the pup forget his agonizing lesson that night intruders are not to be trusted or even to be tolerated. Within a single second, he had graduated from a little friend of all the world into a vigilant watchdog.

With a snarl, he dropped the bag and whizzed forward at his assailant. Needle-sharp milk teeth bared, head low, ruff abristle, friendly soft eyes as ferocious as a wolf's, he charged.

There had been scarce a breathing space between the second report of the pistol and the collie's counterattack. But there had been time enough for the onward-plunging thief to step into the narrow lip of the water-pipe ditch. The momentum of his own rush hurled the upper part of his body forward. But his left leg, caught between the ditch sides, did not keep pace with the rest of him. There was a hideous snapping sound, a screech of mortal anguish; and the man crashed to earth, in a dead faint of pain and shock, his broken left leg still thrust at an impossible angle in the ditch.

Lad checked himself midway in his own fierce charge. Teeth bare, throat agrowl, he hesitated. It had seemed to him right and natural to assail the man who had struck him so painfully. But now this same man was lying still and helpless under him. And the sporting instincts of a hundred generations of thoroughbreds cried out to him not to mangle the defenseless.

Wherefore, he stood, irresolute; alert for sign of movement on the part of his foe. But there was no such sign. And the light bullet-graze on his hip was hurting like the very mischief.

Moreover, every window in the house beyond was blossoming forth into lights. There were sounds—reassuring human sounds. And doors were opening. His deities were coming forth.

All at once, Laddie stopped being a vengeful beast of prey, and remembered that he was a very small and very much hurt and very lonely and worried puppy. He craved the Mistress's dear touch on his wound, and a word of crooning comfort from her soft voice. This yearning was mingled with a doubt lest perhaps he had been transgressing the Place's Law, in some new way; and lest he might have let himself in for a scolding. The Law was still so queer and so illogical!

Lad started toward the house. Then, pausing, he picked up the bag which had been so exhilarating a plaything for him this past few minutes and which he had forgotten in his pain.

It was Lad's collie way to pick up offerings (ranging from slippers to very dead fish) and to carry them to the Mistress. Sometimes he was petted for this. Sometimes the offering was lifted gingerly between aloof fingers and tossed back into the lake. But, nobody could well refuse so jingly and pretty a gift as this satchel.

The Master, sketchily attired, came running down the lawn, flashlight in hand. Past him, unnoticed, as he sped toward the ditch, a collie pup limped—a very unhappy and comfort-seeking puppy who carried in his mouth a blood-spattered brown bag.

"It doesn't make sense to me!" complained the Master, next day, as he told the story for the dozenth time, to a new group of callers. "I heard the shots and I went out to investigate. There he was lying half in and half out of the ditch. The fellow was unconscious. He didn't get his senses back till after the police came. Then he told some babbling yarn about a creature that had stolen his bag of loot and that had lured him to the ditch. He was all unnerved and upset, and almost out of his head with pain. So the police had little enough trouble in 'sweating' him. He told everything he knew. And there's a wholesale roundup of the motor-robbery bunch going on this afternoon as a result of it. But what I can't understand—"

"It's as clear as day," insisted the Mistress, stroking a silken head that pressed lovingly against her knee. "As clear as day. I was standing in the doorway here when Laddie came pattering up to me and laid a little satchel at my feet. I opened it, and—well, it had everything of value in it that had been in the safe over there. That and the thief's story make it perfectly plain. Laddie caught the man as he was climbing out of that window. He got the bag away from him; and the man chased him, firing as he went. And he stumbled into the ditch and—"

"Nonsense!" laughed the Master. "I'll grant all you say about Lad's being the most marvelous puppy on earth. And I'll even believe all the miracles of his cleverness. But when it comes to taking a bag of jewelry from a burglar and then enticing him to a ditch and then coming back here to you with the bag—"

"Then how do you account—?"

"I don't. None of it makes sense to me. As I just said. But, whatever happened, it's turned Laddie into a real watch-dog. Did you notice how he went for the police when they started down the drive last night? We've got a watchdog at last."

"We've got more than a watchdog," amended the Mistress. "An ordinary watchdog would just scare away thieves or bite them. Lad captured the thief and then brought the stolen jewelry back to us. No other dog could have done that."

Lad, enraptured by the note of praise in the Mistress's soft voice, looked adoringly up into the face that smiled so proudly down at him. Then, catching the sound of a step on the drive, he dashed out to bark in murderous fashion at a wholly harmless delivery boy whom he had seen every day for weeks.

A watchdog can't afford to relax vigilance, for a single instant—especially at the responsible age of five months.

*Edward Fenton*

# GUN-SHY

Every day the mornings in the country turned chillier. The sycamore outside the kitchen window was soon bright yellow, and the trees all down the lane made a high arch of burning colors. When Joel stepped out of the house his breathing made little cold clouds of white vapor in front of his face.

This morning was early. Muggsy hadn't even finished his cereal yet. The Duchess ran ahead of him sniffing the air excitedly. With a sudden bound she dashed off into the meadow. Joel watched her weaving through the tall, dry grass, her nose to the ground one moment and the next minute springing up like a jackrabbit, her black ears flying.

Then, suddenly, there was a rustling noise and a mass of feathers rose from the clump of grass ahead over their heads. It glistened across the autumn landscape. Then it was winging out of sight.

The Duchess, now standing stiff in the middle of the field like a dog painted on a calendar picture, was looking after it too. When the bird could no longer be seen, she galumphed back to Joel's side.

Henry came toward them from the barn. Joel noticed at once that he had on his old leather hunting jacket, with the celluloid window on the back of it for his hunting license. Pushed back on his head was a red cap with a visor.

"Hi, Henry," Joel said. "Are you going out today?"

"It's the first day of huntin'," Henry asserted. "Ain't missed it in years. Don't reckon I'll miss it today. Got my license, got my gun all oiled back there in th' barn. Ought to be a good day."

"There are lots of birds around this year," Joel said. "The Duchess just flushed one a minute ago. It was a beauty! It went over that way." He pointed toward the Rocky Pasture.

Henry nodded. "I seen it," he said. "As a matter of fact," he went on, "I was thinkin' of takin' the Duchess along. Ain't never tried her out in the field as yet. Might's well see if she's any good or not."

"I'll bet she'll be better than any other dog you ever took hunting," Joel said stoutly. "Won't you, Duch?"

The Duchess, however, was much too busy pursuing a flea near the base of her tail to do anything in reply to Joel's question.

The porch door slammed just then.

"Well, here's ol' Muggsy, the great trapper!" Henry

called out, swinging him up on his shoulder. Anthony had on a scarlet hunter's cap like Henry's. He looked very proud of it.

"You bet!" Muggsy began. "I'm the best hunter for miles," he announced with no attempt at modesty. "I can catch lions, 'n' bears, 'n', well, anything, 'cause I'm—"

"Oh, come on," Joel said impatiently. "I've got to get you to school. The bus'll be here soon."

They started down the lane together. Joel called back over his shoulder, "Have a good day, Henry. You and the Duchess!"

"Sure," Henry called back. "We'll make out fine together. So long!"

Johnny Nesbitt was in the bus when Joel and Muggsy clambered in. They all sat together, looking out the window. From time to time they could see men, sometimes singly, sometimes in groups, walking along the road. All of them carried guns and had their hunting licenses pinned to their jackets where everyone could see them, and they all wore bright red caps so that other hunters would not mistake them for game as they moved through the woods. Most of them had dogs following along after them.

"Rusty's a good hunter," Johnny Nesbitt said. "He can smell a rabbit a mile away."

"Henry's taking the Duchess out with him," Joel told him in reply. "She's a real hunting dog. I'll bet when I get home Henry'll have so many pheasants he won't hardly be able to carry them all!"

That day school seemed to drag on without end. All through the classes Joel's attention wandered off from his books or the blackboard to the windows. The trees outside blazed against the clear November sky. From time to time he could hear in the distance the sharp crack, crack of a rifle or the high, excited barking of a dog. All his thoughts were with Henry and the Duchess.

The Duchess, so far, had not done anything to demonstrate her true caliber. She hadn't rescued anyone yet, or had a chance to prove herself a heroine. But this time, he knew, she would show her true colors!

The school bus going home seemed to take all afternoon. Why did the driver always have to stop forever, and why did it always take the other kids such a long time to get off? At last it came to a halt with a squeaking of brakes beside the blue letter box marked "Evans."

Joel looked for the Duchess. Usually she knew when it was time for the bus to return, and she sat in the middle of the lane waiting for him. But she wasn't there now. She's probably still out with Henry, Joel thought, although it did seem odd that Henry would be out hunting all day, and it was now nearly milking time.

He ran up the lane to the house. Muggsy had to puff like a locomotive to keep up with him.

No, the Duchess wasn't anywhere around. And there was Henry, going out to the barn.

"Henry, Henry!" Joel cried. "Where is she?"

Henry set down the pails he was carrying.

"Dunno, Joey," he replied slowly.

"Well, didn't you go out hunting and all?"

Henry nodded. "Sure we went out," he said. "She was fine too. Got a good nose on her. In fact she was all right until I raised my gun and fired."

Joel was breathless. "And then what happened?"

"First thing I know there wasn't no Duchess there. She ran off faster'n I could see her go. Looked all over for her. Looked for hours, but I never did find her. Had to come back 'count of it being milking time." Henry put his big hand on Joel's shoulder. "I'm sorry, kid," he said. "I wouldn't have taken her if I'd of known. She's what they call *gun*-shy. She's scared of shootin'."

"But—but where's she now? We've got to find her!" Joel blinked hard.

"No way of tellin'," Henry said, shaking his head. "She's probably hidin' somewheres right now. She won't come back for a while. The woods are full of gunfire."

Supper was dismal. Joel could hardly swallow, and after every few choking mouthfuls he ran out to the porch to whistle. "She might be out there now," he explained.

Mama looked up at the ceiling. "Boys and dogs!" she sighed. "They're the bane of my life!"

But when Joel came back she looked up hopefully. When he shook his head she sighed again, only it was a different kind of sigh.

Muggsy suddenly announced: "Hey, Joey, I got a idea!"

"Can't you *ever* leave me alone, ever?" Joel demanded. "I'm thinking."

"Well, I been thinking too," Muggsy persisted. "I been thinking about how I found her. I betcha you ain't looked under the bridge!"

Joel looked up in amazement. "I never thought of that!" he exclaimed. The next moment he had dashed out of the dining room.

"Put on your jacket!" Mama called, but the front door had already slammed behind him. "Oh, no, you don't, Anthony!" she said firmly as Muggsy began to squirm off his chair. "You're staying right here."

Joel ran headlong into Henry, who had been out in the barn. "I'm goin'—down to—the bridge," he panted. "To see—if—she's there."

Henry went along with him. They whistled for her at every other step, but there was no Duchess to come dashing up to them in response. They went down the lane together. Joel clenched his fists until his fingernails dug into his palms.

But under the bridge there was nothing: just the creek trickling in the dark and the stones shining with wetness when the flashlight went on. Joel had never felt so miserable. "Perhaps she got shot, Henry."

"Dunno," Henry said. He shrugged his shoulders and switched off his flashlight. "Come on, kid, better get back. It's cold out here without your sweater. Your ma won't like it. And it won't bring Her Highness back, just standing here and shivering."

They climbed up to the road again and began trudging back to the house.

Suddenly Joel stopped. "Listen!" he whispered.

They stopped. There was a faint pattering sound. It grew louder as they waited.

"Sure it's her!" Joel cried.

And it was indeed the Duchess. She came toward them at a tired trot. Joel ran forward and put his arms around her. He could feel the burrs sticking to her coat. She was trembling.

Joel looked up at Henry. "Henry, remember when we first found her? Do you think she might have run off that time the same way? I mean—"

Henry shook his head. "Dunno," he said. "Cain't never tell. Could be."

"But—but that means she's no good for hunting, doesn't it?" Joel thought of Johnny Nesbitt's Rusty, and of how he himself had boasted of the Duchess. He swallowed hard. "But I don't care, Henry," he said, running his hands through the shivering dog's coat. "She needs us more than ever now, and there are worse things than being afraid of guns, aren't there, Henry? Aren't there?"

"Sure," Henry said thoughtfully, "sure. Lots worse things."

Joel stroked the Duchess. "See, Duch," he told her, "it's all right now. You're home again." He felt as though something inside him was choking him. But he was happy that he had found her again.

"Come on, Henry," he said. "Let's run back. It's cold out tonight."

One Saturday afternoon Joel Evans and Johnny Nesbitt lay spread out, faces downward, upon a nest of dry leaves. Noisily they munched at a couple of frostbitten apples from the basketful which they had gathered for Johnny's mother. Juice dribbled icily down Joel's chin. "I like 'em best this way," he announced indistinctly.

In the deep grass, not far away, waited their four-legged shadows: Johnny's airedale, Rusty, and the Duchess. Both were panting gently. From time to time one of them stirred, making a dry rattling sound among the crisp leaves.

It was almost evening. The air was getting keen. The faces of the boys were raw from the wind. Their eyes shone. Their ears and the tips of their noses tingled.

It had been an exhausting Saturday, and all four of them were tired. Not that they had, any of them, much to show for it. Sure enough, there was the basket of apples for Mrs. Nesbitt. It had been fun climbing the trees and shaking them down, while the dogs barked furiously at the rain of fruit which thudded and plummeted to the hard ground. And there was a pleasant aching in their arms and legs from all the fields they had scrambled across, the brooks they had jumped over (one of Joel's socks was wet from the time he had missed), the gullies and ravines they had explored all through the sharp, sun-shot day.

For the dogs there were the thousands of exciting smells to remember and the miles of countless mysterious tracks which they had pursued, yipping frantically. Knowingly, they rolled their brown eyes at their masters.

Joel turned his head and stared at the darkening sky. "Gosh, Johnny, it's getting late. I'd better think of making tracks before Mama sends out a posse." He stretched lazily, then rolled back on the ground, folding his arms behind his head.

"My mother'll be worrying too," Johnny said. "It's funny; she knows I'm all right. Nothing ever happens to me. But she always worries just the same. She ought to be used to me by now!"

"I know," Joel agreed. "They ought to relax more, but they never do. I guess that's the way they are. You just can't change them."

They both lay there, wondering why mothers worried the way they did. But neither of them stirred an inch to get up and start home.

The Duchess pulled herself out of her bed of leaves, stretched luxuriously, yawned with a great creaking of her jaws, and looked at Rusty to see what he was doing. He was engrossed in the serious business of licking a forepaw. The Duchess turned her back to him and moseyed over to where Joel lay.

Joel scratched her chin. "How's the girl?" he demanded. "How's Her Highness?" In reply, she licked his face until he had to raise himself, laughing, to a sitting position.

Johnny got up then, too. They both sat among the dead leaves of the past summer and wondered where the day had gone to.

"It's been one super day," Joel said. He looked around him, at the dark trees against the setting sun. Below them—it seemed far, far below, although he knew it was only a few minutes' run—snuggled the Nesbitt farmhouse. The lights were already on. The windows glowed yellow and smoke twisted from the chimney. He picked another apple out of the basket and bit into it.

It was a good apple, firm and juicy. Joel looked at Johnny and winked; Johnny winked back. Then Joel looked at the Duchess. She had her head slightly to one side and her brown eyes were regarding him with all the trust and faith in the world. Suddenly Joel felt an overwhelming contentment sweep over him. It didn't matter about her being gun-shy, about anything. It was just perfect sitting there with her and Johnny as the sun was setting, and eating an apple. It was a moment he wanted to make last forever. "Stop, clock," he wanted to shout. "Just leave your hands where they are for a while."

Finally he said, and it seemed to him as though his voice came out strangely quiet and small, "I don't know any other place I'd rather be than right here now. Do you, Johnny?"

"Sure," Johnny said. "Lots of places. Top of the Empire State Building in New York. Or flying over Shangri-la in my own B-29. The *Johnny N* I'd call it, and I'd have the name painted right on her, big. That's the life!" Johnny's eyes began to glisten with excitement.

"Or I'd like to be in a foxhole at the front with a little old machine gun cradled in my arms. Rattatatattat! I'd show that enemy a thing or two or three. They could shoot and shoot at me all they liked. They'd only miss. I wouldn't even hear it! Then me and Rusty—he'd be my Specially Trained Combat Dog—we'd jump out of that foxhole and give them the rush. Just the two of us; we'd take them all prisoners." Johnny clicked his tongue. "That's where I'd like to be. Not stuck out here where it's the same thing all the time, no excitement.

"And what's more," he added, in a confidential tone, "as soon as I'm old enough to do it, I'm gonna join up. And Rusty's coming right with me. I'll bet they could use a smart dog like him in the Army. He's so tough I bet he could easy get into the Marines!"

Joel was scratching the Duchess slowly behind the ear. He didn't say anything.

"Hey, Joey," Johnny went on—he grew more and more

excited as the idea became clearer—"you could come too. How'd you like that? And take the Duchess!" He looked eagerly at Joel. "What do you think of that?"

The look on Joel's face stopped Johnny short. "Oh, gee, Joey, I forgot about the Duchess. I mean, about her bein'—"

Joel jumped to his feet. "Oh, that's all right, Johnny. We sort of had other plans anyway." He tried to sound offhand. "And anyway, we have to start trekking home now. I guess it's pretty late."

"Sure," Johnny said. "Sure. And my mother will give it to me good if I don't get those apples home to her!"

Johnny and Rusty walked Joel and the Duchess as far as the glen in silence.

"So long, Johnny," Joel called as he turned off. "See you Monday."

"So long," Johnny called back.

The faint trail across the glen was the shortest way home and Joel wanted to get there before dark. The sun was pretty low already.

The Duchess was off after some scent in a clump of bushes. Her nose was to the ground and her white plume of a tail cut through the twilight. Joel whistled to her. She paid no attention to his call.

Joel's mellow mood of happiness and contentment had completely vanished. In its place he was seized by an unreasoning rage.

He whistled again. She was utterly useless, he thought furiously. A gun-shy bird dog. Everybody laughed at her. And now she wouldn't even obey him when he whistled!

"Come here, you!" he shouted harshly.

She bolted out of the bushes and came toward him. Through the growing twilight he could see how uncertain and surprised she was. Already he felt a faint twinge of shame for having spoken to her as he had. But the senseless anger still boiled inside him.

"You come straight off, the next time I call you," he said gruffly.

Then he struck off across the glen toward home. He stopped at one place long enough to cut a maple switch. As he went on, he slashed viciously now and again at the dark trunks of the trees he passed. The Duchess followed faithfully at his heel. He could hear her pattering evenly behind him but he did not turn his head once or stop to speak to her.

By the time Joel reached home, darkness had already fallen. All the lights of the house were on. From the outside, everything had a warm and friendly look.

"We'll catch it for being late," Joel muttered to the Duchess. Resignedly, he made his way to the back door.

Alma was flying about in the kitchen like a demented banshee. She paused long enough to glance up when Joel came in. "Oh, there you are!" she exclaimed. To Joel's surprise, her voice wasn't at all scolding. "Hurry on upstairs and put on your good pants and a clean shirt," she said. "Dinner'll be on soon. You don't want to be late for it."

"I thought I was late already," he said. Then he noticed that she was wearing her best apron, the one with the white ruffles starched as stiff as cardboard.

"Zowie!" he cried. "What's up? Lord Mayor invite himself for dinner?"

"Never you mind," Alma replied. She pushed him to the door and waved him up the staircase. "I've got work to do. You'll find out what's up soon enough when you come down again."

Joel scratched his head and started up the stairs. Halfway up he had a sudden idea. "It's not Ellen home for the weekend, is it, Alma?" he called hopefully down the stairwell.

"It is not," Alma called back. "And don't forget to comb your hair and take that scrubbing brush to your nails," she added. "I'll go tell your ma you'll be right down."

While Joel changed his clothes and washed, the Duchess pattered after him from his bedroom to the bathroom and back again. He could hear, faintly, voices floating up from the living room. He wondered what was happening. At first he decided that Mr. and Mrs. Grant had come to dinner. But then Alma wouldn't have put on her best apron just for them. Maybe it was an important business friend of Papa's.

"Dr. Watson, I am compelled to admit that I am completely baffled this time," Joel said, frowning into the mirror. Then, after a brief tussle between his cowlick and his brush (the cowlick won), he switched off the light and went downstairs to the living room.

He saw Mama first. She had on a long dress and her heavy silver Indian bracelets. She was saying something which he couldn't hear and she smiled as she spoke. She looked different from the way she did every day. Joel had forgotten how young and pretty his mother could look. Papa stood behind her, beaming.

Mama turned her head and saw Joel. "And here's Joey!" she announced. Laughing gaily, she pulled him into the room.

Then, suddenly, Joel realized why Alma was wearing her number-one starched apron and why Mama had on her long dress and such a radiant look and why even Papa was smiling openly. Leaning against the mantelpiece, his back to the fire, stood a tall, grinning young man in the khaki uniform of a lieutenant.

"Uncle Seymour!"

The grin widened. "Hi, Joey!"

It was a long time since Joel had seen his uncle. That had been before Uncle Seymour had gone overseas. Joel ran forward. He wanted to rush up and throw his arms around his uncle. But when he came up to him, Joel suddenly stiffened self-consciously and held out his hand instead.

Gravely they shook hands.

Muggsy, who had been quiet and awed, suddenly came

to life. "Look, Joey," he cried. "He's got a gold bar on his shoulder. That means he's an officer now. And lookit all the medals he won." Muggsy stood on his tiptoes, running his forefinger across the row of service ribbons pinned to his uncle's tunic. "This one's for Good Conduck. This one's for—"

"Anthony!" Mama said. "Must you always handle everything you see?"

"I was only showing Joey!"

"Well, Joel can see for himself."

Joel could indeed see for himself. His uncle seemed to be taller, somehow, than last time. His face had a lean, almost tired look about it. Joel's eyes took in every detail of the uniform, with its knife-sharp creases, the gold insignia, and the row of ribbons. On one of the ribbons there were little stars. They stood for battles, Joel knew.

His uncle was smiling. "Don't pay any mind to those ribbons, Joey," he said. "They're only my brag rags. Fruit salad, we call 'em."

Joel smiled back at him. "Gosh, Uncle Seymour—I mean Lieutenant!—it's good to see you. When did you get back?"

"I hopped a plane over there only three days ago, and here I am!"

Papa began to whistle "Off we go into the wild blue yonder." He caught Uncle Seymour's eye and they both began to laugh.

"Oh, Charlie!" Mama wailed. "There you go. I don't see where that's so funny. Honestly, when you two get together, you carry on just like a couple of overgrown schoolboys."

That only made them laugh harder. "Listen to Grandma!" Uncle Seymour roared. "Relax, Ellie. You look too pretty tonight to pull that stern, serious stuff on us!"

Then Mama gave him a little push. "You!" she said, and she began to laugh too. She didn't look much older than Ellen right then! Joel and Muggsy looked on, grinning. The whole room seemed to be full of happiness and warmth and laughter.

There were candles on the dinner table. Whenever Alma came in, Uncle Seymour teased her and made her blush, but Joel decided that she really liked it, especially when he got up and made a speech.

He said in his speech that he wanted to be on record as being duly, properly, and thoroughly appreciative. Alma had outdone herself as an exponent of the culinary art and Uncle Seymour knew personally of several regiments that would have given their collective eyeteeth to have had her with them overseas.

"Aw, go on with all your talk!" said Alma. She got as red in the face as a poppy, but she loved every word of it.

They remained at table a long time. Papa asked Uncle Seymour a great many serious questions, and Joel didn't dare interrupt. Muggsy tried to several times, but Papa's most sarcastic tone of voice managed to squelch him.

Finally Mama rose, which was the signal for them to go back to the living room. The Duchess was already there, comfortably ensconced on the rug in front of the snapping fire.

"Well, look who's here!" Uncle Seymour said. He turned to Mr. Evans. "Charlie, I thought you hated dogs. Where'd you ever pick this one up?"

"I still abominate the noisome yapping creatures," Mr. Evans answered. "This particularly ill-favored specimen happens to be a waif. It is only suffered on the premises because for some mysterious reason my children seem to have become hysterically attached to it."

"She's a beauty," Uncle Seymour said. He knelt and stroked her warm hair. She thumped her tail lazily against the floor.

"I found her," Muggsy said. "She was under the bridge

and I found her!" Between them, the Evanses poured out the story of how the Duchess came to be with them.

"So!" Uncle Seymour said. He turned to Mr. Evans. "And is she a good hunter, Charlie?" he asked.

Joel swallowed hard. What would Uncle Seymour think if he found out the truth about her? It didn't matter with most people. But Uncle Seymour was different. Besides, he was a soldier.

Tensely, Joel watched his father and waited to hear what he would say.

Mr. Evans cleared his throat.

"Charlie!" Mama said warningly.

Joel didn't dare to swallow again.

"Hm," Papa said. "Well, as a matter of fact—hm—to tell the precise truth—I haven't had her out in the field myself, so-hm—I couldn't exactly testify."

Joel shot his father a grateful glance.

But they had reckoned without Muggsy. The youngest Evans had never been at a loss for words. This time was no exception.

"But Henry took her out, Uncle Seymour. And do you know what? She ran away. She's gun-shy!" He turned triumphantly to his brother. "Isn't she, Joel?"

It was Mama who broke the ensuing silence.

"Up to bed with you," she said. "This Very Minute," she added. It was her firmest tone of voice. From past experience, Muggsy knew that it was the one Mama used when she Meant Every Word She Said.

With a carefully assumed "I don't care" look on his face, Muggsy got up from the footstool where he had been sitting and started for the stairs. Uncle Seymour's voice, booming across the room, stopped him in his tracks.

"What I want to know is, what's so awful about being gun-shy?"

Muggsy turned and looked around at his uncle. His eyes were wary with suspicion.

"I'm gun-shy myself," said Uncle Seymour. Joel gaped incredulously at the bright ribbons awarded for valor which were pinned to his uncle's chest.

"Yes, Joey," his uncle said. "You can look at those all you like. But in spite of them I'm still gun-shy. Most of us were, although we didn't always admit it. It scared the dickens out of us when those big guns used to go off. Only there we were, and there was nothing we could do about it, so we had to be heroes."

"But—but—" Joel stammered.

"Sure, after a while we got used to it," his uncle said more quietly. "But if I'd have been able to bolt the first time, I'd have gone like a lubricated lightning streak. And practically all the other men with me would have, too."

Joel and Anthony stared at him.

Their uncle's voice lowered to a confidential whisper. "And you know, even though it's all over, I still dream about those guns sometimes." He thoughtfully shook his head. "And take it from me, chum, those are pretty bad dreams to have."

Mama broke in. "Seymour," she said, "I do think it's time they went to bed. Both of them, in fact. It's been a big night, and there's all tomorrow ahead of us."

After Joel and Muggsy had said good night and started up the stairs, the Duchess got up and cocked her head after them. Then, wagging her tail, she made her way up to bed behind Joel.

Long after Muggsy had fallen asleep Joel lay awake in the dark, staring at the ceiling. He was trying to make up his mind about what Uncle Seymour had said.

It was hard to figure out exactly. There was something funny somewhere.

Imagine admitting that you were afraid of guns and battle

and all that kind of thing! Especially when you were a soldier! He would never have dreamed of admitting to Johnny Nesbitt that he had often wondered just how exciting being a real soldier would be. But Joel had always had his private doubts.

And now it was Uncle Seymour who had confirmed them! And he was no coward. He'd been through plenty, and he knew what it was like if anyone did, Joel guessed. Joel lay staring at the dark ceiling, trying to imagine what Uncle Seymour had gone through those nights when he lay in his foxhole with the guns going off all around him. The quiet room became alive with imaginary tracer bullets spitting from planes and the whine of artillery shells.

Joel's arm stole around the Duchess. She was breathing quietly in her sleep. Somehow everything had changed around. It was as though a weight which had been pressing against his chest had been miraculously lifted. He wasn't going to be ashamed of her anymore for something she couldn't help.

"Well, Duch," he whispered, "I guess there are lots worse things than being gun-shy." He was sure of that now.

## *Albert Payson Terhune*

# THE GRUDGE

This is the strange yarn of three dogs. If the dogs had been humans, the story would have been on stage and screen long ago.

Frayne's Farms is the alliterative name for the hundred-acre tract of rich bottom land in the shadow of the Ramapo Mountains, a range that splits North Jersey's farm country for some twenty-odd miles.

Back in these mountains are queer folk, whose exploits sometimes serve as a page story for some Sunday newspaper. Within forty miles of New York City as the crow flies, the handful of mountaineers are well nigh as primitive as any

South Sea Islanders. They are as a race apart, and with their own barbarous codes and customs.

Down from the mountains, in the starvingly barren wintertime, every few years, a band of huge black mongrel dogs used to swoop upon the Valley, harrying it from end to end in search of food, and leaving a trail of ravaged hen roosts and sheepfolds in their wake.

These plunderers were the half-wild black dogs of the mountaineers—dogs blended originally from a tangle of diverse breeds, hound predominating, and with a splash of wolf blood in their rangy carcasses.

When famine and cold gripped the folk of the mountains, the dogs were deprived of even such scanty crusts and bones as were their summer portion. And, under the goad of hunger, the black brutes banded for a raid on the richer pickings of the Valley.

At such times, every able-bodied farmer, from Trask Frayne to the members of the Italian garden-truck colony, up Suffern-way, would arm himself and join the hunt. Rounding up the horde of mongrels, they would shoot fast and unerringly. Such few members of the pack as managed to break through the cordon and make a dash for the mountains were followed hotly up into the fastnesses of the gray rocks and were exterminated by trained huntsmen.

The mountaineers were too shrewd to make any effort to protect their sheep-slaying and chicken-stealing pets from the hunters. Much as they affected to despise the stolid toilers of the Valley, yet they had learned from more than one bitter and long bygone experience that the Valley men were not safe to trifle with when once righteous indignation drove them to the warpath.

For years after such a battle, the Valley was wholly free from the marauding black-dog pack. Not only did the dogs seem to shun, by experience, the peril of invading the lowlands; but their numbers were so depleted that there was more than enough food for all of the few survivors, in the meager garbage of the mountain shacks. Not until numbers and forgetfulness again joined hands with famine, did the pack renew its Valley forays.

When this story begins, a mere two years had passed since the latest of the mongrel hunts. Forty farmers and hired men, marshaled and led by young Trask Frayne, had rounded up not less than seventy-five of the great black raiders at the bank of the frozen little Ramapo River, which winds along at the base of the mountain wall, dividing the Valley from the savage hinterland.

The pack's depredations had beaten all records that season. And the farmers were grimly vengeful. Mercilessly, they had poured volley after volley into the milling swarm of freebooters. Led by a giant dog, ebony black and with the forequarters of a timber wolf, the handful of remaining pillagers had burst through the cordon and crossed the river to the safety of the bleak hills.

It was Trask Frayne who guided the posse of trackers in pursuit. For the best part of two days, the farmers kept up the hunt. An occasional faroff report of a shotgun would be wafted to the Valley below, in token of some quarry trailed to within buckshot range.

The gaunt black giant leading the pack seemed to be invulnerable. No less than five times during that two-day pursuit some farmer caught momentary sight of him, only to miss aim by reason of the beast's uncanny craftiness and speed. Trask Frayne himself was able to take a hurried shot at the ebony creature as the fugitive slunk shadowlike between two hillock boulders.

At the report of Trask's gun, the huge mongrel had whirled about, snarling and foaming at the mouth, and had snapped savagely at his own shoulder, where a single buckshot had just seared a jagged groove. But before Frayne could fire a second shot, the dog had vanished.

Thus the hunt ended. Nearly all the black dogs of the mountaineers had met the death penalty. It was the most thorough and successful of the historic list of such battles. The raiders were practically exterminated. Many a year must pass before the pack could hope again to muster numbers for an invasion. And the Valley breathed easier.

Yet Trask Frayne was not content. He knew dog nature, as it is given to few humans to know it. And he could not forget the wily black giant that had led the band of mongrels. The Black was a superdog, for cunning and strength and elusiveness. That had been proven by certain ultradevastating features of the raid, as well as by his own escape from the hunters.

And the Black still lived; still lived, and with no worse reminder of his flight than a bullet-cut on one mighty shoulder. Such a dog was a menace, so long as he should continue alive.

Wherefore, Trask Frayne wanted to kick himself for his own ill luck in not killing him. And he was obsessed by a foreboding that the Valley had not seen the last of the Black. He could not explain this premonition.

He could not explain it, even to himself. For Valley history showed that each battle served as a wholesome lesson to the black dogs for years thereafter. Never, between forays, was one of them seen on the hither side of the Ramapo. Yet the idea would not get out of Frayne's head.

Trask had hated the necessary job of destroying the mongrels. For he loved dogs. Nothing short of stark need would have lured him into shooting one of them. His own two thoroughbred collies, Tam-o'-Shanter and Wisp, were honored members of the Frayne household.

Dogs of the same breed differ as much in character as do humans of the same race. For example, no two humans could have been more widely divergent in nature than were these two collies of Trask's.

Tam-o'-Shanter was deep-chested, mighty of coat, tawny, as befitted the son of his illustrious sire, old Sunnybank Lad. Iron-firm of purpose and staunchly loyal to his master, Tam was as steady of soul as a rock. Whether guarding the farm buildings or rounding up a bunch of scattered sheep that had broken bounds, he was calmly reliable.

He adored Trask Frayne with a worship that was none the less all-absorbing because it was so undemonstrative. And he cared for nothing and nobody else on earth—except Wisp.

Wisp had been the runt of a thoroughbred litter. He was slender and fragile and wholly lovable; a dainty little tricolor, scarce forty pounds in weight. Not strong enough for heavy work, yet Wisp was a gallant guard and a gaily affectionate house dog—the cherished pet and playfellow of the three Frayne babies. Also, he was Tam's dearest friend.

The larger collie, from puppyhood, had established a protection over Wisp, ever conceding to him the warmest corner of the winter hearth, the shadiest spot in the dooryard in summer, the best morsel of their joint daily meal. He would descend from his calm loftiness to romp with the frolicsome Wisp—though the sight of stately Tam, trying to romp, was somehow suggestible of Marshal Joffre playing pat-a-cake.

In short, he loved Wisp, as he loved not even Trask Frayne. More than once, in the village, when a stray cur misunderstood Wisp's gay friendliness and showed his teeth at the frail little dog, Tam so far departed from his wonted noble dignity as to hurl himself upon the aggressor and thrash the luckless canine into howling submission.

He was Wisp's guardian as well as his dearest comrade. Once in a very great while such inseparable friendships spring up between two collies.

One morning in June, Trask set forth for Suffern with a flock of sixty sheep. The day was hot, and the journey promised to be tiresome. So, when the two collies had worked the sixty out from the rest of the Frayne bunch of sheep and had started them, bleating and milling, toward the highroad, Trask whistled Wisp back to him.

"Home, boy!" he ordered, patting the friendly uplifted head and playfully rumpling the collie's silken ears. "Back home, and take care of things there today. It's a long hot trip for a pup that hasn't any more stamina than you have, Wispy. Tam and I can handle them, all right. Chase back home!"

The soft brown eyes of the collie filled with infinitely pathetic pleading. Wisp understood the meaning of his master's words as well as might any of the Frayne children. From birth he had been talked to; and his quick brain had responded, as does every clever collie's.

Wisp knew he had been bidden to stay at home from this delightful outing. And every inch of his body as well as his eloquent eyes cried aloud in appeal to be taken along. Yet when, once more, Frayne patted his head and pointed toward the dooryard, the good little chap turned obediently back.

As he passed Tam, the two dogs touched noses, as if exchanging speech of some sort—as perhaps they were. Then, disconsolately, Wisp trotted to the house and curled up on the doormat in a small and furry and miserably unhappy heap. There he was still lying, his sorrowful eyes fixed on his master and on his busily herding chum, as the huddle of sheep were guided out of the gateway into the highroad beyond.

Glancing back, Frayne smiled encouragingly at the pathetic little waiting figure at the door. Tam, too, paused, as he maneuvered the last silly sheep into the highroad, and stood beside Frayne for a second, peering back at his chum. Under their momentary glance, Wisp made shift to wag his plumy tail once, by way of affectionate farewell.

Long afterward, Trask Frayne could summon up memory of the daintily graceful little dog, lying so obediently on the doormat and wagging such a brave good-bye to the master who had just deprived him of a jolly day's outing. Possibly the picture remained in Tam-o'-Shanter's memory, too.

It is to be hoped so. For never again were Frayne or Tam to see their lovable little collie chum.

Dusk was sifting down the valley from beyond the mountain wall that afternoon, when Trask Frayne turned once more into the gateway leading to his farm. At his side trotted Tam. It had been a hard day, for both dog and man. At best, it is no light task to marshal a flock of sixty bolting sheep along miles of winding road. But when that road is infested with terrifying motorcars and when it goes past two or three blast-emitting stone quarries and a railroad, the labor is spectacular in spots and arduous at all times.

But, at last, thanks to Tam, the sheep had reached Suffern without a single mishap, and had been driven skillfully into the herd pens. The seven-mile homeward tramp had been, by contrast, a mere pleasure stroll. Yet both the collie and his master were glad of the prospect of rest and of supper.

Frayne, reviewing the labor of the day, was pleased with his own foresight in making Wisp stay at home. He knew such an ordeal in such weather would have tired the delicate collie half to death.

Coming up the dusky lane from the house to meet the returning wanderers was a slender, white-clad woman. As he saw her, Frayne waved his hat and hurried forward at new speed. Thus always after one of his few absences from home, his pretty young wife came up the lane to welcome him. And, as ever, the sight of her made him forget his fatigue.

Yet now, after that first glance, worry took the place of eagerness, in Frayne's mind. For his wife was advancing slowly and spiritlessly, and not in the very least with her wonted springy walk.

"The heat's been too much for her!" he muttered worriedly to Tam. "It's been a broiling day. She ought to have—"

But Tam was no longer beside him. The big collie had started ahead, toward the oncoming woman.

Usually, when Mildred Frayne came thus to greet her returning husband, Wisp was with her. The little dog would bound ahead of his mistress as Frayne appeared, and come galloping merrily up to him and Tam. Tam, too, always cantered forward to touch noses with his chum.

But, by this evening's dim light, Frayne could not see Wisp. Nor did Tam rush forward as usual. Instead, he was pacing slowly toward Mildred, with head and tail adroop.

As Tam had turned in at the gate beside his master, the collie had come to a convulsive halt. His nostrils had gone upward in a series of eagerly suspicious sniffs. Then his shaggy body had quivered all over, as if with a spasm of physical pain. At that moment, Mildred's white-clad figure had caught his wandering eye. And he had moved forward, downcast and trembling, to meet her.

It was Tam, long before Trask, who discovered that Mildred was weeping. And this phenomenon, for the instant, turned his attention from his vain search for Wisp and from the confusingly menacing scents which had just assailed his nostrils.

Departing from his lifelong calm, the big dog whined softly as he came up with Mildred; and he thrust his cold muzzle sympathizingly into her loose-hanging hand. Within him stirred all his splendid race's pitiful yearning to comfort a human in grief. So poignant was this craving that it almost made him forget the increasingly keen scents which had put him on his guard when he came in through the gateway.

"Hello!" called Trask, cheerily, as he neared his wife. "Tired, dear? You shouldn't have bothered to walk all this way out to meet me. After a rotten day like this, you ought to be resting. . . . Where's Wisp? Is he 'disciplining' me for making him stay home? I—"

Then he, too, saw Mildred was crying. And before he could speak again, she had thrown her arms around his neck; and was sobbing out an incoherent story, broken by an occasional involuntary shiver. Holding her close to him and asking eagerly futile questions, Trask Frayne, bit by bit, drew forth the reason for her grief.

Harry and Janet, the two older children, had gone down to the river that noon, to fish off the dock for perch. Mildred, at an upper window where she was sewing, had watched them from time to time. For the river was high and rapid from recent rains.

But Wisp was with them; and she had experience in the little collie's sleepless care over the youngsters. More than once, indoors, Wisp had thrust his own slight body between a Frayne child and the fire. Again and again, at the dock, he had interposed his puny bulk and had shoved with all his force, when one or another of the babies ventured too close to the edge.

Today, as she looked up from her sewing, she had seen the trio leave the dock and start homeward. Janet had been in the lead, swinging the string of perch and sunfish and shiners they had caught. They had skirted a riverside thicket on their way to the home path.

Out from the bushes had sprung a gigantic lean dog, jet black except for a zigzag patch of white on one shoulder. The wind had been strong in the other direction. So no scent of the dog had reached Wisp, who was dawdling along a bit to the rear of the children.

The Black had made a lightning grab at the carelessly swung string of fish, and had snatched them away from Janet. As he turned to bolt back into the thicket with his stolen feast, Harry had caught up a stick and had charged in pursuit of the string of laboriously caught fish. The child had brought his stick down with a resounding thwack on the head of the escaping beast.

The blow must have stung. For, instantly, the Black dropped the fish and leaped upon the tiny chap. All this in a single second or less.

But before the mongrel's teeth could reach their mark, Wisp had flashed past the two startled children and had launched his weak body straight at the Black's throat.

Down went the two dogs in a tearing, snarling heap.

Mildred, realizing how hopelessly unequal was the contest, had run to the aid of her beloved Wisp. Fleeing downstairs, she had snatched Trask's gun from its peg above the mantel, had seized at random a handful of shells, and ran out of the house and toward the river, loading the gun as she went.

By the time she came in sight, the Black had already recovered the advantage he had lost by Wisp's unexpected spring. By dint of strength and of weight, he had torn himself free of Wisp's weak grip, had flung the lighter dog to earth and had pinned him there. Right gallantly did little Wisp battle in the viselike grasp of the giant. Fiercely he strove to bite at the rending jaws and to rip free from the crushing weight above him.

But, as ever, mere courage could not atone for dearth of brute strength and ferocity. Undeterred by his foe's puny efforts or by the fusillade of blows from Harry's stick and from Janet's pudgy fists, the Black had slung Wisp to one side and had lunged once more at him.

This time he found the mark he sought: the back of the neck, just below the base of the brain. He threw all his vast jaw power into one terrific bite. And little Wisp's frantic struggles ceased. The valiant collie lay inert and moveless, his neck broken.

Maddened by conquest, the Black tossed the lifeless body in air. It came to ground on the edge of the river. There, from the momentum of the toss, it had rebounded into the water. The swift current had caught it and borne it downstream.

Then, for the first time, the Black seemed to realize that both frantically screaming children were showering futile blows on him. With a snarl he turned on Harry. But, as he did so, Mildred's flying feet brought her within range. Halting, she raised the gun and fired.

She was a good shot. And excitement had not robbed her aim of steadiness. But excitement had made her catch up a handful of cartridges loaded lightly with number-eight shot, instead of anything more deadly.

The small pellets buzzed, hornetlike, about the Black's head and shoulders, several of them stinging hotly. But at that distance, the birdshot could do no lasting damage. Nor did any of it chance to reach one of his eyes.

With a yell of pain he wheeled to face the woman. And she let him have the second barrel. Memories of former clashes with gunners seemed to wake in the brute's crafty brain. Snarling, snapping, shaking his tormented head, he turned and plunged into the narrow river, gaining the farther bank and diving into the waterside bushes before Mildred could think to reload.

The balance of the day had been spent in a vain search of the bank, downstream, for Wisp's lost body; and in trying to comfort the heartbroken children. Not until she had gotten the babies to bed and had soothed them to sleep did Mildred have time to think of her own grief in the loss of the gentle dog who had been so dear to her.

"He—he gave his life for them!" she finished her sobbing recital. "He knew—he *must* have known—that he had no chance against that horrible monster. And Wisp had never fought, you know, from the day he was born. He knew that brute would kill him. And he never hesitated at all. He gave his life for the children. And—and we can't—can't even say a prayer over his grave!"

But Trask Frayne, just then, was not thinking of prayers. Deep down in his throat, he was cursing—softly, but with much venom. And the nails of his hard-clenched fists bit deep into his palms.

"Black, with a white scar on the shoulder?" he said, at last, his own harsh voice not unlike a dog's growl. "Hound ears, and the build of a timber wolf? Almost as big as a Dane; and bone-thin? Hm! That's my buckshot scar on his shoulder, that zigzag white mark. Tomorrow morning, I'm going hunting. Up in the mountains. Want to come along, Tam?"

But, as before, Tam was not there when his master turned to speak to him. The collie had waited only long enough to note that the task of comforting the weeping Mildred had been taken over by more expert powers than his. Then he had trotted off toward the house, not only to solve the problem of these sinister scents which hung so heavy on the moist night air, but to find his strangely absent chum, Wisp.

Circling the house, he caught Wisp's trail. It was some hours old; but by no means too cold to be followed by a collie whose scenting powers had once tracked a lost sheep for five miles through a blizzard. With Wisp's trail was mingled that of two of the children. And it led to the river path.

True, there were other trails of Wisp's that the sensitive nostrils caught. But all of them were older than this which led to the water. Therefore, as any tracking dog would have known, Wisp had gone riverward, since he had been near the house. And down the path, nose to ground, followed Tam-o'-Shanter.

He did not move with his wonted stolidity. For, over and above the mere trail scent, his nostrils were assailed by other and more distressingly foreboding smells—the smells he had caught as he had entered the gate; the smells which grew ranker at every loping step he took.

In half a minute he was at the bank. And before that time, he had abandoned the nose-to-earth tracking. For now all around him was that terrible scent.

Back and forth dashed and circled and doubled Tam. And every evolution told him more of the gruesome story.

Here among the bushes had lain a strange animal, an unwashed and pungent and huge animal, apparently sleeping after a gorge of chicken or lamb. Here, along the path, had come the children, with Wisp behind them. Here the strange dog had leapt forth; and here, alongside that string of forgotten and sun-blown fish on the ground, Wisp and the stranger had clashed.

The dullest of scents could have told the story from that point: the tramped earth, the spatters of dried blood, the indentation in the grass where Wisp's writhing body had striven so heroically to free itself from the crushing weight above it and to renew the hopeless battle.

Wisp was dead. He was slain by that huge and rank-scented creature. His body had touched the river brink, fully five feet from the scene of the fight. After that it had disappeared. For running water will not hold a scent.

Yes, Wisp was dead. He had been murdered. He had been murdered, this adored chum of his, by the great beast whose scent was already graven so indelibly on Tam's heart-sick memory.

There, at the river edge, a few minutes later, Trask Frayne found Tam-o'-Shanter, padding restlessly about, from spot to spot of the tragedy, whimpering under his breath. But the whimper carried no hint of pathos. Rather was it the expression of a wrath that lay too deep for mere growling.

At his master's touch, the great collie started nervously, and shrunk away from the caress he had always craved. And his furtively swift motion, in eluding the loved hand, savored far more of the wolf than of the trained house dog. The collie, in look and in action, had reverted to the wild.

Tam trotted, for the tenth time, to the spot at the river shore where the Black had bounded into the water. Impatiently, always with that queer little throaty whimper, he cast up and down along the bank, in quest of some place where Wisp's slayer might perhaps have doubled back to land.

Presently, Trask called to him. For the first time in his blameless life, Tam hesitated before obeying. He was standing, hock-deep, in the swirling water, sniffing the air and peering through the dusk along the wooded banks on the far side of the stream.

Again, and more imperatively, Frayne called him. With visible distaste, the collie turned and made his way back toward his master. Frayne had finished his own fruitless investigations and was starting homeward.

Halfway to the house he paused and looked back. Tam had ceased to follow him and was staring once more at the patches of trampled and dyed earth. A third and sharper call from Trask brought the collie to heel.

"I can't blame you, old boy," said Frayne, as they made their way toward the lighted kitchen. "But you can't find him that way. Tomorrow you and I are going to take a little trip through the mountains. I'd rather have your help on a hunt like that than any hound's. You won't forget his scent in a hurry. And you know, as well as I, what he's done."

On the way to the house, Frayne paused at the sheepfold, and made a careful detour of it. But the inspection satisfied him that the fence (built long ago with special regard to the mountain pack's forays) was still too stout to permit of any dog's breaking through it. And he passed on to the house, again having to summon the newly furtive collie from an attempt to go back to the river.

"He won't pay us another visit tonight, Tam," he told the sullen dog, as they went indoors. "He's tricky. And if he's really on the rampage, here in the Valley, he'll strike next in some place miles away from here. Wait till tomorrow."

But once more Tam did not follow his overlord's bidding. For, at dawn of the morrow, when Trask came out of the house, shotgun in hand, the dog was nowhere to be found. Never before had Tam forsaken his duties as guardian of the farm to wander afield without Frayne.

The jingle of the telephone brought Trask back into the house. On the other end of the wire was an irate farmer.

"I'm sending word all along the line," came his message. "Last night a dog burst into my hen coop and killed every last one of my prize Hamburgs and fifty-three other chickens, besides. He worked as quiet as a fox. 'Twasn't till I heard a chicken squawk that I came out. That must have been the last of the lot, and the dog had got careless. I had just a glimpse of him as he sneaked off in the dark. Great big cuss he was. As big as a house. Looked something like a wolf by that bum light, and something like a collie, too. Last evening I got news that Gryce, up Suffern-way, lost a lamb, night before, from some prowling dog. D'you s'pose the dogs from the mountains is loose again?"

"One of them is," returned Frayne. "I'm going after him now."

He hung up the receiver, and, gun under arm, made his way to the scow lying at the side of the dock. Crossing the river, he explored the bank for a half mile in both directions. Failing to find sign or trail of the Black, he struck into the mountains.

It was late that night when Trask slouched wearily into his own house and laid aside his gun.

"Any trace of him?" asked Mildred, eagerly.

"Not a trace," answered Frayne. "I quartered the range, farther back than we ever hunted before. And I asked a lot of questions at the godforsaken mountaineer settlement up there. That's all the good it did. I might hunt for a year and not get any track of the beast. Those mountaineers are all liars, of course. Not one of 'em would admit they'd ever seen or heard of the dog. If I'd had Tam with me, I might have caught the trail. Tomorrow, I'll see he goes along. He—"

"Tam?" repeated Mildred in surprise. "Why, wasn't he with you? He hasn't been home all day. He—"

"Hasn't been home? Do you mean to say he didn't come back?"

"No," said his wife, worriedly. "When I got up this morning and found you both gone, I thought of course you'd taken him along, as you said you were going to do. Didn't—"

"He wasn't anywhere around when I started," replied Frayne. "He's—he's never been away for a whole day, or even for a whole hour, before. I wonder . . ."

"Oh, do you suppose that horrible brute has killed Tam, too?" quavered Mildred, in new terror.

"Not he," Trask reassured her. "Not he, or any other mortal dog. But," he hesitated, then went on, shamefacedly, "but I'll tell you what I *do* think. I believe he's trailing that mongrel. If he is, he has a man-size job cut out for him. For the Black is as tricky as a weasel. Tam thought more of Wisp than he thought of anything else. And he was like another animal when he found what had happened down yonder. Take my word for it, he is after the dog that murdered his chum. Whether he'll ever get him is another matter. But if he really is after him, he'll never give up the hunt, as long as he has a breath of life left in him. Either he'll overhaul the cur or—well, either that or we'll never see him again. There's no sense in my poking around in the mountains without him. All we can do is wait. That and try to find Tam and chain him up till he forgets this crazy revenge idea."

But even though the Fraynes did not see their cherished collie when they arose next morning, they did not lack for news of him. In the middle of a silent and doleful breakfast a telephone ring summoned Trask from the table.

"That you, Frayne?" queried a truculent voice. "This is Trippler, at Darlington. I got rotten news for you. But it's a whole lot rottener for *me.* Last night my cowyard was raided by a dog. He killed two of the month-old Jersey calves and pretty near ripped the throat out of one of my yearlings. I heard the racket and I ran out with my gun and a flashlight.

The cowyard looked like a battlefield. The dog had skipped. Couldn't see a sign of him anywheres.

"But about half an hour later he came back. He came back while I was redding up the yard and trying to quiet the scared critters. He came right to the cowyard gate and stood sniffing there as bold as brass, like he was trying to catch the scent of more of my stock to kill. I heard his feet a-pattering and I turned the flashlight on him.

"He was *your* dog, Frayne! That big dark-colored collie dog of yours. I saw him as plain as day. I upped with my gun and I let him have it. For I was pretty sore. But I must have missed him clean. For there wasn't any blood near his footprints in the mud, when I looked. He just lit out. But I'm calling up to tell you you'll have a big bill to pay on this, and—"

"Hold on," interrupted Frayne quietly. "I'll be up there in twenty minutes. Good-bye."

As fast as his car could carry him, Trask made his way up the Valley to Darlington, and to the Trippler farm. There an irately unloving host awaited him.

"Before you go telling me the whole story all over again," Trask broke in on the explosive recital, "take me over to the exact spot where you saw Tam standing and sniffing. The ground all around here is soaked from the shower we had last evening. I want to see the tracks you were speaking of."

Muttering dire threats and whining lamentations for his lost calves, Trippler led the way to the cowyard, pointing presently to a gap in the privet hedge which shut off the barns from the truck garden. Frayne went over to the gap and proceeded to inspect the muddy earth, inch by inch.

"It was here Tam stood when you turned the light on him?" he asked.

"Right just there," declared Trippler. "And I c'n swear to him. He—"

"Come over here," invited Trask. "There are his footprints. As you said, and I'd know them anywhere. There's no other dog of his size with such tiny feet. He gets them from his sire, Sunnybank Lad. Those are Tam's footprints, I admit that. I'd know them anywhere—even if they didn't show the gash in the outer pad of the left forefoot, where he gouged himself on barbed wire when he was a pup."

"You admit it was him, then!" orated Trippler. "That's all I need to hear you say! Now, how much—?"

"No, no," gently denied Frayne. "It isn't anywhere near all you need to hear. Now, let's go back into the cowyard. As I crossed it, just now, I saw dozens of dog footprints, among the hoofmarks of the calves. Let's take another look at them."

Grumblingly, yet eager to add this corroboratory evidence, Trippler followed him to the wallow of churned mud which marked the scene of slaughter. At the first clearly defined set of footprints, Trask halted.

"Take a good look at those," he adjured. "Study them carefully. Here, these, for instance, where the dog planted all fours firmly for a spring. They're the marks of splay feet, a third larger than Tam's; and not one of them has that gash in the pad—the one I pointed out to you, back at the gap. Look for yourself."

"Nonsense!" fumed Trippler, albeit a shade uneasily, as he stood up stiffly after a peering study of the prints. "Anyhow," he went on, "all it proves is that there was two of 'em. This big splayfooted cuss and your collie. They was working in couples, like killers often does."

"Were they?" Frayne caught him up. "Were they? Then suppose you look carefully all through this welter of cowyard mud; and see if you can find a single footprint of Tam's. And while you're looking, let me tell you something."

As Trippler went over the yard's mud with gimlet eyes, Trask related the story of Wisp's killing, and his own theory as to Tam.

"He's trailing that black dog," he finished. "He struck his scent somewhere, and followed him. He got here a half-hour too late. And then when you fired at him he run off, to pick up the trail again. But I doubt if he got it. For the Black would probably be cunning enough to take to the river after a raid like this. He'd have sense enough to know somebody would track him. That brute has true wolf-cunning."

"Maybe—maybe you're right," hesitated Trippler, after a minute search of the yard had failed to reveal a footprint corresponding with Tam's. "And the county's got to pay for 'any damage done to stock by an unknown dog.' That's the law. I'm kind of glad, too. You see, I like old Tam. Besides, I c'n c'llect more damages from the county than I c'd c'llect from a lawsuit with a neighbor. What'll we do now? Fix up a posse like we did the other times?"

"No," replied Trask. "It would do no good. The Black is too clever. And in summer there are too many ways to throw off the scent. Tam will get him—if anyone can. Let's leave it to him."

But other farmers were not so well content to leave the punishment of the mysterious raider to Tam. As the days went on, there were more and more tidings of the killer. Up and down the Valley he worked, never twice in succession in the same vicinity.

Twice, an hour or so after his visits, men saw Tam prowling along the mongrel's cooling tracks. They reported to Frayne that the collie had grown lean and gaunt and that his beautiful coat was one mass of briar and burr; and that he had slunk away, wolf-fashion, when they called to him.

Frayne himself caught no slightest sight of his beloved dog; though, occasionally, in the mornings, he found empty the dish of food he had set out on the previous night. Trask was working out the problem for himself nowadays, deaf to all requests that he head another band of hunters into the mountains. He was getting no sleep to speak of. But he was thrilling with the suspense of what sportsmen know as "the still hunt."

Every evening, when his chores and his supper were finished, Frayne went to the sheepfold and led thence a fat wether that had a real genius for loud bleating. This vocal sheep he would tether to a stake near the riverbank. Then he himself would study the trend of the faint evening breeze; and would take up a position in the bushes, somewhere to leeward of the sheep. There, gun across knees, he would sit, until early daylight.

Sometimes he dozed. Oftener he crouched, tense and wakeful, in his covert; straining his eyes, through the gloom, for the hoped-for sight of a slinking black shadow creeping toward the decoy. Not alone to avenge the death of Wisp and to rid the Valley of a scourge did he spend his nights in this way. He knew Tam, as only a born dogman can know his dog. He missed the collie keenly. And he had solid faith that on the death of the Black, the miserable quest would end and Tam would return to his old home and to his old habits.

So, night after night, Frayne would keep his vigil. Morning after morning he would plod home, there to hear a telephoned tale of the Black's depredations at some other point of the Valley. At first his nightly watch was kept in dense darkness. But soon the waxing moon lightened the riverbank and made the first hours of the sentry duty easier.

Frayne began to lose faith in his own scheme. He had an odd feeling that the Black somehow knew of his presence in the thicket and that Frayne's Farms was left unvisited for that reason. Trask's immunity from the Black's depredations was the theme of much neighborhood talk, as time went on. Once more was revived Trippler's theory that Tam and the Black were hunting in couples and that the collie (like so many dogs which have "gone bad") was sparing his late master's property.

On all these unpleasant themes Trask Frayne was brooding, one night, late in the month, as he sat in uncomfortable stillness amid the bushes and stared glumly out at the occasionally bleating wether. He had had a hard day. And the weeks of semisleeplessness were beginning to tell cruelly on him. His senses had taken to tricking him of late. For instance, at one moment, this night, he was crouching there, waiting patiently for the full moon to rise above the eastern hills, to brighten his vigil. The next moment—though he was certain he had not closed his eyes—the moon had risen and was riding high in the clear heavens.

Frayne started a little, and blinked. As he did so, his disturbed mind told him he had not awakened naturally, but that he had been disturbed by some sound. He shifted his drowsy gaze toward the tethered sheep. And at once all slumber was wiped from his brain.

The wether was lying sprawled on the ground, in a posture that nature neither intends nor permits. Its upflung legs were still jerking convulsively, like galvanized stilts. And above it was bending a huge dark shape.

The moon beat down mercilessly on the tableau of the slain sheep, and of the Black, with his fangs buried deep in the twisting throat.

Now that the longed-for moment had at last come, Trask found himself seized by an unaccountable numbness of mind and of body. By a mighty effort he regained control of his faculties. Slowly and in utter silence he lifted the cocked gun from his knees and put its butt to the hollow of his shoulder.

The Black looked up, in quick suspicion, from his meal. Even in the excitement of the instant, Frayne found scope to wonder at the brute's ability to hear so noiseless a motion. And his sleep-numbed finger sought the trigger.

Then, in a flash, he knew why the Black's great head had lurched so suddenly up from the interrupted meal. From out a clump of alder, twenty feet to shoreward of the riverbank orgy, whirled a tawny shape. With the speed of a flung spear it sped straight for the feasting mongrel. And, in the mere breath of time it took to dash through the intervening patch of moonlight, Frayne recognized the newcomer.

The Black sprang up from beside the dead sheep, and faced the foe he could no longer elude. Barely had he gained his feet when Tam was upon him.

Yet the mongrel was not taken unaware. His crafty brain was alert and the master of his sinewy body. As Tam leaped, the black dog reared to meet him. Then, in practically the same gesture, the Black shifted his direction and dived beneath the charging collie, lunging for the latter's unprotected belly. It was a maneuver worthy of a wolf, and one against which the average dog must have been helpless.

But the Black's opponent was a collie. And, in the back of his brain, though never in his chivalric heart, a collie is forever reverting to his own wolf ancestors. Thus, as the Black changed the course of his lunge, Tam, in midair, changed his. By a violent twist of every whalebone muscle, Tam whirled himself sidewise. And the Black's ravening jaws closed on nothing.

In another instant—even before he had touched ground—Tam had slashed with his curving eyeteeth. This is another trick known to practically no animal save the wolf and the wolf's direct descendant, the collie. The razorlike teeth cut the Black's left ear and cheek as cleanly as might a blade.

But in the same motion, the Black's flying head had veered and his jaws had found a hold above Tam's jugular. Again, with the normal dog, such a hold might well have ended the fight. But the Providence which ordained that a collie should guard sheep on icy Highland moors also gave him an unbelievably thick coat, to fend off the weather. And this coat serves as an almost invulnerable armor, especially at the side of the throat. The Black's teeth closed upon a quantity of tangled fur; but on only the merest patch of skin and on none of the underflesh at all.

Tam ripped himself free, leaving a double handful of ruff between the Black's grinding jaws. As the mongrel spat out the encumbering gag of fur, Tam's curved fang laid bare the scarred shoulder once grazed by Trask Frayne's buckshot. And in a rolling, fighting heap, the two enemies rolled over and over together on the dew-drenched grass.

Frayne's gun was leveled. But the man did not dare fire. By that deceptive light, he had no assurance of hitting one dog without also killing the other. And, chafing at his own impotence, he stood stock-still watching the battle.

Both dogs were on their feet again; rearing and rending in mute fury. No sound issued from the back-curled lips of either. This was no mere dogfight, as noisy as it was pugnacious. It was a struggle to the death. And the dogs realized it.

Thrice more, the Black struck for the jugular. Twice thanks to Tam's lightning quickness, he scored a clean miss. The third time, he annexed only another handful of hair.

With his slashes he was luckier. One of Tam's forelegs was bleeding freely. So was a cut on his belly, where the Black had sought to disembowel him. And one side of his muzzle was laid open. But the collie had given over such mere fencing tactics as slashing. He was tearing into his powerful and wily foe with all the concentrated fury of his month's vain pursuit of vengeance.

The Black dived for the collie's forelegs, seeking to crack their bones in his mighty jaws and thus render his foe helpless. Nimbly, Tam's tiny white forefeet whisked away from the peril of each dive. In redoubled fury he drove for the throat. And the two clashed, shoulder to shoulder.

Then, amid the welter, came the final phase of the fight. The Black, as the two reared, lunged again for the collie's hurt throat. Tam jerked his head and neck aside to avoid the grip. And, as once before, the Black changed the direction of his lunge. With the swiftness of a striking snake he made the change. And, before the other could thwart or so much as divine his purpose, he had secured the coveted hold, far up on Tam's left foreleg.

No mere snap or slash, this; but a death grip. The Black's teeth sank deep into the captured leg; grinding with a force which presently must snap the bones of the upper leg and leave the collie crippled against a practically uninjured and terrible antagonist. The rest would be slaughter.

Tam knew his own mortal peril. He knew it even before Trask Frayne came rushing out from his watching place, brandishing the gun, club-fashion. The collie did not try to wrench free and thereby to hurry the process of breaking his leg or of tearing out the shoulder muscles. He thought, as quickly as the mongrel had lunged.

Rearing his head aloft, he drove down at the Black. The latter was clinging with all his might to the collie's foreleg. And, in the rapture of having gained at last a disabling grip, he ignored the fact that he had left an opening in his own defense—an opening seldom sought in a fight, except by a wolf or a wolf's descendant.

It was for this opening that Tam-o'-Shanter struck. In a trice his white teeth had buried themselves in the exposed nape of the Black's neck.

Here, at the brain's base, lies the spinal cord, dangerously within reach of long and hard-driven fangs. And here Tam had fastened himself.

An instant later—but an instant too late—the Black knew his peril. Releasing his grip on the collie's leg, before the bone had begun to yield, he threw his great body madly from side to side, fighting crazily to shake off the death hold. With all his mighty strength, he thrashed about.

Twice he lifted the seventy-pound collie clean off the ground. Once he fell, with Tam under him. But the collie held on. Tam did more than hold on. Exerting every remaining atom of his waning power, he let his body be flung here and there, in the Black's struggles; and he concentrated his force upon cleaving deeper and deeper into the neck nape.

This was the grip whereby the Black, a month agone, had crushed the life out of friendly little Wisp. And, by chance or by fate, Tam had been enabled to gain the same hold. Spasmodically, he set his fangs in a viselike tightening of his grip.

At one instant, the Black was whirling and writhing in the fullness of his wiry might. At the next, with a sickening snapping sound, his giant body went limp. And his forequarters hung, a lifeless weight, from his conqueror's jaws.

Tam relaxed his hold. The big black body slumped to earth and lay there. The collie, panting and swaying, stood over his dead enemy. The bitterly long quest was ended. Heavenward went his bleeding muzzle. And he waked the solemn stillnesses of the summer night with an eerie wolf howl, the awesome primal yell of victory.

For a few seconds Trask Frayne, unnoticed, stared at his dog. And, as he looked, it seemed to him he could see the collie change gradually back from a wild thing of the forests to the staunch and adoring watchdog of other days. Then the man spoke.

"Tam!" he said quietly. *"Tam!* Old friend!"

The exhausted victor lurched dizzily about, at sound of the voice. Catching sight of Trask, he trembled all over.

He took a dazed step toward Frayne. Then, with something queerly like a human sob, the collie sprang forward, and gamboled weakly about the man, licking Trask's feet and hands, springing up in a groggy effort to kiss his face, patting his master's chest with eager forepaws, crying aloud in an ecstasy of joy at the reunion.

Then, all at once, he seemed to remember he was a staid and dignified middle-aged dog and not a hoodlum puppy. Ceasing his unheard-of demonstrations, he stood beside Frayne; looking up into Trask's eyes in silent worship.

"You've done a grand night's work, Tam," said Frayne, seeking to steady his own voice. "And your hurts need bathing. Come home."

His plumed tail proudly wagging, his splendid head aloft, Tam-o'-Shanter turned and led the way to the house he loved.

*MacKinlay Kantor*

# THE VOICE OF BUGLE ANN

Her voice was something to dream about, on any night when she was running through the hills. The first moment she was old enough to boast an individual voice, Springfield Davis swore that she would be a great dog, and within another month he had given her the name she carried so proudly.

One of her great-grandfathers, many generations removed, had followed Spring Davis away from home when he went off to join General Claiborne Jackson and his homespun army among the prickly-orange hedges, so there was logic in the inheritance which put that trumpet in her throat.

She was slender, like hounds of the Spaulding line, and not as sprawling or cumbersome as the good-natured, long-tongued Walkers. Anyone in Missouri who knew anything about foxhounds had heard of the Davis dogs, but somehow there never came to be a Davis line. It was all in the family, and there existed a haughtiness in the old man which wouldn't permit him to have Davis dogs running anywhere except in the ranges along Heaven Creek. That was why Bugle Ann was still a maiden at five years, long after old Calhoun Royster or the Lanceys would have seen to it that she carried on her business in life.

And Spring Davis was prudish past the point of ridicule, though no one would have dared to laugh at him. He hated the common word for a female dog, and would not let it touch his tongue. He called his she-dogs ladies or girls, and there was a firm beauty about him when he spoke to them. You wouldn't think that a man like that could ever be tried for murder, or become a convict.

Those things did happen to Spring Davis, at eighty-two. They didn't affect him as they would have affected most men of eighty-two. Whenever he heard the gongs and whistles which sent him about his gray routine at Jefferson City, he must have banished those sounds from his consciousness. He must have imagined instead that he was sitting by a fire at the edge of Bachelor's timber, listening to the dogs as they hunted out of Chilly Branch Hollow, with Bugle Ann's cry echoing against the blackness of the sky.

## 2

"Bake," said Old Cal Royster, "put some wood on."

Baker went to the woodpile beyond the red circle and found a piece of rotten stump. "We'll have a good moon by next week," he said, and jammed the wood upon the coals.

"I don't give shucks for moonlight," exclaimed Cal

Royster. "Give me a black-dark night, when the fox ain't shadow-shy. Any fool ought to know that. I don't know where my boys get such notions as moonlight nights."

Across the fire, Spring Davis tapped his pipe against the heel of his boot. He stopped, suddenly, head tilted to one side. The firelight turned his shaggy mustache and eyebrows to fluid metal.

"Listen," he said. "Getting sweet."

His son, Benjy Davis, rose to his feet. He moved like an Indian; so did his father. There was something of the Indian in Benjy's twenty-year-old face, tanned and narrow and bony.

His black eyes glittered. "He's a mighty sweet fox if they've had him away over toward the river! We ain't heard a sound for twenty minutes."

There were five men around that fire at the edge of Bachelor's timber. Four of them—Spring Davis and his only son, Benjy, and Calhoun Royster and his oldest son, Baker—were the most ardent foxhound men in the county. The fifth man was no hound man at all; he was a new insurance agent from Wolf Center. He had eaten supper at the Davises', and he was beside that fire only by invitation and sufferance.

He inquired, "What do you mean, Mr. Davis? 'Getting sweet.' "

"It sweats," Spring told him. "The fox does. They can smell him better after he's been running awhile. That's 'getting sweet.' "

Now even the agent's untrained ears could detect a faint distraction amid the common night sounds—the hush of sleeping forests that never sleep, and which is really no hush at all. The sound came from over past the Armstrong place, far past Chilly Branch and across the ridge beyond, and it was as eerie and elusive as the calling of wild geese.

"You'll hear her in a minute," whispered Springfield Davis.

The confused murmur became a tiny baying: the tongues of many dogs, eager and striving in spite of their two-hour run.

"That's Toul Sector," Bake Royster declared. Bake had been in the war, and all the Royster dogs were named Toul Sector or Border Service or General Bullard or some such name.

"It's not Toul Sector," said Benjy. "Not that nearest one."

Calhoun Royster's tone showed the jealous annoyance which he displayed frequently with the self-assured Davises. "It's no Bugle Ann, neither," he snorted. "Nor no Bill Bryan, nor Cox, nor Frances Cleveland, nor any Davis dog."

"Reckon it is a bit turkey-mouthed for one of ours."

Old Spring Davis loved to hear Cal swear in his beard. So he continued, "I'll tell you, Cal. It's an Armstrong dog. They've picked up an Armstrong as they come past."

Royster stood with head wiggling on his humped shoulders, his bearded lips hanging open as he tried to take that baying apart and examine it.

"What Armstrong dog?" he demanded. He seemed to be weakening.

"I'd say it was Jackie Cooper, that little pale-faced two-year-old."

Old man Royster listened a moment longer. He gave a defeated snort. Then his ire mounted. "Where in hell's Bugle Ann, anyway?"

"Maybe she'll quit, and come in," muttered his son.

Benjy whirled, and for a moment the insurance agent thought that he was going to strike Bake Royster. "No Davis dog ever come in without being called, before a fox holed," Benjy said. "Except one. You remember him. We shot him the next day."

Spring nodded. "Easy, boy. . . . Guess there's bound to be a black sheep in every tribe, though this dog was white.

Don't you folks worry about Bugle Ann. You'll hear her soon enough."

"Pshaw, scat," said Bake, uneasily, "I was just joking."

On such a night as this, with clouds covering the stars and no southeast wind smothering the scent, you could tell that the hounds were running with their heads high. They skirted the eastern boundary of Chilly Branch Hollow, and straightened out along the higher ridge which swung toward Bachelor's woods.

All the men were on their feet.

"You talk moonlight," Royster chided his son. "Never get a fox to keep the high ground except on this kind of night. Lose half the sound when them dogs get in a gulley."

There was a turkey-mouth among those ringing voices; old Spring had been right about the Armstrong dog. The Royster dogs were mainly chop-mouthed, and they sent their clipped bristling bay like a volley across the wooded plateau.

"I don't hear her, Pa," whispered Benjy Davis, with some concern.

The old man held up his hand. Suddenly a new cry was born amid all the hissing of excited crickets.

For some reason, the Wolf Center insurance agent felt the hair prickle on his neck. This was no hound voice such as he had ever heard before, and he would never hear its like again. It was a bugle—the Davises had a rare poetry in their makeup, thought young Mr. Mayor of the National Emblem Liability. He stood there with his nails cutting his palms, and listened.

"That's her, all right," came Cal Royster's admission, "but why's she kiting off by herself? If she hain't lost it, I'm loony."

Spring Davis repeated the word, "Lost," and smiled into the fire. . . . There had never been a sound like that in the Heaven Creek country until Bugle Ann was born; even now the trumpet cry knew its own pride, and swung off toward the southeast, far ahead of the *owk-owk-owk-owk* with which the Royster dogs threatened.

The old man whooped, without any warning: "Now, there they go after her!"

Left, around the last spur of Bachelor's woods, the welter of hounds went sweeping after Bugle Ann. Her cry soared ahead—high, round, with that queer and brassy resonance which made you think that ghosts were out there somewhere, sounding Taps without any armies to follow them.

Springfield Davis came back to the fire and squatted on his heels. "You see," he told the insurance agent, "Bugle Ann was running that same fox night-before-last. I reckon she remembered how he likes to feint west along a little draw that's over there, and then double back and cut his own trail. It's a common fox trick if the fox has got the nerve to try it, and easy for him to work when the scent's heavy."

"I'm afraid," said Mr. Mayor, "that I don't understand."

"Well," said Cal Royster, somewhat reluctantly, "the average dog is bound to foller the way he's headed, if the smell is hauling him."

They were silent for a moment, listening to the baying as it swam fainter and fainter into the darkness.

"I'm afraid I don't understand any of this," Mr. Mayor cried with honesty. "I came from the East, just this year. They gave me this Missouri territory and—fox hunting! If you hunt every night or two, I don't see how you have any foxes left."

Bake Royster added more wood to the fire, and Benjy Davis brought up the sandwich sack. "We never kill the fox," said Spring, sharply. "We don't ride no horses, nor wear funny coats and caps. We raise dogs, and train them."

*Waken, lords and ladies gay,* thought Mr. Mayor in his baffled mind. *All the jolly chase is here, with . . .* "But it's really just a race between fox and dogs, then?"

"Fox holes up when he gets tired, and the dogs come home."

"And the same fox will run again, another night?"

"There's quite a slew of them around. Plenty of mice and ground squirrels for them to eat; they never bother no hen roosts. Yes, they run again. Night after night, and year after year."

Benjy opened a battered vacuum bottle and poured a cup of coffee for his father. The gray-headed man touched the hot tin cup with cautious fingers. "Year after year," he repeated, dreamily.

The insurance agent choked over a bacon sandwich. "Are you folks—and you also, Mr. Royster—the only people who do this sort of thing?"

Spring Davis looked up from the fire. "Young man, did you ever hear of Old Man Spaulding? Reckon not. Or Gentry German, or Alex Parrish, or Colonel Trigg?"

"I suppose," Mr. Mayor replied, "that those are dogs."

"Those are men who made foxhound history in America. And Wash Maupin, and Robert Rodes, and James Kanatzar. You see, sir, it's a matter of breeding good dogs—and understanding them—and—kind of loving them. It—" He broke off suddenly.

Cal Royster blinked at the gems of flame which shone through the whiskey flask in his hand. "Speaking of names, Spring," he began, "you ought to take our friend here, over to the Armstrongs. You see, mister, Ed Armstrong is mighty religious and his boys are mighty the other way."

"Always going to town," put in Bake, "to dances and moving pictures and rotation pool, and things."

His father insisted, "But they do hunt. They name their dogs after moving-picture actors. Old Ed Armstrong, he names his after religious folks. Until you've heard the Armstrong pack after a good, sweet fox, you hain't heard a thing. All turkey-mouthed, or squawl-horn-chop-mouthed at the best. Until you've heard Billy Sunday and Jackie Cooper and Dwight L. Moody and Zasu Pitts and Hoot Gibson and Mary

Magdalene all driving a fox at once, you never have had no treat give to you."

"They're good bench dogs," said Spring Davis. He didn't like to hear too much laughter directed at the Armstrongs. "They mostly got stylish tails and compact feet and good stifles. If you like bench, the Armstrong dogs just hustle in the points."

He held up his hand, and Cal Royster put away the whiskey bottle.

"Coming in," Davis prophesied. "I can get it, from way south, at the top of Heaven Creek."

Benjy swore; his face was very dark. "Blame fox won't give them more'n three hours anymore."

"That's a fact," nodded his father. "We'll have to try farther up Heaven Creek tomorrow."

Mr. Mayor burst out, "Good Lord, do you do this all night, every night? When do you do your farm work?" He began to understand why Spring Davis had been unable to renew his fire insurance policy.

"Not every night," said Springfield. "Sometimes it rains. Or just the opposite, sometimes the weather's been too dry. Or we get long damp spells—too damp—or we get low southeast winds. We don't come out every night."

"Mr. Davis," cried Mr. Mayor of the National Emblem Liability, "how old are you?"

Spring smiled into the fire. "Seventy years ago this season, I ran off to join the Confederate army. I was only twelve, but I had done a sight of fox hunting before that."

The hounds came closer, and once more Bugle Ann's blare was riding high above their hooted chorus.

"He's striking for his hole," Bake said. "In a minute he'll hand them the raspberry."

Spring Davis leaned back and closed his eyes. He drew a deep breath. "Waited seventy years to have a dog like that," he whispered to nobody in particular.

The fox uttered his shout of defiance—that strange yelp which was half a cat cry, half a dog bark, and wholly insulting. Then baffled shrieks told that he had holed.

"Fetch the horn, Benjy," ordered old Davis. "I don't want her sporting around."

Cal Royster bristled. "This ain't August nor yet February. You talk like our dogs was a pack of hoodlums."

"I just like to have her to home, Cal."

From beside a rolled up sweater, Benjy Davis brought a battered army bugle and gave it to his father. The old man wet his lips, fitted the mouthpiece carefully beneath his shaggy mustache, and blew two notes: the *ta-da* of galloping Valkyries, forever a summons and a challenge.

"Will she come for that?" Mr. Mayor asked in amazement.

"Always."

Benjy peered toward the crossing at Heaven Creek. "Looks like some other folks are coming, too."

The dull, yellow lights of an old Ford were rocking toward them, and they could hear the chatter of its motor. "That'll be Tom and Delbert, I reckon," said Cal Royster. "Don't know what's got into them. Been to see the Lancey girls again. They'd ruther spark around with two flibbertigibbets than be out with the dogs."

Slowly the Ford rattled up the hill, and stopped at the wood road. The two younger Royster boys got out with cheers of greeting, which were stilled hastily when they saw a stranger at the fire.

"How's the calf market?" taunted their elder brother.

"Never you mind," grunted Delbert Royster. He and Tom were sunburned, strapping youngsters who would have looked happier in overalls than in the Sunday suits they had worn for their squiring.

Their faces were unwontedly serious, and neither of them headed for the sandwiches.

"What in time ails you two?" demanded Cal.

"You heard about the old Camden place?" countered Delbert.

Everyone except the insurance agent looked automatically toward the northwest. A mile down the valley of Heaven Creek stood an abandoned house and farm buildings, which in daylight showed plainly from their hill.

"I did hear that somebody was moving on it," said the father.

"Some of the Camdens, coming back," added Baker.

Old Spring Davis stood fingering his bugle. "The Camdens was great dog people in their day. That's twenty-thirty year ago."

"Well," said Tom, "we heard about it over at Lancey's. It's a son-in-law of the old Camdens, and his name is Terry, and he aims to raise sheep."

For a long moment no one spoke.

"Fence," said Spring Davis. There was an odd whine in his tone.

Delbert brought out a sack of Bull Durham, and began to make a cigarette. "Martin Lancey was at the lumberyard today, and this Terry was there. He was ordering posts and wire. Wove wire, Lancey said."

"Hog-tight, bull-strong, and horse-high," added Tom.

A coal popped in the fire, and a shower of sparks blew up.

Spring Davis said, thoughtfully: "Man's name is Jacob Terry. I remember him."

"Sure enough," agreed Calhoun Royster, "and he married Effie Camden. I heard she died, up in Jackson County. Had one daughter, seems to me."

Spring Davis put down the bugle. His knee joints creaked as he stood up. "I wouldn't call this Jake Terry a pleasant man. Once he whipped a horse with a piece of board . . . going to put up a wove-wire fence, hey?"

"They're moving in, this week," went on Delbert. "Mrs. Lancey said there was a light in the house early tonight."

Something twitched outside the last reaches of firelight, and Spring Davis went down on one knee. "Come on, little lady," he cried. Bugle Ann trotted into the light, her long ears flapping, her elbows plastered with mud. She was a small hound, but with a strong, well-arched coupling, and she carried her tail like a banner.

Davis took her in his arms. "This here's the angel song you heard, Mr. Mayor."

"She didn't come very prompt," scoffed old Royster.

"Prompt enough," said the veteran. "She set out there past the light, until she was sure about that car. You didn't know the Royster boys would come driving up in their smoke-wagon, did you, honey?"

She wiped his chin with her limp tongue.

"What do you feed her?" asked Mr. Mayor.

"Best cornmeal, bran, and pork cracklings," answered Benjy. "Ma boils it to a thick mush. All our dogs get that."

His father rubbed Bugle Ann's head with his stubbed chin. "I puke out," growled the saturnine neighbor. "Spring, you're plumb foolish over that dog."

The older man shrugged. "I've run dogs for seventy-odd year, but I never heard a voice like this. Nor did you, Cal, nor anybody else. She's galloped forty-five miles tonight. She's the sweetest-mouthed hound in Missouri, and sometimes I reckon I don't deserve her."

Baker asked, "What do you say about the fence, Spring?"

The other hounds were coming in—tan and white, wet ears, drooling jowls—a muddle of tails and snorts and sneezes in the firelight. Benjy took charge of the Davises. There were six of them out, this night, and he handled them with skill and deference and firmness. His father still held Bugle Ann wrapped in his gaunt arms.

"I reckon," decided Spring, "that we'd better make a visit on this Jake Terry tomorrow. Call the Armstrongs and Lanceys and everybody together; even get the Pettigrews down from Big Panther Creek. Nobody has ever put up such a fence in these parts, and this is a mighty poor time to start."

Again Mr. Frank Mayor prayed for information.

"First place," explained Davis, "a fox hates such a fence. He's liable to shy off and leave the country because of it. But some of the foxes do like it, and that's even worse. Because a dog runs about fifteen mile an hour—and he hits a wove-wire fence in the dark. The fox is little—he's gone through without choking to death. The dog is liable to get killed."

He rubbed the homemade collar on Bugle Ann's neck. The collar plate was made from a silver dollar stamped flat, and silver dollars were none too plentiful with Springfield Davis anymore.

"You can't get good hunting in a country where they put such fences across the fox range," Baker Royster summed up.

Bugle Ann was snoring happily in old Spring's arms.

Mr. Mayor had to drive all the way to Wolf Center, and he didn't arrive at home until 4:00 A.M., and his wife was worried to death. He told her that he had just attended the strangest fox hunt in the world; it was a kind of fox hunting in which no killing took place. He was a discerning man, but in this case he spoke too soon.

The men of the Heaven Creek neighborhood waited upon Jacob Terry the next day.

## *3*

That was June. By July, everybody knew that young Benjy Davis was tarnishing some mysterious code which existed among them all, and which no one of them could have explained or accounted for. Benjy was keeping company with Jacob Terry's daughter, and he made no secret of it.

She was named after her mother's people: Camden. She was eighteen, and she had the shaded hazel eyes of her mother's family, the dainty nostrils and firm lower lip which had marked the Camdens as quality folks when they first came to that country on horseback.

From her father Camden inherited the Terry stature, the Terry red hair. All Heaven Creek hoped that she hadn't inherited his surliness, loose tongue, and ugly disposition. Benjy believed that she hadn't.

The crisis began to develop, one night when the grass still reeked from a July flood, and the southeast wind would have drowned any fox smell which rose from last autumn's leaves. Springfield Davis sat on the front porch with his shoes off, and Bugle Ann dreamed on the step beside him.

Spring noticed that Benjy disappeared immediately after the evening chores were done, and later he smelled shoe polish. About eight o'clock Benjy came around the corner of the house, and he was wearing his good trousers and the blue necktie which Grandma Duncan had sent him for Christmas, and which he had never worn.

"It's a wet night," Spring said. He began to fill his pipe.

"I reckon the wind will change," said Benjy. "But anyway it's unlike to dry off the grass before midnight."

Spring put his hand on Bugle Ann. "If it does dry up enough, Cal will be out."

"I'll listen when I get back," Benjy told him. "If I hear you up in the woods, I'll come over. I thought," he said, "that I might go with Camden Terry to see the moving pictures in town."

McKee's Crossing was five miles to the north. Spring thought, I've counted each time they was together. This is eight times. He said aloud, "That's a long way for a buggy. You plowed pretty steady all day, too."

"I wanted to lay by that slow corn," Benjy said. "Camden can drive her Ford. We talked about it out in the field, when she came past today."

"Well," his father muttered. He thought, So I was wrong. Nine times. He cleared his throat. "You might bring me a sack of Sweet Burley from town."

Benjy waved good-bye. "I'll bring it," he said, and went away like a war chief in the dusk.

A long while later, Spring leaned down and blew softly against Bugle Ann's ear, and she roused up to wash his face for him. The April pups, by Billy Bryan out of Miss Wilson, came to tumble across his lap. "I reckon there would be no way to stop that," decided old Davis, "even if I wanted to. She looks more like the Camdens, and they was fine folks. Used to have a beautiful line of Irish-Maryland stock. I hope Benjy has sense enough to pay for the gasoline, if he rides in a Terry car. He will, though."

He sat for hours, thinking of Jacob Terry and how he had greeted the deputation which waited on him a few weeks before. They were men with sober faces, but they were not men who would shoot unless they were called by a certain name, and that was one curse which Jacob Terry had not dared to invoke. He had talked some of shooting dogs, but people didn't believe he really meant it. No man who had married a Camden could be perverted enough to shoot a foxhound wantonly, they thought.

The fence was solidly in place: bull-strong, hog-tight, and horse-high, just as the Royster boys had foretold. It ran across the creek, up the west slope of Heaven Hump, swung its yellow posts to the north, and went downhill for another half mile. On the other two sides it paralleled Heaven Creek and Welsh Run. Jake Terry hadn't bought many sheep yet, but folks said that he was dickering here and there.

It seemed that recently he had inherited some money from an elderly aunt, and likely he would run through with that just as he had done with his wife's share of the Camden property.

When that woven belt of wire encompassed the slope of Heaven Hump, the Davises and Roysters had gone up into the woods and had dug out all the nearer fox dens. Several foxes were captured alive, and later were liberated miles away, east of the Armstrong farm. Their dens were broken in, or stopped with boulders and saturated with chemicals. Now it was hoped that no fox would venture toward that menacing wire sash. The north range of Heaven Creek became a victory for Jacob Terry.

As a matter of fact, the foxes were quick to learn what Terry had done to the hills. Certain of them seemed to take a fiendish delight in slipping through the meshes, whereat the dogs would howl and scramble perilously, knotting themselves in the wire squares.

This night, Spring Davis dozed on the steps until after eleven, and his wife slept on the sofa in the living room. Mrs. Davis was thirty years younger than her husband, eighteen inches shorter, a few degrees less talkative, and she knew that after his dogs Spring loved her well. . . . The breeze did change, and when the old man awoke he found a steady west wind breathing its dryness against his face.

He went out into the yard and felt of the ground. He sniffed several times. Bugle Ann came behind him, stretching and yawning.

"I think a fox would hang on the high ground, after all. The scent'd be fairly free. Reckon you wouldn't have to grind your nose against the ground, little girl," said the master.

She swung her tail, and lifted her muzzle. "Now, hush!" he said, and waited with delight for her to disobey him.

She blew her trumpet.

"What is it?" called Mrs. Davis, sleepily.

The other hounds were answering, from out by the barn, and far in the southwest you could hear the Royster hounds casting about. "We had bugles in the rebel army," said Spring, "but I tell you, Adelaide, I waited a long time to hear the noise that this little girl has got snuggled inside her, all ready to let out when God is willing."

"Are you going up the creek?" asked his wife. They didn't say "down the creek" anymore.

"I reckon I will. Cal is out. I hear General Bullard; sounds like he's striking. Will you fetch me a snack, while I get the lantern?"

She had a lunch ready when the old man came up from the corncrib, with his hands full of Frances Cleveland and Billy Bryan and Old Hickory. "I can't mind more than four, what with Benjy gone," he told Adelaide, and put his lunch in his pocket and the bugle under his suspender strap. He went across the cabbage patch, with the rest of the Davis dogs wailing their grief behind him.

"Poor little folks," he commiserated. "You'll just have to be patient, I reckon. Benjy sure is gone a long time. It must be a mighty good moving picture."

He saw the Royster lanterns opposite the line fence, and he let the dogs loose, one by one. Bugle Ann shot into the lead. "You find the pack, little lady!" Spring shouted at her. "Find the pack if they come high. They got a long jump on you."

Cal Royster chuckled in the shadows. "Talk like she understood every word you said."

"I wager she'll be up with them inside thirty minutes," Spring responded. "And anyway, likely she does know what's what. How could she help it, with that silver cornet the Lord bequeathed her?"

Del and Thomas were off with the Lancey girls again, but Bake and old Cal and Spring Davis all waded Heaven Creek and went up on the south end of the Divide to build their fire.

The bugs were bad, and it was more of a smudge than a camp blaze.

"What's become of Benjy?" asked Bake, who knew well enough what had become of Benjy. "Is he still taking that mail-school lesson about new ways of farming?"

"No, that's been done up for some time," Spring replied. He hesitated, then said: "He's gone to McKee's Crossing to the Wednesday-night moving picture." This seemed neither the time nor the place to elaborate on his statement.

## 4

The hounds came down the valley soon after midnight, with the fox at a tantalizing short lead. The men descended the Divide when the baying sounded first from above them, and they felt rather than saw the truant varmint squeeze past them into the north.

White blur after white blur—like snowy hands whisking before the eyes—the dogs went by.

Cal Royster voiced the apprehension of the others when he spoke. "Fox'll go right up Chilly Branch Holler," he said, and Spring hoped that he was right, for it was hard to forget the menace of the wire which lay beyond.

They heard the dogs crossing Chilly Branch near its mouth, and then Bugle Ann singled out ahead of them all, booming up the steep terraces of Heaven Hump. And Springfield Davis recognized another sound in the universe beyond: the faint clatter of an old Ford rocking along a narrow lane.

He thought, So they're back from the moving pictures. I hope to God the fox switches east to the hilltop. The girl looks more like the Camdens than she does like Jacob. I reckon most of my dogs would be small enough to squeeze through that fence without getting hung up.

Then Bake cracked out, savagely, "They never went up the Hollow. Let's get over there!" and he lumbered away through the darkness. The two older men fumbled after him until their feet touched a deep cattle trail at the base of the hill, and then they could travel rapidly.

They splashed through the rapids near the mouth of Chilly Branch, and far ahead the hounds were rearing and yelling against Jacob Terry's hog-tight fence. One dog (he must have been Wound Stripe, and well named, for Bake Royster swore about it) kiyied, and told the world that an end of the wire had been sharp and gashing.

When the men reached the fence, waving their lanterns, the fox was long since gone. The pack danced and strutted in hysteria beside the barrier.

Wound Stripe's left foreleg was drenched with blood.

"Bugle Ann ain't here," muttered Cal Royster.

The lantern beams had gone their anxious round.

"No," Spring Davis replied, "reckon she sailed right through." He walked up to the fence and tested its strength with his shoe, and prepared to climb over. You couldn't see his face in the lantern light.

Bake was thirty-four, and heavy enough, but he was standing inside Terry's sheep pasture before old Springfield had managed to put his stiff legs astride the fence. Baker was thinking that Benjy should be there, and probably the others were thinking the same thing. The faraway chugging of the Ford car had ceased, but a bright light moved rapidly toward them from the Terry farmhouse.

Sheep scampered here and there in distracted little coteries, appearing suddenly, and vanishing into the thick night amid a rattle of hillside pebbles.

"She'd come up to me, if she was inside the lot," said Spring. "It's possible she squeezed out at the other side, too."

Cal Royster put his arms in the fence meshes, trying vainly to stop their trembling. "She ain't giving voice no more. Maybe you better use your horn, Spring."

The old soldier had the bugle against his lips when Jacob

Terry loomed up the hillside, an electric flashlight in his fist.

"Get out of this pasture," Terry said. He did not yell, and there was added menace in his voice on that account.

"Look out," Cal Royster warned. He saw a shotgun in the curve of the farmer's arm.

Spring Davis turned around and took down the bugle. He rubbed a finger across his mouth. "Jacob," he said, "I come in here after my dog."

"If your damn dog is here, he's got no good business among my sheep." Terry held the flashlight steadily on old Springfield's face, and somehow Bake Royster thought of big searchlights he had seen weaving above the Argonne woods, on another night when hatred paraded on a grander scale.

Spring told Terry, "It's Bugle Ann. She wouldn't hurt your sheep, but she's small enough to come through your fence when a fox brings her here."

In the next silence, they listened for her voice, but could hear only the thudding of sheep which scampered along the slope. The rest of the dogs panted and mourned outside the fence.

"Get this straight, old boy." The flashlight held its unblinking stare in Terry's hand. "I'm gonna raise sheep, and I don't care a stink for all the dogs in Missouri. You keep yours off of my land, or they'll get a dose of number ten-shot in the high end."

Benjy got there a moment later. He had left Camden at the lane entrance, and he had started across a spur of the Davis timber when he heard the hounds working straight down the creek. He had no lantern; the woods were black, so was the creek valley, and it had taken him longer than he anticipated.

Somehow there had been a menace in the entire evening, from the moment when Camden first cried against his clean green shirt.

He asked, "What's the matter?" and his voice sounded like a youth's voice, breaking as it essayed the inflection. He snatched Cal Royster's lantern and investigated the hounds outside the pen. "Pa," he called, "where's Bugle Ann?" and then he came over.

Terry took a couple of steps closer. "There's more than just dogs that give me a peeve, anyway, and you know what I mean. Get out, all of you, and don't bend down my fence when you go over it, neither."

"One of my hounds got cut open," said Bake Royster. "I don't reckon you could be decent enough to staple down those ragged ends of wire, could you? Well, I'll sure come around and staple them for you."

Terry called him a name, and turned the muzzle of the gun toward him, but Benjy stepped out to meet it. He swung wide and openly, for he was not a trained boxer, but he was quicker than a cat in any movement. His fist lifted Terry off his heels and threw him heavily.

The shotgun flew wide; it was still uncocked, and that kept it from going off.

"Take care, Benjy," was all his father said. There were grief and resignation in Spring's voice.

Terry rolled over and got up on his haunches.

"Don't you make a pass at me!" Benjy cried. "If you've killed Bugle Ann, I'll sure kill you."

"No," Spring said, "that'd be my job. But he hasn't, Benjy, he hasn't. . . . I'm plumb certain she went out the other side." Then, all in an instant, he stepped back and flung his arms high; one hand held the bugle.

He appealed, huskily, "For God's sake, listen to that!"

She was far beyond Heaven Hump, far in the timber that blanketed Welsh Run. And she must have passed successfully through the north fence of Terry's pasture, for she had found the fox smell again, and she was telling the whole state of Missouri about it.

It was a bugle, and every man knew that he would never hear its like again after she died.

Bake Royster had Terry's shotgun, and Benjy had his flashlight, and together they eyed the big farmer. "Terry," said Bake, "it's mighty fortunate for you that she's out there running safe and sound."

"You talk smart enough," whispered Jacob Terry. "Four against one! It's easy to talk smart."

"Your having this gun kind of evened it up."

"I'll even up any of your dogs, if they come on my land again." He went on to say what kind of dogs they were.

The hunters returned across the fence—all except Benjy.

"Come on, boy," Spring ordered him.

"Here's your light," said Benjy to Jacob. "I reckoned you had something else to say."

Terry came close to him. "I'm not afraid of no Davises," he bellowed, "but I like to choose my friends! Don't you come near Camden no more—hear me? I'm particular about who my little girl goes places with."

"I reckoned that was it," replied Benjy. The others knew from the drawl with which he spoke that he was enraged almost beyond control. "Well, you can go to hell and fry in your own lard. You know well enough that foxhounds don't go around pulling the hide off of sheep."

The man's voice rose in one shouting shriek. "Why, you young blacksnake, I'll kill every Goddamn cur that steps on this grass!"

"Jacob," Spring called to him, steadily enough, "I can't speak for the Roysters or Lanceys or Armstrongs or anybody else. But if you shoot a Davis dog, I'll blow you clean to glory. Now come out of that hog pen, Benjy Davis."

Benjy climbed over the fence. Terry turned off the flashlight, and stood there like the black stub of a tree, watching him. "How about my gun?" he asked. "Are you folks going around stealing honest people's guns, too?"

"Here," said Bake. He clicked the breech and threw

something far into the valley. He passed the shotgun back through the fence. "Both barrels empty. If you look careful, down by the creek, you'll maybe find the shells."

"Remember what I said!" yelled Jacob Terry. "I got an old cistern needs filling in, and I'd just as soon fill it up with dog meat."

Spring Davis said nothing more, but Cal Royster spat out his tobacco and declared that nobody would forget a word that had been said. He doubted Spring Davis's ability to blow Jacob Terry to glory, and remarked that another destination would be more easy to promise.

They gathered up the dogs and went back to the Divide. Their fire was nearly out, but Bake soon kicked it into activity, and his father found some dry wood stowed away in a hollow basswood at the head of the ravine.

They waited until 2:30 o'clock, and still Bugle Ann didn't come back, nor did they hear her metal baying anymore. Baker took all the Royster dogs home to their straw beds, and then returned to the fireside. The Davis animals lay near the fire and sprawled like the dead, as only hounds can ever do, but there was a nervousness haunting their dreams and you could imagine that the eldest of them moaned in his sleep for Bugle Ann.

Benjy sat like bronze, his arms locked around his knees. From where he watched, Cal Royster studied him and wondered if a strain of Shawnee had not been dropped into the Davis blood a century before. . . . The whiskey got lower and lower in Cal's flask.

Spring Davis walked up and down outside the firelight, tramping a path from the basswood to the nearest clump of hickory sprouts. Once he came back to the fire and spat into the coals.

"Wonder how far the gamest fox would travel, if he set his mind to go in a beeline?" he asked, but Cal Royster couldn't tell him. Then Spring climbed to the highest point of the Divide, and awakened the dozing whippoorwills with his urgent bugle.

## 5

In the darkest half hour, immediately before the sky above the Armstrong farm turned gray, the men heard Jacob Terry's Ford beginning to hiccup. By that time they were scattered far and wide through the hills, but Bake Royster was on top of the Divide. He saw the car lights twist out of Terry's barnyard, and stop for a while, and then go on, smudging away toward the county road.

Bake listened until the car had chugged in the direction of McKee's Crossing. He had started back toward the fire, when a gnome with a lantern waylaid him at the edge of the timber.

"Bake," whispered his father's voice, "I heard a yip."

He asked, "What kind of a yip?" with the unreasoning annoyance of a young man who shuns the mumbling vagaries of the aged.

"A dog yip," said Cal. "I was down the crick, plumb inside Terry's pasture again. And I heard it, up toward the house."

"Just once?"

In the growing fog of dawn, the old man clutched Baker's arm; his fingers tightened and relaxed. "The dog was struck dead, if you ask me. Terry might of done it with an ax, so's Spring wouldn't hear the gun."

Far along the upper twist of Chilly Branch Hollow, Spring Davis's bugle chanted stubbornly. Bake felt stuffed up inside, as he considered what his father had just told him. "Benjy went to take his dogs home, Pa. You wait here for Spring, and I'll go for Del and Tom."

"Don't bring 'em back direct," commanded his father. "Send Tom across fields for the Lanceys, and have Del take the car and go up to the Armstrong place. He can ring the Pettigrews from there. I wish to God I was rich and could afford a telephone."

Bake swallowed. "You want the whole tribe?"

"We can't go off half-cocked, boy. Maybe it was just a notion I had, or something. I would of sworn it was a yip—just one quick one. Don't you dare tell Spring about it. But if that little bitch—"

"Lady," muttered Bake, not realizing he had said it.

"If she's hung up on bob-wire somewhere, we got to find her soon. It'll take a sight of searching. She never was one to try and dig up a foxhole. Maybe she got clear over east on the slab, and some foreigners picked her up in a car."

Bake started for home like a good soldier, with crisp obedience in his mind. At all this talk of killing, he began to tremble inside with a nervousness which had never possessed him since his discharge from the U.S. Veterans' hospital in 1921. *Too much* . . . his big feet found the trampled mire beside Heaven Creek . . . *too much of that sort of thing.* Just now he didn't like the name Springfield. It didn't make him think of a town there in Missouri, but it did make him think of a rifle. Cartridges began to glint in his mind: pointed clips of them, clicking one against the other in a webbed pouch.

Suddenly, he thought he could feel the cold stolidity of a Springfield bolt in the curve of his right index finger.

He decided, She's got to be caught in the wire somewhere. It'll be the best thing that could happen.

He routed Tom and Delbert out, and sent them flying. His mother and Lucy stood in their nightgowns and stared at him with cold, pale eyes, and said they'd do the milking if the men weren't back in an hour and a half. There was a mess of cornmeal in the smelly summer kitchen, stirred up in a huge crock, and Bake took it out to the hounds. Halfway to the barn, he imagined that he heard a frightened voice yapping: "I'm runner—Brigade Headquarters—where's Sixtieth Infantry?" and the rifle bolts clicked in a machine-gun chorus. His throat was dusty, and he smelled pepper in his nose, as if someone had given him a blow that fractured the little blood vessels inside. . . . Then he pulled his nerves together, and went on to feed the dogs.

On the Divide behind his farm, Spring Davis came back to the dead fire with the sunrise smoking behind him. He walked, not like an old man who has been up and on his feet all night, but like a solemn pontiff who has sat in the cruelest judgment.

"It's the first time she ever disobeyed the horn," he said to Cal Royster and Benjy, who were waiting for him.

Cal kicked his empty bottle into the ashes. "Spring, you ought to drink at least a cup of coffee and maybe have a snack, before you go further."

"Why," said Spring, "I don't need—"

Benjy said: "They'll be gathering at the house. Bake and Tom and Del are getting folks."

"I heard her," said Spring. "So did you. She had got through that second fence. I heard her plain, over past the outside of his pasture."

"Sure we heard her," crooned old Royster, "and if she ain't found by high noon—maybe just got a toe caught somewhere, or something, like when she was a pup—I'll give you a four-headed Shorthorn rooster!"

Benjy looked at his father. "Anyway, you got to stop by the house first."

Spring nodded. "Guess that's so. Come along with you."

Roy and Joe Lancey were sitting on the well-curb when they got to the house, and Tom Royster was up at the kitchen door, talking with Mrs. Davis. The Lanceys stood up, awkwardly, as untutored men do at funerals, when Spring strode across the yard.

"Ma," asked Benjy, "you got some coffee?"

She nodded. "I kept hearing the horn, even after you was

here, Benjy. The dogs have been just wild. I got a big coffee-pot on the stove, and a couple skillets of eggs for anybody that wants them."

Bake Royster was coming across the south pasture, and another Lancey—Patterson, the sixteen-year-old one—was advancing up the front road on horseback.

At the back step, Spring Davis surveyed the men in his yard. His eyes were hot enough, but it was a slow and sturdy heat, infinitely ferocious. . . . An orange sun lifted above the Divide and found a whole jewelry store scattered over the clover behind the yard fence. All the remaining Davis dogs seemed to sense the import of this hour, except the April pups. They were smelling around Roy Lancey's legs.

"How about the ears on this one?" muttered Roy.

"They're well set," said Joe, "but she'll never have a stylish tail."

Cal Royster cackled, "Don't ask me! I ain't much on bench, but I'm the darnedest home-plate judge you kids ever seen." The men all tried to laugh, as if he had said something very funny.

They heard the drone of the Armstrongs' old Studebaker from the road, and the rattle of Delbert Royster's Ford behind it. . . . When Spring Davis came out of the house five minutes later, there were thirteen men in the yard, including Benjy.

Spring had a lever action 30-30 Winchester in his hands. He tried it a couple of times, sliding shells into the breech, lowering the hammer with his thumb while he released the trigger, and flicking the cartridges out again. The sun discovered the Winchester; for a moment its barrel looked like mother-of-pearl.

"I'd just as soon go alone," Spring said, mildly.

Benjy cried, "No."

"You might say I'd prefer it."

Benjy said, "I'll go with you."

Cal Royster tried to make an explosion of laughter, but

it was only a vague squawl. "Why, of course we all got to go with you, Spring. It'll take all the men we can raise, to comb real thorough. Maybe that fox took her—" His throat crackled.

"Maybe the fox went clean to the Indian River," supplied young Tom, and there was a murmur of assent.

Spring clamped the rifle under his arm. "Very well, neighbors. . . . I might be wrong, but I reckon I can learn in a hurry when I get there." He stepped down into the yard. "Good-bye, Mother," he said to his wife, and in the doorway she made a sound. The pups scampered to meet him, ears flopping and tails swinging. "Get 'em into the crib or kitchen or somewhere," he requested of the world, and kept going.

The unkempt mob of men started after him. Benjy hustled the pups into the kitchen, and his mother hooked the sagging screen door.

Down in the barn, Frances Cleveland began to bay, and her relatives took up the song. Benjy sprinted ahead and opened the plank gate for his father; the old man headed along the edge of the cornfield, but after twenty yards he struck off between the green fronds, his feet sinking deep into the damp earth and leaving the prints of his heel-corners bright and compressed.

The neighbors followed, all of them; they talked a little about corn. The thinnest corner of the Davis timber swayed forward to meet them, and beyond that lay the lane, and beyond that the Terry house.

They came out into the jet lane, with its golden, morning pools of mud and the grooved ruts where Terry's Ford had plowed through. Nobody tried to avoid the deeper mire; the farmers marched in uneven phalanx behind Spring Davis, and anybody would have guessed that the old man didn't know whether he was walking through mud or last year's oat stubble.

Cal Royster had fallen to the rear, but not through

choice. A little pageant walked with him, and impeded his footsteps . . . it was when he was eighteen, some fifty years earlier, and the neighbors all went up Welsh Run to prosecute Big Cass Strickland when he beat his two children to death. They prosecuted him at the end of his own wagon harness, wrapped around the limb of a white-oak tree, and he hung there seven hours before anyone cut him down. . . .

You couldn't see a soul moving in the Terry yard, and now the men believed most certainly that Jacob Terry had gone far away in the Ford, before dawn. Bake Royster and his father began to watch for tracks, as soon as they came opposite the weed-grown orchard, and it was impossible for them to conceal their search.

Cal felt Spring Davis turning and staring at him, and he held his face closer than ever to the ground.

Then all the men had stopped. Benjy Davis came back and stood between the two Roysters, with his hands clamped over his hip bones.

"The pack never got up this high," he said. "They weren't out of the creek valley, except on the other side."

"No," whispered old Cal. "We was just a-looking."

Benjy grabbed Bake's shoulder and turned him around. "What do you know, Bake?"

"It ain't me," said Bake. "It's Pa. He heard it. I didn't."

Cal stammered, "Now, Benjy Davis. My ears are mighty old and mighty tricky. I can't depend on them no way."

"You better speak up," drawled Benjy. Spring Davis had come back to stand beside them; the rest of the neighbors waited in uneasy silence beyond.

"Well," Cal told them, "it did sound like a yip."

"Up here?" persisted Benjy.

"It was kind of in this general direction. I guess it was a short while before sunup."

Benjy turned to his father, and tried to take the gun. The old man pushed him away with sudden and amazing strength.

"You remember, boy," he said, as if there wasn't another man within twenty miles, "how she got her foot caught in that rat trap before she was weaned."

Bake Royster yowled, without being asked, "Sure, sure! Everybody knows that. But one gone toe never bothered her, because it happened when she was young enough. You'd never pick her as belonging to a Casual Outfit."

"All right, Father," Benjy Davis said. Nobody had ever heard him say "Father" before. "I reckon any tracks that are here would be like cement in the mud. Quite—" He hunted for the word. "Quite unmistakable."

"I'll warrant you," his father replied. Spring drew down the lever of his Winchester the barest part of its arc: there was a shell in the breech. He clicked it back. Then he turned and started east along the lane, with his eyes boring against the ground.

Benjy looked at him as if he were just seeing him for the first time. "Wait," he cried, and the old man turned. Benjy brought out a sack of Sweet Burley, its blue seal blazing in the fresh sunlight. "I just remembered that you wanted me to bring this from town, and I been carrying it in my pants all this time."

Spring nodded. "I'm obliged, Benjy." He thrust the tobacco into his hip pocket. "Before Cal talked about that yip," he told his neighbors, "I had been quite divided. I thought that probably she was in wire, or else somebody had stole her, over on the slab highway. Just possibly."

They didn't find any tracks until they came to the yard gate, almost directly in front of the house. Then there were a few. The imprints were made by the feet of a hound coming from the east, coming slowly and wearily a few inches outside the thick grass which bordered the wood road.

Everybody moved off upon the turf, and let the Davises handle this matter in their own way.

Benjy stood looking into the deserted barnyard, but his

father got down on his knees and examined the smoother patches of drying mud near the intersection of the wheel ruts.

"How about that toe?" asked the boy.

"I think so," answered Spring, haltingly. "I'm not right certain: so many car wheels, and other tracks. She must of turned off on the grass at this point. . . . Wait'll I find a good one."

Then at last he stood up, and took the rifle in both hands. "Oh, I reckon it would stand in court," he declared. "Just like fingerprints and such. That gone toe is as plain as copper plate. And the tracks don't pass this gateway. She did get this far, on the way home."

A drop of water bobbed over his crusty eyelid and spent itself in a quick streak on his face, dividing and splitting when it came to a nest of wrinkles.

Benjy said, "She was all alone, and likely the fox holed over in Lester's timber near the creek mouth. She knew this old wood road come back, and was easier traveling. She knew enough not to go through those wove-wire fences unless a fox took her that way."

"Cal Royster," said Spring, "you owe me a four-headed Shorthorn rooster." He faced the Terry house for the first time.

Old Ed Armstrong cried, "Now, Springfield. Now, brother, wait a spell! The Lord don't smile on wrath in unguarded moments of haste."

"You and the Lord can hold your horses," Spring said, without turning his head. "If I'm looking for rats in my granary, I don't set down and pray on it."

Benjy pleaded, "Give me that Winchester, Pa."

"Pshaw, scat," said his father, and started into the farmyard. "You never bred her, did you? She was mine."

Benjy swung around and glared at the neighbors. "He don't want to go in with a whole parade. I'll stay by this gate. Don't nobody try to come past me."

"Spring!" howled Cal Royster. "He's gone! Spring, I tell you he went away in the car. We all heard it go. We—"

"If he ain't at home," said Benjy, "Pa'll wait."

Jacob Terry came out on the kitchen porch. In the barn lot, his two cows were lowing; they had not yet been milked, and none of the neighbors was surprised to know that Jacob had put off his milking until that hour. There were young chickens on the porch, and in the yard below.

Terry held his shotgun in his hands; of course there had been plenty of other shells in the house. Number-ten shot, Baker remembered. Little bright lights flickered in Bake's eyes, and again he smelled that pepper of a painful smash against his nose.

"Get out of here, you old devil," said Terry.

"What'd you do with her?" asked Spring. His tone was flat. "The tracks are to the gate. Did you haul her inside, then?"

Terry mouthed, "I never killed your damn dog, but I'll put some slugs through you if you don't get out of here." He began to hoist the shotgun toward his shoulder.

Springfield Davis fired from his hip. Terry dropped the shotgun and looked surprised and horrified; a dishpan behind him rang like a gong, and fell from its nail, rolling unsteadily across the floor of the porch. Terry's knees bent; he tried to get hold of his chest, and failed. He fell forward into the mud below the porch, with his arms doubled under him.

A lot of half-feathered chickens scurried away from him, peeping shrilly. When the men had rolled him over, they found that one chicken was dead beneath him—crushed flat when he fell upon it.

Benjy went into the house, but Camden wasn't there, and he was dumbly grateful—even in this calamity, and in the mystery of her absence. But the Ford was gone. She must have driven away in it.

That afternoon, after Springfield Davis had ridden to

Wolf Center with the sheriff, the authorities were able to telephone to the Camdens up in Jackson County. Camden Terry had arrived there about noon, but had driven on to an isolated farm belonging to a bachelor uncle. It was twenty-four hours before she could be notified and could complete the return trip as far as Wolf Center.

On the first day when people sat in the big, hot room among the scarred oak desks, Benjy Davis thought Camden looked prettier than she had ever looked before. Her pallor was the cold pallor of hepaticas; her eyes were excessively deep and shaded and secret.

Benjy didn't look her way when he thought she might be looking at him, but he studied her often when she was watching old Spring and the coroner and the other people. Her story was calm, distant, told without emotion—it might have been translated from some ancient book. Yes, she had been with Benjy Davis the night before the shooting. Yes, she knew that her father had had trouble with the neighbors over his fence and their foxhounds. She knew that there had been threats. . . . After her father came back to the house from the sheep pasture, they had engaged in an argument.

He had slapped her; just once, she said; not very hard. She packed some clothes, and took the Ford. He dared not stop her, because the Ford was hers—not his. Her Aunt Nancy had given it to her after Uncle Newt died; Aunt Nancy couldn't drive.

(She didn't look at Benjy, either, when she thought that he might be observing her. Sometimes their glances crossed, but never seemed to meet and hold. Each understood that Jacob Terry was still between them, standing or lying dead, it didn't make any difference. In a way, Spring Davis also was between them now. And Bugle Ann.)

Her voice continued soberly, a little-girl voice. She thought that she wouldn't stay with her father anymore, after that night. She drove up to Jackson County, and went out to Uncle Elnathan's place, and that was where the news had reached her.

Benjy Davis and the Royster boys spent days in going over the Terry farm, both before and after the sale of farm animals and machinery and household goods. They couldn't find a trace of Bugle Ann's body, even though they took up wooden slabs and explored the old cistern. She could have been buried in any loose earth of the barnyard or hog lot, and no one would have known the difference.

Spring Davis was tried in September; the trial was in no way notable except for the oration on foxhounds by a young attorney who volunteered to assume the defense without pay. The young attorney quoted "Senator Vest's Tribute to the Dog," and added tributes of his own. He discussed fox hunting as practiced in Missouri, and offered a biographical sketch of Old Man Spaulding, who was still alive in those days. In the eastern part of these great United States, said the young attorney, fox hunting was an Anglicized pose of the idle rich, and they had many strange fetishes, not the least of which was the custom never to refer to a foxhound as a "dog." They were all "hounds." Most of his listeners thought that very odd, but they did remember with interest how Spring Davis always called his female dogs Little Ladies or Little Girls.

Fifty years before, certainly, he would never have been convicted. But in this age you must not kill a man, even when another man talks of shooting and has a shotgun in his hands. It was proved that Spring Davis went into the Terry yard armed and ready to kill—he said as much himself. It was proved that Jacob Terry did not fire the first shot, nor did he have his gun at his shoulder when he was struck down.

The most important *corpus delicti*—the body of Bugle Ann—was not available. In short, no one could swear beyond all doubt that Jacob Terry had killed her. Spring Davis had usurped the prerogatives of the Sovereign State of Missouri, and the Sovereign State of Missouri brought that out very pointedly.

Girls made fudge for Spring while he was in jail; women sent in basket dinners. He gave the fudge away, of course, and some of the dinners. There was muttering at his conviction, and men talked darkly of a jail delivery. But such a rebellion belonged fifty years in the past. Springfield Davis went to Jefferson City and served three years, eight months, and twenty-one days, and then he was pardoned by the governor.

## 6

During the first June which Spring spent in prison, the voice of Bugle Ann came back to ring across the dark valleys. Adelaide Davis was the first to hear this banshee, and she ran and told Benjy, and then they were both awake. Over on the next farm, Cal Royster started from his bed screaming, "Bake! Bake! It's her!" and even the youngest Lancey, who was up with a toothache, declared that there was no mistake in the identity.

And from that night rose the sprout of a legend which spread itself over the whole county, and farther than that. It was the legend of a white dog—lean, like hounds of the Spaulding line—who bugled her way through the brush at night, who ran with her head high, calling and hunting for the master who had been carried away from the hills he loved.

They said she ran at the head of a silent pack in which there were thirty-four dogs, all the great and noble sires who had galloped those ranges before the Civil War. There were the hounds brought into Missouri when Daniel Boone came, great sword-mouthed brutes who could pull down a deer if they wanted to. But they all ran silently—their feet made not even a whisper in the dryest leaves of last year, and their baying was not the kind which ordinary people could hear.

Only if you were about to die, you might hear them crying all at once.

But the Davises and the Roysters and one Lancey, and even old Ed Armstrong's hired man—all had heard Bugle Ann on that solitary night, and though they didn't hear her again, it was said that Benjy Davis spent more hours roving the woods than was wise for a young man with a farm on his hands.

No one lived at the Terry farm now. Shortly after Springfield Davis had gone to the penitentiary, men from McKee's Crossing came and took down the hog-tight wire fence. When questioned, they declared that a lawyer had told them they could have the wire and posts if they'd take them down. It was easy to pry out the staples, and they bore the wire away in huge rolls atop their trucks. But the posts were another matter; they quit digging after they had uprooted a few. Still, the wire was the main thing.

And there were those who swore that the pack led by Bugle Ann could go through a hog-tight fence like so much dishwater, but young Benjy Davis was hard to convince. After he had searched and yelled through every ravine between the Indian River and Big Panther Hollow, he declared that it had all been a mistake. Bugle Ann lay somewhere beneath the fresh weeds that grew in Terry's hog lot, and as for her baying —it was another dog, that was all.

"It was her," insisted Adelaide Davis. "If your Pa had been here, he would of got up out of bed and gone for his lantern."

"Well," said Benjy, "I did that, didn't I?"

"But she quit giving voice," his mother said, "and whoever stole her took her away again." Her hands shook, in their cerements of bread dough. "Or else—"

He chided, awkwardly, "I got to get out to the field. . . . It's mighty unnatural to believe in ghosts."

Then he returned to his cultivator seat, and combed the

black earth of the cornfield; he combed the rows early and late, and this year he had planted extra acreage. It was too bad, perhaps, for the price of corn got lower—so low that Benjy said there was no sense in selling. He didn't sell his corn, but he did sell the April pups of the year before, to the Lanceys. He took a corncrib in payment—one fairly new. They moved it over to the Davis place with teams and cables and turnstiles: a three-day job. The Davises were hard put to scratch for a living, and that new corncrib did look like a lot of foolishness.

Benjy stored his 1933 corn, too, and then came the next summer and the drought, and corn at seventy cents. . . . Benjy carried an important slip of pink paper out of the office of the Wolf Center Farmers' Grain Company, and shoved it under a grille at the Wolf Center Savings Bank.

Mr. Mayor came after him and talked of insurance, but the only expenditures which Benjy was known to have made were subscriptions to *The Red Ranger* and *The Hunter's Horn.* You couldn't expect the library at the state prison to have those periodicals in stock.

It was the night of Wednesday, September 26, when Bake Royster came around to the Davis place and got Benjy out of bed. Bake could remember the date forever; that day, sixteen years removed, marked the opening of the Meuse-Argonne offensive. Bake had a great head for names and dates.

He looked green around the gills when Benjy padded out across the kitchen in his nightshirt, and wanted to know what was up.

"I've found something," announced Bake. "Found it in the dark, and I guess you better come and see it."

Benjy's sharp glance made a hole in Royster's face. "I'll get my clothes, Bake. Keep soft, so's not to wake Ma. Her sciatica has been bothering her again."

He came out promptly, and sat on the back step to draw on his shoes. "Where is this—what you found?"

"It's clear in the east side of Bachelor's timber, where the Bachelor used to have a shack. It's a smart piece, but I got my lantern."

"I better take mine, too," said Benjy. He brought a square, scarlet-enameled electric lantern from the porch shelf; Bake thought of that check for the seventy-cent corn.

They went across the yard, with the white disk dancing around their feet and ahead of them. "Maybe you'll want a spade, too," muttered Bake.

"A spade?" Benjy stopped and looked at him in the dark.

Bake said, "Or else a grain sack."

After a moment, Benjy replied, "I'll get a sack, I think," and he found one hanging inside the barn door. Together they crossed the garden patch, and up across the Divide they could hear the Royster dogs and a couple of Armstrongs working intently north into the tangles along Chilly Branch. One or two of the Davis hounds wailed at them, but halfheartedly; the Davis hounds had forgotten what a black-dark night was like, with a fox spraying his oily perfume through the thickets.

"Wound Stripe and Toul Sector had him across the corner of Bachelor's," explained Royster. "Some young dogs was along with them, and that little Elsie Janis got herself twisted in some rusty wire. That's how I come to go down there and—"

He gargled in the dimness, and added with an attempt at being casual, "Tom and Pa are there now."

When they crossed Heaven Creek (its widest pool could have flowed between your shoes, after the drought) Baker began to remonstrate with Benjy Davis.

"I don't see what ails you, Benjy. It's a shame to have good stock tied up and molting away the way yours are."

"You can't sashay around the woods all night, if you're busy farming," the younger man told him.

Bake growled, "Now, I know all about that corn! You

don't need to rub it into me. But you ain't had nothing but dried-up crops to worry you, this year, and since the fall rains began to come there's been *beaucoup* fox around here."

For a while Benjy climbed the incline without speaking, loose pebbles rolling down around Bake Royster as he plodded an arm's length behind. "No stomach for it," Benjy said, at last, and Baker knew that was really the explanation. "Not until he's out of that damn place. I can't set beside a fire and listen to the baying, and know he's at Jefferson City in a cell-house."

It was eerie, passing through the oak woods, with a few katydids throbbing in secret dens under the stiff green leaves, and occasional yellow leaves sailing down into the straight electric ray. There was a feel of frost in the air, and Bake kept thinking of what he had found an hour before. A dog like Bugle Ann could take a thousand ghost hounds across the prairies among the stars, and still her baying would come back to you. Bake had ceased worrying about Springfield rifles and cartridges in webbed pouches, long before; sometimes still he thought of Jacob Terry and the chicken which had been crushed beneath his tumbling body, and he wouldn't get enthusiastic about half-feathered chickens ever again, especially if they made a shrill peeping.

But the death of Jacob Terry had come with its own certain violence, justified and canceled by a rifle bullet, the same as the many deaths Baker had seen in the valley of the Meuse. In Bugle Ann's passing there was too much mystery for any man to ponder. Any man who had ever been a patient in a government hospital.

The Bachelor's cabin was nothing but a heap of mossy shingles and broken crockery among the hickory saplings, for the Bachelor had left the country before Bake Royster was born. Some of his wire existed still: thick, old-fashioned plaits of bent rust amid the stumps. And near one of those barricades Cal Royster and young Tom waited with their lantern.

"Pa," called Bake.

"I'm right here," said the old man. "Evening, Benjy." Tom Royster didn't offer any greeting; embarrassment had frozen him into silence.

Benjy stood beside them and took what Cal Royster handed him. It was a leather collar, now stiff as iron with winter and summer and rain and mold, but the flattened silver dollar on it was unmistakable—you could even scrape away what had gathered over it, and see the Liberty head all flatly distorted, with its crudely scratched legend.

The men waited silently.

"Where's the rest?" asked Benjy, after a long time. He slid the collar, with leaves still clinging to it, inside his shirt.

"Right here, in the bushes. They're a little scattered."

Benjy got down on his knees. If you had seen him, and had not known why he was there, you would have thought that he was praying. . . . Cal Royster had a vague notion that he ought to remove his hat, but Cal had never done such a thing for a dog.

"How long would you say?" asked Benjy presently.

The others murmured, hazarding several opinions. You couldn't tell much about bones. Maybe a doctor could. Animals had been there, probably, and birds. Maybe a year, maybe two, or three, or—

It was the collar which first had attracted Bake's attention. He saw it sticking up out of the leaves while he was releasing Elsie Janis from the wire. The young hound had left some of her blood there, from a lacerated elbow, and it seemed strangely appropriate to have that ground moistened with the blood of a foxhound, even if she wasn't a Davis dog.

"The point is," said Benjy, speaking slowly and gravely, "whether she was here all the time, that night, or whether she come later. Somehow or other. The point is whether we heard her voice two year ago last June, or whether—"

Cal Royster said, "By God, it was her voice. Reckon I heard it."

"And by God," whispered Benjy, "those were her tracks at the edge of Terry's barnyard, in July of 'thirty-one."

"So what?" asked young Tom. It was slang such as he always picked up at the moving pictures, but it seemed unusually apt.

Benjy said, "I reckon there's nothing I can do except tote her home in the grain sack. I'm glad I didn't bring the spade, Bake, because now I'd be tempted to use it; just seem like a lot of old sticks, somehow, and I always did think a dog skull was powerful ugly."

They helped him pick up the relics, and he carried them back home while Bake Royster went ahead with the electric lantern. The men brought a shovel from the woodshed and buried the fragments, grain sack and all, beneath the sweet-crab tree at the corner of Mrs. Davis's little orchard. Benjy washed the collar and wiped it clean, using several dish towels in the process, and then he took it upstairs and hung it over the pointed, upright support of his bureau mirror, on top of his five neckties.

He told his mother the next morning, and of course through the Roysters the story was well around the neighborhood before noon. But Benjy and his mother were positive that no word of it would reach the ears of Springfield Davis at Jefferson City, and they were correct. It was the sort of a tale which might not be welcomed in print, so the *Weekly Clarion-Advocate* held no mention of it. No person except members of the family carried on any correspondence with Spring Davis, anyway, and thus the old man did not learn of how Bugle Ann's skeleton had been found until after he was released from prison.

It gave Bake Royster a fever, however, and he spent four days in bed. His family thought it was a kind of flu, but Baker knew the truth. He'd lie there at night, until he got over it, and watch the whole insane puzzle exploding before his eyes. Desperately he tried to align the formations—to put each separate element in the nook where it belonged; and this was lunacy to attempt.

Camden Terry: take her, now. She was living up in Jackson County, folks said, and she had never offered to sell the farm. Just let it grow to weeds. Nobody seemed to know whether or not she was married, and naturally it would take a hardy soul to mention her name to Benjy. Bake reckoned that Benjy had been mighty sweet on Camden.

Everybody had seen the tracks at Jake Terry's gate; there was no doubt about that missing toe. Not another hound in the neighborhood had a toe gone. So there were her tracks, and why would Bugle Ann have gone across Heaven Creek from the Terry farm—why would she have climbed Heaven Hump, or gone through Chilly Branch Hollow, and south into the timberland to get herself strangled in the Bachelor's wire? Spring Davis was making the hills quiver with his trumpet, and people all knew how Bugle Ann would come to such a summons.

No, she must have lived somehow, somewhere—and then she must have come back to the woods she loved, on another night, in June of 1932. Then they had heard her calling, and then she had met her death, alone beside the windfall of curling shingles.

No, she must have been a ghost, all along. It was not natural for any dog to have a voice like hers, and perhaps she had been sired by one of the silent pack which followed her so willingly in popular imagination. Even now her bones lay wadded in the Davis orchard, but Bugle Ann was up and gone, baying in ranges where no horns could ever summon her, and it would be death to hear her bugling again. It was this surmise, however hysterical, which comforted Baker Royster and let him sleep with no more fever. Yet it was hard for him to forget how Benjy Davis had looked in the lantern light, coming down from the Divide with that sack of bones swinging from his shoulder and Bugle Ann's collar nestling inside his shirt.

## 7

They had less than twenty-four hours' warning, the next June when Springfield Davis was sent home from the penitentiary. There hadn't been such a tornado of festivity in the neighborhood since Delbert Royster and LaVonne Lancey were married two years before, and even then the Davises could not have felt very festive.

At 5:30 P.M. of the great day, Benjy and Bake started for McKee's Crossing in the old Royster car, but the fan belt parted and as a result the train was just pulling out when they careened up to the station. They saw Spring Davis sitting there with a straw suitcase beside him.

His hair and mustache were snow white and his face sagged, as if its fleshy substructure had dried up. His pointed shoulders came forward more noticeably and tried to meet across the front of his chest, but otherwise his appearance was the same as it had been. Benjy expected him to be as pale as a tallow candle, but he was not; Spring explained later that he had worked out of doors a good deal. The worst thing about the whole prison experience, he thought, was having so many of the convicts call him Pop.

He was eighty-six years old, and walked stiffly, and sometimes he'd open his mouth for a moment before he could say anything when he wanted to talk.

They got him into the car, with twenty townspeople staring quietly at him, and started for home. Spring didn't talk much on the way. He took off his old slouch hat and let the wind blow his hair—soft as milkweed silk. Once he said, "I see they've cut down that willow row on the Collins place," and again, "Well, there's no use in my not saying that I was surprised—terribly surprised. It come so sudden! I didn't expect them to let me out for years and years."

He glanced keenly toward the Terry place as they passed its burdock-grown lane, and he seemed about to ask a question. But the next moment the north field of the Davises had swum past, and the car was crunching in at the gate. Adelaide Davis was just opening the screen door; others of the neighborhood women huddled behind her, and a lot of men were squatting on their heels beneath the cottonwood tree. Benjy always remembered how Cal Royster snapped his knife shut and put it into his pocket before he turned. Cal had been whittling a toy dart for one of the Lancey kids.

A long table had been arranged beside the peony bushes, and you could smell everything from fried chicken to beet pickles. After the greetings were made, Spring said that he'd like to put on some other clothes, and Benjy went behind him as he toiled up the narrow stairway to the hot rooms under the eaves. Spring's old work clothes were there, but washed and smooth and foreign to him; he would not feel at home until his crooked knees and elbows had made their appropriate dents in the cloth.

Mrs. Davis had disposed of his old suspenders, and he couldn't get a satisfactory adjustment on the ones he was wearing. He came into Benjy's room for help, and the first thing he saw was Bugle Ann's collar hanging beside the mirror.

If he lived to be a hundred, Benjy would never cease blaming himself for that.

Finally, after working his mouth for a long time, Spring managed to say, "Then you did find her. You never wrote it to me."

"Pa," Benjy groaned, "now you set down, Pa. Set down." And at last the old man sank deep into the narrow feather bed.

He wanted to know, "Where was it? Where?"

"Up in Bachelor's timber. We never found her until last September."

"Bachelor's," echoed Spring. And then: "No, no, couldn't have been there."

"It was right beside the old shack," said his son, as gently as he could.

Spring stared for a while. Downstairs they were yelling and laughing, and LaVonne Lancey Royster was ringing a dinner bell. Out in the yard, old Billy Bryan began to challenge with excitement.

"Then Terry never did it," said Spring.

"Maybe she run up there—after he shot her—or—"

The old man hissed, "Ah, stop your foolish talk!" His eyes were wet and blazing. "Nevertheless," he declared in a rapid whisper, "I'm thankful I done it when I did, for certainly I'd had to do it sometime. He meant it, Benjy. He would of killed her in a minute."

"Sure he would!" cried Benjy. "You don't think anybody in this world is blaming you, do you?"

Springfield had the collar in his hand, turning it slowly around and around.

Benjy mopped his perspiring forehead. "Pa," he began, "that ain't the whole story. There was a time, first June after you went up there—"

He told briefly of the dog's bugling which had echoed in the woods beyond Heaven Creek, and how the neighborhood had taken it, and of the phantom pack which was said to hunt so silently at night, unattended by any hunters.

Spring blew his nose when Benjy was through. "There was a time when I would of laughed my head off at that," he said, simply enough, "but I've had plenty of time to think, these last four years. There were funny things in the war, boy, and there's been funny things other times. My mother knew that brother Rufus was killed by a snapped log cabin, long before they ever brung her the news. She saw it in a kind of dream. . . . I don't say you heard Bugle Ann up there in the timber, that night, but you did hear something. Mighty often I thought I heard her, clear off in Jefferson City."

Then they went downstairs and out into the yard, to the fried chicken and other food, and all the talk, and all the people.

Supper stretched far into the dusk; then the table was cleared, and women began chattering and packing their baskets in the vicious heat of the kitchen. The men sat on the front porch and on the grass, and children shrieked at mysterious games among the berry bushes.

They had tried to enthrone Springfield Davis in the big splint-bottomed rocker, but he preferred to sit with his angular spine against a porch post. The dogs came to pay their respects; there was no one of them that he loved well enough to let it sleep across his lap, though Benjy watched hopefully.

In the first hush of twilight, when conversation had labored away from fox hunting a dozen times, Spring astonished the crowd by rising to his feet and walking slowly down into the yard to feel the grass.

"It's not real wet," he said, so distinctly that all could hear him, "but there's a promising feel of dampness between the blades. When did it rain here?"

Somebody coughed. "Must of been night before last."

The pipes and cigarettes glowed spasmodically, and in the kitchen the younger Lancey girls were trying to harmonize with "Sometimes I'm happy, sometimes I'm blue."

"This night'll be black-dark and that's a fact," came from Cal Royster.

Spring stood listening to the girls' song. "Radio," he muttered. "Well, we had radio music up there, too." He called to Royster, "Cal, I've been smelling at black-dark nights for nigh onto four years."

"I didn't think you'd feel—" Bake started to say, and then he chewed his nervous lip.

Spring Davis echoed, "Feel what?" He looked like a tall, guerrilla ghost in the thickening dusk, and the scent of June flowers was heavy as at a funeral. "Why, when a relative dies we all go on living, don't we? We all have to. I'd like, just as quick as possible, to set beside a fire again."

Benjy stood up. He felt his knees quivering. "The dogs are rusty, Pa. You know I've been farming pretty steady."

"They'll get the kinks out of their noses, once a fox is good and sweet," said Spring. It was as if he alone were trying to whistle up the courage of his neighbors. "I hate to see a good, sticky night go to waste. And there ain't any southeast wind."

There was a stir among the farmers, and more than one stood up. But for all their eagerness a certain delicacy possessed them now. They realized that this pathetic rite—the first journeying of old Spring to the hills of Heaven Creek—was something sacred to the Davises and Roysters, who had hunted together time out of mind.

"I'm afraid Gabe won't look after that colt proper," said old Ed Armstrong. "Awful hard to keep a hock bandaged." The Lanceys spoke of a big day in the field tomorrow, and Henry Pettigrew made lugubrious mention of his rheumatic knee.

"Well," Bake Royster announced, in a sweeping gesture of exclusion, "looks like everybody else has to go home and do chores or go to bed early, but Pa and I might trail up in the timber a spell with you, Spring."

Davis said, "Fetch the hounds, Benjy. I don't reckon we'll need a snack tonight, we're so full of good supper."

In half an hour the four of them had crossed the narrow clover field and were wading the valley darkness: Spring, Benjy, Cal, and Baker. A solid bank of clouds rose slowly out of the west, and rain would come before morning. The air was one great, mossy cellar of humidity.

On the high crest of the Divide, the hounds went loose

—four Davis dogs and five Roysters. All of the Davis dogs were elderly hounds whose voices Spring Davis knew as well as his own name. The white blots went speeding, zigzagging toward the shadows where foxes most often made their path.

The men sat on their haunches and waited.

"One's struck," said Cal, when a haunting moan came from the hilltop. The moan stopped suddenly. "No," Benjy grunted, "you just thought so. If that was Toul Sector . . . has he run on his own trail lately, Bake?"

Bake grinned, in spite of himself. "Not for a good month. Wait awhile."

The insects skirmished around them. At last little Elsie Janis found exciting evidence; she talked about it. Billy Bryan and Old Hickory joined her, and the whole mob went hooting melodiously toward the south slope.

"Good voice she's got," said Spring. "She one of your new ones, Cal?"

"Just small fry," replied Royster, with pride which he couldn't conceal, "and she'll run as long as a fox makes tracks."

Baker thought, Good voice? Well, the old guy said so, and yet Bake was well aware that her yelps were not qualified for a chorus of the best Royster voices, let alone to bring praise from the man who had bred Bugle Ann. He wondered whether it was merely a mistaken kindness on Spring's part, or whether the old man had really lost his ear. Three years, eight months, and twenty-one days were an awful long time.

Bake began to hum "I stood in the jailhouse," and stopped in horror when he realized what he was humming.

He heard the bubbling of his father's whiskey bottle. "Let's have a fire," Cal ordered.

The first curling flame, nursed tenderly through drying twigs, showed Benjy Davis something which made him catch his breath. He had to build the fire higher before he was sure. Yes, old Springfield had gone upstairs before he left the house, but Benjy hadn't given it any thought at the time. And now he saw that the old man wore the battered bugle, tucked neatly beneath his suspender strap.

Stiff little needles rose on Benjy's scalp. He kept fooling with the fire.

"They're well toward Big Panther Holler," Cal estimated.

Spring inclined his head critically. "Yes, that's a beeline fox tonight. Doesn't let no crops grow under his feet." He spoke without a tremor of madness, but his old bugle glowed and shimmered and caught dull flashes from the firelight at every snap of the flames.

Then Benjy saw the shaking of Baker Royster's hands, and he knew that Bake too had seen the trumpet. . . . The son thought crazily, Christ in the Mountains, what would we do if he stood up and started to blow that thing?

Bake was shivering with the same wonder. This was June . . . he knew the month, and the year, and the farm—he knew every scrap of sod beneath his feet—and yet the first blast of that horn would turn the commonplace world to madness. No person could estimate what tribes might come sweeping through the underbrush in answer.

After a few moments, it was impossible to hear the dogs anymore. They had gone deep into the crooked defile of Big Panther Creek; there was no telling just when they might return. The Roysters knew this fox well enough; their dogs had run him frequently during the year. He was a beeliner from the word Go, as Cal often remarked, and he'd just as soon venture into the next county as not. But always he holed at the south end of Bachelor's timber, so they knew the pack would come howling back eventually.

No one talked. The log on the fire shrank to the thinness of a charred bone, and Benjy arose to see whether he could find another one dry enough to burn. There was a V of discarded fence posts nearby, and under their shelter perhaps—

He stopped, frozen in his tracks as the sound pierced him. It was a faint and elvish cry, half lost amid the buzz of tree toads, and it might have been fathered by one of those nighthawks which rode high overhead. . . . Still, it never came from the throat of a bird, and in the first second Benjy wondered what sort of a throat it had come from.

Before the sudden blurring of his gaze, he watched his father's head lifting, nodding. Spring's mouth had opened slightly, in the reflex of one who listens without half knowing. . . .

Again the thin, silver measure—the horn of something which searched the forest away over beyond Heaven Hump. Bake Royster crawled up on his elbow, and his face became yellow instead of red in the firelight.

"Benjy," whispered Spring Davis, "I reckon she's struck."

The young man made a harsh sound. "It's a dog," he said. "Foxhound that belongs to—Running all off by himself, that way. I reckon he's an Armstrong."

The sockets beneath Spring's eyebrows were blank and dark and empty; the weaving shadows did strange things to the contour of his face. He said, "No Armstrong ever had that kind of music in him." Then, creakily, he was on his feet and fingering the lip of his bugle.

"For pity sake," mumbled Cal Royster, "it's just a kind of echo. . . ."

"Cal," said Spring, "if she comes real close to us, I'll blow the bugle for her."

Benjy didn't know why she should have been up again, loping through that timber. It was her voice, of course—no other dog had ever lived with such a melody hidden in its throat. He ventured to suppose that Bugle Ann had loved Spring Davis, much as a woman might have loved him, but it was a cruel and selfish devotion which would rob them all of their sanity, and never let them live in the same world with other men again.

He was repeating, again and again, "Pa! Pa—set down—set down—" and that was the same plea he had made in the bedroom.

Old Spring laughed at them all, and he seemed to tower against the sky. "Are you plumb certain that was her collar, Benjy? . . . I reckon nobody but God seen her bones hop up out of the orchard tonight."

He ceased speaking, then, because the dog's howling was closer and more distinct, as if the trail had swung toward the Hollow; even now the fox might be leaping the gorge of Chilly Branch. But Bugle Ann had learned the last trick of any fox that ever jumped.

Bake Royster was trying to stand up, but for the moment his legs wouldn't support him. He thought, She won't need any help tonight. Spring Davis is in the woods, and naturally she knows it. When he was far off in the penitentiary it had been kind of the Boone dogs, the hounds buried and dust a hundred years ago, to come out and hunt with her and cast in enormous circles to locate the scent . . . big, gobbling shapes, they could drag down the fastest deer in the hills. They could make the black bears afraid of them, and every catamount would slink along the treetops when they went by.

In sudden relief, Bake wanted to laugh out loud. He had hoped that she was a ghost, all along, for that made the whole tale so much easier to understand.

"Sweet mouth," he heard old Davis saying, "the sweetest mouth that ever lived."

Cal groped for his friend's arm. "Now, Spring," he quavered, "you got to get holt of yourself."

Spring laughed.

That clear, baying voice rocketed against the cloudy ceiling, and came down to wash all around them.

"Get holt? Why, I bred the most beautiful tune ever

played in these parts, and I ain't ashamed! Maybe you laughed when you seen me bring this bugle, but I reckoned it would come handy." He paused, grinning slyly, and nodding again as the round pealing broke loose anew.

Then, from blackest distance and seeming to rise behind the hound notes, sounded the yell of a bugle. It blew the same chords which Springfield Davis had always blown for his dog.

The hound's cry ceased, quickly, and the woods seemed to hold out empty hands.

The men looked at one another, pale face reflecting pale face, and for the first time you could see Springfield's eyes. They were bright with bewilderment, and with rage.

Once more the *ta-da,* the shrill witchery and command of it. The strings of old Davis's neck stood out tight against his skin. "I never done it," he cried. "I never gave no one else leave to blow her in!"

"Where was it?" asked Bake, hoarsely.

"Up on Heaven Hump, or past," Benjy answered him. Then he started away through the timber like a runaway steer, with Bake after him.

## *8*

Spring and Cal stumbled cruelly in the underbrush, until the younger men called to each other, remembering, and came back to help them. Only when they had worked their way across Chilly Branch and had crept to the summit beyond, did anyone say a complete sentence. It was Spring who spoke.

"Put out your lights," he ordered. "I see another fire."

A faint ruddiness lived in the north and east, and they went toward it. Benjy grasped his father's arm, pulling him along. The old man moved like a wooden image, but he breathed steadily, and Benjy was certain he'd never drop dead in those woods, no matter who or what they found beside that fire.

Again the tree toads buzzed; the crickets sawed and chuckled, and betty-millers came to kiss the hunters' perspiring faces; these creatures could be merry and could exalt their whispers again, with all those mighty trumpet notes echoed beyond recall.

The woods thinned away. Here was a clearing, stockaded with lonely fence posts, where once Jacob Terry's sheep had lain down in a green pasture.

A black shape grew against the distant core of firelight.

"It's a woman," said Bake.

For a moment he weaved, dizzy, as in the dawn before Jacob Terry was killed.

Camden Terry sat beside the blaze. She was motionless, even as the dry sticks crackled under approaching feet; she must have been expecting this invasion, all along. A dog was with her. The dog bayed, briefly, and Springfield Davis whispered, ". . . World, and they that dwell therein," and his arm tried to twist out of Benjy's manacling grasp.

The girl looked up at them. Benjy thought that she was more beautiful than ever—more beautiful than that day in court, for the fire made red gilt of her hair. Her eyes held dignity and fearlessness, but undoubtedly she was waiting for some immense judgment.

Spring stepped up against the fire, and looked down at the hound which crouched within the curve of the girl's arm. "You blew them notes," were the first words he said, for he saw the bugle in Camden Terry's lap.

She said, "Yes. Twice. Yes, I did."

"That hound . . ." His throat went to pieces on the word. He seemed to build it up again. "What dog is that?"

"I raised her."

"But it's got—her voice."

"Yes, I know. I used to hear her."

He said, scornfully, "I tell you, God never made no two hound voices alike. Same kind of mouth, and all. He never."

The girl looked up at him. "This—she was hers. She's Bugle Ann's. She's by Proctor Pride out of Bugle Ann. There were four more, but only this one had the real bugle mouth."

Springfield staggered. Benjy held him. "She never had no pups," said Spring, thickly.

Camden passed her hand over the little hound's ears, and the dog watched Spring Davis with soft, sad eyes. Her nostrils reached out for the smell of him. Camden Terry stood up; the bugle rolled across the ground. Firelight made her blue dress seem purple, and it did kindly with her eyes, and for a moment Benjy couldn't breathe.

"Mr. Davis," the girl said, "my father never killed her."

Spring cried, "Aw, we know that! The boys found her skeleton over by Bachelor's and they heard her voice in the woods, but I still say she never was bred to any dog."

"That night—" Camden's voice was very low; her hands struggled together. "I drove out of the yard, just like I told in court. She was coming past the gate; I couldn't see her in time. I couldn't—It was an awful sharp turn. . . . I got out and picked her up. . . . She wasn't dead, and even—hurt—she—she didn't seem to blame me. I was afraid there'd be trouble over it—Bugle Ann's being hurt."

Somewhere in the world beyond, Cal Royster was saying, "Car lights. They stopped for a minute. Then they went on. It was when I heard the yip."

"This hound never was hers," Spring Davis snarled. "Where in hell did it get her voice?"

"Wait, Pa," said Benjy.

The girl's hands separated; the fingers flattened stiffly together. "I took her along in the car. The rest of my folks didn't know I'd brought her; just Uncle Elnathan. I told them I had found a run-over dog, on the way, and I hustled her out to Uncle's place. . . . After we heard what had happened, I didn't dare tell the truth. It would have been worse for you, if the jury knew Bugle Ann wasn't really dead at all."

She gasped, "Oh, I hated Pa. He killed my mother with pure meanness. It's the awfulest thing in the world to have a father you've got to hate."

Spring eyed her grimly, and told her to go on.

"Well, it was Bugle Ann's shoulder and leg. . . . She was kind of crippled, but I nursed her to health. When she came in heat in February, I bred her to Proctor Pride. He was a Spaulding hound; the only good one Uncle had, any more. There were five pups. But this was the one—like her."

Camden paused, and there were tears all over her face, but this time it was Benjy who asked her to go on.

"She waited till they were weaned. Then she left one night—there was a moon—she wasn't dried up yet, and she wasn't strong enough to run. But she did go away. We traced her fifteen miles, next day, and then lost her for good. Likely she was heading for home when she struck a fox, and you folks heard her. We never knew she was dead, for sure, but I always thought she'd been killed trying to get back home."

Spring exclaimed, "Benjy, I got to set," and his son eased him quickly to the ground. Cal Royster fumbled around. It took him a long while to find his flask, but at last he did find it.

Soon, Spring opened his eyes and nodded at the girl. "You see," he murmured, "they let me out of Jefferson City."

Her chin trembled. "I knew. That's how I come to be here tonight. I thought you'd maybe be out in the timber."

Benjy stared at her with fierce intensity. "*You* knew. How did you know? They don't talk those things around."

"Well," she told him, "I knew beforehand."

Benjy said, "It wasn't a parole. He was pardoned."

"Yes. The parole board. Sometimes they—kind of recommend. Folks write letters. And talk."

He had taken her hand—both of her hands. He came between her and the Roysters, and he seemed even to have forgotten his father. Camden said, rapidly: "Jacob Terry was my father. I'd like to forget that, but it counted for something when they came to considering and—all my folks weren't Terrys," she cried at him. "Half of them were Camdens, and Camdens mean something in this state, even yet. Some of them are in the legislature."

Bake Royster exploded, "My God! You done it, didn't you?"

She shook her head. "No. I couldn't of done it myself. I just—did what I could. They all knew what kind of a man my father was. And I told them about Mr. Davis."

Inch by inch, the hound had hitched forward to sniff around Spring Davis's feet. At first the old man twisted his legs away, but finally he lay still and watched the dog. "I'm all right, boy," he muttered to Benjy, and then he raised up on his elbow. His eyes took in the whole color and shape and hide of the hound; they studied her slenderness, her strong and well-arched coupling, the stifle built far out from her body. . . . The hound sneezed. She looked at old Davis with curiosity, and then stepped across his legs with tail waving politely, and smelled him from the other side.

"I reckon she could run," said Spring.

"I trained her to the horn. Same as—it seemed like the best thing to do." Camden looked at Benjy, and he nodded slowly, and his face came close to hers.

Spring asked, "What do you call her?"

"Little Lady."

The old man said, "Got a deeper tan, but it's spotted much the same." Stiffly, reluctantly, he put out his hand and touched the hound's muzzle. His eyes were still hard and dry, but he whispered, "Little Lady. You got quite a mouth, Little Lady."

Cal Royster was crying like his own grandchild, but more quietly. Bake took him away from the fire. "Come on, Pa," he grunted, "we got to get out of here. I think I hear the pack coming north again." Baker was certain in his heart that before the other hounds had ever come in, Spring Davis would have sent Little Lady out with Camden and Benjy, to see what she was made of. He prophesied to himself that she would run as long as any fox made tracks; she would be a twenty-hour dog, given to mighty journeyings and chasings, but always she would come back to those black-dark hills when the bugle called her home.

*Mel Ellis*

# MISTER DOG

It had never occurred to me how much I might miss Roggie until the night he and his lead beagle disappeared. The rest of the pack came trailing in at dusk. They stood at the back door for a while waiting to be fed, and then when Roggie didn't come out with a big pail of meal and meat they curled up in dust nests they had rounded for themselves under the porch.

When it came to nine o'clock and I could still see no light in Roggie's three-room cabin, I went over. The pack piled out from under the porch. I lighted a lantern I found in the back hall and counted to make sure: Miss Sue, Miss Sal, Mister Joe,

Mister Jim—all were there except a very special animal that Roggie had named simply Mister Dog.

There was a bag of meal standing in the back hall, and I ran some water from the hand pump into a half pail of it. I couldn't find the meat; so I gave it to them plain.

By the time I had rinsed the pail they were scouting a small swale of willows, making their night toilet before turning in. I watched for a moment, and thought what a fine pack they were for hunting but how they seemed to lack personality, or maybe it was individuality, or—well, I had always been a bird-dog man.

Then I went back to my place across the highway and tried to get on with some writing I had promised. It wouldn't come off, though, because I couldn't keep my eyes on the paper or my mind on the writing. I kept looking out of the window, although there was nothing to see.

The blackness was pushed up solid to my cabin. That was strange too, because usually there was Roggie's yellow light to remind me that I wasn't alone in the valley. There was probably nothing to worry about. Roggie could take care of himself, and Mister Dog could undoubtedly live out the rest of his natural life in the woods without losing more than a few pounds.

It was amazing, I thought as I sat watching for Roggie's light to go on, how much the man resembled the dog—or was it the other way around? Roggie was small, like his breed of hounds. He was just bowlegged enough to give him that hound-leg look and, like Mister Dog, he had gone a little gray where he used to be brown. He wore the quizzical and half-worried look that all dogs and men wear who look out from under perpetually wrinkled brows.

At nine-thirty I gave up. The piece just wouldn't write itself, and I wasn't in the mood to push it. As an excuse to go over to Roggie's place again, I decided that perhaps the pack needed water. They came out stiff-tailed until they smelled me. Then they wriggled a greeting, stood around waiting for a moment, and hustled back to dream more dreams.

They had plenty of water, so I started out of the yard and back across the road. In the middle of the road I stopped to listen. Silence in a valley at night is a friendly thing if you have learned how to live with it; then it has a special meaning. At night the valley becomes a place apart from the rest of the universe. Even the stars seem out of it. Then it becomes a mighty personal place. Perhaps there is no peace anywhere like the feeling of peace that can come to a man in a valley.

I'm glad to say I know what that feeling is like, but tonight it wasn't there. Somehow or other I had a feeling that everything wasn't as it should be. I had the feeling that sometimes comes to a man when a stranger walks into his house without being asked. I shrugged the feeling off and went on up the fieldstone steps. At the door I stopped again to listen, and then went in.

With the light out and the blankets warm at my chin, I lay a long while thinking about Roggie and his pack. I had known him for two years and considered him a friend, but now that I thought about it I realized there was little I really did know about him.

Somewhere in the past there had been a wife and a family, and he did get some kind of pension—either war or railroad. When I first came to Little Bend valley to write a little and get healthy a lot, he had mentioned something about "once riding logs" for somebody. But since he hadn't evinced any desire to know my past, I took it for granted that he didn't put too much stock in what a man had been, but maybe thought it more important to know what he was at the moment and what he might pan out to be.

I must have been awake a couple of hours when I couldn't stand being in bed and not sleeping. I lighted the lamp and crawled into my pants and a woolen shirt. There was a piece of roast beef left from supper and it made good nibbling, but as I nibbled I noticed that my one ear was twitching. Up until then I hadn't realized that I'd been listening that hard.

I walked out of the kitchen and into the front room and looked hard out of the window. Of course, there was nothing to see except a few stars, but I had known it was going to clear off. I felt it at sundown when the air went dry and the wind changed.

I turned to my typewriter and sat looking at the blank piece of paper, but it was no good. Nothing would come out. Nothing good, anyway. The piece was to have been about dogs. Beagles preferably, the note had said. But beagles—what could anyone write about beagles?

I walked over to my bed and was slipping out of my pants when something stopped me with one leg in the air. I sat down on the bed with my pants around my knees, listening. The night held quiet but I had heard something. I pulled my pants back on and slipped a pair of wool socks over my bare feet. After the door had clicked shut I stood outside listening again.

This time I was sure I heard it. It was a dog, all right, and I was fairly positive it was Roggie's Mister Dog. I felt better right away. It seemed I could breath easier. There must have been a little wind blowing up off the ground a way—though it was quiet at earth levels—because the dog's baying was coming more clearly up out of the valley.

But it didn't sound quite right—Mister Dog's baying, that is. It didn't sound as if he was running anything, and it didn't have that confident, bossy ring that so characterized it above others of the pack. The dogs under the porch had heard it too, because I could see a white patch moving here and there, and now and then one of them whined.

Mister Dog's voice puzzled me, though. I had sort of expected that Roggie might have put him down on a fox, because he did that once in a while when he was running the packs for fun, as he'd been doing today. But when Mister Dog ran game he used a throaty cello that hardly ever got yippy or squeaky, like the rest of the pack. This talk of his tonight, however, seemed to carry a note of urgency, and somehow it lacked the confidence of a dog that knows where he is heading and how the chase is going to come out.

Or maybe I'd been beating that typewriter too much, because when a man does he can get to thinking like something out of a magazine instead of the way things really are. Anyway, it was getting cold. It was October already, and I could see a ribbon of mist where the creek was. By the way moisture from my tongue went cold quick on my lips, I knew there would be frost by morning.

Going back in, I pulled on another pair of socks, a light pair of bird-hunting boots, a jacket, some gloves, and a hat, and put a flashlight into my pocket. Then I went outside again to listen.

Mister Dog wasn't running anything—that was certain. His talk was spaced. It was clocklike. On top of that, it wasn't a tree bark—not that Mister Dog wouldn't bark tree, and better than a lot of coon dogs I've met.

Maybe I waited ten minutes before swinging down the road toward the creek. There wasn't much to see along the road, but I could smell where a mink had gotten excited about something, and I knew a deer had probably passed that way because something had crushed a minty patch of greens alongside the bridge.

I figured the creek would be the best way in. There was no path except a small game trail along the west bank that was used by everything from skunk and mink to deer and fox.

I didn't hurry. That would not be good. I walked a little slower than daytime walking so as to let my feelings get out ahead of me a little. That helped, because I could put an arm up in time for branches. Also, I quit speculating about Roggie and Mister Dog. I was on my way to find out, and I wouldn't quit until I did; so it would have been pretty silly to try to weary it out in my mind when I didn't have to.

Instead I thought back upon the few arguments Roggie and I had had since we'd become friends. Argument is the wrong word. Roggie wouldn't argue. He'd talk, and though his eyes sometimes would tell me to go slow he never raised his voice to me—not any more than he would have raised his voice to one of his dogs.

It was about the dogs that we usually disagreed. Living alone as he did, I had tried to convince Roggie that he had picked the wrong kind of dogs for that kind of life. I had tried to convince him that for companionship—intelligent and sympathetic companionship, was the way I had put it—he should have dogs that were capable of more feeling.

"Like a good setter or a spaniel," I had said. "They take to a man more. Now, you take a hound. Can you teach a hound tricks? Will a hound ever learn to do anything except hunt? Why, they won't even come when you call them."

That was as far as I had ever dared to go, but I made it as clear as I could that I thought he would get a lot more satisfaction out of a dog that could understand a man as well as hunt.

Then I stumbled into a collapsed muskrat run, and my mind snapped back to the business of moving through the brush without getting hurt. Mister Dog's talking was coming through mighty clear now, and there was no doubt that he wasn't going anywhere.

I would have to cross the creek; so I watched the mist over the water until I saw a shadow that I knew was an old beaver dam. There were some mighty logs in it; and though the water went around and under it, the main bulwark of the dam stood solid. I crossed there, and then swung on up a slope away from the creek.

It was strange, though, that Roggie took to beagles as he did. I had nothing against the cheerful little fellows, but it had always seemed to me that they cared about nothing except sleeping, eating, and hunting. Which was all right, because that is what they were made for—hunting.

Anyway, I could never get excited about them. I could never picture one guarding a youngster, nor did they seem like the right kind of dog to do the barking when the house was on fire.

Maybe I never knew them too well; but when I'd sit down at my typewriter to do a piece about a dog that had a personality and a character all his own a little beagle just never fitted into the picture.

Anyway, I'd told Roggie that too, and he would tell me I just didn't know what I was talking about. Then he would call Mister Dog to him, and while he was rubbing Mister Dog's ears, he'd look at me as if he thought I was some kind of damn fool. But it would always pass, and for a long while we wouldn't talk about dogs.

Mister Dog was right up ahead of me, maybe a hundred yards by now. The going was hard. I was on a steep, hilly rise that marked the valley's eastern edge. A little moon was showing the closed edges, and most of the stars were clean of cover. I could see better, and I hurried a little.

When I was fifty feet from Mister Dog, he must have scented me, because he set up a yipping that was entirely out of character. In fact, during the two years I had known Mister Dog I couldn't ever remember his becoming so undignified as to give way to a real yip. He came running to meet me, and then led the way back to where he had been doing his talking.

There was a hole in the side of the hill, and out of the hole—I had to put my flashlight on to believe it—stuck Roggie's legs.

I dropped down beside him and shouted: "Roggie! Roggie!"

He grunted, and I knew he wasn't dead. I looked over the ground with my light and saw that one big boulder was pinning him down. I picked up a fallen limb, braced it under the rock, and heaved. It went crackling through the brush downhill and stopped with a thump against a tree.

Roggie stood up. One arm looked bad, but maybe it wasn't too bad. He was shaky but he could smile.

"Fox," he said, pointing. "Damn fox, and I had to crawl in for a look!"

It was funny, but I couldn't laugh.

Mister Dog was making happy with his tail. Roggie picked him up with his good arm and started slowly down the slope, carrying the dog.

I put out the light because the moon was all the way out now, and I walked behind Roggie. Pretty soon Mister Dog wanted to be put down. Roggie put him down, and he was off into the brush, apparently figuring he might just as well hunt on his way home as waste time walking in a straight line.

I felt good now. I could breathe easy, and I felt that maybe when I got back I could get that piece of writing done. Everything was about perfect, because that mighty personal peace that comes to a man in a valley was back with me again.

## *Corey Ford*

# SLIPSTREAM

He could hear them sometimes in his sleep. They would pass right over the house, taking off from Hinman Field nearby, and his paws would begin to twitch, and as the sound of the engines grew louder his toenails would scratch faster and faster on the hardwood floor and he would make an eager whimpering noise in his throat. And then for a moment the roar overhead would seem to shake the entire house, and he would lift his head suddenly, and open his eyes, and stare emptily at the darkness as they faded away and away into the night.

He had lived all his life within the sound of airplane

engines. He had first seen the light of day, one of six squirming pups, in an empty ammo box in the crew chief's shack down on the line. His mother was a collie and belonged to the crew chief, who always insisted she was part full-blooded. He never saw his father, but he must have been a Pomeranian of some kind, because he alone of the litter was born with pointed ears and a great ruff of fur around his neck, and short stubby legs which persisted in flying in all directions and dumping him on his nose when he tried to run. The chief decided to name him Slipstream.

"Slips for short," he told Bill Bentley, "after his mother's getting mixed up with one of them native dogs. You said you wanted a mascot, Lieutenant."

He got his first airplane ride when he was six weeks old. He took it all in stride, sleeping comfortably on Bill Bentley's folded B-10 jacket until they hit an air pocket and he found himself two feet above the floor, clawing at space and wetting all over the cockpit. Thereafter Bill always strapped him down in rough air, or when they were on a combat mission together. He flew quite a few missions with Bill. "It's safer than back at the base," Bill said. "He might get run over by a truck or something." He even got the D.F.C., when Bill's airplane picked up a flak hole in the fuel line, on the way back from Formosa, and Bill went over the side with Slips clasped firmly under one arm. When they were picked up an hour later, Slips was sitting in the inflated rubber raft and Bill was paddling alone in the water, clinging to the side. Some of the maintenance men made him a leather collar with his name spelled out in copper rivets and an imitation Flying Cross hanging from a metal ring, and the colonel presented it to him in a formal ceremony one afternoon after mess.

The sound of airplane engines would always bring back those long steamy afternoons, and the smell of cigars and hair tonic and shoe-dubbing and sweat, and the shuffle and snap of playing cards in the hot Quonset hut. He owned the Quonset, of course. He would burst through the door and scamper heedlessly down the line of cots, leaping from naked chest to naked chest, leaving a wake of cursing pilots and scattered poker hands and beer cans upset on blankets as he made a final spring and landed on the table where Bill was writing a letter home to his wife. "Excuse the blots, Helen, Slips just upset the inkwell." He wrote her every day, and he always mentioned Slips. "Dear Helen, This letter will have to be short, Slips chewed up all the writing-paper. . . ." "Slips sends his love, darling, he's promised to look out for you if anything ever happens. . . ."

Or sometimes, at night, the drone of the engines would recall another afternoon when he lay curled on a folded parachute in the ready room, waiting for Bill to get back from a mission he was flying alone. Waiting and waiting, long after the rest of the squadron had landed again and shuffled past him in heavy flying gear, their eyes lowered. Waiting until Larry Hollis, who flew on Bill's wing, picked him up in silence and carried him back to the Quonset. Some of the other fliers were gathering up Bill's things and putting them into Bill's blue barracks bag, and he growled at them uneasily, and Larry patted him a moment and put him on Bill's cot, and sat down heavily at the table and reached for Bill's writing pad.

"Dear Mrs. Bentley," he began, and crumpled the sheet of paper in his fist, and began again: "Dear Helen . . ."

He had never been quite sure whether Helen liked him. She never laughed at him, or rumpled his ears, or rolled him over and scratched his belly the way Bill did, and now and then he even had the feeling she resented his being there at all. He had felt it the first time he saw her, the night that Larry carried him up the front steps and rang the doorbell. He was dirty and rumpled after flying two days and nights across the Pacific, and his fur was matted with grease and smelled of high-octane gas and creosote from the floor of the cargo plane, and his feet had skidded awkwardly on the polished floor of the small clean living room as Larry set him down. "This is Slips. Bill wanted you to have him, Helen. I hope you don't mind my calling you Helen, but I was Bill's best friend. . . ."

He had wagged his tail and looked into her face expectantly, but she was not looking at him. She was all in black, with her hair pulled back from her white face, and her hands were gripped tight. Her eyes were on Larry. "I want you to tell me frankly, Lieutenant. Is there any hope at all?"

Larry shook his head slowly. "I saw it happen."

The room was full of Bill. There were pictures of Bill in his cadet cap, and Bill in flying helmet and earphones leaning out of the cockpit of his airplane, and Bill's engraved commission, and in an easel frame on the table was a colored photograph of Bill, wearing his shiny new second-lieutenant's bars, beside Helen in a white wedding dress.

"We were married at Lakenan Field, the night he graduated." She spoke in a flat monotone, as though she were talking in her sleep. "Then he was transferred here to Hinman, and we bought this house, and two days after we moved in he got his assignment overseas. I only had him such a little while. Such a little while."

"I'm stationed at Hinman now," Larry said. "Training program. I wish I could call you up sometime. . . ."

"Thank you, Lieutenant," she said in a dull voice, "but I don't go out much."

Mostly she stayed in her room, reading or knitting or listening to the radio. The phone used to ring at first, but she always gave the same answer, and after a few weeks it stopped ringing. Slips moved aimlessly from room to room, feeling unwanted and alone. All the pictures of Bill in uniform disappeared, the day after he arrived; there was only a snapshot, taken when Bill was in college, on the living-room table. Even his leather collar with the Flying Cross disappeared, the first time that Helen gave him a bath and washed away the lingering airplane aroma of gasoline and grease. He had crawled under the sofa after his bath, licking off the scented soap and shivering at the strange sweet way he smelled. He never saw his collar again.

Larry Hollis came to see him once. He barked at the unexpected peal of the doorbell, and then, as he saw in the doorway the polished jodhpur boots and the pinks and the green Army blouse and combat ribbons, he howled and raced toward him and leapt up into his arms, wriggling, frantically lapping his chin and neck. Larry laughed and scratched his ruff and put him down, and he leapt back into his arms again, bowling him backward into a chair. He curled up on his lap and lay still, resting his muzzle against the cool silver wings on Larry's blouse, trying to stop whimpering. Larry looked around him at the bare walls, and at the solitary photograph on the table. "It's funny, you know, but I never saw Bill in civilian clothes."

"I never did, either," Helen said bitterly. "His mother sent it to me. It's the only picture I have of him that doesn't remind me of . . ." She let the sentence die.

Larry fished in his pocket for a paper. "They've just awarded him the Silver Star. I thought maybe you'd like to have the citation."

Helen took it without reading it, and put it on the table. Her face was thinner and older, Larry saw, and her eyes seemed to be fixed on something far away. He fumbled for a cigarette.

"Look, Helen." He flicked a lighter. "Maybe I haven't got any right to say this, but . . ." He lit the cigarette, snapped the lighter shut. "They're having a little dance Saturday at the Field. Wouldn't it be a good thing if you—I mean, got out and saw people again? I mean, after all, Bill wouldn't want you to be like this."

"Thank you, Lieutenant." Her face was a mask. "You're very thoughtful, but . . . I'm afraid I wouldn't be much fun."

Slips could find no way of getting behind that mask. He tagged after her wherever she went, but she did not seem to notice him; she ignored the old glove he brought her to throw for him; when he put his paws on her knee, she pushed him down. She never smiled; he could not make her smile. He slid clownishly on the scatter rugs for her approval; he pretended to hear mice; he put on a great act one day with an ant he discovered on the living-room floor, but she sat rocking in her chair by the window, and at last he abandoned the ant and walked disconsolately down the hall and into the bedroom. The closet door was open; he had never seen it unlocked before. He poked his head inside, and sniffed. A wonderful remembered smell greeted his nostrils. He craned his neck toward a bulky shape at the back of the closet, inhaling deeply, beginning to pant with eagerness. Some boxes stood in front of it; he braced his paws on them and tugged at a dangling cord, until the blue barracks bag toppled toward him, opening as it fell and spilling out a rusted razor and Bill's fountain pen and the framed picture of Helen that had stood on the table beside his cot. The bag was wadded full of moldy flying clothes and he burrowed deeper into it in a frenzy of excitement, pulling out a musty B-10 jacket, a pair of fleece-lined boots tied together by their zippers, Bill's crumpled flight cap—his thousand-hour hat, he always called it—with the sweat-stained visor and the brass emblem bent and tarnished.

Helen looked up as he trotted proudly across the living-room floor toward her, holding the visor in his teeth. She caught her breath with a sharp sob, snatched the cap out of his mouth, and slapped him across the muzzle with it, twice. Her sobbing frightened him so that he forgot to yelp when he was hit. She whirled and ran blindly out of the room, slamming the bedroom door behind her, and a moment later the key turned in the closet door, and he heard the creak of springs as she flung herself on the bed.

He pushed the screen door open with his nose, and slunk out onto the front porch. There was a drone of airplane engines in the distant sky, and he looked up at a pair of red and green lights moving slowly across the stationary stars. It was no use; he was not wanted here. He walked down the steps, and through the front gate and down the street, following the sound of engines fading into the night. . . .

The sergeant saw him first, as he limped across the hard-surfaced runway late the following afternoon. "G'on," he yelled at him, "beat it." The pads of his feet were worn raw, and his tongue lagged as he made his way slowly toward the group of men working around an airplane on the parking area. "You're a hell of a lookin' pooch," the sergeant grumbled. He was too tired to trot; his head hung low, swaying from side to side, and his glassy eyes were fixed ahead. He dropped on his belly in front of a pair of heavy Army shoes. "He's hungry, Sarge," one of the mechanics said. "Let's take him over to the mess hall and get him somepin' to eat."

The warm steamy mess hall; clatter of tin, rumble of masculine voices, the gleam of sweaty bodies behind the counter; the men in oil-stained coveralls straddling the board plank alongside the mess table, handing him chunks of bread, pieces of meat; the big calloused hand, smelling of gasoline, that reached down now and then to rough his fur. "Who the hell's dog is it?" someone asked. "I seen him first," the sergeant said belligerently, "he's mine."

They started back across the field, his well-filled belly as round as a football under the sergeant's shaggy forearm. Larry Hollis, approaching the mess hall, halted in astonishment.

"Isn't that . . . sure it is. Hey, Slips!" He dropped from the sergeant's grasp and ran eagerly toward Larry, leaping up at him. "How in all hell did you get here?" Larry gasped.

"I'm sorry, sir," the sergeant said. "I didn't know it was anybody's dog."

"It's all right, Sergeant. Take him back to your quarters, and just keep an eye on him. I've got to make a phone call. . . ."

Helen's car sounded its horn in front of the barracks, and the sergeant opened the door. He saluted Larry. "The dog's right here, sir," he said. "I'll get him."

Over the sergeant's shoulder, Helen could see the long aisle, the men sprawled asleep on the double row of cots, the bare backs of a group of poker players around a table at the end of the room. Slips jumped off a cot obediently, at the sergeant's whistle, and trotted through the door. He saw Helen, and his pace slowed to a walk. He came toward her dutifully, his ears down.

"Slips," she cried, sweeping him up in her arms and holding him tight, her cheek pressed against his fur. She had never hugged him before. "Oh, Slips."

"I'll put him in the car," Larry offered.

"No, Larry," she said, still hugging Slips. "I . . . I'm leaving him here. It isn't right for him to be all alone."

"It isn't right for anybody to be all alone," Larry said in a low voice. He hesitated. "That dance I was telling you about. It's tonight."

She put Slips down. He looked up at her, and at Larry, and then, as though he were satisfied his job was done, he turned and dashed back into the barracks, hopping onto the end cot and leaping joyously from chest to chest across the sleeping figures until, with a final spring, he landed in the center of the poker game. Cards scattered, a chorus of curses arose, the sergeant hurriedly slammed the door.

Larry was looking at Helen. It was the first time he had ever seen her laugh. It was the first time he had ever seen how young she was when she laughed.

*Vereen Bell*

# BRAG DOG

Eph was outside when it happened. He was sitting under the chinaberry tree, writing in the dirt with a nail, trying, as usual, to study out some way to buy the wheelchair for Addie May. Of course she knew nothing at all about any wheelchair, but Eph guessed that Addie May'd be mighty happy if she could just glide out on the porch to talk to a passerby, and then glide back in when the flies got too bad, without anybody's having to leave their work to tote her.

It was just then that Cleotha came in the house, and there

the puppy was, chewing up her only half fit'n pair of go-to-meetin' shoes. She let go a stick of cordwood at him, and her daughter, little Valentine, screamed like she was stabbed. The puppy was knocked clean under the bed. Eph expected to drag him out cold dead, but before he could kneel down, the puppy came wobbling out, bleeding at the mouth, and one ear torn half off. The puppy sat down, his head tilted to favor his injured ear, and, licking his mouth, he regarded them in puzzlement, blinking that blind, white eye. He wagged his tail uncertainly.

Eph never had felt quite so roused up about anything. "You ever do dat again, Cleotha, and you gwine git hurt. From now on, you bees on prohibition, so you better be keerful, you hear me?"

Little naked Valentine had dropped the shriveled ear of raw corn she had been eating and went to the puppy. Eph knelt beside them, and the puppy began gnawing at his hand as if nothing had happened.

"Ol' hardhead," Eph said tenderly. " 'E got a skull just like a rock in de river."

After that the puppy's name was Hardhead. Mr. Floyd Jessup had given the puppy to Eph. They had been fishing on the lake, and not catching anything. Mr. Floyd didn't mind, though; he kept whipping the fly rod, and popping the bass bug among the lily bonnets.

"How're you making out these days, Eph?" he asked after a while.

Eph hesitated a moment. His crop was no good, because it had been so almighty dry. He hardly had food enough for his family, much less his stock—you could hang your hat on the mule's hip bones. The lake was down low, too, so that the fish weren't biting and hardly anybody wanted a boatman any more. At home, Cleotha was a file-tongue she-cat, and Addie May, his wife, was crippled these eight years, and not long ago the good Lord had taken their boy, Luck, away from them.

Luck had been a first-class hand at tractors and such, and Eph concluded that some of the heavenly machinery had got itself out of fix and they'd just naturally had to call Luck in on the case.

But Eph couldn't bother Mr. Floyd with all that, so he answered, "Tol'able, Mr. Floyd, just tol'able."

"Haven't you a little granddaughter?"

"Yes, suh; Valentine."

"I've got a pointer puppy you can have, Eph. The kid will enjoy him, I guess. A cat scratched his eyes nearly out. One of them's gone, and he'll be blind in the other one within a month or so. But she can have the fun of him for that length of time."

Eph thought it would be fine for Valentine to have a puppy to play with, even a half-blind puppy. So the next time Mr. Floyd came fishing, he brought the puppy with him. That night on the way home the puppy chewed contentedly on Eph's ragged coat, not seeming to mind having one eye milky like a white marble and the other with webby stuff over it.

It was dark when Eph got home, and Addie May and Cleotha and little Valentine were all in bed, but Eph roused them with a shout.

"Guess what I brung home!" he said into the darkness.

"I bet it ain't nothin' to eat," Cleotha said pessimistically.

"I know what it is," Valentine said suddenly, "'cause it's already in the bed with me. It's a little old dog."

Cleotha came out of the bed with an angry bound, and lit a lamp. "A dog?" she shouted. Sure enough, it was a dog, in the bed with Valentine, giving her happy face a lathering.

"Father reserve us!" Cleotha said. "We ain't got a dust a' meal ner a drop a' grease in de house, and de old fool done brung home another mouth to feed."

Addie May turned painfully, so she could get a look at the puppy. "He's purty, ain't he?"

"Purty? I'll purty 'im," Cleotha said in a tight-lipped rage.

The puppy was lucky to be alive next morning. Three or four times during the night Cleotha had tried to slip out and put an end to that extra hungry mouth. But every time Addie May heard her, and called Eph. Sometimes Eph wondered if Addie May ever really went to sleep anymore.

Eph lay awake and thought about the wheelchair. "If'n I was makin' any money," he thought, "I could bury a dime er fi'teen cents a week and in two years er maybe three er four, I'd dig up enough to pay for hit, cash. But I ain't makin' no money."

His brain began to ache from a confusion of thought. It wasn't possible for an old nigger like him to buy a wheelchair for his crippled wife. Yet he wanted it so bad he was tempted to call on the good Lord to pass a miracle. He was even tempted to point out to Him how wrong things had been going, with Luck dying, and Addie May getting crippled, and little Valentine being half hungry all the time; but he was afraid the Lord might think he was criticizing, so he kept his mouth shut.

With morning, rain came. Not a gully-washer, the kind they needed to bring the lake up, but enough of one to help the corn some. By late summer they had bread to eat with their greens, and occasionally Eph would get his old Long Tom single-barreled full-choke shotgun and kill a rabbit or a crow for dinner.

Eph and little Valentine saw to it that the puppy got a little something to eat all the time. He seemed to prosper on corn bread and greens; in fact, his bones grew faster than his flesh, it looked like, giving him a gawky, thick-legged appearance.

The dog's good eye got better instead of worse, and gradually the spidery film over it was gone and the puppy could see almost as good as anybody.

"Well, now, let me see," Eph said, puzzled. "I guess I got to take de Hardhead back to Mr. Floyd."

"How come?" Cleotha asked.

"Well, he ain't went complete blind like Mr. Floyd thought. He goan make a bird dog now."

"You old fool, didn't Mr. Floyd gi'm to you? We gwine sell dat dog and git some money for him, maybe two dollars er two and a quarter. He's sho your dog."

But Eph thought he ought to take him back, so he rose before Valentine woke next morning, and he and the puppy started sadly to Tallahassee. When he finally got there, they went straight to Mr. Floyd's enormous country house on the other side of town.

"You walked twenty miles from the lake with this dog?" Mr. Floyd asked. "You lunatic, I gave you that dog. Now, you keep him."

"Yes, suh, but I feel kinda gilted 'bout him re-gittin' back his sights. He ought to be your little dog, Mr. Floyd."

"I gave him to you, understand? And listen, I don't want to hear of you selling that dog for two or three dollars. He's worth thirty right now, if that eye's all right. Take him to the kennels and let my dog man give him a distemper shot and some worm medicine and a square meal." He drew out a dollar bill and gave it to Eph. "That's bus money back, understand? I don't want you walking down here again, keeping a bird-dog puppy out in the hot sun all day."

Afterward, on the way to the department store, Eph had a curious mixture of feelings. Now that he was about to get the wheelchair, his fingers trembled violently in glad excitement. At the same time, the thought of parting with Hardhead put a sickness in his heart. He hurried into the store before he could change his mind.

"How much your w'eelchairs costes, suh?"

"We got one for twenty-five dollars," the clerk told him.

It was beautiful, with rubber tires and shiny bright wood and black spokes.

Eph didn't hesitate. "Well, dis yere's a thutty-dollar puppy, and I wants to turn him in on dat w'eelchair."

The clerk looked at Hardhead's gaunt frame and unsightly imperfections, and he had to put his hand over his mouth. "I'm afraid we couldn't do that, old man," he said. "Tell you what, though; you train that puppy and he'll be easier to sell. Won't make much difference what he looks like then."

Eph went out with the curious mixture of feelings, only this time they were backward. His hand on Hardhead's scrawny neck was glad. At the same time his whole insides seemed touched by his disappointment. He hadn't got the wheelchair.

Eph told Cleotha what Mr. Floyd had said about harming the puppy. " 'E says if you boddered dis puppy, he gwine have you put in de callyboots, in de blackest corner of hit."

Addie May had them put her out on the porch, so she could tell passersby about Eph's trip from town. They sat her down carefully. Addie May looked at her yard and said, "If'n I had me a nickel, I'd buy me some flar seed, and I'd plant 'em right around this 'ere poach. Zeenies. Blue uns and yaller uns and pank uns." It wasn't often that Addie May let on about wanting anything. The next nickel Eph got his hand on, he was sure going to buy her some zinnia seed.

All afternoon Addie May sat there, speaking to the people who occasionally went by with fish poles and sacks on their way to the lake.

"Mawnin', Miz Davis," they would say to her, "how you?"

"Just tol'able," Addie May would answer. "It's sho Lawd hot, ain't it?"

"Ain't it?"

"Eph went to Ta'hassee, yestiddy, right in de b'ilin' sun."

"Did? W'en 'e comin' back, Miz Davis?"

" 'E come back yestiddy," Addie May would say casually. "On de bust."

Mr. Floyd had given Eph about a dozen cans of dog food to feed the Hardhead. "Feed him a can every three or four days, to sort of balance his diet. A dog needs more than corn bread, you know."

But when Eph came in from pulling fodder one afternoon, Cleotha had found the dog food. She cooked two cans of it in the frying pan. It looked like beef hash.

"Dat ain't people's sump'm-to-eat," Eph said. "Dat's dog rations."

"It eats good," Cleotha said complacently.

Eph dubiously took a spoonful of the stuff and sampled it, and it wasn't bad, sure enough. They had dog food for supper, but Eph couldn't eat any of it, knowing he wasn't supposed to. After supper, he went out and fed Hardhead corn bread and pot licker and tried to explain as best he could.

"It doan seem eggsactly fair," Eph admitted, "but at the same time we been sharin' up wid you, so I guess you don't objeck to sharin' up wid us, specially since you don't know nothin' 'bout it nohow."

The lake got into such a shape that nobody fished it anymore, and Eph had lots of time to spend trying to make his eroded clay farmland grow something. Hardhead always went with him plowing. While Eph plodded up and down the dry furrows, Hardhead would crouch under the sassafras bushes along the rail and wait for the birds. Presently they would come fluttering in, one or two at a time—larks and bluebirds and grassbirds, prospecting in Eph's plowed earth. Suddenly Hardhead, now a half-grown, long-legged dog, would come bounding out and circle the field with whippet-like speed, raising a considerable dust, and chase every bird out of the field. Then he went back to the sassafras bushes, panting, and waited for them to come back into the field again.

Eph watched his antics with pride. "Yes, suh, you got de bird-dog instank. W'en de fust frost comes, you and me is gwine a bird huntin', and I gwine learn you your bird-dog manners." A trained dog would bring a fine price, he thought with a sudden unhappiness.

Along about the first week in December, Eph got his old Long Tom down from the rafters, and the five shells he had saved.

Eph said, as they walked out of the yard, "All right, now git out and go. And recollect 'bout dis, Hardhead. Fum now on, I ain't your sugar tit to chaw on. I de Boss Man, and w'en I holler, you got to hear my voice."

Hardhead ran about excitedly, going faster and faster. Every now and then a field lark would jump up in front of him, and Hardhead would chase it, springing up in the air after the bird. Suddenly the dog cut short one of his absurdly long casts with a flash point, then moved in boldly and held.

Eph grinned in pleasure. "I hope dee's sup'm dere. I kin tolerate a bird-eatin' dog er a flushin' dog, but I can't abide no false pointer."

Hardhead's ears moved, listening to the man's voice. The muscles in his big-boned hind legs quivered. Eph came up until he stood beside the dog. Slowly he stroked the dog from his head to the tip of his shaking tail, and talked to him soothingly.

"Yes, suh, dat's de way a brag dog behaves hisself, and you's de brag dog fo' sho." He saddened momentarily. "Dog-gone, I do wish ol' Luck was here now, a-lookin'. Me and you and Luck could had us some ideal hunts together, couldn't us, now?"

Hardhead's tremors gradually passed. Eph stopped stroking him and stepped in front of him. A rabbit came out in great frightened bounds. Hardhead went after him with a happy yelp. Eph chuckled.

"Chase him plumb out de county, and see do I keer," he said. "You in grammy school now, and you ain't sposed to be reading de high-school books." He walked on in the direction the dog had gone. "Anyhow, dat ol' rabbit did smell like a pa'tridge. He even fooled me."

That night, he told his family, "We gwine have us a ideal bird dog."

"How much he goan be wuth w'en you git 'em trained up?" Cleotha asked interestedly. "Ten or twelve dollars, you reckon?"

"Sheh, gal. Time I work on him three-four months, I 'spect he be wuth forty dollars."

"Y'ain't plannin' to seel him off?" Addie May asked. Little Valentine began to pucker up around the mouth like she had eaten a green persimmon.

"I ain't sure," Eph said unhappily.

"Yes, you is," Cleotha said ominously. "I ain't goin' round raggedy w'en dey's a forty-dollar dog in de yard!"

"Maybe he turn out bad," Addie May said hopefully. "If'n he ain't a bird dog, he ain't wuth nothin', is he, Eph?"

"Ain't wuth a nickel," Eph agreed.

"In dat case," Cleotha said, "be better to knock 'im in de haid, and den dey'll be one lesser hongry mouth to feed."

For a while, Hardhead improved. But approaching maturity, he became a wild dog. Soon as they left the yard, Hardhead lit out, fast as he could run. For maybe ten minutes he was in sight, then he'd disappear in the distance, going hell-a-lickety. Eph's shouting never seemed to mean a thing to him. And that would be the last Eph saw of him that day usually. Sometimes Eph would see him find birds way off. He flushed them immediately, without hesitation, and chased them out of sight.

Finally Eph thought of putting a drag chain on Hardhead. The dog stood patiently while it was being attached, blinking that white-marble eye and twitching his mutilated ear and grinning in excitement. He ran somewhat one-sided, but he still ran wild, and presently he would be out of sight.

"Dang your fool time," Eph finally said when the dog came in one night, brier-scratched and happy, "how come you don't listen at me? I hope you run dem legs off up to de yelbows." The dog got up and came to Eph, and began biting imaginary fleas on the Negro's leg. "Git away fum here," Eph said. He was thinking about the lost wheelchair, and Hardhead's worthlessness made him sicklike. His hand fell upon the dog's big head, and he softened. "If de truth be told, you jist ain't no bird dog. You jist ain't got it into you. You jist a high-class yard dog, and fum now on dat's all you claims to be."

Cleotha, standing behind him, said, "I heered you say he wasn't no bird dog."

From then on, Cleotha was out to get rid of that hungry mouth, and several times, when Eph was in the field, she almost did it. Hardhead knew well enough how Cleotha felt about him, and he never let her get close to him. When he saw her coming, he got up and moved elsewhere. Being one-eyed didn't seem to make him any less alert. Sometimes Cleotha would come out with a plate of corn bread and pot licker in her outstretched hand, and a stick of cordwood behind her back, but hungry as he was, Hardhead wasn't fooled. He wagged his tail politely and went under the sagging old barn.

When Mr. Floyd came back from Europe, the first thing he did was to drive to the lake to fish with Eph. In the past year the rains had done fine, and the bass were roiling the water.

"I guess you didn't know I was going to be your neighbor, Eph," Mr. Floyd said. "I'm buying the old Humphrey plantation that joins your little farm. Ten thousand acres of it. Plenty of birds on that place."

"Oh, Lawd, de birds on dat Humphrey place!" Eph said.

"By the way, what ever happened to that bird-dog puppy I gave you about three years ago?"

"We still got 'im, and proud of 'im. 'Course Cleotha, she don't keer 'bout him mightily. But ol' Hardhead, 'e de best yard dog in Floridy."

"Is that so?" Mr. Floyd asked. "How is he on birds?"

Eph sighed, " 'E ain't no 'count as a bird dog, Mr. Floyd. We jist got him for a pet dog, sort of."

"Gun-shy?"

"Oh, no, suh; 'e like to hear de guns."

"What's wrong with him?"

" 'E's a pure wild dog in de woods, Mr. Floyd. Sometime I wish you could see de way 'e lickety-splits, like a fitified dog. Den, too, 'e hardheaded as a light'rd knot."

"Does he find birds?"

"Well, I can't rightly say what-all he do do. I don't see him but jist a very few minutes, once I let 'im go. Ev'y now and den I see him find a covey. Den—blip!—he done fleshed 'em."

"Did you ever try hunting him from horseback?" Mr. Floyd asked.

"No, suh. Ner muleback either, 'cause ol' Kate's backbone would split me right in two."

"I want to see that dog hunt, Eph. Bring him over to the place Monday morning. We'll have a horse saddled for you."

Monday, Mr. Floyd told Mr. Mac, his dog man, to get out Bob, one of his best pointers. The horses were saddled when Hardhead arrived, followed at the end of a taut plowline by Eph.

Eph wiped his face with the back of his hand. "Dis lunytic done drug me two miles," he said. "W'en I gits back, I gwine hitch 'im up to de plow, and let ol' Kate loafer a w'ile."

Mr. Floyd looked at Hardhead. He saw a seventy-pound liver-and-white pointer with a great chest, long, big-boned legs, and a lithe waist hardly bigger than your two fists together. His ribs flared out under his tough hide like keg staves, and you could tell that fat would no more stay on him than it would stay on a white-hot stove. Eph tied him to a tree, and when the dog finally decided that the tree was too sturdy to be moved, he half-crouched at the end of his rope, panting excitedly and blinking at them with that milky eye.

They took the two dogs down to Blue Pasture on leash, and Mr. Floyd said, "All right, let's see what they'll do. Leave that check cord on Hardhead."

The dogs were released. "Better watch de big fool close right now, suh," Eph said, " 'cause you ain't gwine see him for long, dog bite his bullheaded time."

Mr. Floyd's dog, Bob, made a long swinging cast toward the branch at the left of Blue Pasture. But Hardhead split the middle, going wide open like a racing greyhound, the fifty-foot check cord they'd tied to him dancing and leaping wildly into the air. The horses spurred after him, and they did well to keep him in sight for fifteen minutes. Once they saw him swing with startling abruptness from a dead run to a cold point, never having slowed or put his nose to the ground. For that one instant, his work was perfect. There he stood, with his tail pointing at the pine tops and his head up as if he were looking over a stump, and that crooked ear twisted lopsided on top of his head. It lasted only a second. Hardhead ducked his head and bolted, busting the covey into twenty frightened pieces, slashing at them with his teeth. He came in with such a lightning rush he even caught one of the birds. He gave it a quick crunch, flung it aside, and then went helling it after the others, chasing them out of sight.

"See dere how 'e do?" Eph said. "Ain't no 'count as a bird dog. But round de house he minds good, and he keeps de possums out de chicken house and de pigs out de yard, and he's a ideal play-pretty for Valentine."

That night when they came in, Mr. Floyd asked, "Well, Mac, what do you think?"

"It'll be a hell of a job to break him, Mr. Floyd," the dog man answered, "but if we can do it, he'll be one everlastin' pistol ball."

"That's what I think, too," Mr. Floyd said. "Eph, you've got a dog we figure can run in field trials. He's your dog, but I want to see a winner that was bred in my kennels; and I'm going to let you and Mac try to break him. I need another man around the kennels anyway, and from now you're working for me—and you better keep your lazy bones in a hustle."

That night as Hardhead dragged Eph home at a trot, the Negro said, "Now, ain't you sump'm! Mr. Floyd done made up his mind dat you a field-trial dog, and 'e want us to train you up. But 'e gwine find out just how hardhead you is, 'fo' he gits through, and he gwine be plumb disagusted. But I ain't. It ain't gwine make de fust bit of diffe'nce. You gwine still be de ol' nigger's brag dog, even if it ain't nothin' but de brag yard dog."

They went to work trying to break Hardhead, but he seemed to get wilder. In the woods they could never get near him. He ran wild as a buck deer and he never held a point for more than twenty seconds. They couldn't train him when they couldn't touch him. Sometimes Hardhead would come back that night, and then again he might be gone three days. After a day of fruitless search in the woods, they would wake up to find the dog lying wearily by the house, muddy and brier-slashed, and twitching in his sleep as he chased dream quail. One time he showed up with blood spots here and there on him. They dug the shot out, and found them to be number fours. Whoever let go at him had meant to kill him. They investigated and found out Hardhead had run down a yearling calf and killed it, just for the fun of it. The calf belonged to Mr. Donnelson, a farmer friend of Mr. Floyd's who lived fifteen miles away. Mr. Floyd paid for the calf and got everything straightened out.

"Damn his wild soul," he said afterward, "my ten thousand acres just cramped his style. He wanted room to stretch out and hunt."

Eph thought of the trick that they used finally to break Hardhead. Down in the Blue Pasture there were two coveys that Hardhead knew, and he inevitably went straight to them, first off, and sent them a-scattering. One day they took another bird dog out and located the two coveys precisely, without flushing them. Then Mr. Mac hid in the brush near the first covey, and Eph hid near the second covey, nearly a quarter mile down the pasture. Presently, far up the woods, they heard Mr. Floyd's shout, and they knew Hardhead was loose. Then Mr. Mac could see him coming, his big feet drumming on the ground like a wild mustang's hoofs. Hardhead got wind of this first covey and swerved in and flash-pointed.

Mr. Mac made a dive for the trailing check cord. He got it just as Hardhead lunged forward to pop the birds. "Whoa!" he yelled, and braced himself, but when the big dog hit the end of the cord the man was jerked to his knees.

Hardhead turned a complete end-over-end flip, and hopped to his feet with an expression of mixed incredulity and frustration, his tongue hanging out sideways. He got another whiff of the quail, and stiffened. Then he tried to bust into 'em again, and Mr. Mac turned him tail over head again. Every time Hardhead moved he got snatched back on his tail. Mr. Mac made him stand there twenty minutes, with the birds not ten yards from him. Then he walked in and flushed the birds, shooting one of them down. He made Hardhead stand another minute, then let him go retrieve the bird the way he'd learned to do it in the yard. He retrieved with tender mouth, too, because the last bird he bit had had nails in it.

When Mr. Mac sent him on, he headed straight as a bullet for that second covey. He held his point a good bit longer this time, and when he did charge, Eph was on the other end of the cord, and Hardhead hit the ground again.

Later, when they were talking about it, they laughed about the look on Hardhead's face after he'd been stopped by the cord.

Mr. Mac observed, "He come up with a surprised expression, and he said to me: 'Well, Judas Priest, is that what you been wanting me to do all this time?' "

Eph shook his head. "Dat ain't what he said to me. After nearbout snatching my arms out de sockeys, de ol' scoun'l looked at me, a-spittin' de dirt out'n his mouth, and he said, plain as day, 'Well, you finely cotched me, but I sho give you a time of it!' "

When they had worked on him a few more months, they ran him at Quitman, at the Continentals—"Mr. Gerald Livin'ston's trials," Eph called them afterward—but Hardhead was too wild. Mr. Mac handled him, and Eph scouted. Hardhead found two coveys and held them staunchly. Then he got lost. The time was up when Eph finally found Hardhead three miles off the course, on point.

At Shuqualak, Mississippi, Hardhead won second. A big lemon pointer named Kentucky Buckaroo beat him, a hard-going young dog that had been burning up the field-trial circuit.

"Buck's the next champion, absolutely," they said.

After Shuqualak, Mr. Floyd came to Eph and handed him two hundred-dollar bills.

Eph's eyes widened. "W'at's dis yere for, Mr. Floyd?"

"That's what you get for having the next-best dog in the trials."

"Father, do!" Eph whispered. "I didn't know dey gave you no money for jist bird huntin'. Dese Sugar Log people is sho fine folks."

Mr. Floyd started to go, then turned back. "When we get back, I've got a brood bitch I'm going to send over to your place. We want to be getting some Hardhead puppies."

Grand Junction, Tennessee, on field-trial week is dog men's paradise. Any talk but bird-dog talk is beside the point. The great old dogs live again; dogs like Mary Montrose, who first won the National when she was a Derby, and Becky Broomhill and Feagin's Mohawk Pal, both of whom also won it three times; John Proctor, champion and famous sire, whose blood has run hot as ever in his descendants, like Comanche Rap, and Ferris Jake, who won the 1921 championship, and Muscle Shoals Jake, who missed the championship, but took everything else, and his son, Air Pilot, who was headed for the top until automobile fumes in a garage ruined his nose, and his son, Air Pilot's Sam, who won in 1937, twenty-one years after his great-great-great-grandfather, John Proctor.

The wealthy dog owners are there, Johnsons and Teagles and Fleischmanns and Sages, and such, and field-trial judges like Hobart Ames, who owns the course, and Dr. Benton King, a little man on a big horse; and the professional handlers, the real dog men—the Farriors, father and son, and Ches Harris, who has won more championships than any other living handler, and Dewey English and Clyde Morton and the Bevan Brothers and all the rest of them.

Eph had never seen so many handsome saddle horses in his life. He held Hardhead's collar and said, "Yes, suh, Hardhead, if'n you win next-best ag'in, we goan buy Addie May that sump'm-another!"

The first day was perfect, clear and brittle-cold and breathless. Hardhead was paired with a dog from Oklahoma who hunted well the first half of the long heat, then tired and slowed. Hardhead got off to a bad start, ambling too wide and getting lost, but Eph found him; from then on he hunted the course at a ground-eating pace.

"I'll bet he's in the second series," Mr. Mac said after the heat, as he put the leash on Hardhead's collar.

"He sure hustled," Mr. Floyd grinned. "Take him to the dog truck, Eph."

But it was Hardhead who took Eph to the dog truck. After three hours of the hardest bird hunting, most dogs would have been content to trot wearily at heel. Hardhead hunched his gaunt shoulders, stretched the leash taut as a fiddle string, and pulled.

Two or three men were watching. One of them asked Eph, "Hey, George, ain't that the one they call Hardhead? The one they just took up?"

Jogging along, Eph grinned and said, "Dis de ol' fool hisse'f, gen'lemen."

"I'll bet a hundred to two on that dog against the field," the man said to his friends, "provided they call him back for the second series."

"You think I didn't see the way he drug that nigger by here?" one of the others said. "You trying to catch a fish?"

"I throwed out my net."

But when night of the second day came, there was a new favorite. He was a yellow pointer from Oklahoma, and his name was Ambling Sam. When he ran he outhunted everything that had been put down, finding five coveys and nailing them tight. He traveled wide and fast, with a happy, lighthearted style, and he handled like a show dog.

Eight dogs were called back for the second series, but everybody was pretty sure that the real race was between Hardhead, Ambling Sam, and Kentucky Buckaroo. Hardhead and Buck were paired in the last brace. In the brace preceding them, Ambling Sam threw his chances away. After hunting nicely for two hours—though not so spectacularly as he had in his previous run—he jumped a doe deer, forgot his training, and chased her clean out of the country.

The judges called the last brace. Mr. Mac and Mr. Floyd

and Eph took Hardhead out of the dog truck and gave him a tiny bit of water. The dog yawned nervously and looked things over, his leathery muscles quivering and his one good eye glinting fiercely.

Mr. Floyd pulled at his cigarette and whispered, "Look at him. He's right today."

Mr. Mac gave Eph a hard glance. "Don't lose him, Eph. He's sure hot. He can be the best dog in the world today—or he can be the wildest."

They brought him out front, Mr. Mac leaning back as the dog strained mulelike against the rope. Eph held the rope until Mr. Mac found the leash snap. "All right, I got him," he said, unsnapping the rope. He muttered, "He's hot as a pistol, Eph. Don't lose him now."

Buck stood waiting, eager, too, but well-mannered. A smooth-turned bird dog, Buck made an odd contrast with the gaunt, big-boned Hardhead, with his wild impatience and his bad eye and ear.

"Let 'im go!" the starting judge said.

Both dogs broke fast, but Hardhead jumped with the suppressed power of a spring out of a clock. He ran furiously, straining almost agonizingly for a longer stride. Easily losing Buckaroo, he was still going like this when he hit game, five minutes later. He was right in the middle of the covey in one bound, and they exploded around him. For one split second he seemed about to lunge forward after them. But he stood, on point, until the judges came.

"It's a stop to flush," one of them said. "I saw the birds."

Mr. Mac sent Hardhead on. The dog resumed his wicked wind-scorching stride. He swung out to the right, skirting a cornfield and leaving a vapor of dust behind him.

"Go hard, dog," Eph muttered, "but don't come up on no birds till you run off some o' dat hot."

Then Hardhead found two coveys within five minutes. The first he almost flushed again. Running wild, he suddenly stopped his front feet dead. His rear end kept going, swinging him around, and when he had stopped he was on birds.

Eph rode to the edge of the woods and shouted to the judges, waving his battered hat.

The brown body of the gallery shifted and broke, and the riders galloped to the point. Mr. Mac dismounted, his little twenty-eight-gauge gun in his left hand, and his quirt in the other. Hardhead stood frozen, his tail good and his front quarters still in the slight crouch in which he had stopped. Mr. Mac walked rapidly out front, kicking the bushes and flinging his quirt against the grass. When the birds got up, he fired the gun with one hand, watching to see that Hardhead didn't break.

The next find was a bit on the spectacular side. Slicing rapidly across a thinly covered grass field, Hardhead picked up a vagrant scent and wheeled at right angles. He didn't slow down, but his head was higher as he read the wind. The birds were feeding quietly two hundred yards away. He drew on them boldly, cockily, and abruptly pointed with high head and tail and all feet planted solid. Two birds were not eight feet from him, their frightened little black eyes shining as they squatted motionlessly in a barren furrow in plain view of everybody. Mr. Mac flushed the covey.

Kentucky Buckaroo had come to be known as one of the biggest going dogs on the field-trial circuit. Hardhead was bigger. Buck made several good finds, and handled nicely, but it was Hardhead that everybody watched. In the distance they saw the Negro ride out to the edge of the woods and wave his hand, and again his shout of point drifted clearly down.

"That big dog's got 'em again," a brown man called. When the judge rode up, Mr. Mac dismounted and walked toward the motionless dog. Before he got close to him, Hardhead left the point and ran fifty yards out into the sedge and pointed again.

"Dey runnin' fum 'im," Eph thought nervously. This time the birds held, and Mr. Mac's boots exploded them out. Hardhead stood to wing and shot, and was sent on.

Eph grinned his relief. "De reason dat ol' head's so hard is 'cause she's packed plumb tight with brains!"

Hardhead swung out into the woods again, going like a ball of light through the cold shadows. An ice-water brook wandered down the woods; Eph hoped the dog would stop and drink, and get a few seconds of rest. Hardhead drank, but he did it galloping up the shallow stream, splashing the chilled waters on the damp leaves of the banks. Then he jumped out and headed for the cornfield.

In ten minutes he was out of Eph's sight. Twenty minutes later Hardhead was lost and Mr. Mac had joined the search. They quirted their horses, riding high in the saddle and intently studying every distant whitish object that might be a pointer on birds.

Dog take my sorry time, Eph thought fearfully, I done gone and let 'im lost hisse'f!

Another ten minutes they searched, without success. If they didn't find him before taking-up time, Hardhead was out of it. "Lemme find 'im, Lord, lemme find 'im," Eph kept muttering. Then he thought of Luck, and he said, "If'n you kin look any better fum where you is, Luck, glance round and see do you see 'im."

A man shouted, "Hey, Mac, yon's your dog!"

Eph saw him, a mile away, beyond the gallery, slashing his way down a rise, moving with incredible swiftness, as always. At the bottom of the rise, Kentucky Buckaroo stood on point; even that far away, Eph could tell the judges were watching to see what Hardhead would do.

When Hardhead was two hundred yards away, he saw the point and stopped on the hillside, stylishly honoring; he held until the birds were flushed and Buck sent on.

"For a dog with one eye," a man was saying as Eph

approached the gallery again, "he can see a damn long way."

"That's the most dog you'll ever look at, bud," another answered. "I've watched 'em all from Eugene M right on down, and that hardheaded son of a gun right yonder's my pick."

"Comanche Frank would've showed him a thing or two."

"Comanche Frank, hell."

"You wait a while. This race isn't over. See if your Hardhead is still balling the jack like that after three hours of it."

That's what the judges were watching too. Buckaroo was running a good race, and finding birds; and ordinarily his performance would have won. But Hardhead was too much dog. He had covered more ground, found more birds, and handled as well as Buck.

The gallery rode in quiet excitement. Hardhead was far out to the left, almost, it seemed, on the horizon. Buck was on the right and closer in. Buck cut across in front of the gallery. Ahead of him was a ravine, ten feet or so across. Buck slid down one side and galloped up the other, hardly slowing.

"Buck can't be very tired," somebody said, "the way he come out of that hole like a bat out of hell."

While the riders looked for a place to cross the ravine, Hardhead came back in, his big feet thrumming on the red earth. Before he even reached the place, it was apparent that he was going to cross the ravine at exactly the same place Buck had crossed. Everybody stopped—the judges and reporters and spectators and dog men—to see if Hardhead would reveal any weariness in crossing that deep ravine.

The dog came on, that torn ear lying inside out on his head the way it did sometimes. For a split second it seemed that Hardhead didn't even see the ravine. Then he was there. He left the ground. In midair his tail gave a convulsive flirt that seemed to send him over. That unbelievable leap carried him across with two feet to spare. Within a few minutes he had overtaken Buckaroo and was headed for the horizon again.

The judges looked at their watches. Doctor King said, "You can take your dogs up."

Addie May didn't know exactly what to make of the wheelchair. A lot of the neighbors heard that Eph had bought it, and they were there when it came.

"How you do it, Eph?" Addie May said uncertainly.

"You jist gits in it and rolls right around," Eph said happily.

Addie May hesitated. "Ise scared of hit."

Eph laughed. "Hit's plumb harmless, honey."

They sat her in it, and she rolled carefully across the room, and, with growing confidence, turned it around and came back.

"Doggone," said Joe Ben Brown, "I gwine borry dat to ride to de store in!"

Cleotha looked at Eph angrily. "I see you aims to just th'ow dat best-dog money away."

Eph paid no attention to her. "How you likes it, Addie May?"

"Hit's sho Lord purty," she said, almost ready to cry in her happiness. "We'll put us a sheet over hit to keep it nice, and just let comp'ny set in it."

"Honey, dat ain't no comp'ny chair. Dat's your ev'yday chair, and you kin roll right where you pleases," Eph said. Hardhead came up and hassled the chair with his flaring nostrils, and his tail gave a perfunctory wag. "Look at de ol' scoun'l," Eph said, "he know he done bought you dat fancy sump'm."

*Dion Henderson*

# THE TEST

We had the clearing between us, the open space between the green tents of the cedars marked with the bright patches of the wintergreen vines that didn't pay any attention to the frost, and we could hear the deer running before we saw her. She bounced out of the brush into the clearing—too far into the clearing, and she knew it—stopping with all four feet under her and the big white-lined ears coming up in alarm.

She was real pretty that way for just a second, which is all it took the sheriff to open his big, flapping red mouth on the other side of the clearing and bawl, "It's a doe!"

The doe's ears went up and her tail went up and she went across the clearing and down the ridge.

I moved out of the cedars, trying not to look any more ornery than necessary, and I'm here to tell you I had a lot of practice. A game warden has to learn to put up with a lot of things, but putting up with a big, noisy sheriff as a hunting partner over fifteen or twenty years makes a good many of the other things seem right trivial.

The sheriff came out from behind his tree.

"That," he said proudly, "was a doe, all right."

"I'm glad you said something," I told him. "There wasn't hardly time for me to get out my field guide to North American mammals and make sure it wasn't no rhinoceros."

"I was just being on the safe side," the sheriff said. "I recollect the time you saw that there big rack of elk antlers in the brush and shot the top out of a forty-dollar walnut tree."

Now, that was a durn lie and he knew it; in the first place, it was a pecan tree, and in the second place, he was the one who shot it. We stood there jawing around and suddenly there was a gunshot down the ridge. We kept on standing there, not jawing anymore, and the fun went out of the afternoon just as quick as that.

"Sounds like work for you, Warden," the sheriff said.

"Sounds like it," I said.

There really wasn't much doubt that somebody had shot the doe. It was a middling straight ridge, and there aren't many bucks about to go charging downwind along ridges when the traffic is all headed the other way.

"We'll swing out off the ridge," I said. "Then if the fellow missed her and decided to hike for his car, we'll be between him and the road. If he hit her, we can walk him up easy."

This was the kind of a bind you get into, where having a sheriff as a hunting partner offers something besides trouble.

He's kind of a handy fellow, times like this. Maybe he feels the same way about me, come occasions when somebody sets up in the bank-robbing business. Anyhow, between us we save the county the cost of a deputy sheriff and a deputy game warden.

Anyway, we cut for the road, but it took a little longer than I figured. The sun was dropping fast, and the dark came up faster out of the hollows. We came out on the road without cutting any trail, and for a minute it looked as though our friend heard us coming.

Then the sheriff pointed suddenly to an open sandy spot as big as your hand in the middle of the trail and a wisp of smoke from where a pipe had been emptied.

We didn't have to discuss it. He went off the trail on one side and I went off on the other, and I had the right side. Anyway, that's one way of looking at it. I wasn't ten feet into the brush when somebody humped up ahead of me and ran, just a blur in the dark woods. I took after him and lost him for a second and tripped over a log, and while I was still on my hands and knees I got belted over the head with a tree branch.

"Oh, my gosh!" a young voice said thankfully. "It's you, Warden. I thought it was that durned sheriff."

"I wish it was," I said, rubbing my head. "But you're lucky it wasn't. Now, give me that gun and let's talk about this."

"I didn't mean to hurt you," he said apologetically, and by this time I figured out who he was. The old single-barrel shotgun was most as tall as he was. When I broke it the fired shell still was in it, because the ejector was busted. After a shot, you'd have to pry out the old shell with a jackknife.

"Benjy Gauge," I said, "you ain't old enough to take up pipe smoking, say nothing about deer poaching."

"It was only corn silk," he said. "I made me a cob pipe."

We were back on the trail now, and the sheriff met us.

He glowered at Benjy, who was kind of scrawny, even for a boy of twelve.

"That's a middling poor excuse for the pipe-smoking part," I said. "You got a better one for shooting a doe in buck season?"

Benjy blushed. The sheriff said, "Starting to take after your old man just a little early, ain't you?"

"Never mind my old man," Benjy said, flaring up. "He maybe don't see eye to eye with you lawmen about making whiskey and borrowing things and stuff, and you got him in your old jail to account for it."

"I ain't got him," the sheriff said. "They got him in the next county. Maybe I'll get him next, though."

"Anyway"—Benjy's embarrassment was close to tears—"he'll be home by Thanksgiving, and then us Gauges'll be all right. And what's more, I was just fixing to shoot a deer, and that ain't stealing."

I cleared my throat. "Reckon it's the next thing to it, Benjy. The deer running around out in the woods, they belong to everybody. We fix us up a set of rules so we don't kill off too many deer but always leave enough for next year, and yet so's everybody gets his fair chance at shooting one. Then some feller gets kind of sneaky and takes a deer he ain't got any right to, because it might've belonged to somebody else fair and square. Ain't that wrong, Benjy?"

"Well," he said, "I guess maybe it is wrong. I guess maybe I even figured it was wrong when I saw that old doe coming right at me, otherwise I wouldn't have missed her."

"All right, then," I said and clapped him on the shoulder. "Now, you go to work and remember that, and you won't have any more trouble with the likes of the sheriff and me."

Benjy looked kind of baleful at the sheriff, who was muttering something sort of ominous himself; then the youngster grinned. We walked down the fire trail to where my station wagon was parked, then drove on through the straight section road to where the Gauge place was, in a halfhearted sort of a clearing.

It wasn't much of a house. If you want to get right down to it, I'd say the house probably started out as the horse barn and got itself converted when the original house burned down. The sheriff claimed he could remember when it was quite a place, when Benjy's old man married one of the pretty Renfrew girls, despite all the kicking and hollering her kinfolks did, and settled on this place Helen Renfrew's father gave them. Partly it was for a wedding present, I guess, and partly it was to keep them out of town. Marrying Helen Renfrew, the sheriff said, was the only sign of good sense Benjy Gauge's old man ever showed. There'd been a lot of progressively worse signs since, and the worst of all, of course, was when he stole the highway-department truck to move his still from the next county. That's how he got to being a boarder of the neighboring sheriff.

We pulled into the clearing where the brush was getting up some, and Benjy's mother came out with a worried look; the red light and the aerial and the siren on the fender made my old station wagon look mighty official.

Right off, I told her nothing serious was the matter; we'd just had a little talk with Benjy and everything was going to be all right. She didn't ask us in, but I saw through the door that while there wasn't much to speak of in the way of furniture, everything was neat. The pine floor was scrubbed white and there were curtains at the windows. After all, she was a Renfrew, and it appeared that she gave up hard on some things.

Anyway, after Benjy was in she stayed outside with us. She wasn't exactly cordial, but she wanted to talk. Her face was calm; I guess you might say it had a still look about it, as though she'd seen some things she'd just as soon not looked at and expected to see more, and figured she could stand it but she didn't have to like it.

"I'm not one to come asking favors for nothing," she said, "but it appears to me you lawmen have an interest in this. And I tell you I'm some worried about how Benjy's going to turn out."

"Well," I said, feeling more uncomfortable by the minute.

She looked at me, lamplight from the window shining on that quiet face with the level eyes. Pushing women and kids around isn't quite my line, and I can't work up a good glower to cover it up the way the sheriff does.

"My brother Ted Renfrew is alone in the big house in town since his wife died," Benjy's mother said. "He'd be right glad to have the boy with him. Benjy could go to school there and have a proper bringing up."

I was getting tired of saying, "Well."

"I know what you're thinking," Benjy's ma said. "But the boy is set against going. We haven't had much in his time, but we've got the place, such as there is left of it." She let the sheriff share that level look. "And I can't very well explain to him how it's been run down and how come he'd be in a lot better shape to make something of it in after years if he had some bringing up now."

It was the sheriff's turn. He said, "Well—"

"A woman can't hold a boy's father up just to shame him," Benjy's mother said quietly. "It isn't proper. And, on the other hand, I have an idea what it does to folks inside, to make them do things they don't want to do, things they can't see reason to."

Her voice never got away from her at all. But it dropped a little when she said, "He's not much more than a little boy, and he hasn't had much except crowding, most of his days."

"Maybe we can think of something," I said.

She watched us get in the car. Just before I closed the door she said civilly, "I thank you kindly, Warden."

Most of the way back to town the station wagon was

pretty quiet. Finally the sheriff said, "All right. You got something in mind. Let's hear it."

"Nothing at all," I said. "Matter of fact, I was just sitting here driving and reflecting to myself on the great benefits accruing to a man in connection with his associating with bird dogs. That's one of the things I got against deer hunting, outside of a few personal items. Deer hunting, I don't have the beneficial company of a class bird dog to offset the ornery human company."

"You," said the sheriff, alert now, "are trying to distract me with some irrelevant insults. What've bird dogs got to do with Benjy Gauge?"

"Nothing," I said. "Nothing at all. He ain't even got one."

"Now, just a minute," the sheriff said. "You ain't going to take one of the Maid's pups out there to that old shack and deliver it to a certain bad end?"

"It ain't the end that a dog, or a man, either, comes to that worries me," I said. "Not so much as how he gets there. Anyhow, the Maid went and had herself nine spanking puppies, you know."

"Yes, sure she did. And you know good and well you got 'em all sold; you got some of them sold to bird-dog men five hundred miles away before they were born."

"I know," I said. "But Maid ain't so terrible old yet. And some of them city fellows are real patient. Some of them been waiting for two litters past now and won't mind waiting another."

The next morning I went out to the kennel and picked Benjy out a dog. The pups were past three months old and starting out for their regular homes any minute. They were getting rangy and starting to grow teeth, and there was this big one with liver ears and a cocky white blaze on his forehead, bold and brassy and just right for what I wanted. He was marked out for a city hunter who was a real nice fellow and who would be real disappointed, too. I don't know, though. Maybe I know more about dogs than I do about kids, but I figured there were some kids worth risking a good dog on.

I put the pup in the wagon and drove on out to the Gauge place. Benjy was in the clearing, back near to where the old house used to be before the fire, chopping wood. His mother came out, too, and stood on the stoop of the shack. Neither one said anything.

I took the pup out and set him down and he looked around, sort of testing the air; then he saw Benjy and his ears came up, those liver ears that on a pup his age seem twice as big as he'll ever have any use for. The long white tail flagged and the pup, big-footed and wagging, started for the boy. Benjy's face lighted up and he squatted down. The pup put his front feet on Benjy's knees, unmannerly as anything.

Then Benjy stood up suddenly, and his face had that funny look you don't like to see very often.

"What's the puppy for?" he asked warily. "Why you want to bring a puppy around here?"

"Thought you might like to see him," I said casually. "Thought you might like to handle a class puppy like that."

"Well," he said, trying not to look down at the ears and the wagging, "there ain't no call for you to be doing me any favors."

A grimy hand strayed toward ears, then was jerked back.

"I bet my ma talked to you about this," he said indignantly. "I bet she asked you to bring this puppy out here for a joy gift."

I could see his mother's face there on the stoop. It hurt a little. I said briskly, "Your mother didn't say anything about joy gifts. And neither did I, that I know of. Did I now?"

He blushed, seeing that he'd been impolite.

"Main reason I stopped," I said, "was to see if you might

do me a favor. This here pup, now, is a right promising dog. But he needs a lot of handling and this is a busy time of year for me. I ain't got time to spend fooling with puppies. I thought you might tell me somebody who'd keep him and give him a little handling now and then—see how he turns out."

"Well," Benjy said, "that's different. Yes, sir." He took a big, important breath. "I'm right busy myself, too," he said. "But it might so happen I could handle him a little, were you willing to let me try."

"You know," I said, "I never thought of that. But it sure would be nice of you to accommodate me that way."

Benjy squatted down again, and his face was all right this time. His face was fine. I got into the station wagon and said, "He's a class dog, now, like I told you. And he has to eat kind of fancy, so I'll bring a sack of feed out for him."

"I'll be real careful about feeding him," Benjy said.

"His name is Chippewa Boy."

Benjy said, "I think I'll call him Chip."

That was the day after deer season opened, which was early that year. Every week or so I stopped out at the Gauge place, and I want to tell you it was a wonder the way that boy worked with the pup. By some lights, I suppose it was throwing away a good dog, because no boy like Benjy could possibly train a bird dog to regular standards, the standards being about as well known to him as the rules for conduct at a White House reception. But a high-bred dog is born knowing more about the hunting part of the bird-dog business than any man can teach him, and the rest doesn't really amount to so much.

The deer season went on and closed without any more trouble than usual, and the bird season came on. The sheriff was with me one time when we stopped out at the Gauges', and Benjy showed us how he'd taught Chip to hunt dead and to make the search for a downed bird that he hadn't seen fall.

The way they performed pretty near made the sheriff grin before he caught himself.

I said something about how I'd bet there wasn't another boy in the whole eighth grade back in the town school who could train a five-month-old pup to hunt dead, and the sheriff said he'd bet that, too. And I said maybe some of the other boys knew about tying neckties and even dancing with girls, but, shucks, a fellow could learn things like that right smart, but he couldn't just go out and pick up handling sense.

Benjy glowed at the talk, but when we were through, he looked up and said, "I know what you fellers are driving at, but I ain't going. I got to cut another cord of wood right now."

We figured we'd been dismissed. His mother told us about the woodcutting. It turned out he'd made a deal with some of the neighbors to take some cordwood off the place so's he could buy a turkey and all the trimmings for Thanksgiving, when his father would be home. Benjy sure had big plans, his mother said.

If nothing more had happened, the whole thing would have turned out the way most things turn out in this life—not real good nor real bad, maybe, and maybe not even very decisive one way or another.

But then one night—two days before Thanksgiving, it was—the rangers called up from the fire tower and said they'd been watching some flickering out in the woods that they thought first was a little fire. But it wasn't. It looked more like my kind of business. When a man back in the hills figures he needs himself a deer out of season, he generally goes out and shoots it and goes home. But when the lights keep showing up, it's more likely a sign of regular commercial poaching, a gang shooting a whole truckful of deer in one night to take into the city and sell. And since this is what you might call the combined bank holdup and grand larceny of the game-management business, I invited the sheriff along to look into it. We talked to a couple of the towers on the radio, and they finally pinned down a reading on the map for us.

There was a good moon and we could drive along the back roads without the car lights on, which is a good idea. But when we turned off on a fire lane that looked close to the spot where the light had been, there was no sign of any other car or truck being in ahead of us. We got out of the station wagon and listened until the small brush noises that had been quieted by our coming came back again.

The sheriff leaned over and said against my ear, "Only about a half mile from the Gauge place. And I got a release notice from the next county. They turned Benjy's old man loose today."

I didn't say anything, because I didn't have to. We were both thinking about how Benjy's pa was just the kind who might decide to go out and poach a few deer while he got the still working, and how the things we had tried to do to help Benjy and his mother could all go for nothing.

We waited a little longer, and suddenly there was a flash of light down off the ridge, only a couple of hundred yards away. There was the light, and then there was a gunshot. The big noise set the little rustling noises in the woods going away from it quickly, like water rings.

We started running. There was enough moon so that you could keep from running into the big trees, but the brush and the deadfalls were in shadow and you thumped your shins on them. Then we were in close enough to hear thrashing and a dog barking and somebody yelling, and then we were right on it, with the moon giving one kind of eerie light and a flashlight on the ground giving another kind, even more eerie.

There was a big buck deer, down behind but still pivoting on his forelegs, a good deer with antlers glinting in the light and the whites of his eyes showing and puffs of steam coming from his nostrils. There was a pointer pup barking and the kid—no doubt about the kid with the dog and the old gun—trying frantically to get an empty shell out of the gun because the ejector didn't work, and the deer lunging and almost getting up, and the kid crying and swearing at the gun and finally swinging it at the deer. But a big buck is nothing to fool with at some times of the year, especially when the antler points are polished and the neck is swelled and the whites of the eyes show. The buck made a lunging kind of a scramble. The kid tripped and fell almost under him, and the pointer pup made a shrill challenge and charged the deer.

The buck met him with a forefoot as quick and sharp as a hatchet, and there was the crunch you do not have to think about when you hear it—it is the sound of things breaking.

The kid saw the dog fall as he was rolling away himself. With the dog down, the kid found his feet and suddenly started to walk with a crazy bare-handed lurch toward that buck, and while I still was slipping the rifle sling off my shoulder, the sheriff's hand came out from under his coat. There was a big blossom of orange flame and the crashing sound of the .357. The deer went down and over and halfway over again, and was very quiet.

And then everything was quiet. The kid looked at the deer, then he turned to look at the dog, and then he went down on his knees very slowly, as though something in him was breaking apart in sections, and put his arms around the dog.

I looked at him for a minute, using the flashlight that had been on the ground but keeping the light away from the dog. Benjy kept his face down against the puppy. The puppy didn't move.

"I didn't calculate to do anything like this," Benjy said. "Things kind of got to crowding me."

"Your old man made you do it. Where is he?"

My voice sounded harsh even to me. Anger can do that,

and disappointment and some other feelings you might have under the circumstances. Later you might sort them out.

"I guess he did make me, at that," Benjy said. "But not the way you think. My old man came home today. We all run out to see him and tell him about the swell Thanksgiving dinner we were going to have, with him back and all." He pressed his face against the dog. "My old man said never mind. He told us we never brought him nothing but trouble and he was going to leave us. So he took some stuff from the house and left."

The sheriff whistled through his teeth, remembering. "A woman can't hold a boy's father up to shame him," Benjy's mother had said. Well, the way this worked out, she didn't need to.

"He took the money I got from the cordwood," Benjy said. "I was fixing to buy a turkey tomorrow, all by myself. But he took the money when he went away. There ain't nothing in the house to eat but grits and a few eggs, and Thanksgiving day after tomorrow."

"So you killed a deer," I said.

"It's an old buck and won't hurt the herd none," Benjy said. "I let a couple others go by. I done wrong, but it don't seem right that a man's mother should have to eat grits and eggs for Thanksgiving after a feller made her a promise."

He huddled there, looking up at us. The sheriff did not say anything, and I did not want to say anything, either, but this was the time to say something. There would never be any better time to say the hard things that needed to be said.

"Seems to me," I said, "that there are times when a man has to do something, right enough. The thing he has to decide is—does he do something easy, even if it's wrong, or does he do something right, even if it's hard."

The kid looked at me. It probably wasn't such a long time, but it seemed most of the night.

"Like going to school and living in town," he said, just

a touch of the old curl on his lips. "Reckon that would make everything all right again."

"Seems to me—" I wasn't going to let go of it now— "seems to me that when things been going wrong long enough and far enough, you can't do one right thing and expect everything will be all right again. You have to start kind of gradual, and it's hard. But you have to start."

Benjy looked at me. His eyes were wide, but he wasn't crying anymore. The puppy made a small movement in his arms and he said, "What can we do for Chip?"

The puppy moved again, but he did not try to bite, the way they will when they are hurting badly. He moved his nose up against the boy's face, but he did not lick, either. His eyes came open, and now he was not hurting anymore. He had stopped hurting. The look in his face meant that he was seeing into a far field and he would be there soon and it was all right, except that he was sorry he had not had a chance to learn all the things he was born wanting to know. Then he put his muzzle down very sadly against the boy's hand and closed his eyes and sighed. The boy held him tightly with both arms and put his face against him.

"Benjy," I said, "he's dead now."

"I know," Benjy said. "There's nothing we can do."

"Yes," I said. "Though it's not an easy thing, either. But we can bury him proper. That's the last thing anybody can do for anybody, to bury him proper."

"I know a place," Benjy said. "There's an old apple tree out behind the house. It's back by the foundation of where the big house used to be, before the fire. I can remember when I was a little kid there was a swing there, and my ma used to push me on it. I was a little bit of a kid. I can remember swinging when there was blossoms on it, and later on when there was apples and I'd try to grab one when I was swinging. Once I fell out of the swing trying."

"That sounds like a good place," I said.

The sheriff coughed.

"If you two are fixing to do something with that dog," he said, "I'll dress out the deer and bring it along in the station wagon."

I took the guns and the flashlight, and Benjy walked ahead carrying the dog, the puppy legs dangling awkwardly from his arms. We walked the half mile to the shack and walked past it, back to the old foundation. There was the apple tree, bare-branched and kind of strange in the moonlight. There was a shovel against an outbuilding, and I started digging. There was a little frost in the ground, but after the first couple of inches it went all right.

"I'll help," Benjy said.

"Digging a grave for a friend ain't among the easiest things you can do."

"I want to."

"You don't really have to."

"I helped him all I could, up to now."

"All right."

"After this I can't do anything for him."

"Well, in a way you can," I said. "You want to remember that the only reason we keep dogs is for the help and comfort we get from them. We don't keep a penful of kyoodles just to hear the racket. We keep dogs that are gentlefolk, and we do what we can for them and they do what they can for us, and Chip here tried to do something for you."

Benjy's mother had seen the light and came out of the shack. She had an old shawl over her shoulders. She looked at me and the boy and the dog, her face very still, but she did not say anything. There had been some good things in her life, but I guess there'd been a quantity more of the other kind, and she was always ready for them.

"He done a lot of things for me." Benjy was still talking about the dog.

"Main thing," I said, "he showed that when the time

comes, you do what you have to do. I don't reckon he wanted to charge that buck much. But according to his lights, he had to."

"He didn't have much chance," Benjy said.

"Sometimes you don't get much chance," I said. "And you do it anyway. That's better than when you have the chance and don't even try."

Benjy said, "He showed me something, all right." Then he said, "It's kind of cold to put him in the ground there with nothing to lay on. In the house, he most generally figured out some way to get a old piece of rug or something to lay on. Ma," he said, "do you reckon it would be all right to wrap him up in this old shirt?"

His mother said quietly, "I reckon it would be all right, Son."

So the boy took off his jacket and peeled off the old shirt. His bare skin gleaming in the cold moonlight, he wrapped the puppy in the shirt and put him gently in the bottom of the hole. He did not cry anymore. We filled in the dirt and walked back to the shack. The sheriff was driving my station wagon into the clearing.

Benjy said, "Ma, reckon Uncle Ted would like to have you and me both move into town with him?"

His mother looked at him quickly and sharply, then looked away.

"I reckon he might be right pleased," she said. Her voice was perfectly casual. "I wouldn't be surprised at all, the way things turned out, if he was right tickled."

"Reckon we could do it before school starts, after the holiday vacation?"

"I'll study on it," his mother said. "If you really want to go."

"A man," Benjy said, "does what he has to do, when the time comes." Then he said, "It ain't even a very hard thing to do, Ma, now I got to do it. It ain't like we're leaving the place for good. We can come out here most anytime, and after a while maybe I'll be able to fix things up a little, like they used to be."

He worked up to spit on the ground and said, "What kind of a game preserve would this place make, anyway, and what kind of studying would I have to do for that?"

"That takes a parcel of studying," I said. "Some of us figure we never quite get to the end of studying about wildlife management. But you kind of get used to it."

His mother went past him into the shack. They weren't much for clouding up and raining all over people, the Renfrews weren't.

From inside, she said, "I can offer you lawmen a cup of chicory to warm you."

The sheriff made a face, but I said, "We'd be right proud to join you, ma'am."

The sheriff went on in with Benjy. I said I happened to think of something and went back to the station wagon. There was something I had to put into the lean-to behind the shack. Then I went back inside and we drank a cup of the hot, bitter, black stuff, and after that we left.

On the way back to town the sheriff said, "Well, maybe a brand got saved from the burning, after all."

"You do what you can, but you don't deserve any credit unless you want to count the times you messed things up," I said. "Reckon my average ain't too good. Even this time, it took some burning first."

"It most generally does," the sheriff said. Then he said, "But if that kid's old man shows up again, I'll burn him to where he'll stay burned."

"He won't," I said. "Seems like he played out the string."

We drove quite a distance in silence, then the sheriff turned in the seat to scratch a match on the rear deck.

"Hey," he said. "What happened to that deer?"

I drove another quarter mile. "What deer?" I said.

The sheriff said, "You know good and well what deer. You're supposed to confiscate that deer and turn it over to the welfare people."

"Well," I said. "I do seem to remember that part. But this here deer you're talking about, now—killed out of season, was it?"

"Dang it," the sheriff said righteously, "not only out of season, but by unlawful means, jacklighting and all."

I clucked my tongue.

"Sounds powerful illegal, all right. Was this deer killed by a sidearm, too, instead of a proper shotgun or rifle? A three fifty-seven maybe?"

The sheriff kept an uneasy silence all of a sudden.

"Does seem a little clearer now," I said. "Was this deer killed out of season and with a sidearm, by a real honest-to-John officer of the law, a feller sworn to uphold the statutes?" The sheriff didn't say anything at all. I went on, kind of thoughtfully. "Seems to me if that was the case, I'd probably have to bring all kinds of charges. The governor'd probably hear about it, too. Misfeasance, malfeasance—all them unpleasant words."

"You're letting your imagination run away with you," the sheriff said, kind of grinning. "Like you said, I don't remember any deer."

## *Dion Henderson*

# BROKEN TREATY

We had walked down the beach and around the bay and finally out to where the point stabbed into the lake to watch the ducks come home from the cornfields. While we were watching the ducks we saw Doc's old dog and watched him, too. He was old, incredibly old, more than a hundred years old as you reckon the age of a man, and he walked very carefully on the little stones as though he knew that everything inside him was very fragile and might break if he jarred any of it.

We watched him move down the steps, a big taffy-colored dog, still very handsome, as some golden retrievers are, and at the bottom of the steps he did not hesitate at all but turned after us, tracking easily on the beach. "Old, old," Doc said. "Golden Recollection. I hope I do not grow so old."

"Or if you do, that you grow old as beautifully as Wreck," I added.

"What's the difference?" Doc asked. "You get so terribly old, and then you are at the end of it."

I didn't say anything. Maybe it makes no difference how you get there. Maybe it does. The old dog was still tracking us, not wasting any motion, and down at the far end of the bay he stopped altogether. For a moment I thought he was resting, but he hadn't stopped for that. It was something the wind told him, and he had turned his head out toward the lake.

The ducks were coming in occasionally now, crossing us high up and heading for their rafts in open water, and the bay was rippling lightly in the breeze. Earlier the wind had been stronger from the bluffs, and now the water was flecked with floating oak leaves.

Abruptly the old dog gathered himself and slid into the water, still being very careful but clearly very determined, too.

"Chasing a leaf," Doc said wearily. "And with his rheumatism. It'll take me an hour to rub some life back into him."

But it wasn't a leaf. You do not smell a leaf, and the old dog went into the water because the nose he had by rightful inheritance from Lord Tweedmouth's long-ago bloodhound told him to go. He swam very low in the water and so slowly that it sometimes seemed he did not move at all. Nearly a hundred yards out a leaf that was not a leaf flapped a startled wing and quacked once in alarm as it was engulfed. The old dog then veered toward the nearest shore, which was very close to us. He took a long time, and you could hear him breathing all the way. When he was in shallow water, he stopped and let the water support him until his breathing was even again. Then he came out and started casting for our trail again, and Doc called him.

Wreck came on, wavering a little, and sat down proudly with the crippled duck and held it until Doc said, "Thank you, sir," and put out his hand. The old dog put the bird there and stood up to shake, but he could not quite make it. He tried, looked up with a wry expression on his face as though it did not surprise him greatly, and then lay down on the stones and suddenly was exhausted. I took the duck, and Doc wrapped the big dog in his jacket and carried him all the way home.

"You see what I mean?" Doc said over his shoulder. "What can you do with a dog like this?"

"I don't know," I replied, because I did not want any part of the decision he was trying to make. "I don't know very much about retrievers."

When the old kennel hands begin to talk of memorable dogs, one of the things they remember best is the royal manner—the flashing stride, the relentless courage, the flare of style, and the champion's heart. Such dogs do not always achieve royal standing in the world of dog competitions because they do not always have the chance, but when they do, they know that they do, and they are as proud as a man of the achievement.

Golden Recollection won his bench championship on the main line when the majors were few and far between, and he had finished the campaigning with a sporting-group win. His field work was very distinguished, too, although his best seasons were before the face-to-face competition of the National as it is today. He was aging during the time of the compiled championships, and I suppose you would say he was the dawn of the goldens' day that came in with Midas, who either won or did not win the first real National, and Nitro Express, and the later great ones.

He wasn't Doc's dog, you understand. His registration was dated the year Doc had entered fourth grade, and this summer that they came to the lakeshore together was the year Doc finished his internship. It did not seem possible that a dog's life could span such a time. Most people have to accustom themselves to living through several generations of dogs. But in Wreck's case it was reversed, and he was well along in his second generation of people, because men don't live forever, either.

So Doc and the dog who had been his father's contemporary were living in the same house again, but conditions were changed considerably from the time they had been the famous champion and the schoolboy, and naturally there were many complications. For one thing, Doc got married in the spring before he was quite ready to set up a practice, and he had quite a few problems that were strictly his own. His wife was very pretty and very brave, as any girl has to be who marries a young doctor, and she was very good about the dog, too.

But there is one thing about a handsome and polite dog you pet occasionally when you visit his home, and it is another thing entirely to have a heedless old monarch with all the weakness of that age and condition accept you as his handmaiden. I don't think she complained, then or later, about the obvious nuisance that Wreck was around the house. The first morning I met her, when she and Doc came to the old cottage from the city, I heard something special in the way she looked at the dog and said, "Poor old fellow."

There is a way a woman has of saying things like that; you can tell when you hear the sadness in her voice. She does not say exactly what she means, and maybe she does not even know exactly what she means; but you know, and a dog knows, too, after a while. So I did not become involved any of the times that Doc asked sort of casually, "What do you do with an old dog?" The time I came closest was the day after Wreck went for the duck. It was a cool morning, the dew not quite a frost but glistening very close to it on the shady side of the trees.

Doc and his wife were having breakfast on the porch and called me in for coffee. Wreck was lying where the morning sun streamed in on him, and once I heard him move and looked at him sharply. He was inching his way across the floor to keep fully in the sun, because that was how he had to move, with the chill and dampness of night heavy on the old bones. But he saw me watching him, and though he looked back at me he did not invite help, so I let him alone. Two or three other times he moved the same way, but when I left an hour later the sun had soaked through the caramel-colored hide and the blood was moving. A warm dog is not nearly so old as a cold dog.

Outside, Doc explained, "It hurts his pride if you help him. What are you going to do with a dog like that?"

"It depends on you and it depends on the dog," I said. "And it depends on the association that has developed between you and the way each of you has accepted it and a number of other things that there is no point discussing."

"We've negotiated a treaty," Doc said. "The old guy is happy—I guess he's happy."

And I guess he was, in his way. He did not really feel very bad about being old. He moved carefully always, and on warm, dry afternoons when he had been in the sun quite a while he would play very sedately all by himself. Then he would draw a very clear line to the playing and look at you wryly, and you knew he was up against the boundary he had made for himself. It was a little like being around a famous old athlete who occasionally worked out ever so little, in imitation of himself as a young man, then paused apologetically because he could not in modesty indicate just how beautifully and easily he had done the physical things that hardly anyone could do so well anymore.

And plainly Golden Recollection did not think of himself as a nuisance, not to anybody. Sometimes when he was sleeping on the pier and the sun moved away from him behind the trees he could not move very well, but he was very patient and expected someone would come for him after a while. Someone always did and might say, "Poor old dog," which made a strange, flat look come in his eyes, as though he heard what I heard in the words.

"He earned a lot of things in his time," Doc said. "I guess he figures he earned enough to retire on."

Then it was getting to be time for Doc and his wife to move back to the city to a little apartment, and there got to be a feeling of strain around the cottage. Every time his wife looked at Wreck she looked as though she might cry, and one time Doc told her, "You couldn't take a dog who's been a house dog all that length of time and put him in a boarding kennel. You might as well kill him outright."

When he said that, his wife did start to cry, and I thought it was a pretty good time for me not to be around anymore. Doc walked out with me and we headed along the shore toward my place, but he did not say anything and neither did I. Opposite the point, we stopped for a while and watched the big mergansers working in the bay. Presently there was a rustling in the leaves behind us, and there was Wreck, walking very carefully but coming on just the same.

"Fifteen years ago," Doc said, sounding partly proud and partly exasperated, "my father told Wreck to look after me, and he's still doing it. When I was a kid and wanted to go fishing in the canoe by myself, he used to make me take Wreck with me, and he'd say, 'Look after the kid, Wreck.' And all the time we were fishing, the dog would lie there in the canoe and watch me."

"I remember. He pulled you out once, didn't he?"

"He sure did." Doc grinned a little. "It was in four feet of water, but it was swimming depth for him, so he pulled me out. Pretty near broke my arm in the process, but Dad thought it was fine."

The dog reached us by then and sat down next to Doc and looked at him briefly with those old, old eyes.

"That's the same expression." Doc was almost angry. "He doesn't really give a hoot about me. But the old man said he should look out for me, and he'll do it if he has to live thirty years more."

I guess that pretty well stated the case. Wreck did not really love anyone anymore; he had outlived all his young loves, but he still had a job to do, and he did not propose to quit. You never know what goes on in a dog's head. He will do a thing, and there are various ways to explain it. The best way usually is the simple and instinctive way, but I am not sure it is always right. In the end there is really no way to tell.

The next day I went past Doc's cottage in a boat, well out, but I could see they were taking down screens and putting boxes in the car. I wondered about the dog. It was automatic to think of him at that point, and soon I saw the golden heap lying in the sun in sight of everything or at least in range of ear and nose. When you have dogs for a long time and keep them for the quality they have that is quite beyond compromise, you make many treaties that are hard to keep.

I thought about the dogs and treaties, and I was grateful for the dog in the boat with me. She was one of the German dogs who was far from home and who, knowing she would never see her home again, looked at the world with ice-cold eyes. She did her work marvelously and she gave me puppies who would love passionately and cling hard to life, but she did not offer anything like that and she wouldn't accept it, and I was grateful for her.

But however they are, you do whatever you have to do, and I expected that Doc and his wife would take the old dog with them. Long after dark the two of them came to my door.

"Wreck's gone," Doc blurted out. "We've been looking for hours."

"My boots are in the closet," I said. "Just a minute. What happened?"

"He followed Doc out in the field." His wife had been crying again. "Then he started to come back by himself and got lost."

I stopped putting on my boots. There was an expression on Doc's face.

"All right. What happened?" I asked.

"He left me." Doc's voice was a little hoarse. "The gun misfired, and he looked at me and left me."

"No," his wife said. "You didn't!"

"It seemed like the best thing to do," Doc said. "I didn't plan it. I could have given him an intravenous a lot more easily. But then he'd have known. The way it was, I heard crows tormenting something up in the field, and I took the gun and went back to see what it was. I was away back there watching them, and Wreck came along trailing me. It wasn't a good day for him, and he had a lot of trouble walking. Once he fell down, and I was afraid he couldn't get up again, but he did. He got up to me, breathing very hard and pretty shaky, but he gave me that quick glance, then went on out into the field to see what the crows were doing." Doc was sweating now.

"All of a sudden I thought, Here it is. No fuss, and it won't hurt him at all. And I brought up the gun and pulled the trigger." He wiped his face like a kid, and the sweat followed right after it. "It misfired," he said. "It never did that before. And there he was, looking at me right down the barrel, with the little gold bead right on his head. I put the gun down, and I knew that I couldn't ever do it again and that we'd keep him as long as he was happy. And I called him to come."

"But he didn't come," I prompted.

"No," Doc said. "He looked at me in a way that he'd never looked before, sort of relieved, and took a big breath and walked away from me better than he's walked for months."

"And you thought he was going home?"

"No," Doc said. "I knew he wasn't going home. I knew it, all right."

There was not much else for anyone to say, and there really wasn't any need to look for him that night. In the morning we went out to the field and lined ourselves up with the place that had been home to Wreck for so long and then suddenly was not home anymore, and we walked in a straight line away from it. After a while we came to the water's edge, and there was all that remained of Golden Recollection.

"I wonder what happened," said Doc's wife.

"He did not need to live anymore," I told her. "Your husband knows what that means."

"Yes," Doc said. "Now I do."

## *Walter D. Edmonds*

# MOSES

It was a long climb. The scent was cold, too; so faint that when he found it behind the barn he could hardly trust himself. He had just come back from Filmer's with a piece of meat, and he had sat down behind the barn and cracked it down; and a minute later he found that scent reaching off, faint as it was, right from the end of his nose as he lay.

He had had the devil of a time working it out at first, but up here it was simple enough except for the faintness of it. There didn't appear to be any way to stray off this path; there wasn't any brush, there wasn't any water. Only he had to make sure of it, when even for him it nearly faded out, with so many other stronger tracks overlaying it. His tail drooped, and he stumbled a couple of times, driving his nose into the dust. He looked gaunt when he reached the spot where the man had lain down to sleep.

The scent lay heavier there. He shuffled round over it, sifting the dust with an audible clapping of his nostrils to work out the pattern the man had made. It was hard to do, for the dust didn't take scent decently. It wasn't like any dust he had ever come across, either, being glittery, like mica, and slivery in his nose. But he could tell after a minute how the man had lain, on his back, with his hands under his head, and probably his hat over his eyes to shield them from the glare, which was pretty dazzling bright up this high, with no trees handy.

His tail began to cut air. He felt better, and all of a sudden he lifted up his freckled nose and let out a couple of short yowps and then a good chest-swelled belling. Then he struck out up the steep going once more. His front legs may have elbowed a little, but his hind legs were full of spring, and his tail kept swinging.

That was how the old man by the town entrance saw him, way down below.

The old man had his chair in the shadow of the wall with a black-and-yellow parasol tied to the back of it as an extra insurance against the sun. He was reading the "Arrivals" in the newspaper, the only column that ever interested him; but he looked up sharply when he heard the two yowps and the deep chest notes that, from where he sat, had a mysterious floating quality. It was a little disturbing; but when he saw a dog was the cause he reached out with his foot and shoved the gate hard, so that it swung shut and latched with a sound like a gong. Only one dog had ever come here, and that sound had been enough to discourage him; he had hung round for a while, though, just on the edge, and made the old man nervous. He said to himself that he wasn't going to watch this one, anyway, and folded the paper in halves the way the subway commuter had showed him and went on with the "Arrivals."

After a while, though, he heard the dog's panting coming close and the muffled padding of his feet on the marble gate stone. He shook the paper a little, licked his thumb, and turned over half a sheet and read on through the "Arrivals" into the report of the Committee on Admissions. But then, because he was a curious old man, and kindhearted, noticing that the panting had stopped—and because he had never been quite up to keeping his resolves, except once—he looked out of the gate again.

The dog was sitting on the edge of the gate stone, upright, with his front feet close under him. He was a rusty-muzzled, blue-tick foxhound, with brown ears, and eyes outlined in black like an Egyptian's. He had his nose inside the bars and was working it at the old man.

"Go away," said the old man. "Go home."

At the sound of his voice the hound wrinkled his nose soberly and his tail whipped a couple of times on the gate stone, raising a little star dust.

"Go home," repeated the old man, remembering the dog that had hung around before.

He rattled the paper at him, but it didn't do any good. The dog just looked solemnly pleased at the attention, and a little hopeful, and allowed himself to pant a bit.

This one's going to be worse than the other, the old man thought, groaning to himself as he got up. He didn't know much about dogs anyway. Back in Galilee there hadn't been dogs that looked like this one—just pariahs and shepherds and the occasional Persian greyhound of a rich man's son.

He slapped his paper along the bars; it made the dog suck in his tongue and move back obligingly. Peter unhooked his shepherd's staff from the middle crossbar, to use in case the dog tried to slip in past him, and let himself out. He could tell by the feeling of his bare ankles that there was a wind making up in the outer heavens and he wanted to get rid of the poor creature before it began really blowing round the walls. The dog backed off from him and sat down almost on the edge, still friendly, but wary of the shepherd's staff.

Why can't the poor dumb animal read? thought Peter, turning to look at the sign he had hung on the gatepost.

The sign read:

*TAKE NOTICE*
NO
DOGS
SORCERERS
WHOREMONGERS
MURDERERS
IDOLATERS
LIARS
WILL BE
ADMITTED

When he put it up, he had thought it might save him a lot of trouble; but it certainly wasn't going to help in the case of this dog. He expected he would have to ask the Committee on Admissions to take the matter up; and he started to feel annoyed with them for not having got this animal on the list themselves. It was going to mean a lot of correspondence and probably the Committee would send a memorandum to the Central Office suggesting his retirement again, and Peter liked his place at the gate. It was quiet there, and it was pleasant for an old man to look through the bars and down the path, to reassure the frightened people, and, when there was nothing else to do, to hear the winds of outer heaven blowing by.

"Go away. Go home. Depart," he said, waving his staff;

but the dog only backed down on to the path and lay on his wishbone with his nose between his paws.

Peter went inside and sat down and tried to figure the business out. There were two things he could do. He could notify the Committee of the dog's arrival, or he could give the information to the editor. The Committee would sit up and take notice for once if they found the editor had got ahead of them. It would please the editor, for there were few scoops in Heaven. And then, as luck would have it, the editor himself came down to the gate.

The editor wasn't Horace Greeley or anybody like that, with a reputation in the newspaper world. He had been editor of a little country weekly that nobody in New York, or London, or Paris had ever heard of. But he was good and bursting with ideas all the time. He was now.

"Say, Saint Peter," he said, "I've just had a swell idea about the 'Arrivals' column. Instead of printing all the 'Arrivals' on one side and then the 'Expected Guests' on the other, why not just have one column and put the names of the successful candidates in uppercase type? See?" He shoved a wet impression under Peter's nose and rubbed the back of his head nervously with his ink-stained hand. "Simple, neat, dignified."

Peter looked at the galley and saw how simple it would be for him, too. He wouldn't have to read the names in lowercase at all. It would make him feel a lot better not to know. Just check the uppercase names as they came to the gate.

He looked up at the flushed face of the editor and his white beard parted over his smile. He liked young, enthusiastic men, remembering how hard, once, they had been to find.

"It looks fine to me, Don," he said. "But the Committee won't like losing all that space in the paper, will they?"

"Probably not," the editor said ruefully. "But I thought you could pull a few wires with the Central Office for me."

Peter sighed.

"I'll try," he said. "But people don't pay attention to an old man, much, Don. Especially one who's been in service."

The editor flushed and muttered something about bums.

Peter said gently, "It doesn't bother me, Don. I'm not ashamed of the service I was in." He looked down to his sandals. He wondered whether there was any of the dust of that Roman road left on them after so long a time. Every man has his one great moment. He'd had two. He was glad he hadn't let the second one go. "I'll see what I can do, Don."

It was a still corner, by the gate; and, with both of them silently staring off up the avenue under the green trees to where the butterflies were fluttering in the shrubbery of the public gardens, the dog decided to take a chance and sneak up again.

He moved one foot at a time, the way he had learned to do behind the counter in the Hawkinsville store, when he went prospecting toward the candy counter. These men didn't hear him any more than the checker players in the store did, and he had time to sniff over the gatepost thoroughly. It puzzled him; and as the men didn't take any notice, he gumshoed over to the other post and went over that, too.

It was queer. He couldn't smell dog on either of them and they were the best-looking posts he had ever come across. It worried him some. His tail drooped and he came back to the gate stone and the very faint scent on it, leading beyond the gate, that he had been following so long. He sat down again and put his nose through the bars, and after a minute he whined.

It was a small sound, but Peter heard it.

"That dog," he said.

The editor whirled round, saying, "What dog?" and saw him.

"I was going to let you know about him, only I forgot," said Peter. "He came up a while ago, and I can't get rid of him. I don't know how he got here. The Committee didn't give me any warning and there's nothing about him in the paper."

"He wasn't on the bulletin," said the editor. "Must have been a slip-up somewhere."

"I don't think so," said Peter. "Dogs don't often come here. Only one other since I've been here, as a matter of fact. What kind of a dog is he anyway? I never saw anything like him." He sounded troubled and put out, and the editor grinned, knowing he didn't mean it.

"I never was much of a dog man," he said. "But that's a likely-looking foxhound. He must have followed somebody's scent up here. Hi, boy!" he said. "What's your name? Bob? Spot? Duke?"

The hound lowered his head a little, wrinkled his nose, and wagged his tail across the stone.

"Say," said the editor. "Why don't I put an ad in the 'Lost and Found?' I've never had anything to put there before. But you better bring him in and keep him here till the owner claims him."

"I can't do that," said Peter. "It's against the Law."

"No dogs. Say, I always thought it was funny there were no dogs here. What happens to them?"

"They get removed," said Peter. "They just go."

"That don't seem right," the young editor said. He ruffled his back hair with his hand. "Say, Saint," he asked, "who made this law anyway?"

"It's in Revelation. John wasn't a dog man, as you call it. Back in Galilee we didn't think much of dogs, you see. They were mostly pariahs."

"I see," said the editor. His blue eyes sparkled. "But say! Why can't I put it in the news? And write an editorial? By golly, I haven't had anything to raise a cause on since I got here."

Peter shook his head dubiously.

"It's risky," he said.

"It's a free country," exclaimed the editor. "At least nobody's told me different. Now probably there's nothing would mean so much to the owner of that dog as finding him up here. You get a genuine dog man and this business of passing the love of women is just hooey to him."

"Hooey?" Peter asked quietly.

"It just means he likes dogs better than anything. And this is a good dog, I tell you. He's cold-tracked this fellow, whoever he is, Lord knows how. Besides, he's only one dog, and look at the way the rabbits have been getting into the manna in the public garden. I'm not a dog man, as I said before, but believe me, Saint, it's a pretty thing on a frosty morning to hear a good hound hightailing a fox across the hills."

"We don't have frost here, Don."

"Well," said the editor, "frost or no frost, I'm going to do it. I'll have to work quick to get it in before the forms close. See you later."

"Wait," said Peter. "What's the weather report say?"

The editor gave a short laugh.

"What do you think? Fair, moderate winds, little change in temperature. Those twerps up in the bureau don't even bother to read the barometer anymore. They just play pinochle all day, and the boy runs that report off on the mimeograph machine."

"*I* think there's a wind making up in the outer heavens," Peter said. "When we get a real one, it just about blows the gate stone away. That poor animal wouldn't last a minute."

The editor whistled. "We'll have to work fast." Then suddenly his eyes blazed. "All my life I wanted to get out an extra. I never had a chance, running a weekly. Now, by holy, I will."

He went off up the Avenue on the dead run. Even Peter, watching him go, felt excited.

"Nice dog," he said to the hound; and the hound, at the deep gentle voice, gulped in his tongue and twitched his haunches. The whipping of his tail on the gate stone made a companionable sound for the old man. His beard folded on his chest and he nodded a little.

He was dozing quietly when the hound barked.

It was a deep, vibrant note that anyone who knew dogs would have expected the minute he saw the spring of those ribs; it was mellow, like honey in the throat. Peter woke up tingling with the sound of it and turned to see the hound swaying the whole hind half of himself with his tail.

Then a high loud voice shouted, "Mose, by Jeepers! What the hell you doing here, you poor dumb fool?"

Peter turned to see a stocky, short-legged man who stuck out more than was ordinary, both in front and behind. He had on a gray flannel shirt, and blue denim pants, and a pair of lumberman's rubber packs on his feet, with the tops laced only to the ankle. There was a hole in the front of his felt hat where the block had worn through. He wasn't, on the whole, what you might expect to see walking on that Avenue. But Peter had seen queer people come to Heaven and he said mildly, "Do you know this dog?"

"Sure," said the stout man. "I hunted with him round Hawkinsville for the last seven years. It's old Mose. Real smart dog. He'd hunt for anybody."

"Mose?" said Peter. "For Moses, I suppose."

"Maybe. He could track anything through hell and high water."

"Moses went through some pretty high water," said Peter. "What's your name?"

"Freem Brock. What's yours?"

Peter did not trouble to answer, for he was looking at the hound; and he was thinking he had seen some people come to Heaven's gate and look pleased, and some come and look shy, and some frightened, and some a little shamefaced, and some satisfied, and some sad (maybe with memories they couldn't leave on earth), and some jubilant, and a whole quartet still singing "Adeline" just the way they were when the hotel fell on their necks in the earthquake. But in all his career at the gate he had never seen anyone express such pure, unstifled joy as this rawboned hound.

"Was he your dog?" he asked Freeman Brock.

"Naw," said Freem. "He belonged to Pat Haskell." He leaned his shoulder against the gatepost and crossed one foot over the other. "Stop that yawping," he said to Mose, and Mose lay down, wagging. "Maybe you ain't never been in Hawkinsville," he said to Peter. "It's a real pretty village right over the Black River. Pat kept store there and he let anybody take Mose that wanted to. Pretty often I did. He liked coming with me because I let him run foxes. I'm kind of a fox hunter," he said, blowing out his breath. "Oh, I like rabbit hunting all right, but there's no money in it. . . . Say," he broke off, "you didn't tell me what your name was."

"Peter," said the old man.

"Well, Pete, two years ago was Mose's best season. Seventy-seven fox was shot ahead of him. I shot thirty-seven of them myself. Five crosses and two blacks in the lot. Yes, sir. I heard those black foxes had got away from the fur farm and I took Mose right over there. I made three hundred and fifty dollars out of them hides."

"He was a good dog, then?" asked Peter.

"Best foxhound in seven counties," said Freem Brock. He kicked the gate with his heel in front of Mose's nose and Mose let his ears droop. "He was a fool to hunt. I don't see no fox signs up here. Plenty rabbits in the Park. But there ain't nobody with a gun. I wish I'd brought my old Ithaca along."

"You can't kill things here," said Peter.

"That's funny. Why not?"

"They're already dead."

"Well, I know that. But it beats me how I got here. I never did nothing to get sent to this sort of place. Hell, I killed them farm foxes and I poached up the railroad in the *pre*-serve. But I never done anything bad."

"No," said St. Peter. "We know that."

"I got drunk, maybe. But there's other people done the same before me."

"Yes, Freem."

"Well, what the devil did I get sent here for, Pete?"

"Do you remember when the little girl was sick and the town doctor wouldn't come out at night on a town case, and you went over to town and made him come?"

"Said I'd knock his teeth out," said Freem, brightening.

"Yes. He came. And the girl was taken care of," said Peter.

"Aw," Freem said, "I didn't know what I was doing. I was just mad. Well, maybe I'd had a drink, but it was a cold night, see? I didn't knock his teeth out. He left them in the glass." He looked at the old man. "Jeepers," he said. "And they sent me here for that?"

Peter looked puzzled.

"Wasn't it a good reason?" he asked. "It's not such a bad place."

"Not so bad as I thought it was going to be. But people don't want to talk to me. I tried to talk to an old timber-beast named Boone down the road. But he asked me if I ever shot an Indian, and when I said no he went along. You're the only feller I've seen that was willing to talk to me," he said, turning to the old man. "I don't seem to miss likker up here, but there's nowhere I can get to buy some tobacco."

Peter said, "You don't have to buy things in Heaven."

"Heaven?" said Freeman Brock. "Say, is that what this is?" He looked frightened all at once. "That's what the matter is. I don't belong here. I ain't the kind to come here. There must have been a mistake somewhere." He took hold of Peter's arm. "Listen," he said urgently. "Do you know how to work that gate?"

"I do," said Peter. "But I can't let you out."

"I got to get out."

Peter's voice grew gentler.

"You'll like it here after a while, Freem."

"You'll let me out."

"You couldn't go anywhere outside," Peter said.

Freem looked through the bars at the outer heavens and watched a couple of stars like water lilies floating by below. He said slowly, "We'd go someplace."

Peter said, "You mean you'd go out there with that dog?"

Freem flushed.

"I and Mose have had some good times," he said.

At the sound of his name, Mose's nose lifted.

Peter looked down at the ground. With the end of his shepherd's staff he thoughtfully made a cross and then another overlapping it and put an *X* in the upper left-hand corner. Freem looked down to see what he was doing.

"You couldn't let Mose in, could you, Pete?"

Peter sighed and rubbed out the pattern with his sandal.

"I'm sorry," he said. "The Committee don't allow dogs."

"What'll happen to the poor brute, Pete?"

Peter shook his head.

"If you ask me," Freem said loudly, "I think this is a hell of a place."

"What's that you said?"

Peter glanced up.

"Hello, Don," he said. "Meet Freem Brock. This is the editor of the paper," he said to Freem. "His name's Don."

"Hello," said Freem.

"What was that you said about Heaven being a hell of a place?" asked the editor.

Freem drew a long breath. He took a look at old Mose lying outside the gate with his big nose resting squashed up and sideways against the bottom crossbar; he looked at the outer heavens, and he looked at the editor.

"Listen," he said. "That hound followed me up here. Pete says he can't let him in. He says I can't go out to where Mose is. I only been in jail twice," he said, "but I liked it better than this."

The editor said, "You'd go out there?"

"Give me the chance."

"What a story!" said the editor. "I've got my extra on the Avenue now. The cherubs will be coming this way soon. It's all about the hound, but this stuff is the genuine goods. Guest prefers to leave Heaven. Affection for old hunting dog prime factor in his decision. It's human interest. I tell you it'll shake the Committee. By holy, I'll have an editorial in my next edition calling for a celestial referendum."

"Wait," said Peter. "What's the weather report?"

"What do you think? Fair, moderate winds, little change in temperature. But the Central Office is making up a hurricane for the South Pacific and it's due to go by pretty soon. We got to hurry, Saint."

He pounded away up the Avenue, leaving a little trail of stardust in his wake.

Freem Brock turned on Saint Peter.

"He called you something," he said.

Peter nodded.

"Saint."

"I remember about you now. Say, you're a big shot here. Why can't you let Mose in?"

Peter shook his head.

"I'm no big shot, Freem. If I was, maybe—"

His voice was drowned out by a shrieking up the Avenue.

"Extry! Extry! Special Edition. Read all about it. Dog outside Heaven's Gate. Dog outside . . ."

A couple of cherubs were coming down the thoroughfare, using their wings to make time. When he saw them, Freem Brock started. His shoulders began to itch self-consciously and he put a hand inside his shirt.

"My gracious," he said.

Peter, watching him, nodded.

"Everybody gets them. You'll get used to them after a while. They're handy, too, on a hot day."

"For the love of Pete," said Freem.

"Read all about it! Dog outside Heaven's Gate. Lost Dog waiting outside . . ."

"He ain't lost!" cried Freem. "He never got lost in his life."

" 'Committee at fault,' " read Peter. "Thomas Aquinas isn't going to like that," he said.

"It don't prove nothing," said Freem.

"Mister, please," said a feminine voice. "The editor sent me down. Would you answer some questions?"

"Naw," said Freem, turning to look at a young woman with red hair and a gold pencil in her hand. "Well, what do you want to know, lady?"

The young woman had melting brown eyes. She looked at the hound. "Isn't he cute?" she asked. "What's his name?"

"Mose," said Freem. "He's a cute hound all right."

"Best in seven counties," said Peter.

"May I quote you on that, Saint?"

"Yes," said Peter. "You can say I think the dog ought to be let in." His face was pink over his white beard. "You can say a hurricane is going to pass, and that before I see that animal blown off by it I'll go out there myself—I and my friend Freem. Some say I'm a has-been, but I've got some standing with the public yet."

The girl with red hair was writing furiously with a little gold glitter of her pencil. "Oh," she said.

"Say I'm going out too," said Freem. "I and Pete."

"Oh," she said. "What's your name?"

"Freeman Brock, Route Five, Boonville, New York, U.S.A."

"Thanks," she said breathlessly.

"How much longer before we got that hurricane coming?" asked Freem.

"I don't know," said the old man anxiously. "I hope Don can work fast."

"Extry! Owner found. Saint Peter goes outside with hound, Moses. Committee bluff called. Read all about it."

"How does Don manage it so fast?" said Peter. "It's like a miracle."

"It's science," said Freem. "Hey!" he yelled at a cherub.

They took the wet sheet, unheeding of the gold ink that stuck to their fingers.

"They've got your picture here, Pete."

"Have they?" Peter asked. He sounded pleased. "Let's see."

It showed Peter standing at the gate.

"It ain't bad," said Freem. He was impressed. "You really mean it?" he asked. Peter nodded.

"By cripus," Freem said slowly, "you're a pal."

Saint Peter was silent for a moment. In all the time he had minded Heaven's Gate, no man had ever called him a pal before.

Outside the gate, old Mose got up on his haunches. He was a weather-wise dog, and now he turned his nose outward. The first puff of wind came like a slap in the face, pulling his ears back, and then it passed. He glanced over his shoulder and saw Freem and the old man staring at each other. Neither of them had noticed him at all. He pressed himself against the bars and lifted his nose and howled.

At his howl both men turned.

There was a clear gray point way off along the reach of the wall, and the whine in the sky took up where Mose's howl had ended.

Peter drew in his breath.

"Come on, Freem," he said, and opened the gate.

Freeman Brock hesitated. He was scared now. He could see that a real wind was coming, and the landing outside looked almighty small to him. But he was still mad, and he couldn't let an old man like Peter call his bluff.

"All right," he said. "Here goes."

He stepped out, and Mose jumped up on him, and licked his face.

"Get down, darn you," he said. "I never could break him of that trick," he explained shamefacedly to Peter. Peter smiled, closing the gate behind him with a firm hand. Its gonglike note echoed through Heaven just as the third edition burst upon the Avenue.

Freeman Brock was frightened. He glanced back through the bars, and Heaven looked good to him. Up the Avenue a crowd was gathering. A couple of lanky, brown-faced men were in front. They started toward the gate.

Then the wind took hold of him and he grasped the bars and looked outward. He could see the hurricane coming like an express train running through infinity. It had a noise like an express train. He understood suddenly just how the victim of a crossing accident must feel.

He glanced at Peter.

The old saint was standing composedly, leaning on his staff with one hand, while with the other he drew Mose close between his legs. His white robe fluttered tight against his shanks and his beard bent sidewise like the hound's ears. He had faced lack of faith, in others; what was worse, he had faced it in himself; and a hurricane, after all, was not so much. He turned to smile at Freem. "Don't be afraid," he said.

"Okay," said Freem, but he couldn't let go the gate.

Old Mose, shivering almost hard enough to rattle, reached up and licked Peter's hand.

One of the brown-faced men said, "That's a likely-looking hound. He the one I read about in the paper?"

"Yep," said Freem. He had to holler now.

Daniel Boone said, "Let us timber-beasts come out with you, Saint, will you?"

Peter smiled. He opened the gate with a wave of his hand, and ten or a dozen timber-beasts—Carson, Bridger, Nat Foster—all crowded through, and started shaking hands with him and Freeman Brock. With them was a thin, mild-eyed man.

"My name's Francis," he said to Freem when his turn came. "From Assisi."

"He's all right," Daniel Boone explained. "He wasn't much of a shot, but he knows critters. We better get holt of each other, boys."

It seemed queer to Freem. Here he was going to get blown to eternity and he didn't even know where it was, but all of a sudden he felt better than he ever had in his life. Then he felt a squirming round his legs and there was Mose, sitting on his feet, the way he would on his snowshoes in cold weather when they stopped for a sandwich on earth. He reached down and took hold of Mose's ears.

Let her blow to blazes, he thought.

She blew.

The hurricane was on them. The nose of it went by, sweeping the wall silver. There was no more time for talk. No voices could live outside Heaven's Gate. If a man had said a word, the next man to hear it would have been some poor heathen aborigine on an island in the Pacific Ocean, and he wouldn't have known what it meant.

The men on the gate stone were crammed against the bars. The wind dragged them bodily to the left, and for a minute it looked as if Jim Bridger were going, but they caught him back. There were a lot of the stoutest hands that ever swung an ax in that bunch holding onto Heaven's Gate, and they weren't letting go for any hurricane—not yet.

But Freem Brock could see it couldn't last that way. He didn't care, though. He was in good company, and that was what counted the most. He wasn't a praying man, but he felt his heart swell with gratitude, and he took hold hard of the collar of Mose and felt the license riveted on. A queer thing to think of, a New York State dog license up there. He managed to look down at it, and he saw that it had turned to gold, with the collar gold under it. The wind tore at him as he saw it. The heart of the hurricane was on him now like a million devils' fingers.

Well, Mose, he thought.

And then in the blur of his thoughts a dazzling bright light came down and he felt the gate at his back opening and he and Peter and Francis and Daniel and the boys were all drawn back into the peace of Heaven, and a quiet voice belonging to a quiet man said, "Let the dog come in."

"Jesus," said Freem Brock, fighting for breath, and the quiet man smiled, shook hands with him, and then went over and placed his arm around Peter's shoulders.

They were sitting together, Freem and Peter, by the gate, reading the paper in the morning warmth, and Peter was having an easy time with the editor's new type arrangement. "Gridley," he was reading the uppercase names, "Griscome, Godolphin, Habblestick, Hafey, Hanlon, Hartwell, Haskell . . ."

"Haskell," said Freem. "Not Pat?"

"Yes," said Peter. "Late of Hawkinsville."

"Not in big type?"

"Yes."

"Well, I'll be . . . Well, that twerp. Think of that. Old Pat."

Peter smiled.

"By holy," said Freem. "Ain't he going to be amazed when he finds Mose up here?"

"How's Mose doing?"

"He's all right now," said Freem. "He's been chasing the rabbits. I guess he's up there now. The dew's good."

"He didn't look so well, I thought," Peter said.

"Well, that was at first," said Freem. "You see, the rabbits just kept going up in the trees and he couldn't get a real run on any of them. There, he's got one started now."

Peter glanced up from the paper.

Old Mose was doing a slow bark, kind of low, working out the scent from the start. He picked up pace for a while, and then he seemed to strike a regular knot. His barks were deep and patient.

And then, all of a sudden, his voice broke out—that deep, ringing, honey-throated baying that Freem used to listen to in the late afternoon on the sand hills over the Black River. It went away through the public gardens and out beyond the city, the notes running together and fading and swelling and fading out.

"He's pushing him pretty fast," said Freem. "He's going to get pretty good on these rabbits."

The baying swelled again; it came back, ringing like bells. People in the gardens stopped to look up and smile. The sound of it gave Peter a warm tingling feeling.

Freem yawned.

"Might as well wait here till Pat Haskell comes in," he said.

It was pleasant by the gate, under the black-and-yellow parasol. It made a shade like a flower on the hot stardust. They didn't have to talk, beyond just, now and then, dropping a word between them as they sat.

After a while they heard a dog panting and saw old Mose tracking down the street. He came over to their corner and lay down at their feet, lolling a long tongue. He looked good, a little fat, but lazy and contented. After a minute, though, he got up to shift himself around, and paused as he sat down, and raised a hind leg, and scratched himself behind his wings.

## *Zane Grey*

# DON

It has taken me years to realize the greatness of a dog; and as often as I have told the story of Don—his love of freedom and hatred of men—how I saved his life and how he saved mine—it never was told as I feel it now.

I saw Don first at Flagstaff, Arizona, where arrangements had been made for me to cross the desert with Buffalo Jones and a Mormon caravan en route to Lee's Ferry on the Colorado River. Jones had brought a pack of nondescript dogs. Our purpose was to cross the river and skirt the Vermilion Cliffs, and finally work up through Buckskin Forest to the north rim of the Grand Canyon, where Jones expected to lasso mountain lions and capture them alive. The most important part of our outfit, of course, was the pack of hounds. Never had I seen such a motley assembly of canines. They did not even have names. Jones gave me the privilege of finding names for them.

Among them was a hound that seemed out of place because of his superb proportions, his sleek dark smooth skin, his noble head, and great solemn black eyes. He had extraordinarily long ears, thick-veined and faintly tinged with brown. Here was a dog that looked to me like a thoroughbred. My friendly overtures to him were unnoticed. Jones said he was part bloodhound and had belonged to an old Mexican don in Southern California. So I named him Don.

We were ten days crossing the Painted Desert, and protracted horseback riding was then so new and hard for me that I had no enthusiasm left to scrape acquaintance with the dogs. Still I did not forget and often felt sorry for them as they limped along, clinking their chains under the wagons. Even then I divined that horses and dogs were going to play a great part in my Western experience.

At Lee's Ferry we crossed the Colorado, and I was introduced to the weird and wild canyon country, with its golden-red walls and purple depths. Here we parted with the caravan and went on with Jones's rangers, Jim and Emmet, who led our outfit into such a wonderful region as I had never dreamed of. We camped several days on the vast range where Jones let his buffalo herd run wild. One day the Arizonians put me astride a white mustang that apparently delighted in carrying a tenderfoot. I did not then know what I was soon to learn—that the buffalo always chased this mustang off the range. When I rode up on the herd, to my utter amaze and terror they took after me and—but I am digressing, and this is a dog story.

Once across the river, Jones had unchained the dogs and

let them run on ahead or lag behind. Most of them lagged. Don for one, however, did not get sore feet. Beyond the buffalo range we entered the sage, and here Jones began to train the dogs in earnest. He carried on his saddle an old blunderbuss of a shotgun, about which I had wondered curiously. I had supposed he meant to use it to shoot small game.

Moze, our black-and-white dog, and the ugliest of the lot, gave chase to a jackrabbit.

"Hyar, you Moze, come back!" bawled Jones in stentorian tones. But Moze paid no attention. Jones whipped out the old shotgun and before I could utter a protest he had fired. The distance was pretty far—seventy yards or more—but Moze howled piercingly and came sneaking and limping back. It was remarkable to see him almost crawl to Jones's feet.

"Thar! That'll teach you not to chase rabbits. You're a lion dog!" shouted the old plainsman as if he were talking to a human.

At first I was so astounded and furious that I could not speak. But presently I voiced my feeling.

"Wal, it looks worse than it is," he said, with his keen gray-blue eyes on me. "I'm usin' fine birdshot an' it can't do any more than sting. You see, I've no time to train these dogs. It's necessary to make them see quick that they're not to trail or chase any varmints but lions."

There was nothing for me to do but hold my tongue, though my resentment appeared to be shared by Jim and Emmet. They made excuses for the old plainsman. Jim said, "He shore can make animals do what he wants. But I never seen the dog or hoss that cared two bits for him."

We rode on through the beautiful purple sageland, gradually uphill, toward a black-fringed horizon that was Buckskin Forest. Jackrabbits, cottontails, coyotes and foxes, prairie dogs and pack rats infested the sage and engaged the attention of our assorted pack of hounds. All the gods except Don fell victim to Jones's old blunderbuss; and surely stubborn Moze received a second peppering, this time at closer range. I espied drops of blood upon his dirty white skin. After this it relieved me greatly to see that not even Moze transgressed again. Jones's method was cruel, but effective. He had captured and subdued wild animals since his boyhood. In fact, that had been the driving passion of his life, but no sentiment entered into it.

"Reckon Don is too smart to let you ketch him," Jim once remarked to our leader.

"Wal, I don't know," responded Jones, dubiously. "Mebbe he just wouldn't chase this sage trash. But wait till we jump some deer. Then we'll see. He's got bloodhound in him, and I'll bet he'll run deer. All hounds will, even the best ones trained on bear an' lion."

Not long after we entered the wonderful pine forest the reckoning of Don came as Jones had predicted. Several deer bounded out of a thicket and crossed ahead of us, soon disappearing in the green blur.

"Ahuh! Now we'll see," ejaculated Jones, deliberately pulling out the old shotgun.

The hounds trotted along beside our horses, unaware of the danger ahead. Soon we reached the deer tracks. All the hounds showed excitement. Don let out a sharp yelp and shot away like a streak on the trail.

"Don, come hyar!" yelled Jones, at the same time extending his gun. Don gave no sign he had heard. Then Jones pulled the trigger and shot him. I saw the scattering of dust and pine needles all round Don. He doubled up and rolled. I feared he might be badly injured. But he got up and turned back. It seemed strange that he did not howl. Jones drew his plunging horse to a halt and bade us all stop.

"Don, come back hyar," he called in a loud, harsh, commanding voice.

The hound obeyed, not sneakingly or cringingly. He did not put his tail between his legs. But he was frightened and no doubt pretty badly hurt. When he reached us I saw that he was trembling all over and that drops of blood dripped from his long ears. What a somber sullen gaze in his eyes!

"See hyar," bellowed Jones, "I know you was a deer chaser. Wal, now you're a lion dog."

Later that day, when I had recovered sufficiently from my disapproval, I took Jones to task about this matter of shooting the dogs. I wanted to know how he expected the hounds to learn what he required of them.

"Wal, that's easy," he replied curtly. "When we strike a lion trail I'll put them on it—let them go. They'll soon learn."

It seemed plausible, but I was so incensed that I doubted the hounds would chase anything; and I resolved that, if Jones shot Don again, I would force the issue and end the hunt unless assured there would be no more of such drastic training methods.

Soon after this incident we made camp on the edge of a beautiful glade where a snowbank still lingered and a stream of water trickled down into a green swale. Before we got camp pitched a band of wild horses thudded by, thrilling me deeply. My first sight of wild horses! I knew I should never forget that splendid stallion, the leader, racing on under the trees, looking back at us over his shoulder.

At this camp I renewed my attempts to make friends with Don. He had been chained apart from the other dogs. He ate what I fetched him, but remained aloof. His dignity and distrust were such that I did not risk laying a hand on him then. But I resolved to win him if it were possible. His tragic eyes haunted me. There was a story in them I could not read. He always seemed to be looking afar. On this occasion I came to the conclusion that he hated Jones.

Buckskin Forest was well named. It appeared to be full of deer, the large black-tailed species known as mule deer. This species must be related to the elk. The size and beauty of them, the way they watched with long ears erect and then bounded off as if on springs, never failed to thrill me with delight.

As we traveled on, the forest grew wilder and more beautiful. In the parklike glades a bleached white grass waved in the wind and bluebells smiled wanly. Wild horses outnumbered the deer, and that meant there were some always in sight. A large gray grouse flew up now and then; and most striking of the forest creatures to fascinate me was a magnificent black squirrel, with a long bushy white tail, and tufted ears, and a red stripe down its glossy sides.

We rode for several days through this enchanting wilderness, gradually ascending, and one afternoon we came abruptly to a break in the forest. It was the north rim of the Grand Canyon. My astounded gaze tried to grasp an appalling abyss of purple and gold and red, a chasm too terrible and beautiful to understand all at once. The effect of that moment must have been tremendous, for I have never recovered from it. To this day the thing that fascinates me most is to stand upon a great height—canyon wall, or promontory, or peak—and gaze down into the mysterious colorful depths.

Our destination was Powell's Plateau, an isolated cape jutting out into the canyon void. Jones showed it to me—a distant gold-rimmed black-fringed promontory, seemingly inaccessible and unscalable. The only trail leading to it was a wild-horse hunter's trail, seldom used, exceedingly dangerous. It took us two days over this canyon trail to reach the Saddle—a narrow strip of land dipping down from the Plateau and reaching up to the main rim. We camped under a vast looming golden wall, so wonderful that it kept me from sleeping. That night lions visited our camp. The hounds barked for hours. This was the first chance I had to hear Don. What a voice he had! Deep, ringing, wild, like the bay of a wolf!

Next morning we ascended the Saddle, from the notch

of which I looked down into the chasm still asleep in purple shadows; then we climbed a narrow deer trail to the summit of the Plateau. Here indeed was the grand wild isolated spot of my dreams. Indeed I was in an all-satisfying trance of adventure.

I wanted to make camp on the rim but Jones laughed at me. We rode through the level stately forest of pines until we came to a ravine, on the north side of which lay a heavy bank of snow. This was very necessary, for there was no water on the Plateau. Jones rode off to scout while the rest of us pitched camp. Before we had completed our tasks a troop of deer appeared across the ravine, and motionless they stood watching us. There were big and little deer, blue-gray in color, sleek and graceful, so tame that to me it seemed brutal to shoot at them.

Don was the only one of the dogs that espied the deer. He stood up to gaze hard at them, but he did not bark or show any desire to chase them. Yet there seemed to me to be a strange yearning light in his dark eyes. I had never failed to approach Don whenever opportunity afforded, to continue my overtures of friendship. But now, as always, Don turned away from me. He was cold and somber. I had never seen him wag his tail or whine eagerly, as was common with most hounds.

Jones returned to camp jubilant and excited, as far as it was possible for the old plainsman to be. He had found lion trails and lion tracks, and he predicted a great hunt for us.

The Plateau resembled in shape the ace of clubs. It was perhaps six miles long and three or four wide. The body of it was covered with a heavy growth of pine, and the capes that sloped somewhat toward the canyon were thick with sage and cedar. This lower part, with its numerous swales and ravines and gorges, all leading down into the jungle of splintered crags and thicketed slopes of the Grand Canyon, turned out to be a paradise for deer and lion.

We found many lion trails leading down from the cedared broken rim to the slopes of yellow and red. These slopes really constituted a big country, and finally led to the sheer perpendicular precipices, three thousand feet lower.

Deer were numerous and as tame as cattle on a range. They grazed with our horses. Herds of a dozen or more were common. Once we saw a very large band. Down in the sage and under the cedars and in ravines we found many remains of deer. Jones called these lion-kills. And he frankly stated that the number of deer killed yearly upon the Plateau would be incredible to anyone who had not seen the actual signs.

In two days we had three captive lions tied up to pine saplings near camp. They were two-year-olds. Don and I had treed the first lion; I had taken pictures of Jones lassoing him; I had jumped off a ledge into a cedar to escape another; I had helped Jones hold a third; I had scratches from lion claws on my chaps, and—but I keep forgetting that this is not a story about lions. Always before when I have told it I have slighted Don.

One night, a week or more after we had settled in camp, we sat round a blazing red fire and talked over the hunt of the day. We all had our part to tell. Jones and I had found where a lioness had jumped a deer. He showed me where the lioness had crouched upon a little brushy knoll, and how she had leaped thirty feet to the back of the deer. He showed me the tracks the deer had made—bounding, running, staggering with the lioness upon its back—and where, fully a hundred paces beyond, the big cat had downed its prey and killed it. There had been a fierce struggle. Then the lioness had dragged the carcass down the slope, through the sage, to the cedar tree where her four two-year-old cubs waited. All that we found of the deer were the ragged hide, some patches of hair, cracked bones, and two long ears. These were still warm.

Eventually we got the hounds on this trail and soon put up the lions. I found a craggy cliff under the rim and sat there watching and listening for hours. Jones rode to and fro above me, and at last dismounted to go down to join the other men. The hounds treed one of the lions. How that wild canyon slope rang with barks and bays and yells! Jones tied up this lion. Then the hounds worked up the ragged slope toward me, much to my gratification and excitement. Somewhere near me the lions had taken to cedars or crags, and I strained my eyes searching for them.

At last I located a lion on top of an isolated crag right beneath me. The hounds, with Don and Ranger leading, had been on the right track. My lusty yells brought the men. Then the lion stood up—a long, slender, yellowish cat—and spat at me. Next it leaped off that crag, fully fifty feet to the slope below, and bounded down, taking the direction from which the men had come. The hounds gave chase, yelping and baying. Jones bawled at them, trying to call them off, for what reason I could not guess. But I was soon to learn. They found the lion Jones had captured and left lying tied under a cedar, and they killed it, then took the trail of the other. They treed it far down in the rough jumble of rocks and cedars.

One by one we had ridden back to camp that night, tired out. Jim was the last in and he told his story last. And what was my amazement and fright to learn that all the three hours I had sat upon the edge of the caverned wall, the lioness had crouched on a bench above me. Jim on his way up had seen her, and then located her tracks in the dust back of my position. When this fact burst upon me I remembered how I had at first imagined I heard faint panting breaths near me somewhere. I had been too excited to trust my ears.

"Wal," said Jones, standing with the palms of his huge hands to the fire, "we had a poor day. If we had stuck to Don there'd have been a different story. I haven't trusted him. But now I reckon I'll have to. He'll make the greatest lion dog I ever had. Strikes me queer, too, for I never guessed it was in him. He has faults though. He's too fast. He outruns the other hounds, an' he's goin' to be killed because of that. Someday he'll beat the pack to a mean old Tom lion or a lioness with cubs, an' he'll get his everlastin'. Another fault is, he doesn't bark often. That's bad, too. You can't stick to him. He's got a grand bay, shore, but he saves his breath. Don wants to run an' trail an' fight alone. He's got more nerve than any hound I ever trained. He's too good for his own sake—an' it'll be his death."

Naturally I absorbed all that Buffalo Jones said about dogs, horses, lions, everything pertaining to the West, and I believed it as if it had been gospel. But I observed that the others, especially Jim, did not always agree with our chief in regard to the hounds. A little later, when Jones had left the fire, Jim spoke up with his slow Texas drawl:

"Wal, what does he know about dawgs? I'll tell you right heah, if he hadn't shot Don we'd had the best hound thet ever put his nose to a track. Don is a wild strange hound, shore enough. Mebbe he's like a lone wolf. But it's plain he's been mistreated by men. An' Jones has just made him wuss."

Emmet inclined to Jim's point of view. And I respected this giant Mormon who was famous on the desert for his kindness to men and animals. His ranch at Lee's Ferry was overrun with dogs, cats, mustangs, burros, sheep, and tamed wild animals that he had succored.

"Yes, Don hates Jones and, I reckon, all of us," said Emmet. "Don's not old, but he's too old to change. Still, you can never tell what kindness will do to animals. I'd like to take Don home with me and see. But Jones is right. That hound will be killed."

"Now I wonder why Don doesn't run off from us?" inquired Jim.

"Perhaps he thinks he'd get shot again," I ventured.

"If he ever runs away it'll not be here in the wilds," replied Emmet. "I take Don to be about as smart as any dog ever gets. And that's pretty close to human intelligence. People have to live lonely lives with dogs before they understand them. I reckon I understand Don. He's either loved one master once and lost him, or else he has always hated all men."

"Humph! That's shore an idee," ejaculated Jim, dubiously. "Do you think a dog can feel like that?"

"Jim, I once saw a little Indian shepherd dog lie down on its master's grave and die," returned the Mormon, sonorously.

"Wal, dog-gone me!" exclaimed Jim, in mild surprise.

One morning Jim galloped in, driving the horses pell-mell into camp. Any deviation from the Texan's usual leisurely manner of doing things always brought us up short with keen expectation.

"Saddle up," called Jim. "Shore thar's a chase on. I see a big red lioness up heah. She must have come down out of the tree whar I hang my meat. Last night I had a haunch of venison. It's gone. . . . Say, she was a beauty. Red as a red fox."

In a very few moments we were mounted and riding up the ravine, with the eager hounds sniffing the air. Always overanxious in my excitement, I rode ahead of my comrades. The hounds trotted with me. The distance to Jim's meat tree was a short quarter of a mile. I knew well where it was and, as of course the lion trail would be fresh, I anticipated a fine opportunity to watch Don. The other hounds had come to regard him as their leader. When we neared the meat tree, which was a low-branched oak shaded by thick silver spruce, Don elevated his nose high in the air. He had caught a scent even at a distance. Jones had said more than once that Don had a wonderful nose. The other hounds, excited by Don, began to whine and yelp and run around with noses to the ground.

I had eyes only for Don. How instinct he was with life and fire! The hair on his neck stood up like bristles. Suddenly he let out a wild bark and bolted. He sped away from the pack and like a flash passed that oak tree, running with his head high. The hounds strung out after him and soon the woods seemed full of a baying chorus.

My horse, Black Bolly, well knew the meaning of that medley and did not need to be urged. He broke into a run and swiftly carried me up out of the hollow and through a brown-aisled pine-scented strip of forest to the canyon.

I rode along the edge of one of the deep indentations on the main rim. The hounds were bawling right under me at the base of a low cliff. They had jumped the lioness. I could not see them, but that was not necessary. They were running fast toward the head of this cove, and I had hard work to hold Black Bolly to a safe gait along that rocky rim. Suddenly she shied, and then reared, so that I fell out of the saddle as much as I dismounted. But I held the bridle, and then jerked my rifle from the saddle sheath. As I ran toward the rim I heard the yells of the men coming up behind. At the same instant I was startled and halted by sight of something red and furry flashing up into a tree right in front of me. It was the red lioness. The dogs had chased her into a pine the middle branches of which were on a level with the rim.

My skin went tight and cold and my heart fluttered. The lioness looked enormous, but that was because she was so close. I could have touched her with a long fishing pole. I stood motionless for an instant, thrilling in every nerve, reveling in the beauty and wildness of that great cat. She did not see me. The hounds below engaged all her attention. But when I let out a yell, which I could not stifle, she jerked spasmodically to face me. Then I froze again. What a tigerish yellow flash of eyes and fangs! She hissed. She could have sprung from the tree to the rim and upon me in two bounds. But she leaped to a ledge below the rim, glided along that, and disappeared.

I ran ahead and with haste and violence clambered out upon a jutting point of the rim, from which I could command the situation. Jones and the others were riding and yelling back where I had left my horse. I called for them to come.

The hounds were baying along the base of the low cliff. No doubt they had seen the lioness leap out of the tree. My eyes roved everywhere. This cove was a shallow V-shaped gorge, a few hundred yards deep and as many across. Its slopes were steep with patches of brush and rock.

All at once my quick eye caught a glimpse of something moving up the opposite slope. It was a long red pantherish shape. The lioness! I yelled with all my might. She ran up the slope and at the base of the low wall she turned to the right. At that moment Jones strode heavily over the rough loose rocks of the promontory toward me.

"Where's the cat?" he boomed, his gray eyes flashing. In a moment more I had pointed her out. "Ha! I see. . . . Don't like that place. The canyon boxes. She can't get out. She'll turn back."

The old hunter had been quick to grasp what had escaped me. The lioness could not find any break in the wall, and manifestly she would not go down into the gorge. She wheeled back along the base of this yellow cliff. There appeared to be a strip of bare clay or shale rock against which background her red shape stood out clearly. She glided along, slowing her pace, and she turned her gaze across the gorge.

Then Don's deep bay rang out from the slope to our left. He had struck the trail of the lioness. I saw him running down. He leaped in long bounds. The other hounds heard him and broke for the brushy slope. In a moment they had struck the scent of their quarry and given tongue.

As they started down Don burst out of the willow thicket

at the bottom of the gorge and bounded up the opposite slope. He was five hundred yards ahead of the pack. He was swiftly climbing. He would run into the lioness.

Jones gripped my arm in his powerful hand.

"Look!" he shouted. "Look at that fool hound! . . . Runnin' uphill to get to that lioness. She won't run. She's cornered. She'll meet him. She'll kill him. . . . Shoot her! Shoot her!"

I scarcely needed Jones's command to stir me to save Don, but it was certain that the old plainsman's piercing voice made me tremble. I knelt and leveled my rifle. The lioness showed red against the gray—a fine target. She was gliding more and more slowly. She saw or heard Don. The gunsight wavered. I could not hold steady. But I had to hurry. My first bullet struck two yards below the beast, puffing the dust. She kept on. My second bullet hit behind her. Jones was yelling in my ear. I could see Don out of the tail of my eye. Again I shot. Too high! But the lioness jumped and halted. She lashed with her tail. What a wild picture! I strained—clamped every muscle, and pulled trigger. My bullet struck right under the lioness, scattering a great puff of dust and gravel in her face. She bounded ahead a few yards and up into a cedar tree. An instant later Don flashed over the bare spot where she had waited to kill him, and in another his deep bay rang out under the cedar.

"Treed, by gosh!" yelled Jones, joyfully pounding me on the back with his huge fist. "You saved that fool dog's life. She'd have killed him shore. Wal, the pack will be there pronto, an' all we've got to do is go over an' tie her up. But it was a close shave for Don."

That night in camp Don was not in the least different from his usual somber self. He took no note of my proud proprietorship or my hovering near him while he ate the supper I provided, part of which came from my own plate. My interest and sympathy had augmented to love.

Don's attitude toward the captured and chained lions never ceased to be a source of delight and wonder to me. All the other hounds were upset by the presence of the big cats. Moze, Sounder, Tige, Ranger would have fought these collared lions. Not so Don! For him they had ceased to exist. He would walk within ten feet of a hissing lioness without the slightest sign of having seen or heard her. He never joined in the howling chorus of the dogs. He would go to sleep close to where the lions clanked their chains, clawed the trees, whined and spat and squalled.

Several days after that incident of the red lioness we had a long and severe chase through the brushy cedar forest on the left wing of the Plateau. I did well to keep the hounds within earshot. When I arrived at the end of that run I was torn and blackened by the brush, wet with sweat, and hot as fire. Jones, lasso in hand, was walking round a large cedar under which the pack of hounds was clamoring. Jim and Emmet were seated on a stone, wiping their red faces.

"Wal, I'll rope him before he rests up," declared Jones.

"Wait till—I get—my breath," panted Emmet.

"We shore oozed along this mawnin'," drawled Jim.

Dismounting, I untied my camera from the saddle and then began to peer up into the bushy cedar.

"It's a tom lion," declared Jones. "Not very big, but he looks mean. I reckon he'll mess us up some."

"Haw! Haw!" shouted Jim, sarcastically. The old plainsman's imperturbability sometimes wore on our nerves.

I climbed a cedar next to the one in which the lion had taken refuge. From a topmost fork, swaying to and fro, I stood up to photograph our quarry. He was a good-size animal, tawny in hue, rather gray of face, and a fierce-looking brute. As the distance between us was not far, my situation was as uncomfortable as thrilling. He snarled at me and spat viciously. I was about to abandon my swinging limb when the lion turned away from me to peer down through the branches.

Jones was climbing into the cedar. Low and deep the lion growled. Jones held in one hand a long pole with a small fork at the end, upon which hung the noose of his lasso. Presently he got far enough up to reach the lion. Usually he climbed close enough to throw the rope, but evidently he regarded this beast as dangerous. He tried to slip the noose over the head of the lion. One sweep of a big paw sent pole and noose flying. Patiently Jones made ready and tried again, with similar result. Many times he tried. His patience and perseverance seemed incredible. One attribute of his great power to capture and train wild animals here asserted itself. Finally the lion grew careless or tired, on which instant Jones slipped the noose over its head.

Drawing the lasso tight, he threw his end over a thick branch and let it trail down to the men below. "Wait now!" he yelled and quickly backed down out of the cedar. The hounds were leaping eagerly.

"Pull him off that fork an' let him down easy so I can rope one of his paws."

It turned out, however, that the lion was hard to dislodge. I could see his muscles ridge and bulge. Dead branches cracked, the treetop waved. Jones began to roar in anger. The men replied with strained hoarse voices. I saw the lion drawn from his perch and, clawing the branches, springing convulsively, he disappeared from my sight.

Then followed a crash. The branch over which Jones was lowering the beast had broken. Wild yells greeted my startled ears and a perfect din of yelps and howls. Pandemonium had broken loose down there. I fell more than I descended from that tree.

As I bounded erect I espied the men scrambling out of the way of a huge furry wheel. Ten hounds and one lion comprised that brown whirling ball. Suddenly out of it a dog came hurtling. He rolled to my feet, staggered up.

It was Don. Blood was streaming from him. Swiftly I dragged him aside, out of harm's way. And I forgot the fight. My hands came away from Don wet and dripping with hot blood. It shocked me. Then I saw that his throat had been terribly torn. I thought his jugular vein had been severed. Don lay down and stretched out. He looked at me with those great somber eyes. Never would I forget! He was going to die right there before my eyes.

"Oh, Don! Don! What can I do?" I cried in horror.

As I sank beside Don one of my hands came in contact with snow. It had snowed that morning and there were still white patches in shady places. Like a flash I ripped off my scarf and bound it round Don's neck. Then I scraped up a double handful of snow and placed that in my bandana handkerchief. This also I bound tightly round his neck. I could do no more. My hope left me then, and I had not the courage to sit there beside him until he died.

All the while I had been aware of a bedlam near at hand. When I looked I saw a spectacle for a hunter. Jones, yelling at the top of his stentorian voice, seized one hound after the other by the hind legs and, jerking him from the lion, threw him down the steep slope. Jim and Emmet were trying to help while at the same time they avoided close quarters with that threshing beast. At last they got the dogs off and the lion stretched out. Jones got up, shaking his shaggy head. Then he espied me and his hard face took on a look of alarm.

"Hyar—you're all—bloody," he panted plaintively, as if I had been exceedingly remiss.

Whereupon I told him briefly about Don. Then Jim and Emmet approached and we all stood looking down on the quiet dog and the patch of bloody snow.

"Wal, I reckon he's a goner," said Jones, breathing hard. "Shore I knew he'd get his everlastin'."

"Looks powerful like the lion has aboot got his too," added Jim.

Emmet knelt by Don and examined the bandage round his neck. "Bleeding yet," he muttered, thoughtfully. "You did all that was possible. Too bad! . . . The kindest thing we can do is to leave him here."

I did not question this but I hated to consent. Still, to move him would only bring on more hemorrhage and to put him out of his agony would have been impossible for me. Moreover, while there was life there was hope! Scraping up a goodly ball of snow I rolled it close to Don so that he could lick it if he chose. Then I turned aside and could not look again. But I knew that tomorrow or the following day I would find my way back to this wild spot.

The accident to Don and what seemed the inevitable issue weighed heavily upon my mind. Don's eyes haunted me. I very much feared that the hunt had reached an unhappy ending for me. Next day the weather was threatening and, as the hounds were pretty tired, we rested in camp, devoting ourselves to needful tasks. A hundred times I thought of Don, alone out there in the wild brakes. Perhaps merciful death had relieved him of suffering. I would surely find out on the morrow.

But the indefatigable Jones desired to hunt in another direction next day and, as I was by no means sure I could find the place where Don had been left, I had to defer that trip. We had a thrilling hazardous luckless chase, and I for one gave up before it ended.

Weary and dejected I rode back. I could not get Don off my conscience. The pleasant woodland camp did not seem the same place. For the first time the hissing, spitting, chain-clinking, tail-lashing lions caused me irritation and resentment. I would have none of them. What was the capture of a lot of spiteful vicious cats to the life of a noble dog? Slipping my saddle off, I turned Black Bolly loose.

Then I imagined I saw a beautiful black long-eared hound enter the glade. I rubbed my eyes. Indeed there was a dog coming. Don! I shouted my joy and awe. Running like a boy I knelt by him, saying I knew not what. Don wagged his tail! He licked my hand! These actions seemed as marvelous as his return. He looked sick and weak but he was all right. The handkerchief was gone from his neck but the scarf remained, and it was stuck tight where his throat had been lacerated.

Later, Emmet examined Don and said we had made a mistake about the jugular vein being severed. Don's injury had been serious, however, and without the prompt aid I had so fortunately given he would soon have bled to death. Jones shook his gray old locks and said, "Reckon Don's time hadn't come. Hope that will teach him sense." In a couple of days Don had recovered and on the next he was back leading the pack.

A subtle change had come over Don in his relation to me. I did not grasp it so clearly then. Thought and memory afterward brought the realization to me. But there was a light in his eyes for me which had never been there before.

One day Jones and I treed three lions. The largest leaped and ran down into the canyon. The hounds followed. Jones strode after them, leaving me alone with nothing but a camera to keep those two lions up that tree. I had left horse and gun far up the slope. I protested. I yelled after him, "What'll I do if they start down?"

He turned to gaze up at me. His grim face flashed in the sunlight.

"Grab a club an' chase them back," he replied.

Then I was left alone with two ferocious-looking lions in a piñon tree scarcely thirty feet high. While they heard the baying of the hounds they paid no attention to me, but after that ceased they got ugly. Then I hid behind a bush and barked like a dog. It worked beautifully. The lions grew quiet. I barked and yelped and bayed until I lost my voice. Then they got ugly again! They started down. With stones and clubs I kept them up there, while all the time I was wearing to collapse. When at last I was about to give up in terror and despair I heard Don's bay, faint and far away. The lions had heard it before I had. How they strained! I could see the beating of their hearts through their lean sides. My own heart leaped. Don's bay floated up, wild and mournful. He was coming. Jones had put him on the back trail of the lion that had leaped from the tree.

Deeper and clearer came the bays. How strange that Don should vary from his habit of seldom baying! There was something uncanny in this change. Soon I saw him far down the rocky slope. He was climbing fast. It seemed I had long to wait, yet my fear left me. On and up he came, ringing out that wild bay. It must have curdled the blood of those palpitating lions. It seemed the herald of that bawling pack of hounds.

Don espied me before he reached the piñon in which were the lions. He bounded right past it and up to me with the wildest demeanor. He leaped up and placed his forepaws on my breast. And as I leaned down, excited and amazed, he licked my face. Then he whirled back to the tree, where he stood up and fiercely bayed the lions. While I sank down to rest, overcome, the familiar baying chorus of the hounds floated up from below. As usual they were far behind the fleet Don, but they were coming.

Another day I found myself alone on the edge of a huge cove that opened down into the main canyon. We were always getting lost from one another. And so were the hounds. There were so many lion trails that the pack would split, some going one way, some another, until it appeared each dog finally had a lion to himself.

It was a glorious day. From far below, faint and soft, came

the strange roar of the Rio Colorado. I could see it winding, somber and red, through the sinister chasm. Adventure ceased to exist for me. I was gripped by the grandeur and loveliness, the desolation and loneliness of the supreme spectacle of nature.

Then as I sat there, absorbed and chained, the spell of enchantment was broken by Don. He had come to me. His mouth was covered with froth. I knew what that meant. Rising, I got my canteen from the saddle and poured water into the crown of my sombrero. Don lapped it. As he drank so thirstily I espied a bloody scratch on his nose.

"Aha! A lion has batted you one, this very morning," I cried. "Don—I fear for you."

He rested while I once more was lost in contemplation of the glory of the canyon. What significant hours these on the lonely heights! But then I only saw and felt.

Presently I mounted my horse and headed for camp, with Don trotting behind. When we reached the notch of the cove the hound let out his deep bay and bounded down a break in the low wall. I dismounted and called. Only another deep bay answered me. Don had scented a lion or crossed one's trail. Suddenly several sharp deep yelps came from below, a crashing of brush, a rattling of stones. Don had jumped another lion.

Quickly I threw off sombrero and coat and chaps. I retained my left glove. Then, with camera over my shoulder and revolver in my belt, I plunged down the break in the crag. My boots were heavy soled and studded with hobnails. The weeks on these rocky slopes had trained me to fleetness and surefootedness. I plunged down the sliding slant of weathered stone, crashed through the brush, dodged under the cedars, leaped from boulder to ledge and down from ledge to bench. Reaching a dry streambed, I espied in the sand the tracks of a big lion, and beside them smaller tracks that were Don's. And as I ran I yelled at the top of my lungs, hoping to help Don tree the lion. What I was afraid of was that the beast might wait for Don and kill him.

Such strenuous exertion required a moment's rest now and then, during which I listened for Don. Twice I heard his bay, and the last one sounded as if he had treed the lion. Again I took to my plunging, jumping, sliding descent; and I was not long in reaching the bottom of that gorge. Ear and eye had guided me unerringly for I came to an open place near the main jump-off into the canyon, and here I saw a tawny shape in a cedar tree. It belonged to a big tom lion. He swayed the branch and leaped to a ledge, and from that down to another, and then vanished round a corner of wall.

Don could not follow down those high steps. Neither could I. We worked along the ledge, under cedars, and over huge slabs of rock toward the corner where our quarry had disappeared. We were close to the great abyss. I could almost feel it. Then the glaring light of a void struck my eyes like some tangible thing.

At last I worked out from the shade of rocks and trees and, turning the abrupt jut of wall, I found a few feet of stone ledge between me and the appalling chasm. How blue, how fathomless! Despite my pursuit of a lion I was suddenly shocked into awe and fear.

Then Don returned to me. The hair on his neck was bristling. He had come from the right, from round the corner of wall where the ledge ran, and where surely the lion had gone. My blood was up and I meant to track that beast to his lair, photograph him if possible, and kill him. So I strode onto the ledge and round the point of wall. Soon I espied huge cat tracks in the dust, close to the base. A well-defined lion trail showed there. And ahead I saw the ledge—widening somewhat and far from level—stretch before me to another corner.

Don acted queerly. He followed me, close at my heels. He whined. He growled. I did not stop to think then what he wanted to do. But it must have been that he wanted to go back. The heat of youth and the wildness of adventure had gripped me, and fear and caution were not in me.

Nevertheless my sensibilities were remarkably acute. When Don got in front of me there was something that compelled me to go slowly. Soon, in any event, I should have been forced to that. The ledge narrowed. Then it widened again to a large bench with cavernous walls overhanging it. I passed this safe zone to turn on to a narrowing edge of rock that disappeared round another corner. When I came to this point I must have been possessed, for I flattened myself against the wall and worked round it.

Again the way appeared easier. But what made Don go so cautiously? I heard his growls; still, no longer did I look at him. I felt this pursuit was nearing an end. At the next turn I halted short, suddenly quivering. The ledge ended—and there lay the lion, licking a bloody paw.

Tumultuous indeed were my emotions, yet on that instant I did not seem conscious of fear. Jones had told me never, in close quarters, to take my eyes off a lion. I forgot. In the wild excitement of a chance for an incomparable picture I forgot. A few precious seconds were wasted over the attempt to focus my camera.

Then I heard quick thuds. Don growled. With a start I jerked up to see the lion had leaped or run half the distance. He was coming. His eyes blazed purple fire. They seemed to paralyze me, yet I began to back along the ledge. Whipping out my revolver I tried to aim. But my nerves had undergone such a shock that I could not aim. The gun wobbled. I dared not risk shooting. If I wounded the lion it was certain he would knock me off that narrow ledge.

So I kept on backing, step by step. Don did likewise. He stayed between me and the lion. Therein lay the greatness of that hound. How easily he could have dodged by me to escape along the ledge! But he did not do it.

A precious opportunity presented when I reached the

widest part of the bench. Here I had a chance and I recognized it. Then, when the overhanging wall bumped my shoulder, I realized too late. I had come to the narrow part of the ledge. Not reason but fright kept me from turning to run. Perhaps that might have been the best way out of the predicament. I backed along the strip of stone that was only a foot wide. A few more blind steps meant death. My nerve was gone. Collapse seemed inevitable. I had a camera in one hand and a revolver in the other.

That purple-eyed beast did not halt. My distorted imagination gave him a thousand shapes and actions. Bitter despairing thoughts flashed through my mind. Jones had said mountain lions were cowards, but not when cornered—never when there was no avenue of escape!

Then Don's haunches backed into my knees. I dared not look down but I felt the hound against me. He was shaking yet he snarled fiercely. The feel of Don there, the sense of his courage caused my cold thick blood to burst into hot gushes. In another second he would be pawed off the ledge or he would grapple with this hissing lion. That meant destruction for both, for they would roll off the ledge.

I had to save Don. That mounting thought was my salvation. Physically, he could not have saved me or himself, but this grand spirit somehow pierced to my manhood.

Leaning against the wall, I lifted the revolver and steadied my arm with my left hand, which still held the camera. I aimed between the purple eyes. That second was an eternity. The gun crashed. The blaze of one of those terrible eyes went out.

Up leaped the lion, beating the wall with heavy thudding paws. Then he seemed to propel himself outward, off the ledge into space—a tawny spread figure that careened majestically over and over, down—down—down to vanish in the blue depths.

Don whined. I stared at the abyss, slowly becoming unlocked from the grip of terror. I staggered a few steps forward to a wider part of the ledge and there I sank down, unable to stand longer. Don crept to me, put his head in my lap.

I listened. I strained my ears. How endlessly long seemed that lion in falling! But all was magnified. At last puffed up a sliding roar, swelling and dying until again the terrific silence of the canyon enfolded me.

Presently Don sat up and gazed into the depths. How strange to see him peer down! Then he turned his sleek dark head to look at me. What did I see through the somber sadness of his eyes? He whined and licked my hand. It seemed to me Don and I were more than man and dog. He moved away then round the narrow ledge, and I had to summon energy to follow. Shudderingly, I turned my back on that awful chasm and held my breath while I slipped round the perilous place. Don waited there for me, then trotted on. Not until I had gotten safely off that ledge did I draw a full breath. Then I toiled up the steep rough slope to the rim. Don was waiting beside my horse. Between us we drank the rest of the water in my canteen, and when we reached camp night had fallen. A bright fire and a good supper broke the gloom of my mind. My story held those rugged Westerners spellbound. Don stayed close to me, followed me of his own accord, and slept beside me in my tent.

There came a frosty morning when the sun rose red over the ramparts of colored rock. We had a lion running before the misty shadows dispersed from the canyon depths.

The hounds chased him through the sage and cedar into the wild brakes of the north wing of the Plateau. This lion must have been a mean old tom for he did not soon go down the slopes.

The particular section he at last took refuge in was impassable for man. The hounds gave him a grueling chase, then one by one they crawled up, sore and thirsty. All but Don!

He did not come. Jones rolled out his mighty voice, which pealed back in mocking hollow echoes. Don did not come. At noonday Jones and the men left for camp with the hounds.

I remained. I had a vigil there on the lofty rim, alone, where I could peer down the yellow-green slope and beyond to the sinister depths. It was a still day. The silence was overpowering. When Don's haunting bay floated up it shocked me. At long intervals I heard it, fainter and fainter. Then no more!

Still I waited and watched and listened. Afternoon waned. My horse neighed piercingly from the cedars. The sinking sun began to fire the Pink Cliffs of Utah, and then the hundred miles of immense chasm over which my charmed gaze held dominion. How lonely, how terrifying that stupendous rent in the earth! Lion and hound had no fear. But the thinking, feeling man was afraid. What did they mean—this exquisitely hued and monstrous canyon—the setting sun—the wildness of a lion, the grand spirit of a dog—and the wondering sadness of a man?

I rode home without Don. Half the night I lay awake waiting, hoping. But he did not return by dawn, nor through that day. He never came back.

## *D. H. Lawrence*

# REX

Since every family has its black sheep, it almost follows that every man must have a sooty uncle. Lucky if he hasn't two. However, it is only with my mother's brother that we are concerned. She had loved him dearly when he was a little blond boy. When he grew up black, she was always vowing she would never speak to him again. Yet when he put in an appearance, after years of absence, she invariably received him in a festive mood, and was even flirty with him.

He rolled up one day in a dogcart, when I was a small boy. He was large and bullet-headed and blustering, and this time, sporty. Sometimes he was rather literary, sometimes colored with business. But this time he was in checks, and was sporty. We viewed him from a distance.

The upshot was, would we rear a pup for him. Now, my mother detested animals about the house. She could not bear the mix-up of human with animal life. Yet she consented to bring up the pup.

My uncle had taken a large, vulgar public house in a large and vulgar town. It came to pass that I must fetch the pup. Strange for me, a member of the Band of Hope, to enter the big, noisy, smelly plate-glass-and-mahogany public house. It was called The Good Omen. Strange to have my uncle towering over me in the passage, shouting, "Hello, Johnny, what d'yer want?" He didn't know me. Strange to think he was my mother's brother, and that he had his bouts when he read Browning aloud with emotion and éclat.

I was given tea in a narrow, uncomfortable sort of living-room, half kitchen. Curious that such a palatial pub should show such miserable private accommodations, but so it was. There was I, unhappy, and glad to escape with the soft fat pup. It was wintertime, and I wore a big-flapped black overcoat, half cloak. Under the cloak sleeves I hid the puppy, who trembled. It was Saturday, and the train was crowded, and he whimpered under my coat. I sat in mortal fear of being hauled out for traveling without a dog ticket. However, we arrived, and my torments were for nothing.

The others were wildly excited over the puppy. He was small and fat and white, with a brown-and-black head: a fox terrier. My father said he had a lemon head—some such mysterious technical phraseology. It wasn't lemon at all, but colored like a field bee. And he had a black spot at the root of his spine.

It was Saturday night—bath night. He crawled on the hearthrug like a fat white teacup, and licked the bare toes that had just been bathed.

"He ought to be called Spot," said one. But that was too ordinary. It was a great question, what to call him.

"Call him Rex—the King," said my mother, looking down on the fat, animated little teacup, who was chewing my sister's little toe and making her squeal with joy and tickles. We took the name in all seriousness.

"Rex—the King!" We thought it was just right. Not for years did I realize that it was a sarcasm on my mother's part. She must have wasted some twenty years or more of irony on our incurable naïveté.

It wasn't a successful name, really. Because my father, and all the people in the street, failed completely to pronounce the monosyllable Rex. They all said Rax. And it always distressed me. It always suggested to me seaweed, and rack-and-ruin. Poor Rex!

We loved him dearly. The first night we woke to hear him weeping and whinnying in loneliness at the foot of the stairs. When it could be borne no more, I slipped down for him, and he slept under the sheets.

"I won't have that little beast in the beds. Beds are not for dogs," declared my mother callously.

"He's as good as we are!" we cried, injured.

"Whether he is or not, he's not going in the beds."

I think now my mother scorned us for our lack of pride. We were a little infra dig, we children.

The second night, however, Rex wept the same and in the same way was comforted. The third night we heard our father plod downstairs, heard several slaps administered to the yelping, dismayed puppy, and heard the amiable, but to us heartless, voice saying "Shut it then! Shut thy noise, 'st hear? Stop in thy basket, stop there!"

"It's a shame!" we shouted in muffled rebellion, from the sheets.

"I'll give you shame if you don't hold your noise and go to sleep," called our mother from her room. Whereupon we shed angry tears and went to sleep. But there was a tension.

"Such a houseful of idiots would make me detest the little beast, even if he was better than he is," said my mother.

But as a matter of fact, she did not detest Rexie at all. She only had to pretend to do so, to balance our adoration. And in truth, she did not care for close contact with animals. She was too fastidious. My father, however, would take on a real dog's voice, talking to the puppy: a funny, high, singsong falsetto which he seemed to produce at the top of his head. " 'S a pretty little dog! 'S a pretty little doggy! Ay! Yes! He is, yes! Wag thy strunt, then! Wag thy strunt, Raxie! Ha-ha! Nay, tha munna—" This last as the puppy, wild with excitement at the strange falsetto voice, licked my father's nostrils and bit my father's nose with his sharp little teeth.

" 'E makes blood come," said my father.

"Serves you right for being so silly with him," said my mother. It was odd to see her as she watched the man, my father, crouching and talking to the little dog and laughing strangely when the little creature bit his nose and tousled his beard. What does a woman think of her husband at such a moment?

My mother amused herself over the names we called him.

"He's an angel—he's a little butterfly—Rexie, my sweet!"

"Sweet! A dirty little object!" interpolated my mother. She and he had a feud from the first. Of course he chewed boots and worried our stockings and swallowed our garters. The moment we took off our stockings he would dart away with one, we after him. Then as he hung, growling vociferously, at one end of the stocking, we at the other, we would cry:

"Look at him, Mother! He'll make holes in it again." Whereupon my mother darted at him and spanked him sharply.

"Let go, sir, you destructive little fiend."

But he didn't let go. He began to growl with real rage, and hung on viciously. Mite as he was, he defied her with a manly fury. He did not hate her, nor she him. But they had one long battle with one another.

"I'll teach you, my jockey! Do you think I'm going to spend my life darning after your destructive little teeth! I'll show you if I will!"

But Rexie only growled more viciously. They both became really angry, whilst we children expostulated earnestly with both. He would not let her take the stocking from him.

"You should tell him properly, Mother. He won't be driven," we said.

"I'll drive him further than he bargains for. I'll drive him out of my sight for ever, that I will," declared my mother, truly angry. He would put her into a real temper, with his tiny, growling defiance.

"He's sweet! A Rexie, a little Rexie!"

"A filthy little nuisance! Don't think I'll put up with him."

And to tell the truth, he was dirty at first. How could he be otherwise, so young! But my mother hated him for it. And perhaps this was the real start of their hostility. For he lived in the house with us. He would wrinkle his nose and show his tiny dagger teeth in fury when he was thwarted, and his growls of real battle-rage against my mother rejoiced us as much as they angered her. But at last she caught him in flagrante. She pounced on him, rubbed his nose in the mess, and flung him out into the yard. He yelped with shame and disgust and indignation. I shall never forget the sight of him as he rolled over, then tried to turn his head away from the disgust of his own muzzle, shaking his little snout with a sort of horror, and trying to sneeze it off. My sister gave a yell of despair, and dashed out with a rag and a pan of water, weeping wildly. She sat in the middle of the yard with the befouled puppy, and shedding bitter tears, she wiped him and washed him clean. Loudly she reproached my mother. "Look how much bigger you are than he is. It's a shame, it's a shame!"

"You ridiculous little lunatic, you've undone all the good it would do him, with your soft ways. Why is my life made a curse with animals! Haven't I enough as it is—"

There was a subdued tension afterward. Rex was a little white chasm between us and our parent.

He became clean. But then another tragedy loomed. He must be docked. His floating puppy tail must be docked short. This time my father was the enemy. My mother agreed with us that it was an unnecessary cruelty. But my father was adamant. "The dog'll look a fool all his life, if he's not docked." And there was no getting away from it. To add to the horror, poor Rex's tail must be *bitten* off. Why bitten? we asked, aghast. We were assured that biting was the only way. A man would take the little tail and just nip it through with his teeth, at a certain joint. My father lifted his lips and bared his incisors, to suit the description. We shuddered. But we were in the hands of fate.

Rex was carried away, and a man called Rowbotham bit off the superfluity of his tail in the Nags Head, for a quart of best and bitter. We lamented our poor diminished puppy, but agreed to find him more manly and *comme il faut.* We should always have been ashamed of his little whip of a tail if it had not been shortened. My father said it had made a man of him.

Perhaps it had. For now his true nature came out. And his true nature, like so much else, was dual. First he was a fierce, canine little beast, a beast of rapine and blood. He longed to hunt, savagely. He lusted to set his teeth in his prey. It was no joke with him. The old canine Adam stood first in him, the dog with fangs and glaring eyes. He flew at us when we annoyed him. He flew at all intruders, particularly the postman. He was almost a peril to the neighborhood. But not quite. Because close second in his nature stood that fatal need to love, the *besoin d'aimer* which at last makes an end of liberty. He had a terrible, terrible necessity to love, and this trammeled the native, savage hunting beast which he was. He was torn between two great impulses: the native impulse to hunt and kill, and the strange, secondary, supervening impulse to love and obey. If he had been left to my father and mother, he would have run wild and got himself shot. As it was, he loved us children with a fierce, joyous love. And we loved him.

When we came home from school we would see him standing at the end of the entry, cocking his head wistfully at the open country in front of him, and meditating whether to be off or not: a white, inquiring little figure, with green savage freedom in front of him. A cry from a far distance from one of us, and like a bullet he hurled himself down the road, in a mad game. Seeing him coming, my sister invariably turned and fled, shrieking with delighted terror. And he would leap straight up her back, and bite her and tear her clothes. But it was only an ecstasy of savage love, and she knew it. She didn't care if he tore her pinafores. But my mother did.

My mother was maddened by him. He was a little demon. At the least provocation, he flew. You had only to sweep the floor, and he bristled and sprang at the broom. Nor would he let go. With his scruff erect and his nostrils snorting rage, he would turn up the whites of his eyes at my mother as she wrestled at the other end of the broom. "Leave go, sir, leave go!" She wrestled and stamped her foot, and he answered with horrid growls. In the end it was she who had to let go. Then she flew at him, and he flew at her. All the time we had him he was within a hairsbreadth of savagely biting her. And she knew it. Yet he always kept sufficient self-control.

We children loved his temper. We would drag the bones from his mouth, and put him into such paroxysms of rage that he would twist his head right over and lay it on the ground upside down, because he didn't know what to do with himself, the savage was so strong in him and he must fly at us. "He'll fly at your throat one of these days," said my father. Neither he nor my mother dared have touched Rex's bone. It was enough to see him bristle and roll the whites of his eyes when they came near. How near he must have been to driving his teeth right into us cannot be told. He was a horrid sight snarling and crouching at us. But we only laughed and rebuked him. And he would whimper in the sheer torment of his need to attack us.

He never did hurt us. He never hurt anybody, though the neighborhood was terrified of him. But he took to hunting. To my mother's disgust, he would bring large dead bleeding rats and lay them on the hearthrug, and she had to take them up on a shovel. For he would not remove them. Occasionally he brought a mangled rabbit, and sometimes, alas, fragmentary poultry. We were in terror of prosecution. Once he came home bloody and feathery and rather sheepish-looking. We cleaned him and questioned him and abused him. Next day we heard of six dead ducks. Thank heaven no one had seen him.

But he was disobedient. If he saw a hen he was off, and calling would not bring him back. He was worst of all with my father, who would take him for walks on Sunday morning. My mother would not walk a yard with him. Once, walking with my father, he rushed off at some sheep in a field. My father yelled in vain. The dog was at the sheep, and meant business. My father crawled through the hedge, and was upon him in time. And now the man was in a paroxysm of rage. He dragged the little beast into the road and thrashed him with a walking stick.

"Do you know you're thrashing that dog unmercifully?" said a passerby.

"Ay, an' mean to," shouted my father.

The curious thing was that Rex did not respect my father any the more for the beatings he had from him. He took much more heed of us children, always.

But he let us down also. One fatal Saturday he disappeared. We hunted and called, but no Rex. We were bathed, and it was bedtime, but we would not go to bed. Instead we sat in a row in our nightdresses on the sofa, and wept without stopping. This drove our mother mad.

"Am I going to put up with it? Am I? And all for that hateful little beast of a dog! He shall go! If he's not gone now, he shall go."

Our father came in late, looking rather queer, with his hat over his eye. But in his staccato tippled fashion he tried to be consoling.

"Never mind, my duckie, I s'll look for him in the morning."

Sunday came—oh, such a Sunday. We cried, and didn't eat. We scoured the land, and for the first time realized how empty and wide the earth is when you're looking for something. My father walked for many miles—all in vain. Sunday dinner, with rhubarb pudding, I remember, and an atmosphere of abject misery that was unbearable.

"Never," said my mother, "never shall an animal set foot in this house again, while I live. I knew what it would be! I knew."

The day wore on, and it was the black gloom of bedtime, when we heard a scratch and an impudent little whine at the door. In trotted Rex, mud-black, disreputable, and impudent. His air of offhand "How d'ye do!" was indescribable. He trotted round with *suffisance,* wagging his tail as if to say, "Yes, I've come back. But I didn't need to. I can carry on remarkably well by myself." Then he walked to his water, and drank noisily and ostentatiously. It was rather a slap in the eye for us.

He disappeared once or twice in this fashion. We never

knew where he went. And we began to feel that his heart was not so golden as we had imagined.

But one fatal day reappeared my uncle and the dogcart. He whistled to Rex, and Rex trotted up. But when he wanted to examine the lusty, sturdy dog, Rex became suddenly still, then sprang free. Quite jauntily he trotted round—but out of reach of my uncle. He leaped up, licking our faces, and trying to make us play.

"Why, what ha' you done wi' the dog—you've made a fool of him. He's softer than grease. You've ruined him. You've made a damned fool of him," shouted my uncle.

Rex was captured and hauled off to the dogcart and tied to the seat. He was in a frenzy. He yelped and shrieked and struggled, and was hit on the head, hard, with the butt end of my uncle's whip, which only made him struggle more frantically. So we saw him driven away, our beloved Rex, frantically, madly fighting to get to us from the high dogcart, and being knocked down, whilst we stood in the street in mute despair.

After which, black tears, and a little wound which is still alive in our hearts.

I saw Rex only once again, when I had to call just once at The Good Omen. He must have heard my voice, for he was upon me in the passage before I knew where I was. And in the instant I knew how he loved us. He really loved us. And in the same instant there was my uncle with a whip, beating and kicking him back, and Rex cowering, bristling, snarling.

My uncle swore many oaths, how we had ruined the dog forever, made him vicious, spoiled him for showing purposes, and been altogether a pack of mard-soft fools not fit to be trusted with any dog but a gutter mongrel.

Poor Rex! We heard his temper was incurably vicious, and he had to be shot.

And it was our fault. We had loved him too much, and he had loved us too much. We never had another pet.

It is a strange thing, love. Nothing but love has made the dog lose his wild freedom, to become the servant of man. And this very servility or completeness of love makes him a term of deepest contempt—"You dog!"

We should not have loved Rex so much, and he should not have loved us. There should have been a measure. We tended, all of us, to overstep the limits of our own natures. He should have stayed outside human limits, we should have stayed outside canine limits. Nothing is more fatal than the disaster of too much love. My uncle was right, we had ruined the dog.

My uncle was a fool, for all that.

## *Booth Tarkington*

# BLUE MILK

Mr. and Mrs. Stone, little Orvie's parents, should not be blamed for a special prejudice they had. After all, they were only a young couple, took pride in the neatness of their house, didn't wish to incur bills for reupholstering furniture, and both were fond of Kitty, Mrs. Stone's cat. They loved their child more than they did Kitty or their furniture, no question; nevertheless, their steadfast refusal to add a pup to the family is comprehensible.

Orvie had more than a longing for a pup, he had a determination to possess one, gave his father and mother little rest from the topic, and did all he could to impose his will upon theirs. Their great question had thus become whether it would be worse to have a pup or to have Orvie go on everlastingly asking for one. Then suddenly, without warning, he stopped.

Overnight he ceased to entreat, eschewed the subject completely, and yet was cheerful. This change in him was welcomed by his father; but his mother, who, of course, saw more of Orvie, could not feel it to be natural. She perceived a strangeness in the matter, something morbid, especially as the alteration was accompanied by peculiar manifestations. Disturbed, she spoke to her husband apprehensively.

"Nonsense!" he said. "Let's be grateful for a little peace and thank heaven he's got pups out of his head at last—at least for a little while! Home seems like a different place to me; I'd almost forgotten it could be restful. Two whole days—and he hasn't once asked for a pup! I suppose it's too soon to hope; but maybe—maybe—maybe—oh, maybe he's forgotten pups altogether!"

"No." She shook her head. "You haven't watched him. Really it's very queer. Haven't you even noticed these peculiar noises he's making?"

"What peculiar noises?" Mr. Stone, preparing to leave the breakfast table, moved back his chair, but remained seated. "When does he make 'em?"

"Why, almost any time. He was making some just a few minutes ago before he finished his breakfast, and he made some more in the hall after he left the table. Didn't you notice?"

"Notice? I thought he was trying to hum some terrible kind of whining tune and not succeeding. Usually when children try to sing, they do make peculiar—"

"No," Mrs. Stone interrupted seriously. "He wasn't singing; he was making noises like a pup's whining and barking—at least he was trying to. He does it all the time. I haven't told you what happened last night when I put him to bed, because you didn't get home till so late, how could I? I don't even know what time you finally did get home, and really I think when you feel you have to go to these stag card parties all the time—"

"The first!" her husband said sternly. "The first since way last Easter—the only one in five months! Listen. You were talking about what happened when you put Orvie to bed last night. Can't you stick to the subject? Did he ask for a pup again?"

"No. He did the strangest thing I ever knew him to do. Right in the middle of his prayers, kneeling by the bed, he began to bark."

"What?"

"He did," Mrs. Stone insisted. "He'd just said, 'Bless Mamma and Papa' and then he made a noise like this: 'Muff! Muff! Muff!' " Untalented in mimicry, she gave a squeaky imitation of the sounds her son had made. "Yes, he seemed to be barking, or trying to, the way a very young pup does. Then he got into bed and did it some more."

Mr. Stone laughed. "I don't see anything very—"

"Don't you? Wait. I haven't told you the rest of it. After I'd put out the light and gone to my own room, I heard him doing it again; and then a little while later he began whining like a pup. He kept it up so long that I went back to his room and asked him what was the matter. He just said, 'Nothing, Mamma' and then made the whining sound again. I told him to stop doing that and go to sleep, and the minute I was out of the room he began again; and not until I opened the door and said 'Orvie!' did he stop. What's more, I'd heard him making sounds like that every now and then all yesterday. What do you think of it?"

"Nothing. Children often imitate animals; it's kind of an instinct. You hear 'em meowing or barking or—"

"No," Mrs. Stone said. "Not the way Orvie's doing it. There are times when he sounds almost exactly like a real pup.

He—" She paused, lifted a warning hand, and nodded her head toward the open window. "Listen!"

Her husband listened, and then, rising, went to the window and looked out. Upon the cement path just below, his son was passing round the house on his way to the backyard and apparently amusing himself as he went by barking and whining realistically in a small but accurately puplike voice. At the same time he seemed to be scratching himself intimately upon the body; for his right hand and forearm were thrust within the breast of his polka-dotted shirtwaist, so that bulk and motion were visible in that locality. Disregarding this scratching, which, though it seemed vigorous, appeared to have no significance, Mr. Stone laughed again.

"Nonsense!" he said. "Orvie's just playing at something or other in his own imagination. Likely enough he's seen or heard some ventriloquist at a movie theater and maybe he's trying to learn to be one himself. Children imitate frogs and cows and dogs and cats and ventriloquists and—"

"No." Mrs. Stone remained serious. "There's something different about this and I'm afraid it might be getting deep-seated—something very peculiar."

Evidently she had a theory, or the beginnings of one; but her husband did not press her to explain it, and, more amused than disquieted, went out to the small garage in the rear of the yard, got into his car, and set forth for his morning's work in good spirits. Little Orvie immediately came from the vicinity of the alley gate, where he had been lurking, entered the garage, closed the sliding door, smiled happily, and began to stroke the front of his polka-dotted waist, which still bulked and moved, though he had withdrawn his hand and forearm from within it.

"Good ole Ralph," he said affectionately. "Good ole Ralphie!"

One button of the polka-dotted waist was already unbuttoned, so to speak; Orvie unbuttoned two more and there promptly emerged upon his front the small black bright-eyed head and immature whiskers of a somewhat Scottish-seeming very young pup.

"Good ole Ralphie!" Orvie said, and fondly placed the pup upon the floor.

Then he went to the garage window and looked forth toward the house. Corbena, the colored cook, had just put a pan upon the top step of the rear veranda, Kitty's morning milk, though Kitty himself had not yet arrived from a night's excursion out amongst 'em, a too-frequent habit of his. Corbena retired within the kitchen, leaving the milk exposed, and little Orvie, opening a closet in the garage, brought therefrom two empty tomato cans.

One of these he half filled with fair water at a spigot, and the other he left empty; then he tenderly placed Ralph in a smallish wooden box inside the closet. This box was comfortable for the occupant, having been made soft and warm with rags and straw, and, though Orvie closed down its hinged lid securely, there were holes bored through the wood, here and there, so that the interior air remained, if not precisely fresh, at least breathable. For greater security, Orvie closed the closet door upon that precious box; then, with his two cans, he went forth, and, keeping an eye upon the screen door of the kitchen, made a chemical alteration of Kitty's morning milk.

When he returned to the garage, the tomato can that had held water was empty; but the other contained milk, and Ralph, released from box and closet, enjoyed it. Afterward he was replaced in the open box, and little Orvie sat beside it upon the floor of the closet and stroked Ralph from nose to tail repeatedly, shook hands with Ralph gently, opened Ralph's mouth, looked long within, and then delicately examined the interiors of both Ralph's ears.

During this orgy of ineffable possession, little Orvie should have been painted by Sir Joshua Reynolds or even by

Sir Thomas Lawrence, who carried further than did Sir Joshua the tradition that children at times glow with an unearthly sweetness surpassing the loveliness of flowers. Little Orvie, intrinsically, was anything but a beautiful child; but if Sir Joshua or Sir Thomas had painted him as he was at this moment, modernists would have execrated the portrait for its prettiness.

The intricate insides of Ralph's ears added an element to little Orvie's expression, the element of pride; and he shone with that radiance of young motherhood in discovery that the firstborn is not only alive but consists of incredible structural miracles. Into little Orvie there entered the conviction that Ralph, gloriously his own, was incomparably the most magnificently constructed as well as the strongest, handsomest, best-blooded and most unconquerable dog in the whole world.

Such convictions take little account of facts; Orvie was of course not affected by the circumstance that Ralph was a dubious stray, an outcast wandering loosely upon the very streets a few days earlier. In regard to another fact or circumstance, moreover, little Orvie's conviction was likewise obtuse. Ralph, in reality, was a girl; but Orvie had no more doubt that Ralph was a boy than he had that he himself was a boy. His mind couldn't have entertained for one moment a question upon the matter, and, to avoid unnecessary confusion, it seems best for the rest of us to adopt Orvie's view, to regard Ralph in that light and think of her as "he"—at least whenever that is not impossible.

Suddenly the beauteousness of Orvie's expression vanished; he became alert, and his hand, pausing, permitted Ralph's left ear to become less inside out and return to its customary posture. Two voices were heard from without, a little distant; one was Kitty's and the other Corbena's. Kitty meowed clearly and persistently, and Corbena responded with sympathetic inquiries, such as are addressed to one in trouble. Orvie closed the lid upon little Ralph, stepped out of the closet, closed it, too, went to the door of the garage, opened it slightly, and looked toward the house. His mother had just joined Corbena and Kitty upon the back veranda.

"Yes'm," Corbena was saying. "Kitty ack thataway right along lately, mew and meow breakfast and supper, too, and don' look right to me—Kitty kind o' gaunt-lookin'. Then look at that milk, gone and done the same thing again. Look to me like the minute I pour it in the pan it up and turn bluish on me, so Kitty won't take more'n just a li'l some of it and commence meowin' and mewin'. I thought maybe somep'n in the pan do it, so I changed pans; but no, ma'am, there that milk bluish again as ever!"

"Poor Kitty!" Mrs. Stone said. "She does seem to look rather thin. Corbena, are you sure the milk you put in the pan was—" She paused, and, instead of continuing her thought about the milk, stared in troubled fascination at her son, who was approaching from the garage.

Little Orvie, walking slowly, had the air of an absent-minded stroller concerned with the faraway. He did not look toward his mother, or Corbena, or Kitty, seemed unaware of them and in a muse. At the same time, however, he allowed his lips to move slightly in the production of a dreamy sort of barking and whining: "Muff! Muff! Muff! Um-oo-ee! Um-oo-ee! Um-oo-ee!"

Kitty continued to meow. Mrs. Stone and Corbena, saying nothing, stared at little Orvie.

"Muff! Muff! Muff!" he said dreamily. "Um-oo-ee! Um-oo-ee! Um-oo-ee!"

Then, continuing his apparently absentminded barking and whining, and paying no attention to the three upon the veranda, he passed round the corner of the house and from their sight. "Dear me!" Mrs. Stone murmured. "What in the world's the matter with him?"

"Yes'm," Corbena agreed. "That child is somep'n more

whut turn queer lately. The way he all time bark and whine like li'l pup look to me, Miz Stone, like maybe you better git doctor come and 'tend to him. Child can git out of his right mind same as grown people can."

"Nonsense!" Mrs. Stone said. "Don't be silly, Corbena. It's just one of those habits children get sometimes."

She spoke with some sharpeness; nevertheless, her uneasiness about Orvie was increased by this additional barking and whining; for thus not infrequently do the most promising cerebrations of childhood fail to obtain recognition from adults. Little Orvie, if she had but known the truth, was for the first time in his life really using his mind.

Not forward in school, not quotable for bright sayings, Orvie in his own field was accomplishing more than either of his parents would have dared to attempt in theirs. They were both more than four times his age; yet he had completely hoodwinked them, had introduced the forbidden stranger into their very house, not a large one, and, undetected, had repeatedly provided Ralph with food from their very table and from their Kitty's very pan. More, he had made Ralph his bedfellow, and the technique he here employed, though it necessarily involved risk, could not have been improved upon.

In the evenings while Orvie was at dinner, Ralph occupied a drawer in Orvie's bureau upstairs. Later, when Mrs. Stone had heard Orvie's prayers and seen him in bed, Orvie rose, took Ralph from the drawer, gave him more of Kitty's milk, and then slept with him.

In the morning Orvie returned Ralph to the drawer, descended to breakfast, came up afterward and again removed Ralph from the drawer. Ralph then was borne outdoors in the concealment of little Orvie's shirtwaist and thus carried to the box in the garage, whence, during the day, all manner of excursions became feasible. Thus the periods of greater danger—when Ralph occupied the bureau drawer—were reduced to a minimum; the only really crucial moments were those during which Mrs. Stone was putting Orvie to bed, and Orvie and Ralph had twice survived them encouragingly.

Here then was ingenuity, true thinking; Mr. and Mrs. Stone could not possibly have concealed a dog from him as he did from them. But, as if this were not enough, little Orvie's mind soared higher still. There were matters in which Ralph could not be made to understand the requisites for his own safety. As valet, so to say, Orvie did the best he could; but, in the detail of barking and whining, proved himself open to those inspirations sometimes called streaks of genius.

By barking and whining frequently himself, he accustomed his parents and Corbena to hear such sounds in and about the house, and thus planned to provide Ralph—if Ralph's own voice should sometimes be heard—with an alibi.

Such was little Orvie's single-hearted purpose, and such had been his skill in carrying it out that Ralph was now well into his third day of residence with Mr. and Mrs. Stone without their even dreaming they were that hospitable. Mentally, little Orvie was growing.

Intellectual progress, however, was anything but his mother's interpretation of what was the matter with him, and Mr. Stone also began to take a gloomy view of him at lunch that day. He sent an annoyed side glance in his son's direction. "Orvie, don't sing at the table."

"No, Papa," Orvie said, and barked reticently, as if to himself, "Muff!"

"Don't imitate animals either."

"Animals?" Orvie asked. "No, Papa. Muff! Um-oo-ee!"

"Orvard, did you hear me?"

"Yes, Papa." Orvie was silent; but, after a moment or two, ventured to bark again softly.

"Orvard!" Mr. Stone, staring imperiously at his son, became aware of the odd appearance of Orvie's plate. "Well, I declare!"

Mrs. Stone, preoccupied, looked up. "What's the matter?"

"His plate," her husband said. "Look at it! I just gave him a chop and French fried potatoes and now there's nothing there. Not a thing! Why, he must eat like an anaconda!"

"Oh, no," Mrs. Stone protested gently; but she added, "You must learn not to gulp down your food, Orvie; it'll give you indigestion."

"Indigestion!" Orvie's father exclaimed, and he stared harder at the empty plate. "Why, even the bone's gone! Where is it? Orvie, did you drop that chop bone on the floor? Where is it?"

"Where's what, Papa?"

"That chop!" Mr. Stone got up and looked at the rug upon which the table stood. "No, there's nothing there. Where'd it go?"

"Where'd what go, Papa?"

"That chop!" Mr. Stone sat down at his place again. "That chop, or at least the bone! You could eat the chop; but you certainly couldn't eat the bone. Nobody could. What became of it? Did you see it fall?"

"Fall?" Orvie asked. "Fall, Papa?"

"Yes, fall! Fall, fall, fall! If it didn't fall off your plate, where did it go?"

"You mean my chop, Papa?"

"Yes, I do! What became of it?"

Orvie was thoughtful; then seemed to brighten a little. "Maybe it fell out the window, Papa."

"The window?" Mr. Stone breathed heavily. "Ten feet away and with a wire screen in it? Fell out of it?"

Orvie looked absentminded. "Muff! Muff! Muff!" he said. "Um-oo-ee!"

"Oh, dear!" his father exclaimed, depressed. "Oh, dear me!"

"What, Papa?"

"Nothing!" Mr. Stone simply gave up thinking about the chop bone. Fathers and mothers, confronted frequently by the inexplicable, acquire this rather helpless habit of allowing mysteries to pass unsolved. Orvie applied himself to bread and milk, having just proved that for the sake of Ralph he was glad to deprive himself as well as Kitty. Unobserved legerdemain had removed the chop, with only one small bite out of it, to the interior of his shirtwaist, where also were a handful of French fried potatoes and a few of Ralph's hairs. Beneath Orvie's polka-dotted surface and about his upper middle, that is to say, little Orvie for two days had been far from neat. Bacon, toast, buttered bread, bits of steak and broiled chicken, and even cereal had lain against him there during and after recent meals; he was no dietitian and fondly offered Ralph as wide a choice as he could.

"Muff!" he said, finishing his milk. "Um-oo-ee! I'm all through. Can I go out in the yard now, Mamma?"

She nodded gravely, not speaking; whereupon, uttering a few petty barks as he went, he ran outdoors. Mr. Stone, who had arrived after his wife and son had sat down to lunch, glanced across the table inquiringly. "Well, what's on your mind?" he asked, alluding to the preoccupation that had made her unusually silent.

"I'm really getting worried," she informed him. "Really, I mean. Something else happened this morning."

"Something else? Something else than what?"

"Than his barking," she said. "Listen, please. This summer I've been trying to have Orvie begin to cultivate self-reliance, so I've been having him look after his clothes, to a certain extent, himself. That is, he's supposed to hang them up when he takes them off, put what's soiled in the clothes basket and when he puts on fresh ones, get them out of his bureau drawer himself. This morning about eleven the laundry came and Corbena took Orvie's to his room to put in his bureau. I wish you'd seen what she found in the middle drawer! One of his best little white cambric waists with ruffled collars absolutely mangled—almost torn to pieces. She knew when she put it there last week it was in perfect condition. What's your explanation? What do you think made him do such a thing?"

"Who?" Mr. Stone asked. "Orvie? You don't mean he did it himself?"

She nodded solemnly. "He admitted it."

"What?"

"He did," Mrs. Stone said. "I called him in and he came in barking. I showed him the waist and asked him what had happened to it. First he said he thought Kitty must have done it; but when I showed him how absurd that was, he admitted he did it himself. I asked him how, and he said he 'guessed he must have gnawed it'! Those were his very words! What do you say to that?"

"I don't know, I'm sure. It seems odd, but—"

"Odd!" she exclaimed. "Don't you think maybe it's a case for one of these psychopathic doctors or whatever they call them? Corbena thinks it is. Corbena said herself we ought to get—"

"Never mind," Mr. Stone said. "I don't care what Corbena thinks we ought to do. Why did Orvie gnaw it? How did he explain doing such a thing?"

"He didn't explain it. When I asked him why he did it, he'd just say, 'What, Mamma?' and then make those noises, and that's what upset me the worst. Do you suppose it could be possible that a child could want something so long and talk about it so much and brood upon it so intensely that in time he'd—well, that in time he'd almost begin to have the delusion that he'd turned into the thing he'd wanted so much?"

"What?" Mr. Stone stared at his wife incredulously, and then, in despair over the elasticities of her imagination, laughed aloud. "Your theory is that Orvie's wanted a dog so long that now he's begun to believe he's a dog himself? So you want a psychoanalyst to prove to him that he's really a boy? Is that your idea?"

"No," she said, annoyed; but nevertheless added, "Still, it's certainly very strange. It's easy for you to make fun of me; but will you kindly tell me why he does all this barking and whining and why he gnawed his little cambric waist like that?"

"Good heavens! There's nothing very strange about a boy's playing to himself that he's a pup. You've heard him playing he's a whole railroad engine, haven't you?" This was spoken confidently; nevertheless, a meeting he had with his son, a few minutes later in the front yard, brought curious doubts into Mr. Stone's mind. As was his custom at noon, he had left his car before the house at the curbstone, and he was on his way to it when Orvie came from the backyard, barking indistinctly.

"Orvie! Where are you going?"

Until thus questioned, Orvie had not observed his father; he betrayed hesitation and embarrassment. Walking slowly, he again had his right hand inside his shirtwaist and seemed to be scratching himself strongly. "What, Papa?" He paused at a distance from his father and turned partly away.

"Where are you going?"

"Only across the street to Freddie and Babe's house, Papa," Orvie said, and added quickly and with some emphasis, "Muff! Muff! Um-oo-ee! Um-oo-ee! Muff! Muff!"

"Come here," Mr. Stone said. "What do you want to bark all the time for like that? Come here!"

Orvie moved a few sidelong steps and paused, still keeping his shoulder and back toward his father as much as seemed plausible. The situation, indeed, appeared critical; for Ralph, whom he was carrying inside his shirtwaist to show confidentially to the little cousins, Babe and Freddie, had all at once begun to feel lively. Ralph, in fact, was not only squirming in an almost unbearably tickling manner but was also chewing at his young master's fragile undergarment, rending it and at the same time abrading actual surfaces of the young master. To have so much going on sub rosa yet directly under Mr. Stone's eye, and simultaneously to maintain an air of aplomb, was difficult.

For more than two days Ralph had been accustomed to seclusions and enclosures; his adaptation of himself to these environments had hitherto been such a marvel of meekness, or inanity, that Orvie had been encouraged to believe the routine might be carried on permanently, or at least during his own lifetime. Now, however, Ralph, it seemed, desired to frolic, and did frolic—wished, too, a broader field and to gambol in the open air, though apparently he thought that his route thither lay not through the shirtwaist but through Orvie. No doubt the legend of the Spartan boy who permitted the fox to gnaw his vitals arose from some such affair and was later poetically garbled; probably the Spartan boy's parents wouldn't let him have a fox.

"Stop scratching yourself!" Mr. Stone said. "Have you got chiggers? What's the matter with you?"

"Nothing, Papa. I—" Orvie interrupted himself, for to his horror Ralph, though briefly, became vocal in a slight bark, which had to be covered. Orvie turned his back upon his father and began to walk toward the street, barking loudly.

"Stop that!" Mr. Stone said. "Stop that silly barking, stand still, and listen to me!"

"Yes, Papa." Orvie halted tentatively and looked back over his shoulder. "What you want, Papa? Muff! Muff! Um-oo-ee! Um-oo-ee! I got to go over to Babe and Freddie's now, Papa. Muff!"

"Listen to me!" Mr. Stone said, advancing. "Stop all this barking. At your age if you get a habit like that—"

"Yes, Papa. I—Muff!" Orvie said hurriedly, and moved on toward the sidewalk. "Muff! Muff! Ouch! I got to go now, Papa. Honest, I—Um-oo-ee! Papa, I—Muff! Muff!"

Mr. Stone let him go, and, frowning, watched him as he ran barking across the street and into the yard opposite. It could not be denied that little Orvie's behavior was peculiar, at least tinged with something suggestive of a kind of lunacy; and his father, stepping into the waiting automobile, nervously recalled the mystery of the chop bone at lunch. Could it be that Orvie had hidden that bone about his person, intending to bury it later and then dig it up, perhaps? A canine impersonation that would go to such lengths did seem almost unnaturally realistic, and Mr. Stone, as he drove down town, was in fact a little disturbed about his son.

That son, meanwhile, in Freddie's and Babe's yard, had stopped barking, and, after employing his voice for some time in an attempt at yodeling meant to let those within know that he waited for them without, was joined upon the lawn by his two little cousins. He had kept his happy secret to himself about as long as he could; his constantly swelling pride in Ralph, and in himself as owner, now resistlessly pressed him to excite the envy of pupless contemporaries.

"What you want, Orvie?" Babe inquired, and she added, "You look awful dirty. Little Cousin M'ree from Kansas City and Cousin Sadie and Cousin Josie are comin' to play with me this afternoon pretty soon. You and Freddie better go somewheres and play by yourselfs because the rest of us'll be all girls and clean."

"Listen," Orvie said. "Freddie, if I show you and Babe a secret will you promise you'll never tell anybody?"

Interested, both Babe and Freddie promised.

"I mean you haf to promise you'll never tell anybody in the whole world or you rather die," Orvie said; and, when they agreed to this, he led them behind a clump of lilac bushes, opened his shirtwaist and displayed his treasure.

"Look there," he said. "Its name's Ralph."

Both Freddie and Babe were immediately ecstatic, though Babe interrupted herself to tell Orvie he looked terrible inside the shirtwaist and ought to be ashamed to keep Ralph in such an awful place; then shouting, she had something like a little fight with Freddie, as both claimed the privilege simultaneously of holding Ralph against their cheeks to feel how soft he was.

Orvie became nervous. "For good heavens goodnesses sakes hush up!" he said, glancing toward the house. "Here! You give me back my dog!" Decisively he took Ralph from them and restored him into the interior of his shirtwaist. "I guess I got enough trouble having Papa and Mamma not find out Ralph's my dog without your making all this fuss!"

Babe resented the sequestration of Ralph; she wanted to play with him, made efforts to obtain possession of him, and, when forcibly repulsed, became threatening. "You just wait, Orvie Stone! Wait till your papa and mamma find out you got a dog!"

Orvie had to remind her of the consequences of broken honor. "You promised you'd never tell and you'll be a dirty ole storyteller if you do and I'll tell everybody you are one too!"

"I won't tell, Orvie," Babe said coaxingly. "Orvie, please give me that dear little puppy."

"No!"

"I mean just to play with," Babe said. "Orvie, please let me play with that dear little puppy just half an hour. Please, Orvie—"

"No!"

"Of course he won't," Freddie said to Babe. "Orvie's going to let me have Ralph to play with now because I and Orvie are boys and—"

"No!" Orvie said, and buttoned up his shirtwaist, enclosing Ralph from view.

At this, naturally, both Freddie and Babe were antagonized, and, as it happened that a sedan just then deposited three speckless little girls upon the sidewalk before the gate, the brother and sister ran to greet the newcomers and to speak at once unfavorably of Orvie, who remained behind the clump of lilacs.

" 'Lo, M'ree, 'lo, Josie, 'lo, Sadie," Babe said. "Dirty ole Orvie's here. He's over behind those bushes because he's got a secret."

"It's in his clo'es," Freddie explained. "It's a secret and I and Babe promised not to tell; but he's got it in his clo'es. Come on look at him and see if you can guess what it is; it's alive."

Little Marie from Kansas City, little Josie, and little Sadie shouted with cruel pleasure. "Dirty ole Orvie!" they cried. "Come on! Come on! Come on!"

Thus Orvie, rushed upon, found himself driven from the shelter of the lilac bushes, and decided to leave for home. His five little cousins, however, made his departure difficult; they surrounded him, screaming merrily and spitefully, jostled him, poked him; and in this process the right forefinger of little Marie from Kansas City was electrified by the sensation of encountering a protuberance that squirmed.

She shrieked sincerely in horror. "Oh, oh, oh! He's got a rat in there! It's a rat or a cat or maybe a snake! Oh, you bad dirty little Orvie!"

"I am not!" Orvie cried. "It is not!" Infuriated, both on his own account and Ralph's, and, too, because he never did get on well with little Marie from Kansas City, he became indiscreet. "I have not got any ole rat or ole dirty cat or any snake in here! It's something I wouldn't let you touch even its tail if you cried your ole eyes out begging me!"

"Tail! Tail! Tail!" shouted little Josie and little Sadie, prodding insanely at Orvie. "It's got a tail! It's got a tail! It's got a tail!"

"Its name's Ralph!" Babe cried. "I didn't promise I wouldn't tell what its name was, Orvie. I'm not a storyteller for only tellin' what its name is."

Upon this, little Josie, little Sadie, and little Marie from Kansas City were inspired to guess the rest. "It's a dog!" they cried simultaneously. "It's a dog!"

"Yes," Freddie said. "And his papa and mamma won't let him have one either. I didn't promise I wouldn't tell that, because everybody knows it anyways, Orvie."

"Storytellers!" Orvie shouted at the top of his voice. "Babe and Freddie are dirty ole storytellers and so's everybody else! You're all every one dirty ole storytellers!"

"We are not! You're one yourself!" they all assured him, and then, as he bitterly hustled his way out from among them and ran to the street, they ran after him.

Little Marie made her voice piercing. "Orvie's got! Orvie's got! Orvie's got!" she cried, leaving what Orvie had to the imagination of dangerous adult listeners and terrifying him with this imminent menace to his secret. "Orvie's got! Orvie's got! Orvie's got!"

The others took it up. "Orvie's got! Orvie's got! Orvie's got!" they chanted delightedly, pursued him across the street and into his own yard. There he knew not where to turn. With the pack upon him, and the windows of the house open, so that at any moment his mother might hear, comprehend, and look forth, he did not dare go to the garage to hide Ralph, nor to enter the house, nor to remain in the yard—nor to run away, when Freddie, Babe, Josie, Sadie, and little Marie from Kansas City would certainly run whooping after him. All resources failed him.

"You go home!" he shouted, knowing helplessly how futile this assertion of his rights. "This is my yard and you got to everyone go home, you ole dirty storytellers, you! Go home!"

They enlarged their threat by a monosyllable. "Orvie's got a!" they chanted. "Orvie's got a! Orvie's got a! Orvie's got a!"

Corbena appeared at a kitchen window, obviously interested. Orvie, perceiving her and in terror lest the chanters should complete their chorus with the fatal word *dog,* bawled incoherences at the top of his voice to drown them out. "Baw! Waw! Waw! Boo! Yoo! Yoo!"

Tauntingly little Marie chanted the first sound of the word *dog.* "Orvie's got a duh!"

The rest took this up immediately. "Orvie's got a duh! Orvie's got a duh! Orvie's got a duh!"

"Baw! Waw! Waw! I have not! You're all storytellers! Baw! Waw! Waw! Yoo! Yoo!"

They danced about him, encircling him. "Orvie's got a duh!" And then little Josie, the youngest of the group, piercingly added, "awg!" So that Orvie, though he bawled his loudest, feared Corbena might have heard the ruinous completion, "Orvie's got a duh—awg!"

Corbena had, in fact, heard just that. Her interest increased as she looked from the window and listened to the screeching. Then, returning to a polishing of the stove, she engaged herself in thought; but presently, looking forth again, saw that the five little cousins, following some new caprice, were racing back to the yard across the street.

Orvie, brooding, was walking toward the garage, and Corbena decided upon a line of conduct she would follow. No doubt she was influenced by an ill-founded partiality she had always felt for Kitty.

Kitty, as a matter of fact, was usually no bad hand at looking out for himself. True, he was subject to the seemingly haphazard misfortunes of life, as are we all, and the long arm of disastrous coincidence could at any time reach him; but he lived with a bold craftiness solely for himself and seldom failed to take care of number one. Orvie, entering the garage with Ralph in his bosom, or a little below, heard a sinisterly eloquent sound as he approached the door of the closet, which he had carelessly left open as he had the lid of the box also.

Ralph, rather overfed, had been indifferent to the chop and French fried potatoes brought him from the lunch table, had allowed them to remain in the box almost untouched, and now, later, when he might have taken pleasure in them, another was doing that for him.

Kitty, though not aware to whom he owed the blueness of his daily milk, was getting even and didn't intend to be balked. Kitty, that is to say, was in Ralph's box eating Ralph's chop, and the eloquent sound Orvie heard as he came near was the police siren inside of Kitty turned on in nasty warning.

"Get out o' there!" Orvie cried indignantly, and accompanied his words with furious gestures. "Get out o' my dog's own box, you bad ole cat you!"

Kitty rose up out of the box in a tall, dangerous manner, sirening and with his teeth fixed in the chop and the bone projecting like a deformity ever to be part of him; anesthetics and surgeons might remove this chop from him, he made clear, but nothing less should do it. Stepping testily, and with head and chop and rigid tail held high, he went forth with no undue haste, daring all hell to intercept him. He disappeared proudly into the golden light of outdoors.

"You bad ole cat, you!" Intimidated, Orvie spoke feebly, though none the less bitterly; for this was the second time Kitty had been caught—so to speak—robbing Ralph's box. "You'll see, you ole cat you! I'll show you!"

Orvie didn't know how or what he was going to show Kitty, but later in the afternoon seized upon an opportunity to show him at least a little something. Having made a sketchy leash and collar out of a length of discarded clothesline, he gave Ralph some too-early lessons in "heeling" in the alley, and, returning, found Kitty again in the box. This time, however, Orvie neither bellowed nor made threatening gestures, but quietly closed the lid on Kitty. Kitty made a few objections; and then, after trifling with cold French fried potatoes in the dark, philosophically took a nap until Orvie came back from another excursion, raised the lid, and said severely, "There! That'll teach you, I guess, you ole cat you!"

Kitty yawned, left the box, and walked languidly away; showed so much indifference, indeed, that Orvie was galled.

"You listen, you ole Kitty, you!" he called fiercely. "Next time I catch you in my dog's box I'm goin' to slam the lid down and fasten it and keep you in there all day! You better look out!"

Kitty paid not the slightest attention and even had the hardihood to return within the hour, seat himself in Orvie's presence, look at the box and meow inquiringly.

"You—" Orvie began; but a summons into the house prevented him from further expressing his emotion. Corbena called loudly from the kitchen door.

"Li'l Orvie! You out 'n 'at garage? You come in here. You' mamma want you ri' now."

Orvie put Ralph in the box, fastened the lid down, closed the door of the closet, and noisily gave himself the pleasure of seeing Kitty precede him into the house.

"Shame!" Corbena said, holding open the screen door of the kitchen for Kitty, but closing it before Orvie arrived. "Shame on you to holler and chase Kitty thataway! No, you ain' go' come in my kitchen and holler and chase Kitty some more. You go round and go in front door and walk upstairs to you' mamma. Go on now! I got somep'n else to do 'cept argue!"

Her words held a meaning hidden from little Orvie, a meaning that would have chilled his blood had he understood it; and, while he was following the route she had insisted upon, and being kept upstairs for a sufficient time by his mother, Corbena completed a brief but thorough investigation. Mrs. Stone, who made a pretext to have little Orvie change his clothes under her own eye, also learned much; and, when Mr. Stone arrived at the house after his day's work, she met him at the front door, drew him into the living room, and told him all.

"Two days!" she said, approaching the conclusion of her narrative. "Three days really by this time, and two nights! In the daytime he keeps it in that box in the garage whenever he hasn't got it out playing with it; though when he slips it into the house and up to his room he must carry it inside his waist—I wish you'd seen conditions there!—and Corbena found a rope collar and leash that he leads it by, probably in the alley. Then, when he comes in and goes upstairs to wash his hands and face before dinner, he hides it in his bureau drawer—that's what happened to his cambric ruffled waist—then, after I put him in bed, he gets up and takes it out of the drawer and sleeps with it. Oh, there's no doubt about it! Corbena and I worked it all out. What makes us sure he's had this dog for two whole days without our knowing it, Corbena remembered it was day before yesterday he brought down that box from the attic and carried it out to the garage. What on earth do you think?"

"I don't know." Mr. Stone sighed; then blew out an audible breath suggesting a faint kind of laughter. "In a way it's almost a relief—I mean, to know that he hasn't been getting woozy in the head on account of this dog mania of his. Of course that's why he's been barking—in the hope we mightn't notice if the dog himself barked. Not so dumb, you know! Really seems to show he has ideas—peculiar ones, but at least ideas. What have you done about it? What have you said to Orvie?"

"Nothing. He doesn't dream we even suspect. I waited to see what you'd say, so we could decide together."

"I see." Mr. Stone pondered. "What sort of a dog is he?"

"He?" Mrs. Stone uttered a half-hushed outcry. "It isn't! Corbena says it's very small but terribly mongrel, and the worst of it is it's a she!"

"Well, that settles it," Mr. Stone said. "Of course that settles it."

"Yes, of course; but how am I to—"

"Wait," he said. "Let me handle this. I see just what to do."

"Do you?" Mrs. Stone was doubtful. "If you simply mean to call Orvie in and take that dog away from him and tell him he can't have it, I won't answer for the shock to his nervous system. I don't think it should be managed that way."

"Neither do I!" her husband protested. "Don't you think I have any regard for the child's feelings? Don't you suppose I know it's one thing to tell him he can't have a dog and quite another thing to take a dog away from him after he's actually got one? Naturally, I intend to use some diplomacy."

"What kind of diplomacy? I don't see—"

"Listen," he interrupted. "We don't want to get Orvie all harrowed up, or to be harrowed up ourselves. We'll simply let him believe the pup's got out of the box, wandered away, and got lost. If we do that, why, of course Orvie'll think maybe he'll find it again someday, so he won't feel too badly about it. For a while he'll poke around looking for it and whistling, of course; then he'll forget all about it."

"I hope so."

"Of course he will," Mr. Stone said. "We won't say a thing to Orvic, and you mustn't let Corbena speak of it to him, either. What's more, he can have the pup sleep with him tonight and we'll let him have another morning and most of the afternoon, too, for that matter, playing with it—pretty near a whole day—and then, toward evening, it'll simply be missing and he won't have so very long to worry about it before bedtime comes and he goes to sleep. Next morning when he wakes up, he'll hardly think of it at all."

"I hope so," she said again. "I do hope so!"

"Why, certainly!" Mr. Stone reassured her. "Tomorrow after lunch I'll have Elmore Jones come down to my office and

I'll give him a couple of dollars to drive up here later in his car and take the pup quietly away."

"Elmore Jones? You mean that awful old colored man who used to be a sort of gardener at your father's and stole the lawn mower?"

"That was when Elmore was drinking," Mr. Stone explained, and laughed, though he was a little nettled by the criticism of his judgment she seemed to imply. "Father was rather hard on him about that and the rest of us give Elmore little jobs when we can, to help him out. He's got an old car now that he uses as a sort of a truck, and he's perfectly reliable."

"But if he comes in here and walks out to the garage and takes the pup out of that box, and Orvie sees him—"

"Oh, dear me!" Mr. Stone sighed. "Orvie won't be here to see him—not unless you let him. I'll instruct Elmore Jones to come and get the pup tomorrow afternoon at five o'clock exactly; and you can arrange for Orvie to be across the street at Babe's and Freddie's, playing with them, from half-past four to half-past five, can't you?"

"Yes," she said thoughtfully, then looked more cheerful. "Why, yes, I believe that would work out all right. I'll tell Winnie about it this evening and ask her to make sort of a little party of it. I'll get her to ask some of the other children and I'll take Orvie over there myself, between four and half past, and tell him he can stay till almost six o'clock. I'll ask Winnie to have cookies and lemonade and little games, so he'll have a nice happy time; and that way, it seems to me, with a long happy day and a little party to remember—and of course just thinking his pup's lost and may come back sometime—why, probably, he won't be much upset."

"Of course he won't," her husband agreed. "Besides that, it isn't as if we were doing anything rather cruel to this pup, because Elmore Jones'll simply take it out in the country twenty-five or thirty miles and leave it near some farmhouse or other, where people usually are glad to have a dog and—"

"Yes," Mrs. Stone said, almost with enthusiasm. "People who live way out in the country like that are kind to dogs. They're nearly always glad to find one and give it a good home; so of course we're really not—"

"No, of course we're not. It isn't like telling Elmore Jones to take Orvie's pup out and drown it. No; we're doing the best we can under the circumstances, and I really don't think Orvie'll mind at all."

"No," Mrs. Stone agreed. "I don't think he will, either —not to speak of."

Then, though both parents were thoughtful and perhaps slightly apprehensive, not to say remorseful, they ended by stimulating themselves with something like an exchange of congratulations upon having discovered a plan that would depress their little son's spirits in the least possible degree. On the following afternoon, however, at about ten minutes before six, when Mr. Stone came into the house, he found his wife in a pathetic mood. She was looking out of one of the living-room windows and didn't turn when he approached her.

"How—how did it go?" he asked somewhat hesitantly. "How did Orvie take it?"

"I don't know." She sniffled abruptly, turned, and allowed him to see that her eyes were moist and not free from reproachfulness. "Oh, your plan was carried out—carried out quite perfectly! Your old Elmore Jones was here at five. I heard him in the kitchen and Corbena telling him what to do; so it's gone. Orvie's just come back from Winnie's. He's upstairs."

"What did he say?"

"Nothing," Mrs. Stone replied huskily. "Of course he knows, because this is the time he always takes it upstairs and puts it in the bureau drawer, so of course he's been out there —to the empty box. I kept out of his way—just listened to him running upstairs—I felt I simply couldn't face him. I do wonder if you've been really right in doing this to him. I do wonder."

"I!" her husband exclaimed. "Wonder if I'm really right? Me? Didn't you tell me—" He paused. Corbena stood in the doorway.

"Dinner serve'," she said, glanced about the room questioningly, and added in a solemn voice, addressing herself to Mrs. Stone, "Milk in 'at pan I set on back porch fer Kitty done gone blue on me again."

"Blue?" Mr. Stone said. "Blue milk? What do you mean, Corbena?"

Corbena's solemnity increased. "Blue," she said. "Milk blue again. Elmore Jones come five o'clock like Miz Stone tell me he goin' to; but he ain't no right bright nice-actin' colored man, Elmore Jones ain't. He come in my kitchen, say he goin' be rich man soon. I say, 'Don't blow all 'at gin in my face, Elmore Jones! Go on open the closet in the garage, git that pup out that box in the closet and go on away from here.' He say, yes'm that box whut he come fer, not me, and shambled on out. I tooken a look in my oven, then I heard him shut the garage door and I went and looked out and he was goin' out the alley gate wif 'at box under his arm. 'I got him!' Elmore Jones holler at me. 'He in here all right,' Elmore Jones holler. Then I heard Elmore Jones's ole clatterbox automobile buzz-chuggin' away. How fur you tell Elmore to go, Mr. Stone?"

"Why, I told him to go twenty-five or thirty—"

Corbena, though interrupting, seemed merely to meditate aloud. "Li'l Orvie come back from his aunt's house 'cross the street li'l while after you tooken him over there this afternoon, Miz Stone. Then he gone back again. I see him pass my kitchen window; and, come to 'member, I didn't tooken no notice then, but seem to me now like he was actin' like he scratchin' hisself under his li'l shirt." Corbena paused and again looked about the room questioningly. "Kitty nowhere in here, Miz Stone?"

"Kitty? No."

"No, Kitty certainly ain't here," Corbena said. "Elmore Jones tell me Mr. Stone done hand him fi'-dolluh bill; tell me he ain't spen' more'n half of it. Miz Stone, you see poor Kitty anywheres at all since about four o'clock?"

"No!" Mrs. Stone gasped. "Oh, my goodness!"

Mr. Stone, staring haggardly, strode out into the hall and halfway up the stairs, but there he paused.

His ascending footsteps must have been heard overhead, for, as he halted, little Orvie's voice promptly became audible.

"Muff! Muff! Muff!" The barking grew louder as Orvie approached the head of the stairway to descend for dinner. "Muff! Um-oo-ee! Um-oo-ee! Um-oo-ee!"

Artistically, the imitated whining was of course plaintive; yet the voice that produced it had never sounded more contented. "Muff! Muff!" said little Orvie: "Um-oo-ee!"

Mr. Stone returned down the stairs he had just impetuously ascended and made a pitiable effort to seem unconscious of how his wife and Corbena were looking at him.

## *Lester del Rey*

# THE FAITHFUL

Today, in a green and lovely world, here in the mightiest of human cities, the last of the human race is dying. And we of Man's creation are left to mourn his passing, and to worship the memory of Man, who controlled all that he knew save only himself.

I am old, as my people go, yet my blood is still young and my life may go on for untold ages yet, if what this last of Men has told is true. And that also is Man's work, even as we and the Ape People are his work in the last analysis. We of the Dog People are old, and have lived a long time with Man. And yet, but for Roger Stren, we might still be baying at the

Moon and scratching the fleas from our hides, or lying at the ruins of Man's empire in dull wonder at his passing.

There are earlier records of dogs who mouthed clumsily a few Man words, but Hungor was the pet of Roger Stren, and in the labored efforts at speech, he saw an ideal and a lifework. The operation on Hungor's throat and mouth, which made Man-speech more nearly possible, was comparatively simple. The search for other "talking" dogs was harder.

But he found five besides Hungor, and with this small start he began. Selection and breeding, surgery and training, gland implantation and X-ray mutation were his methods, and he made steady progress. At first money was a problem, but his pets soon drew attention and commanded high prices.

When he died, the original six had become thousands, and he had watched over the raising of twenty generations of dogs. A generation of my kind then took only three years. He had seen his small backyard pen develop into a huge institution, with a hundred followers and students, and had found the world eager for his success. Above all, he had seen tail wagging give place to limited speech in that short time.

The movement he had started continued. At the end of two thousand years, we had a place beside Man in his work that would have been inconceivable to Roger Stren himself. We had our schools, our houses, our work with Man, and a society of our own. Even our independence, when we wanted it. And our life span was not fourteen, but fifty or more years.

Man, too, had traveled a long way. The stars were almost within his grasp. The barren Moon had been his for centuries. Mars and Venus lay beckoning, and he had reached them twice, but not to return. That lay close at hand. Almost, Man had conquered the universe.

But he had not conquered himself. There had been many setbacks to his progress because he had to go out and kill the others of his kind. And now, the memory from his past called again, and he went out in battle against himself. Cities crumbled to dust, the plains to the south became barren deserts again, Chicago lay covered in a green mist. That death killed slowly, so that Man fled from the city and died, leaving it an empty place. The mist hung there, clinging days, months, years—after Man had ceased to be.

I, too, went out to war, driving a plane built for my people, over the cities of the Rising Sun Empire. The tiny atomic bombs fell from my ship on houses, on farms, on all that was Man's, who had made my race what it was. For my Men told me I must fight.

Somehow, I was not killed. And after the last Great Drive, when half of Man was already dead, I gathered my people about me and we followed to the north, where some of my Men had turned to find a sanctuary from the war. Of Man's work, three cities still stood—wrapped in the green mist, and useless. And Man huddled around little fires and hid himself in the forest, hunting his food in small clans. Yet hardly a year of the war had passed.

For a time, the Men and my people lived in peace, planing to rebuild what had been, once the war finally ceased. Then came the Plague. The antitoxin which had been developed was ineffective as the Plague increased in its virulency. It spread over land and sea, gripped Man who had invented it, and killed him. It was like a strong dose of strychnine, leaving Man to die in violent cramps and retchings.

For a brief time, Man united against it, but there was no control. Remorselessly it spread, even into the little settlement they had founded in the north. And I watched in sorrow as my Men around me were seized with its agony. Then we of the Dog People were left alone in a shattered world from whence Man had vanished. For weeks we labored at the little radio we could operate, but there was no answer; and we knew that Man was dead.

There was little we could do. We had to forage our food as of old, and cultivate our crops in such small way as our somewhat modified forepaws permitted. And the barren north country was not suited to us.

I gathered my scattered tribes about me, and we began the long trek south. We moved from season to season, stopping to plant our food in the spring, hunting in the fall. As our sleds grew old and broke down, we could not replace them, and our travel became even slower. Sometimes we came upon our kind in smaller packs. Most of them had gone back to savagery, and these we had to mold to us by force. But little by little, growing in size, we drew south. We sought Men; for two hundred thousand years we of the Dog People had lived with and for Man.

In the wilds of what had once been Washington State we came upon another group who had not fallen back to the law of tooth and fang. They had horses to work for them, even crude harnesses and machines which they could operate. There we stayed for some ten years, setting up a government and building ourselves a crude city. Where Man had his hands, we had to invent what could be used with our poor feet and our teeth. But we had found a sort of security, and had even acquired some of Man's books by which we could teach our young.

Then into our valley came a clan of our people, moving west, who told us they had heard that one of our tribes sought refuge and provender in a mighty city of great houses lying by a lake in the east. I could only guess that it was Chicago. Of the green mist they had not heard—only that life was possible there.

Around our fires that night we decided that if the city were habitable, there would be homes and machines designed for us. And it might be there were Men, and the chance to bring up our young in the heritage which was their birthright. For weeks we labored in preparing ourselves for the long march to Chicago. We loaded our supplies in our crude carts, hitched our animals to them, and began the eastward trip.

It was nearing winter when we camped outside the city, still mighty and imposing. In the sixty years of its desertion, nothing had perished that we could see; the fountains to the west were still playing, run by automatic engines.

We advanced upon the others in the dark, quietly. They were living in a great square, littered with filth, and we noted that they had not even fire left from civilization. It was a savage fight, while it lasted, with no quarter given nor asked. But they had sunk too far, in the lazy shelter of Man's city, and the clan was not as large as we had heard. By the time the sun rose there was not one of them but had been killed or imprisoned until we could train them to our ways. The ancient city was ours, the green mist gone after all those years.

Around us were abundant provisions, the food factories which I knew how to run, the machines that Man had made to fit our needs, the houses in which we could dwell, power drawn from the bursting core of the atom which needed only the flick of a switch to start. Even without hands, we could live here in peace and security for ages. Perhaps here my dreams of adapting our feet to handle Man's tools and doing his work were possible, even if no Men were found.

We cleared the muck from the city and moved into Greater South Chicago, where our people had had their section of the city. I, and a few of the elders who had been taught by their fathers in the ways of Man, set up the old regime, and started the great water and light machines. We had returned to a life of certainty.

And four weeks later, one of my lieutenants brought Paul Kenyon before me. Man! Real and alive, after all this time! He smiled, and I motioned my eager people away.

"I saw your lights," he smiled. "I thought at first some Men had come back, but that is not to be; but civilization still has its followers, evidently, so I asked one of you to take me to the leader. Greetings from all that is left of Man!"

"Greetings," I gasped. It was like seeing the return of the

gods. My breath was choked; a great peace and fulfillment surged over me. "Greetings, and the blessings of your God. I had no hope of seeing Man again."

He shook his head. "I am the last. For fifty years I have been searching for Men—but there are none. Well, you have done well. I should like to live among you, work with you—when I can. I survived the Plague somehow, but it comes on me yet, more often now, and I can't move nor care for myself then. That is why I have come to you.

"Funny." He paused. "I seem to recognize you. Hungor Beowulf, XIV? I am Paul Kenyon. Perhaps you remember me? No? Well, it was a long time, and you were young. But that white streak under the eye still shows." A greater satisfaction came to me that he remembered me.

Now one had come among us with hands, and he was of great help. But most of all, he was of the old Men, and gave point to our working. But often, as he had said, the old sickness came over him, and he lay in violent convulsions, from which he was weak for days. We learned to care for him, when he needed it, even as we learned to fit our society to his presence. And at last, he came to me with a suggestion.

"Hungor," he said, "if you had one wish, what would it be?"

"The return of Man. The old order, where we could work together. You know as well as I how much we need Man."

He grinned crookedly. "Now, it seems, Man needs you more. But if that were denied, what next?"

"Hands," I said. "I dream of them at night and plan for them by day, but I will never see them."

"Maybe you will, Hungor. Haven't you ever wondered why you go on living, twice normal age, in the prime of your life? Have you never wondered how I have withstood the Plague which still runs in my blood, and how I still seem only in my thirties, though nearly seventy years have passed since a man has been born?"

"Sometimes," I answered. "I have no time for wonder, now, and when I do—Man is the only answer I have."

"A good answer," he said. "Yes, Hungor, Man is the answer. That is why I remember you. Three years before the war, when you were just reaching maturity, you came into my laboratory. Do you remember?"

"The experiment," I said. "That is why you remember me?"

"Yes, the experiment. I altered your glands somewhat, implanted certain tissues into your body, as I had done to myself. I was seeking the secret of immortality. Though there was no reaction at the time, it worked, and I don't know how much longer we may live—or you may; it helped me resist the Plague, but did not overcome it."

So that was the answer. He stood staring at me a long time. "Yes, unknowingly, I saved you to carry on Man's future for him. But we were talking of hands.

"As you know, there is a great continent to the east of the Americas, called Africa. But did you know Man was working there on the great apes, as he was working here on your people? We never made as much progress with them as with you. We started too late. Yet they spoke a simple language and served for common work. And we changed their hands so the thumb and fingers opposed, as do mine. There, Hungor, are your hands."

Now Paul Kenyon and I laid plans carefully. Out in the hangars of the city there were aircraft designed for my people's use; heretofore I had seen no need of using them. The planes were in good condition, we found on examination, and my early training came back to me as I took the first ship up. They carried fuel to circle the globe ten times, and out in the lake the big fuel tanks could be drawn on when needed.

Together, though he did most of the mechanical work

between spells of sickness, we stripped the planes of all their war equipment. Of the six hundred planes, only two were useless, and the rest would serve to carry some two thousand passengers in addition to the pilots. If the apes had reverted to complete savagery, we were equipped with tanks of anesthetic gas by which we could overcome them and strap them in the planes for the return. In the houses around us, we built accommodations for them strong enough to hold them by force, but designed for their comfort if they were peaceable.

At first, I had planned to lead the expedition. But Paul Kenyon pointed out that they would be less likely to respond to us than to him. "After all," he said, "Men educated them and cared for them, and they probably remember us dimly. But your people they know only as the wild dogs who are their enemies. I can go out and contact their leaders, guarded of course by your people. But otherwise, it might mean battle."

Each day I took up a few of our younger ones in the planes and taught them to handle the controls. As they were taught, they began the instruction of others. It was a task which took months to finish, but my people knew the need of hands as well as I; any faint hope was well worth trying.

It was late spring when the expedition set out. I could follow their progress by means of television, but could work the controls only with difficulty. Kenyon, of course, was working the controls at the other end, when he was able.

They met with a storm over the Atlantic Ocean, and three of the ships went down. But under the direction of my lieutenant and Kenyon the rest weathered the storm. They landed near the ruins of Cape Town, but found no trace of the Ape People. Then began weeks of scouting over the jungles and plains. They saw apes, but on capturing a few they found them only the primitive creatures which nature had developed.

It was by accident they finally met with success. Camp

had been made near a waterfall for the night, and fires had been lit to guard against the savage beasts which roamed the land. Kenyon was in one of his rare moments of good health. The telecaster had been set up in a tent near the outskirts of the camp, and he was broadcasting a complete account of the day. Then, abruptly, over the head of the Man was raised a rough and shaggy face.

He must have seen the shadow, for he started to turn sharply, then caught himself and moved slowly around. Facing him was one of the apes. He stood there silently, watching the ape, not knowing whether it was savage or well disposed. It, too, hesitated; then it advanced.

"Man—Man," it mouthed. "You came back. Where were you? I am Tolemy, and I saw you, and I came."

"Tolemy," said Kenyon, smiling. "It is good to see you, Tolemy. Sit down; let us talk. I am glad to see you. Ah, Tolemy, you look old; were your father and mother raised by Man?"

"I am eighty years, I think. It is hard to know. I was raised by Man long ago. And now I am old; my people say I grow too old to lead. They do not want me to come to you, but I know Man. He was good to me. And he had coffee and cigarettes."

"I have coffee and cigarettes, Tolemy." Kenyon smiled. "Wait, I will get them. And your people, is not life hard among them in the jungle? Would you like to go back with me?"

"Yes, hard among us. I want to go back with you. Are you many here?"

"No, Tolemy." He set the coffee and cigarettes before the ape, who drank eagerly and lit the smoke gingerly from a fire. "No, but I have friends with me. You must bring your people here, and let us get to be friends. Are there many of you?"

"Yes. Ten times we make ten tens—a thousand of us,

almost. We are all that was left in the city of Man after the great fight. A Man freed us, and I led my people away, and we lived here in the jungle. They wanted to be in small tribes, but I made them one, and we are safe. Food is hard to find."

"We have much food in a big city, Tolemy, and friends who will help you, if you work for them. You remember the Dog People, don't you? And you would work with them as with Man if they treated you as Man treated you, and fed you, and taught your people?"

"Dogs? I remember the Man-dogs. They were good. But here the dogs are bad. I smelled dog here; it was not like the dog we smell each day, and my nose was not sure. I will work with Man-dogs, but my people will be slow to learn them."

Later telecasts showed rapid progress. I saw the apes come in by twos and threes and meet Paul Kenyon, who gave them food, and introduced my people to them. This was slow, but as some began to lose their fear of us, others were easier to train. Only a few broke away and would not come.

Cigarettes that Man was fond of—but which my people never used—were a help, since they learned to smoke with great readiness.

It was months before they returned. When they came there were over nine hundred of the Ape People with them, and Paul and Tolemy had begun their education. Our first job was a careful medical examination of Tolemy, but it showed him in good health, and with much of the vigor of a younger ape. Man had been lengthening the ages of his kind, as it had ours, and he was evidently a complete success.

Now they have been among us three years, and during that time we have taught them to use their hands at our instructions. Overhead the great monorail cars are running, and the factories have started to work again. They are quick to learn, with a curiosity that makes them eager for new knowledge. And they are thriving and multiplying here. We need no longer bewail the lack of hands; perhaps, in time to come, with their help, we can change our forepaws further, and learn to walk on two legs, as did Man.

Today I have come back from the bed of Paul Kenyon. We are often together now—perhaps I should include the faithful Tolemy—when he can talk, and among us there has grown a great friendship. I laid certain plans before him today for adapting the apes mentally and physically until they are Men. Nature did it with an apelike brute once; why can we not do it with the Ape People now? The Earth would be peopled again, science would rediscover the stars, and Man would have a foster child in his own likeness.

And we of the Dog People have followed Man for two hundred thousand years. That is too long to change. Of all Earth's creatures, the Dog People alone have followed Man thus. My people cannot lead now. No dog was ever complete without the companionship of Man. The Ape People will be Men.

It is a pleasant dream, surely not an impossible one.

Kenyon smiled as I spoke to him, and cautioned me in the jesting way he uses when most serious, not to make them too much like Man, lest another Plague destroy them. Well, we can guard against that. I think he, too, had a dream of Man reborn, for there was a hint of tears in his eyes, and he seemed pleased with me.

There is but little to please him now, alone among us, racked by pain, waiting the slow death he knows must come. The old trouble has grown worse, and the Plague has settled harder on him.

All we can do is give him sedatives to ease the pain now, though Tolemy and I have isolated the Plague we found in his blood. It seems a form of cholera, and with that information, we have done some work. The old Plague serum offers a clue, too. Some of our serums have seemed to ease the spells a little, but they have not stopped them.

It is a faint chance. I have not told him of our work, for only a stroke of luck will give us success before he dies.

Man is dying. Here in our laboratory, Tolemy keeps repeating something; a prayer, I think it is. Well, maybe the God whom he has learned from Man will be merciful, and grant us success.

Paul Kenyon is all that is left of the old world which Tolemy and I loved. He lies in the ward, moaning in agony, and dying. Sometimes he looks from his windows and sees the birds flying south; he gazes at them as if he would never see them again. Well, will he? Something he muttered once comes back to me:

"For no man knoweth—"

## *Don Marquis*

# BLOOD WILL TELL

I am a middle-size dog, with spots on me here and there, and several different colors of hair mixed in even where there aren't any spots, and my ears are frazzled a little on the ends where they have been chewed in fights.

At first glance you might not pick me for an aristocrat. But I am one. I was considerably surprised when I discovered it, as nothing in my inmost feelings up to that time, nor in the treatment which I had received from dogs, humans, or boys, had led me to suspect it.

I can well remember the afternoon on which the discovery was made. A lot of us dogs were lying in the grass, up by the swimming hole, just lazying around, and the boys were doing the same. All the boys were naked and comfortable, and no humans were about, the only thing near being a cow or two and some horses, and although large they are scarcely more human than boys. Everybody had got tired of swimming, and it was too hot to drown out gophers or fight bumblebees, and the boys were smoking grapevine cigarettes and talking.

Us dogs was listening to the boys talk. A Stray Boy, by which I mean one not claimed or looked out for or owned by any dog, says to Freckles Watson, who is my boy:

"What breed would you call that dog of yours, Freck?"

I pricked up my ears at that. I cannot say that I had ever set great store by breeds up to the time that I found out I was an aristocrat myself, believing, as Bill Patterson, a human and the town drunkard, used to say when intoxicated, that often an honest heart beats beneath the outcast's ragged coat.

"Spot ain't any *one* particular breed," says Freckles. "He's considerably mixed."

"He's a mongrel," says Squint Thompson, who is Jack Thompson's boy.

"He ain't," says Freckles, so huffy that I saw a mongrel must be some sort of a disgrace. "You're a link, link liar, and so's your Aunt Mariar, and you're another."

"A dog," chips in the Stray Boy, "has either got to be a thoroughbred or a mongrel. He's either an aristocrat or else he's a common dog."

"Spot ain't any common dog," says Freckles, sticking up for me. "He can lick any dog in town within five pounds of his weight."

"He's got some spaniel in him," says the Stray Boy.

"His nose is pointed like a hound's nose," says Squint Thompson.

"Well," says Freckles, "neither one of them kind of dogs is a common dog."

"Spot has got some bulldog blood in him, too," says Tom Mulligan, an Irish boy owned by a dog by the name of Mutt Mulligan. "Did you ever notice how Spot will hang on so you can't pry him loose, when he gets into a fight?"

"That proves he is an aristocratic kind of dog," says Freckles.

"There's some bird-dog blood in Spot," says the Stray Boy, sizing me up careful.

"He's got some collie in him, too," says Squint Thompson. "His voice sounds just like a collie's when he barks."

"But his tail is more like a coach dog's tail," says Tom Mulligan.

"His hair ain't, though," says the Stray Boy. "Some of his hair is like a setter's."

"His teeth are like a mastiff's," says Mutt Mulligan's boy Tom. And they went on like that; I never knew before there were so many different kinds of thoroughbred dog. Finally Freckles says:

"Yes, he's got all them different kinds of thoroughbred blood in him, and he's got other kinds you ain't mentioned and that you ain't slick enough to see. You may think you're running him down, but what you say just *proves* he ain't a common dog."

I was glad to hear that. It was beginning to look to me that they had a pretty good case for me being a mongrel.

"How does it prove it?" asked the Stray Boy.

"Well," says Freckles, "you know who the king of Germany is, don't you?"

They said they'd heard of him from time to time.

"Well," says Freckles, "if you were a relation of the king of Germany you'd be a member of the German royal family. You fellows may not know that, but you would. You'd be a swell, a regular high-mucky-muck."

They said they guessed they would.

"Now, then," says Freckles, "if you were a relation to the king of Switzerland, too, you'd be just *twice* as swell, wouldn't you, as if you were only related to one royal family? Plenty of people are related to just *one* royal family."

Tom Mulligan butts in and says that way back, in the early days, his folks was the kings of Ireland; but no one pays any attention.

"Suppose, then, you're a cousin of the queen of England into the bargain and your granddad was king of Scotland, and the prince of Wales and the emperor of France and the sultan of Russia and the rest of those royalties were relations of yours, wouldn't all that royal blood make you *twenty times* as much of a high-mucky-muck as if you had just *one* measly little old king for a relation?"

The boys had to admit that it would.

"You wouldn't call a fellow with all that royal blood in him a *mongrel,* would you?" says Freckles. "You bet your sweet life you wouldn't! A fellow like that is darned near on the level with a congressman or a vice-president. Whenever he travels around in the old country they turn out the brass band; and the firemen and the Knights of Pythias and the Modern Woodmen parade, and the mayor makes a speech, and there's a picnic and firecrackers, and he gets blamed near anything he wants. People kowtow to him, just like they do to a swell left-handed pitcher or a champion prize fighter. If you went over to the old country and called a fellow like that a mongrel, and it got out on you, you would be sent to jail for it."

Tom Mulligan says yes, that is so; his granddad came to

this country through getting into some kind of trouble about the king of England, and the king of England ain't anywhere near as swell as the fellow Freckles described, nor near so royal, neither.

"Well, then," says Freckles, "it's the same way with my dog Spot here. *Any* dog can be full of just *one* kind of thoroughbred blood. That's nothing! But Spot here has got more different kinds of thoroughbred blood in him than any dog you ever saw. By your own say-so he has. He's got *all* kinds of thoroughbred blood in him. If there's any kind he ain't got, you just name it, will you?"

"He ain't got any Great Dane in him," yells the Stray Boy, hating to knuckle under.

"You're a liar—he has, too," says Freckles.

The Stray Boy backed it, and there was a fight. All us dogs and boys gathered around in a ring to watch it, and I was more anxious than anybody else. For the way that fight went, it was easy to see, would decide what I was.

Well, Freckles licked that Stray Boy, and rubbed his nose in the mud, and that's how I come to be an aristocrat.

Being an aristocrat may sound easy. And it may look easy to outsiders. And it may really be easy for them that are used to it. But it wasn't easy for *me.* It came on me suddenly, the knowledge that I was one, and without warning. I didn't have any time to practice up being one. One minute I wasn't one, and the next minute I was; and while, of course, I felt important over it, there were spells when I would get kind of discouraged, too, and wish I could go back to being a common dog again. I kept expecting my tastes and habits to change. I watched and waited for them to. But they didn't. No change at all set in on me. But I had to pretend I was changed. Then I would get tired of pretending, and be downhearted about the whole thing, and say to myself: "There has been a mistake. I am *not* an aristocrat after all."

I might have gone along like that for a long time, partly

in joy over my noble birth, and partly in doubt, without ever being certain, if it had not been for a happening which showed, as Freckles said, that blood will tell.

It happened the day Wilson's World's Greatest One-Ring Circus and Menagerie came to our town. Freckles and me, and the other dogs and boys, and a good many humans, too, followed the street parade around through town and back to the circus lot. Many went in, and the ones that didn't have any money hung around outside a while and explained to each other they were going at night, because a circus is more fun at night anyhow. Freckles didn't have any money, but his dad was going to take him that night, so when the parade was over him and me went back to his dad's drugstore on Main Street, and I crawled under the soda-water counter to take a nap.

Freckles' dad, that everyone calls Doc Watson, is a pretty good fellow for a human, and he doesn't mind you hanging around the store if you don't drag bones in or scratch too many fleas off. So I'm there considerable in right hot weather. Under the soda-water counter is the coolest place for a dog in the whole town. There's a zinc tub under there always full of water, where Doc washes the soda-water glasses, and there's always considerable water slopped onto the floor. It's damp and dark there always. Outdoors it may be so hot in the sun that your tongue hangs out of you so far you tangle your feet in it, but in under there you can lie comfortable and snooze, and when you wake up and want a drink there's the tub with the glasses in it. And flies don't bother you because they stay on top of the counter where soda water has been spilled.

Circus day was a hot one, and I must have drowsed off pretty quick after lying down. I don't know how long I slept, but when I waked up it was with a start, for something important was going on outside in Main Street. I could hear people screaming and swearing and running along the wooden sidewalk, and horses whinnying, and dogs barking, and old Tom Cramp, the city marshal, was yelling out that he was an officer of the law, and the steam whistle on the flour mill was blowing. And it all seemed to be right in front of our store. I was thinking I'd better go out and see about it, when the screen doors crashed like a runaway horse had come through them, and the next minute a big yellow dog was back of the counter, trying to scrooch down and scrouge under it like he was scared and was hiding. He backed me into the corner without seeing me or knowing I was there, and like to have squashed me.

No dog—and it never struck me that maybe this wasn't a dog—no dog can just calmly sit down on me like that when I'm waking up from a nap, and get away with it, no matter *how* big he is, and in spite of the darkness under there I could see and feel that this was the biggest dog in the world. I had been dreaming I was in a fight, anyhow, when he crowded in there with his hindquarters on top of me, and I bit him on the hind leg.

When I bit him he let out a noise like a thrashing machine starting up. It wasn't a bark. Nothing but the end of the world coming could bark like that. It was a noise more like I heard one time when the boys dared Freckles to lie down between the cattle guards on the railroad track and let a train run over him about a foot above his head, and I laid down there with him and it nearly deefened both of us. When he let out that noise I says to myself, "Great guns! What kind of a dog have I bit?"

And as he made that noise he jumped, and over went the counter, marble top and all, with a smash, and jam into the show window he went, with his tail swinging, and me right after him, practically on top of him. It wasn't that I exactly intended to chase him, you understand, but I was rattled on account of that awful noise he had let out, and I wanted to get away from there, and I went the same way he did. So when he bulged through the window glass onto the street I bulged right after him, and as he hit the sidewalk I bit him again. The first time I bit him because I was sore, but the second time I bit him because I was so nervous I didn't know what I was doing, hardly. And at the second bite, without even looking behind him, he jumped clean over the hitch rack and a team of horses in front of the store and landed right in the middle of the road with his tail between his legs.

And then I realized for the first time he wasn't a dog at all. He was the circus lion.

Mind you, I'm not saying that I would have bit him at all if I'd a-known at the start he was a lion.

And I ain't saying I *wouldn't* 'a' bit him, either.

But actions speak louder than words, and records are records, and you can't go back on them, and the fact is I *did* bite him. I bit him twice.

And that second bite, when we came bulging through the window together, the whole town saw. It was getting up telephone poles, and looking out of second-story windows, and crawling under sidewalks and into cellars, and trying to hide behind the town pump; but no matter where it was trying to get to, it had one eye on that lion, and it saw me chasing him out of that store. I don't say I would have chased him if he hadn't been just ahead of me, anyhow, and I don't say I wouldn't have chased him, but the facts are I *did* chase him.

The lion was just as scared as the town—and the town was so scared it didn't know the lion was scared at all—and when his trainer got hold of him in the road he was tickled to death to be led back to his cage, and he lay down in the far corner of it, away from the people, and trembled till he shook the wagon it was on.

But if there was any further doubts in any quarter about me being an aristocrat, the way I bit and chased that lion settled 'em forever. That night Freckles and Doc went to the circus, and I marched in along with them. And every kid in town, as they saw Freckles and me marching in, says:

"There goes the dog that licked the lion!"

And Freckles, every time anyone congratulated him on being the boy that belonged to that kind of a dog, would say:

"Blood will tell! Spot's an aristocrat, he is."

And him and me and Doc Watson, his dad, stopped in front of the lion's cage that night and took a good long look at him. He was a kind of an old moth-eaten lion, but he was a lion all right, and he looked mighty big in there. He looked so big that all my doubts come back on me, and I says to myself: "Honest, now, if I'd *a-known* he was a lion, and that *big* a lion, when I bit him, *would* I have bit him, or would I not?"

But just then Freckles reached down and patted me on the head and said: "You wasn't afraid of him, was you, old Spot! Yes, sir, blood will tell!"

*Eric Knight*

# LASSIE COME-HOME

The dog had met the boy by the school gate for five years. Now she couldn't understand that times were changed and she wasn't supposed to be there anymore. But the boy knew.

So when he opened the door of the cottage, he spoke before he entered.

"Mother," he said, "Lassie's come home again."

He waited a moment, as if in hope of something. But the man and woman inside the cottage did not speak.

"Come in, Lassie," the boy said.

He held open the door, and the tricolor collie walked in

obediently. Going head down, as a collie when it knows something is wrong, it went to the rug and lay down before the hearth, a black-white-and-gold aristocrat. The man, sitting on a low stool by the fireside, kept his eyes turned away. The woman went to the sink and busied herself there.

"She were waiting at school for me, just like always," the boy went on. He spoke fast, as if racing against time. "She must ha' got away again. I thought, happen this time, we might just—"

"No!" the woman exploded.

The boy's carelessness dropped. His voice rose in pleading.

"But this time, mother! Just this time. We could hide her. They wouldn't ever know."

"Dogs, dogs, dogs!" the woman cried. The words poured from her as if the boy's pleading had been a signal gun for her own anger. "I'm sick o' hearing about tykes round this house. Well, she's sold and gone and done with, so the quicker she's taken back the better. Now get her back quick, or first thing ye know we'll have Hynes round here again. Mr. Hynes!"

Her voice sharpened in imitation of the Cockney accent of the south: " 'Hi know you Yorkshiremen and yer come-'ome dogs. Training yer dogs to come 'ome so's yer can sell 'em hover and hover again.'

"Well, she's sold, so ye can take her out o' my house and home to them as bought her!"

The boy's bottom lip crept out stubbornly, and there was silence in the cottage. Then the dog lifted its head and nudged the man's hand, as a dog will when asking for patting. But the man drew away and stared, silently, into the fire.

The boy tried again, with the ceaseless guile of a child, his voice coaxing.

"Look, feyther, she wants thee to bid her welcome. Aye, she's that glad to be home. Happen they don't tak' good care on her up there? Look, her coat's a bit poorly, don't ye think? A bit o' linseed strained through her drinking water—that's what I'd gi' her."

Still looking in the fire, the man nodded. But the woman, as if perceiving the boy's new attack, sniffed.

"Aye, tha wouldn't be a Carraclough if tha didn't know more about tykes nor breaking eggs wi' a stick. Nor a Yorkshireman. My goodness, it seems to me sometimes that chaps in this village thinks more on their tykes nor they do o' their own flesh and blood. They'll sit by their firesides and let their own bairns starve so long as t' dog gets fed."

The man stirred, suddenly, but the boy cut in quickly.

"But she does look thin. Look, truly—they're not feeding her right. Just look!"

"Aye," the woman chattered. "I wouldn't put it past Hynes to steal t' best part o' t' dog meat for himself. And Lassie always was a strong eater."

"She's fair thin now," the boy said.

Almost unwillingly the man and woman looked at the dog for the first time.

"My gum, she is off a bit," the woman said. Then she caught herself. "Ma goodness, I suppose I'll have to fix her a bit o' summat. She can do wi' it. But soon as she's fed, back she goes. And never another dog I'll have in my house. Never another. Cooking and nursing for 'em, and as much trouble to bring up as a bairn!"

So, grumbling and chatting as a village woman will, she moved about, warming a pan of food for the dog. The man and boy watched the collie eat. When it was done, the boy took from the mantelpiece a folded cloth and a brush, and began prettying the collie's coat. The man watched for several minutes, and then could stand it no longer.

"Here," he said.

He took the cloth and brush from the boy and began working expertly on the dog, rubbing the rich, deep coat, then brushing the snowy whiteness of the full ruff and the apron, bringing out the heavy leggings on the forelegs. He lost himself in his work, and the boy sat on the rug, watching contentedly. The woman stood it as long as she could.

"Now will ye please tak' that tyke out o' here?"

The man flared in anger.

"Well, ye wouldn't have me tak' her back looking like a mucky Monday wash, wouldta?"

He bent again, and began fluffing out the collie's petticoats.

"Joe!" the woman pleaded. "Will ye tak' her out o' here? Hynes'll be nosing round afore ye know it. And I won't have that man in my house. Wearing his hat inside, and going on like he's the duke himself—him and his leggings!"

"All right, lass."

"And this time, Joe, tak' young Joe wi' ye."

"What for?"

"Well, let's get the business done and over with. It's him that Lassie runs away for. She comes for young Joe. So if he went wi' thee, and told her to stay, happen she'd be content and not run away no more, and then we'd have a little peace and quiet in the home—though heaven knows there's not much hope o' that these days, things being like they are." The woman's voice trailed away, as if she would soon cry in weariness.

The man rose. "Come, Joe," he said. "Get thy cap."

The Duke of Rudling walked along the gravel paths of his place with his granddaughter, Philippa. Philippa was a bright and knowing young woman, allegedly the only member of the duke's family he could address in unspotted language. For it was also alleged that the duke was the most irascible, vile-tempered old man in the three Ridings of Yorkshire.

"Country going to pot!" the duke roared, stabbing at the walk with his great blackthorn stick. "When I was a young man! Hah! Women today not as pretty. Horses today not as fast. As for dogs—ye don't see dogs today like—"

Just then the duke and Philippa came round a clump of rhododendrons and saw a man, a boy, and a dog.

"Ah," said the duke, in admiration. Then his brow knotted. "Damme, Carraclough! What're ye doing with my dog?"

He shouted it quite as if the others were in the next county, for it was also the opinion of the Duke of Rudling that people were not nearly so keen of hearing as they used to be when he was a young man.

"It's Lassie," Carraclough said. "She runned away again and I brought her back."

Carraclough lifted his cap, and poked the boy to do the same, not in any servile gesture, but to show that they were as well brought up as the next.

"Damme, ran away again!" the duke roared. "And I told that utter nincompoop Hynes to—where is he? Hynes! Hynes! Damme, Hynes, what're ye hiding for?"

"Coming, your lordship!" sounded a voice, far away behind the shrubberies. And soon Hynes appeared, a sharp-faced man in check coat, riding breeches, and the cloth leggings that grooms wear.

"Take this dog," roared the duke, "and pen her up! And damme, if she breaks out again, I'll—I'll—"

The duke waved his great stick threateningly, and then, without so much as a thank-you or kiss-the-back-of-my-hand to Joe Carraclough, he went stamping and muttering away.

"I'll pen 'er up," Hynes muttered, when the duke was gone. "And if she ever gets awye agyne, I'll—"

He made as if to grab the dog, but Joe Carraclough's hobnailed boot trod heavily on Hynes's foot.

"I brought my lad wi' me to bid her stay, so we'll pen her up this time. Eigh—sorry! I didn't see I were on thy foot. Come, Joe, lad."

They walked down the crunching gravel path, along by

the neat kennel buildings. When Lassie was behind the closed door, she raced into the high wire run where she could see them as they went. She pressed close against the wire, waiting.

The boy stood close, too, his fingers through the meshes touching the dog's nose.

"Go on, lad," his father ordered. "Bid her stay!"

The boy looked around, as if for help that he did not find. He swallowed, and then spoke, low and quickly.

"Stay here, Lassie, and don't come home no more," he said. "And don't come to school for me no more. Because I don't want to see ye no more. 'Cause tha's a bad dog, and we don't love thee no more, and we don't want thee. So stay there forever and leave us be, and don't never come home no more."

Then he turned, and because it was hard to see the path plainly, he stumbled. But his father, who was holding his head very high as they walked away from Hynes, shook him savagely, and snapped roughly: "Look where tha's going!"

Then the boy trotted beside his father. He was thinking that he'd never be able to understand why grown-ups sometimes were so bad-tempered with you, just when you needed them most.

After that, there were days and days that passed, and the dog did not come to the school gate anymore. So then it was not like old times. There were so many things that were not like old times.

The boy was thinking that as he came wearily up the path and opened the cottage door and heard his father's voice, tense with anger: ". . . walk my feet off. If tha thinks I like—"

Then they heard his opening of the door and the voice stopped and the cottage was silent.

That's how it was now, the boy thought. They stopped talking in front of you. And this, somehow, was too much for him to bear.

He closed the door, ran out into the night, and onto the moor, that great flat expanse of land where all the people of that village walked in lonesomeness when life and its troubles seemed past bearing.

A long while later, his father's voice cut through the darkness.

"What's tha doing out here, Joe lad?"

"Walking."

"Aye."

They went on together, aimlessly, each following his own thoughts. And they both thought about the dog that had been sold.

"Tha maun't think we're hard on thee, Joe," the man said at last. "It's just that a chap's got to be honest. There's that to it. Sometimes, when a chap doesn't have much, he clings right hard to what he's got. And honest is honest, and there's no two ways about it.

"Why, look, Joe. Seventeen year I worked in that Clarabelle Pit till she shut down, and a good collier too. Seventeen year! And butties I've had by the dozen, and never a man of 'em can ever say that Joe Carraclough kept what wasn't his, nor spoke what wasn't true. Not a man in his Riding can ever call a Carraclough mishonest.

"And when ye've sold a man summat, and ye've taken his brass, and ye've spent it—well, then done's done. That's all. And ye've got to stand by that."

"But Lassie was—"

"Now, Joe! Ye can't alter it, ever. It's done—and happen it's for t' best. No two ways, Joe, she were getting hard to feed. Why, ye wouldn't want Lassie to be going around getting peaked and pined, like some chaps round here keep their tykes. And if ye're fond of her, then just think on it that now she's got lots to eat, and a private kennel, and a good run to herself, and living like a varritable princess, she is. Ain't that best for her?"

"We wouldn't pine her. We've always got lots to eat."

The man blew out his breath, angrily. "Eigh, Joe, nowt pleases thee. Well then, tha might as well have it. Tha'll never see Lassie no more. She run home once too often, so the duke's taken her wi' him up to his place in Scotland, and there she'll stay. So it's good-bye and good luck to her, and she'll never come home no more, she won't. Now, I weren't off to tell thee, but there it is, so put it in thy pipe and smoke it, and let's never say a word about it no more—especially in front of thy mother."

The boy stumbled on in the darkness. Then the man halted.

"We ought to be getting back, lad. We left thy mother alone."

He turned the boy about, and then went on, but as if he were talking to himself.

"Tha sees, Joe, women's not like men. They have to stay home and manage best they can, and just spend the time in wishing. And when things don't go right, well, they have to take it out in talk and give a man hell. But it don't mean nowt, really, so tha shouldn't mind when thy mother talks hard.

"Ye just got to learn to be patient and let 'em talk, and just let it go up t' chimney wi' th' smoke."

Then they were quiet, until, over the rise, they saw the lights of the village. Then the boy spoke: "How far away is Scotland, feyther?"

"Nay, lad, it's a long, long road."

"But how far, feyther?"

"I don't know—but it's a longer road than thee or me'll ever walk. Now, lad. Don't fret no more, and try to be a man —and don't plague thy mother no more, wilta?"

Joe Carraclough was right. It is a long road, as they say in the North, from Yorkshire to Scotland. Much too far for a man to walk—or a boy. And though the boy often thought of it, he remembered his father's words on the moor, and he put the thought behind him.

But there is another way of looking at it; and that's the distance from Scotland to Yorkshire. And that is just as far as from Yorkshire to Scotland. A matter of about four hundred miles, it would be, from the Duke of Rudling's place far up in the Highlands, to the village of Holdersby. That would be for a man, who could go fairly straight.

To an animal, how much farther would it be? For a dog can study no maps, read no signposts, ask no directions. It could only go blindly, by instinct, knowing that it must keep on to the south, to the south. It would wander and err, quest and quarter, run into firths and lochs that would send it side-tracking and backtracking before it could go again on its way —south.

A thousand miles, it would be, going that way—a thousand miles over strange terrain.

There would be moors to cross, and burns to swim. And then those great, long lochs that stretch almost from one side of that dour land to another would bar the way and send a dog questing a hundred miles before it could find a crossing that would allow it to go south.

And, too, there would be rivers to cross, wide rivers like the Forth and the Clyde, the Tweed and the Tyne, where one must go miles to find bridges. And the bridges would be in towns. And in the towns there would be officials—like the one in Lanarkshire. In all his life he had never let a captured dog get away—except one. That one was a gaunt, snarling collie that whirled on him right in the pound itself, and fought and twisted loose to race away down the city street—going south.

But there are also kind people, too; ones knowing and understanding in the ways of dogs. There was an old couple in Durham who found a dog lying exhausted in a ditch one night—lying there with its head to the south. They took that dog into their cottage and warmed it and fed it and nursed it.

And because it seemed an understanding, wise dog, they kept it in their home, hoping it would learn to be content. But, as it grew stronger, every afternoon toward four o'clock it would go to the door and whine, and then begin pacing back and forth between the door and the window, back and forth as the animals do in their cages at the zoo.

They tried every wile and every kindness to make it bide with them, but finally, when the dog began to refuse food, the old people knew what they must do. Because they understood dogs, they opened the door one afternoon and they watched a collie go, not down the road to the right, or to the left, but straight across a field toward the south; going steadily at a trot, as if it knew it still had a long, long road to travel.

Ah, a thousand miles of tor and brae, of shire and moor, of path and road and plowland, of river and stream and burn and brook and beck, of snow and rain and fog and sun, is a long way, even for a human being. But it would seem too far —much, much too far—for any dog to travel blindly and win through.

And yet—and yet—who shall say why, when so many weeks had passed that hope against hope was dying, a boy coming out of school, out of the cloakroom that always smelled of damp wool drying, across the concrete play yard with the black, waxed slides, should turn his eyes to a spot by the school gate from force of five years of habit, and see there a dog? Not a dog, this one, that lifted glad ears above a proud, slim head with its black-and-gold mask; but a dog that lay weakly, trying to lift a head that would no longer lift, trying to wag a tail that was torn and blotched and matted with dirt and burs, and managing to do nothing much except to whine in a weak, happy, crying way as a boy on his knees threw arms about it, and hands touched it that had not touched it for many a day.

Then who shall picture the urgency of a boy, running, awkwardly, with a great dog in his arms running through the village, past the empty mill, past the Labor Exchange, where the men looked up from their deep ponderings on life and the dole? Or who shall describe the high tones of a voice—a boy's voice, calling as he runs up a path: "Mother! Oh, mother! Lassie's come home! Lassie's come home!"

Nor does anyone who ever owned a dog need to be told the sound a man makes as he bends over a dog that has been his for many years; nor how a woman moves quickly, preparing food—which might be the family's condensed milk stirred into warm water; nor how the jowl of a dog is lifted so that raw egg and brandy, bought with precious pence, should be spooned in; nor how bleeding pads are bandaged, tenderly.

That was one day. There was another day when the woman in the cottage sighed with pleasure, for a dog lifted itself to its feet for the first time to stand over a bowl of oatmeal, putting its head down and lapping again and again while its pinched flanks quivered.

And there was another day when the boy realized that, even now, the dog was not to be his again. So the cottage rang again with protests and cries, and a woman shrilling: "Is there never to be no more peace in my house and home?" Long after he was in bed that night the boy heard the rise and fall of the woman's voice, and the steady, reiterative tone of the man's. It went on long after he was asleep.

In the morning the man spoke, not looking at the boy, saying the words as if he had long rehearsed them.

"Thy mother and me have decided upon it that Lassie shall stay here till she's better. Anyhow, nobody could nurse her better than us. But the day that t' duke comes back, then back she goes, too. For she belongs to him, and that's honest, too. Now tha has her for a while, so be content."

In childhood, "for a while" is such a great stretch of days when seen from one end. It is a terribly short time seen from the other.

The boy knew how short it was that morning as he went to school and saw a motorcar driven by a young woman. And in the car was a gray-thatched, terrible old man, who waved a cane and shouted: "Hi! Hi, there! Damme, lad! You there! Hi!"

Then it was no use running, for the car could go faster than you, and soon it was beside you and the man was saying: "Damme, Philippa, will you make this smelly thing stand still a moment? Hi, lad!"

"Yes, sir."

"You're What's-'is-Name's lad, aren't you?"

"Ma feyther's Joe Carraclough."

"I know. I know. Is he home now?"

"No, sir. He's away to Allerby. A mate spoke for him at the pit and he's gone to see if there's a chance."

"When'll he be back?"

"I don't know. I think about tea."

"Eh, yes. Well, yes. I'll drop round about fivish to see that father of yours. Something important."

It was hard to pretend to listen to lessons. There was only waiting for noon. Then the boy ran home.

"Mother! T' duke is back and he's coming to take Lassie away."

"Eigh, drat my buttons. Never no peace in this house. Is tha sure?"

"Aye. He stopped me. He said tell feyther he'll be round at five. Can't we hide her? Oh, mother."

"Nay, thy feyther—"

"Won't you beg him? Please, please. Beg feyther to—"

"Young Joe, now it's no use. So stop thy teasing! Thy feyther'll not lie. That much I'll give him. Come good, come bad, he'll not lie."

"But just this once, mother. Please beg him, just this once. Just one lie wouldn't hurt him. I'll make it up to him.

I will. When I'm growed up, I'll get a job. I'll make money. I'll buy him things—and you, too. I'll buy you both anything you want if you'll only—"

For the first time in his trouble the boy became a child, and the mother, looking over, saw the tears that ran openly down his contorted face. She turned her face to the fire, and there was a pause. Then she spoke.

"Joe, tha mustn't," she said softly. "Tha must learn never to want nothing in life like that. It don't do, lad. Tha mustn't want things bad, like tha wants Lassie."

The boy shook his clenched fists in impatience.

"It ain't that, mother. Ye don't understand. Don't yer see—it ain't me that wants her. It's her that wants us! Tha's wha made her come all them miles. It's her that wants us, so terrible bad!"

The woman turned and stared. It was as if, in that moment, she were seeing this child, this boy, this son of her own, for the first time in many years. She turned her head down toward the table. It was surrender.

"Come and eat, then," she said. "I'll talk to him. I will that, all right. I feel sure he won't lie. But I'll talk to him, all right. I'll talk to Mr. Joe Carraclough. I will indeed."

At five that afternoon, the Duke of Rudling, fuming and muttering, got out of a car at a cottage gate to find a boy barring his way. This was a boy who stood, stubbornly, saying fiercely: "Away wi' thee! Thy tyke's net here!"

"Damme, Philippa, th' lad's touched," the duke said. "He is. He's touched."

Scowling and thumping his stick, the old duke advanced until the boy gave way, backing down the path out of the reach of the waving blackthorn stick.

"Thy tyke's net here," the boy protested.

"What's he saying?" the girl asked.

"Says my dog isn't here. Damme, you going deaf? I'm supposed to be deaf, and I hear him plainly enough. Now, ma lad, what tyke o' mine's net here?"

As he turned to the boy, the duke spoke in broadest Yorkshire, as he did always to the people of the cottages—a habit which the Duchess of Rudling, and many more members of the duke's family, deplored.

"Coom, coom, ma lad. Whet tyke's net here?"

"No tyke o' thine. Us hasn't got it." The words began running faster and faster as the boy backed away from the fearful old man who advanced. "No tyke could have done it. No tyke can come all them miles. It isn't Lassie. It's another one that looks like her. It isn't Lassie!"

"Why, bless ma heart and sowl," the duke puffed. "Where's thy father, ma lad?"

The door behind the boy opened, and a woman's voice spoke.

"If it's Joe Carraclough ye want, he's out in the shed—and been there shut up half the afternoon."

"What's this lad talking about—a dog of mine being here?"

"Nay," the woman snapped quickly. "He didn't say a tyke o' thine was here. He said it wasn't here."

"Well, what dog o' mine isn't here, then?"

The woman swallowed, and looked about as if for help. The duke stood, peering from under his jutting eyebrows. Her answer, truth or lie, was never spoken, for then they heard the rattle of a door opening, and a man making a pursing sound with his lips, as he will when he wants a dog to follow, and then Joe Carraclough's voice said: "This is t' only tyke us has here. Does it look like any dog that belongs to thee?"

With his mouth opening to cry one last protest, the boy turned. And his mouth stayed open. For there he saw his father, Joe Carraclough, the collie fancier, standing with a dog at his heels—a dog that sat at his left heel patiently, as any well-trained dog should do—as Lassie used to do. But this dog was not Lassie. In fact, it was ridiculous to think of it at the same moment as you thought of Lassie.

For where Lassie's skull was aristocratic and slim, this dog's head was clumsy and rough. Where Lassie's ears stood in twin-lapped symmetry, this dog had one ear draggling and the other standing up Alsatian fashion in a way to give any collie breeder the cold shivers. Where Lassie's coat was rich tawny gold, this dog's coat had ugly patches of black; and where Lassie's apron was a billowing stretch of snow-white, this dog had puddles of off-color blue-merle mixture. Besides, Lassie had four white paws, and this one had one paw white, two dirty-brown, and one almost black.

That is the dog they all looked at as Joe Carraclough stood there, having told no lie, having only asked a question. They all stood, waiting the duke's verdict.

But the duke said nothing. He only walked forward slowly, as if he were seeing a dream. He bent beside the collie, looking with eyes that were as knowing about dogs as any Yorkshireman alive. And those eyes did not waste themselves upon twisted ears, or blotched marking, or rough head. Instead they were looking at a paw that the duke lifted, looking at the underside of the paw, staring intently at five black pads, crossed and recrossed with the scars where thorns had lacerated, and stones had torn.

For a long time the duke stared, and when he got up he did not speak in Yorkshire accents any more. He spoke as a gentleman should, and he said: "Joe Carraclough. I never owned this dog. 'Pon my soul, she's never belonged to me. Never!"

Then he turned and went stumping down the path, thumping his cane and saying: "Bless my soul. Four hundred miles! Damme, wouldn't ha' believed it. Damme—five hundred miles!"

He was at the gate when his granddaughter whispered to him fiercely.

"Of course," he cried. "Mind your own business. Exactly what I came for. Talking about dogs made me forget. Carraclough! Carraclough! What're ye hiding for?"

"I'm still here, sir."

"Ah, there you are. You working?"

"Eigh, now. Working," Joe said. That's the best he could manage.

"Yes, working, working!" The duke fumed.

"Well, now—" Joe began.

Then Mrs. Carraclough came to his rescue, as a good housewife in Yorkshire will.

"Why, Joe's got three or four things that he's been considering," she said, with proper display of pride. "But he hasn't quite said yes or no to any of them yet."

"Then say no, quick," the old man puffed. "Had to sack Hynes. Didn't know a dog from a drunken filly. Should ha' known all along no damn Londoner could handle dogs fit for Yorkshire taste. How much, Carraclough?"

"Well, now," Joe began.

"Seven pounds a week, and worth every penny," Mrs. Carraclough chipped in. "One o' them other offers may come up to eight," she lied, expertly. For there's always a certain amount of lying to be done in life, and when a woman's married to a man who has made a lifelong cult of being honest, then she's got to learn to do the lying for two.

"Five," roared the duke—who, after all, was a Yorkshire-man, and couldn't help being a bit sharp about things that pertained to money.

"Six," said Mrs. Carraclough.

"Five pound ten," bargained the duke, cannily.

"Done," said Mrs. Carraclough, who would have been willing to settle for three pounds in the first place. "But, o' course, us gets the cottage too."

"All right," puffed the duke. "Five pound ten and the cottage. Begin Monday. But—on one condition. Carraclough, you can live on my land, but I won't have that thick-skulled, screw-lugged, gay-tailed eyesore of a misshapen mongrel on my property. Now never let me see her again. You'll get rid of her?"

He waited, and Joe fumbled for words. But it was the boy who answered, happily, gaily: "Oh, no, sir. She'll be waiting at school for me most o' the time. And, anyway, in a day or so we'll have her fixed up and coped up so's ye'd never, never recognize her."

"I don't doubt that," puffed the duke, as he went to the car. "I don't doubt ye could do just exactly that."

It was a long time afterward, in the car, that the girl said: "Don't sit there like a lion on the Nelson column. And I thought you were supposed to be a hard man."

"Fiddlesticks, m'dear. I'm a ruthless realist. For five years I've sworn I'd have that dog by hook or crook, and now, egad, at last I've got her."

"Pooh! You had to buy the man before you could get his dog."

"Well, perhaps that's not the worst part of the bargain."

## *Sholom Aleichem*

# RABCHIK, A JEWISH DOG

Rabchik was a dog with white spots. Not a big dog—middle-size—quiet, not a grabber. He did not, as other dogs do, like to jump at one from behind to snatch at a hem or take a bite out of a leg. He was happiest just to be left alone. So it follows that every God-fearing person picked on him. Giving Rabchik a blow with a stick, or kicking him when his back was turned, or throwing a rock at his head, or emptying a slop pail at him, was sport for everyone—almost a pious duty. Rabchik, attacked this way, did not, as other dogs might, pause to discuss the matter or bark his distress, or show his teeth. No. After receiving his blows,

Rabchik would grovel, belly nearly to the ground, and whine: *"Aie, aie, aie."* Then, his tail between his legs, he would run off to hide in some corner where he sank into deep thought and snapped at flies.

Who was Rabchik? Where did he come from? That's hard to know. It may be that he was left behind by the former landlord of the yard. It may be that he missed his way, lost his owner, adopted a new one, and stayed on. You know how such things happen: One is taking a walk, and then—there's a lost dog in your tracks. You think, Hey, what's this tagging along? You raise your hand to the dog and shout, "Beat it!" The dog stops, bow like a human, and just as you're trying to smack him one, manages to get even closer. Now you bend; you make a feint with your hand, pretending to throw a rock at him. It does no good. You stand watching the dog; the dog stands watching you. You look silently into each other's eyes. You spit, and start off again. The dog follows, and you're going out of your mind. You grab a stick and go at him fiercely, which gives the dog an idea: He lies down, sticks his feet in the air, trembles and shivers and gazes into your eyes as if to say, "Well, you want to beat me? Beat away."

That's the kind of dog our Rabchik was.

Rabchik was not one to snatch at food. You could leave the finest things lying around the house and he would not touch them. He understood clearly that whatever was put *under* the table was meant for him. Anything else was none of his business—though it was said that Rabchik, as a youngster, had been something of a brat. One time, the story goes, as he stalked the meat-salting board, meaning to steal the leg of a goose, he was seen by Breinah the cook, who set up a dreadful racket, crying, "Isaac, Isaac!" Issac, the handyman, came running in just at the moment when Rabchik was trying to make off with the stolen goose leg. Isaac managed to squeeze Rabchik in the doorway so that Rabchik's front end was on one side of the door, and his hind end on the other. Oh, they really made Rabchik pay: On one side of the door, Isaac banged away at his head with a stick, while on the other side, Breinah beat at him with a chunk of wood, screaming all the while, "Isaac, Isaac!"

That incident left its mark on him. The minute anyone went up to him, looked into his face, and said, "Isaac, Isaac," he ran off wherever his legs would take him.

Paraska bothered Rabchik more than anyone. Paraska was the one who did our laundry, whitewashed the walls, and milked the cows. What did she have against Rabchik? It's hard to say, but he annoyed her on sight. The moment she saw him, she was inflamed: "A plague on you, you scurvy hound." And Rabchik, as if on purpose, was invariably under her feet. Paraska, as she worked, avenged herself on him as we do on Haman. If she was washing clothes, she would pour a basin of cold water over him. Rabchik hated such a bath, after which he had to shake himself long and hard. If she was whitewashing the walls, she would spatter his face so that he had to lick at himself for an hour at a stretch to get clean. If she was milking the cow, she would throw a chunk of wood at his legs.

Rabchik learned to leap. When he saw a chunk coming his way, he learned to dodge like an elf. There was one time when Rabchik got the worst of such attentions. Paraska had flung a piece of wood which struck his front paw with such force it made him cry out strangely, *"Aie, aie, aie."* Everyone in the courtyard came running. No sooner did Rabchik see that people were gathering than he began to whimper, showing everyone his broken foot, as if to say, "See, see what Paraska has done," thinking, evidently, that they would take his side and that Paraska would be blamed. Perhaps he expected that they would decapitate her for what she had done.

Actually, what happened was that everyone burst out laughing. Mustached Breinah flew out of her kitchen with a big spoon in her hands. Wiping her nose with her bare elbow, she said, "Did they break his stupid foot? Good. Good." As for the street urchins, those delinquents came running from all sides, yelling and whistling, after which Paraska came up and really let him have it, pouring a pitcherful of scalding water over his back. Rabchik howled and yammered, *"Aie, aie, aie,"* as he leaped and twirled, biting his own tail, all the while keeping up such a racket that it excited the youngsters to further laughter. The sight of Rabchik dancing on three legs seemed to unleash their pent-up ugliness, and they went at him with sticks. Rabchik ran off, howling, stumbling, followed by the street boys with their sticks and their stones, whistling and hooting, driving him farther and farther out of the village and beyond the mill.

Rabchik ran on, convinced that he would never come back to the village. He was off, into the wide world, anywhere at all that his legs would carry him. He ran . . . and ran . . . until he reached the next village, where he was met by the local dogs. They sniffed him up and down and said, "Welcome, dog. Where are you from? And what sort of decoration is that on your back? It looks as if someone had singed a hunk of hide in the middle of your back."

"Ah, don't ask," says Rabchik sadly. "There's a lot to tell but little worth hearing. Can I spend the night here?"

"With the greatest pleasure," the local dogs say. "The outdoors is roomy enough, and it's even more spacious under the sky."

"What do you do for food?" asks Rabchik. "How do you ease your hungry stomach when it makes its demands?"

"Not bad. Slops can be found everywhere. As for meat—well, God created bones. If the householders eat meat, we get bones. One way or another, our stomachs are filled."

"And your householders? How are they?" asks Rabchik, making an inquiring gesture with his tail.

"The householders are . . . householders," say the dogs, making an end of the matter.

"Well. And . . . Paraska?" Rabchik inquires.

"Paraska? What Paraska?" reply the dogs.

"The Paraska who does the laundry, whitewashes the walls, and milks the cow. You don't know Paraska?"

The village dogs study Rabchik as if he has lost his mind. "What kind of Paraska-stuff is this?" Again, they sniff him over from every side and one by one they drift away, each to his personal garbage heap.

Rabchik thinks, What fortunate dogs, and stretches out on God's earth, under God's sky, thinking to doze a bit. But he can't sleep. First, there is the matter of his scalded hide; it bites and smarts terribly; and the tormenting flies—no way to drive them off. Second, his stomach is growling. He would like to gnaw on something, but there is nothing to chew. He'll have to wait until morning. And third, he can't sleep because of all the things he heard from the village dogs. There were no Isaacs among them to squeeze him with a door and bang him with a hunk of wood; there were no Paraskas to scald him with boiling water; there were no street boys to whistle at him or beat him with sticks or chase him. There were fortunate dogs in the world! And I thought my world was the whole world. Well, a worm in horseradish can't imagine anything sweeter.

Rabchik falls asleep and dreams of a huge, brimful slop bucket with bread and plenty of tripes and meat scraps, groats, and a mixture of millet and beans. And bones! A whole treasure house of bones. Shin bones, rib bones, marrow bones. Fish bones—whole fish heads waiting to be sucked. Rabchik doesn't know where to begin. The village dogs standing respectfully by say, "Blessed are those who partake," and watch him prepare for his feast.

For politeness' sake, Rabchik says, "Come. Eat."

"Eat in good health," say the village dogs in a friendly way.

Suddenly, he hears a voice in his ear crying, "Isaac!"

Rabchik starts up. It was only a dream.

In the morning, Rabchik prowls the yards looking for a slop kettle, a piece of zwieback, a bit of bone, but wherever he goes, the garbage heaps are taken. "Can one get a bite here?" Rabchik asks.

"You? No. Maybe in the next yard."

Rabchik trots about from yard to yard—everywhere, the same tune. He thinks the matter over and decides that politeness doesn't pay. Much better to make a grab at whatever offers, but at the very first "grab," the local dogs really let him have it. First, they glare at him; then they show their teeth. Then several of them jump him, biting and tearing, ruining his tail; after which they give him an honorable send-off well beyond the village gates.

His tail between his legs, Rabchik starts off to the next village. Arrived there, it is the same story all over again. First, pleasant words; treated like a guest; but the moment he approaches a slop bucket, there are angry looks, growls, bared teeth, then tearing and biting and "Beat it!" from all sides.

Finally, this prowling from place to place disgusts him and he decides that people are no good, and dogs not much of an improvement. Better to live in the forest among the beasts.

So Rabchik went off to the forest and wandered there alone. One day, two, then three, until he felt his guts shriveling and his stomach cramping more tightly the farther he walked. In the last throes of hunger and thirst, he felt there was nothing left for him but to lie down in midforest and perish. It was an annoying thought, because what he wanted most to do was to live.

Tucking his tail under him, Rabchik stretches out his front paws, puts out his tongue, and settles down under a tree to think a dog's thought: Where to find a bit of bread, a morsel of meat, even a bone, a drop of water? Thus anguish makes a seeker of him, a philosopher. And he speculates, wondering why he, a dog, is being punished rather than the beasts or the birds or the rest of the world's creatures. For instance, the bird that flies to its nest, or the lizard scurrying home to its hole, or the crawling worm, or the beetle or the ant—they all have their homes and can provide for themselves. "Only I, a dog . . . *bark, bark, bark.*"

"Who barks in the forest?" inquires a hungry wolf, his tongue lolling as he runs.

Rabchik, who has never seen a wolf before, thinks it is a dog. Slowly, he gets to his feet, stretches, and approaches the wolf. "Who are you?" the wolf asks arrogantly. "Where are you from, and what are you doing here?"

Rabchik is delighted to have met such a friendly brother, someone to whom he can at least tell his troubles, and he pours out his bitter heart to the wolf. "I'll tell you the truth," says Rabchik, after reciting his list of woes, "I would be just as glad now to meet with a lion or a bear, or even a wolf."

"What would happen, do you suppose?" asks the wolf with a sinister smile.

"Nothing," says Rabchik, "but if I'm destined to die, I'd just as soon a wolf killed me rather than die of hunger among my own kind—among dogs."

"In that case," says the wolf, breathing hard and clicking its teeth, "you should know that *I* am a wolf, and I have a great urge to tear you to bits and make a meal of you. Because I'm terribly hungry. Eight days have gone by since I've had anything to eat."

At these words, Rabchik was so frightened that his singed skin began to tremble. "My lord king, O reverend wolf," Rabchik said tearfully, making a pitiful face, "may God send you a better meal. What will you get eating me? Hide and bones, as you can see. Take my advice, take pity on my dog's bones and let me be."

With that, Rabchik tucked in his tail, arched his back, crawled on his belly, and made such ugly gestures that they turned the wolf's stomach so that it was nearly faint with revulsion. "Take your filthy tail," said the wolf, "and get to hell out of my sight, you hound. I can't bear to look at your ugly face."

More dead than alive, Rabchik ran off, so fast he could hardly feel the earth under his feet, afraid even to look around. Running, away . . . away from the forest. Back to the village.

Arrived back in his village, Rabchik overshot the yard where he had grown up (though he was drawn to the place where he had been constantly beaten, where he had had his foot broken and his back scalded). He found himself instead in the butchers' market among the butchers' dogs, that is, among his own kind.

"Well, look who's here. Where are you from?" the butchers' dogs say, yawning as they get ready for bed.

"To tell the truth, I'm from right here," says Rabchik. "Don't you recognize me? I'm Rabchik."

"Rabchik. Rabchik . . . the name sounds familiar," say the butchers' dogs, pretending not to know him.

"What sort of mark is that on your back?" asks a small dog named Tsutsik, springing impudently at him.

"Must be a sign to make him easy to recognize—or else it's a beauty mark," jokes Rudek, a shaggy red dog.

Sirkeh, a gray bachelor dog with one eye and one ear missing, says, "If it comes to that, I'm the one to tell you about marks. What he has is a mark of battle—against other dogs, whole gangs of them."

"Talk, talk. Everyone talks," says Zhuk, a black dog without a tail. "Let Rabchik talk. He can tell us better himself."

Rabchik lies down and starts to tell his story, leaving out not the smallest detail. All the dogs listen, except red Rudek, the jokester who interrupts constantly with his quips.

"Rudek, are you going to shut up?" asks Zhuk, the black dog with no tail, and gives a great yawn. "Tell, tell, Rabchik. We like hearing stories after our meals."

Rabchik tells on and on, reciting his doleful story, but no one is listening. Tsutsik talks quietly with Sirkeh. Rudek makes jokes, and Zhuk snores louder than ten soldiers. From time to time he starts from his sleep to say, "Tell, tell. We like hearing stories after our meals."

Rabchik is up early the next morning. Keeping his distance, he watches the butchers wielding their cleavers. Here, a forequarter of beef is being hacked, its neck dangling and dripping blood; there, a hindquarter—a lovely treasure, marbled with fat. Rabchik looks on, swallowing his saliva. The butchers cut the meat up. From time to time they throw a piece of skin, or meat, or a bone to the dogs who leap to catch it. Rabchik watches the dogs outsmarting each other, making skillful jumps in the right places, never missing a bone. No sooner does a dog catch its share than it goes off to one side, full of self-importance, and lies down to preside over its feast, looking about at the other dogs as if to say, "You see this bone. *My* bone. *I* am eating it."

The others pretend not to notice, though they are thinking, "May you choke on your bone; may the plague take you. Gobbling away all morning, and we have to watch you eat. May the worms eat you."

Another dog sneaks off, a piece of skin in its mouth, looking for a corner in which to eat without being seen—afraid of the evil eye.

Still another stands watching an angry butcher shouting and quarreling with his fellows. Fawning, the dog wags its tail and says, "You see this butcher," (they all look as if they were angry), "I know him. I give you my word—he's a fine man, a precious stone, a diamond, with a character of gold. These butchers have a real sympathy for us. Truly 'Friends of the Dog.' Watch. In a minute, you'll see a bone with meat still on it come flying—hup!" It leaps into the air to give the other dogs the impression it has really caught something worthwhile.

A nearby dog calls out, "That one—he's two things: first, a flattering dog, and then, a liar. May the devil take him."

One dog stands at a chopping block, and the moment the butcher turns his back, it leaps to the block and licks at the blood. Seeing this, several of the dogs bark, betraying it to the butcher, swearing up and down that the dog has stolen a bit of meat. "As we hope to prosper," they say, "we saw it with our own eyes. May we die on the spot if we are not telling the truth. May we choke on the very first bit of bone that we eat. May we never have anything but sheep's horns and hooves to gnaw on."

"Ugh. It's repulsive . . . enough to turn one's stomach," says an old dog nearby who would have been glad to lick a little at the chopping block itself.

Rabchik thinks: "How will it all end?" Is he merely going to stand by and watch as the dogs leap and snatch? Better to do some leaping and snatching himself. But even as he is considering the matter, several dogs are at his throat, tearing and biting precisely where he is already in great pain.

Rabchik tucks up his tail, finds his way into a corner, lifts his chin, and howls.

"Why are you crying?" asks Zhuk, licking his lips after his meal.

"What's to keep me from crying?" says Rabchik. "I'm the

unluckiest dog in the world. I thought that here, among my own kind, I'd be able to get something. Believe me, I don't usually crawl but I'm dying of hunger. I'm at my last gasp."

"I believe you," says Zhuk with a sigh. "I know about hunger and I understand your situation, but there's no way I can help you. It's been all worked out: here each butcher has his special dog, and every dog his own butcher."

"Is that really fair?" Rabchik says. "What about justice? What about dogmanity? Is it possible that a dog can perish among dogs, that one can die of hunger among those who have fed?"

"I sigh for you," Zhuk says. "It's as much as I can do." He yawns deliciously and gets ready for his usual after-breakfast nap.

"If that's how it is," says Rabchik, plucking up his courage, "I'll go right to the butchers. It may be I can bark one up for myself."

"Go in good health," Zhuk replies. "Just as long as you keep away from *mine.* If you don't, I'll turn you into a tailless dog—like me. Get it?"

Rabchik went directly to the butchers, bypassing the other dogs. He jumped into the butchers' faces, wagged his tail. But a loser drags bad luck. One of the butchers, a huge, playful fellow with broad shoulders, threw a cleaver at him. Fortunately, Rabchik was a good jumper, or he would have been hacked in two. "You're not a bad dancer," quipped Rudek. "Much better than our Tsutsik. Tsutsik, come and watch some real dancing."

Tsutsik runs up and jumps right in Rabchik's face. Rabchik can stand it no longer. He grabs Tsutsik, throws him down, and bites him in the stomach, venting all his misery on him. Then he takes to his heels and runs off.

At last, all alone in a field, he lies down in the path and puts his chin between his paws. He feels so deeply ashamed he does not care if he ever sees the light of day again. He does not even mind the biting flies that now attack him. Let them bite; let them tear. To hell with it.

It's the end of the world, thinks Rabchik. When a dog among dogs, among his own kind, can't survive a single day, then the world has been turned topsy-turvy.

*Translated by Leonard Wolf*

*Ray Bradbury*

# THE EMISSARY

Martin knew it was autumn again, for Dog ran into the house bringing wind and frost and a smell of apples turned to cider under trees. In dark clocksprings of hair, Dog fetched goldenrod, dust of farewell-summer, acorn-husk, hair of squirrel, feather of departed robin, sawdust from fresh-cut cordwood, and leaves like charcoals shaken from a blaze of maple trees. Dog jumped. Showers of brittle fern, blackberry vine, marsh grass sprang over the bed where Martin shouted. No doubt, no doubt of it at all, this incredible beast was October!

"Here, boy, here!"

And Dog settled to warm Martin's body with all the bonfires and subtle burnings of the season, to fill the room with soft or heavy, wet or dry odors of far-traveling. In spring, he smelled of lilac, iris, lawn-mowered grass; in summer, ice-cream-mustached, he came pungent with firecracker, Roman candle, pinwheel, baked by the sun. But autumn! Autumn!

"Dog, what's it like outside?"

And lying there, Dog told as he always told. Lying there, Martin found autumn as in the old days before sickness bleached him white on his bed. Here was his contact, his carryall, the quick-moving part of himself he sent with a yell to run and return, circle and scent, collect and deliver the time and texture of worlds in town, country, by creek, river, lake, down-cellar, up-attic, in closet or coalbin. Ten dozen times a day he was gifted with sunflower seed, cinderpath, milkweed, horse chestnut, or full flame smell of pumpkin. Through the looming of the universe Dog shuttled; the design was hid in his pelt. Put out your hand, it was there. . . .

"And where did you go this morning?"

But he knew without hearing where Dog had rattled down hills where autumn lay in cereal crispness, where children lay in funeral pyres, in rustling heaps, the leaf-buried but watchful dead, as Dog and the world blew by. Martin trembled his fingers, searched the thick fur, read the long journey. Through stubbled fields, over glitters of ravine creek, down marbled spread of cemetery yard, into woods. In the great season of spices and rare incense, now Martin ran through his emissary, around, about, and home!

The bedroom door opened.

"That dog of yours is in trouble again."

Mother brought in a tray of fruit salad, cocoa, and toast, her blue eyes snapping.

"Mother . . ."

"Always digging places. Dug a hole in Miss Tarkins's garden this morning. She's spittin' mad. That's the fourth hole he's dug there this week."

"Maybe he's looking for something."

"Fiddlesticks, he's too darned curious. If he doesn't behave he'll be locked up."

Martin looked at this woman as if she were a stranger. "Oh, you wouldn't do that! How would I learn anything? How would I find things out if Dog didn't tell me?"

Mom's voice was quieter. "Is that what he does—tell you things?"

"There's nothing I don't know when he goes out and around and back, *nothing* I can't find out from him!"

They both sat looking at Dog and the dry strewings of mold and seed over the quilt.

"Well, if he'll just stop digging where he shouldn't, he can run all he wants," said Mother.

"Here, boy, here!"

And Martin snapped a tin note to the dog's collar:

MY OWNER IS MARTIN SMITH
TEN YEARS OLD
SICK IN BED
VISITORS WELCOME.

Dog barked. Mother opened the downstairs door and let him out.

Martin sat listening.

Far off and away you could hear Dog run in the quiet autumn rain that was falling now. You could hear the barking-jingling fade, rise, fade again as he cut down alley, over lawn, to fetch back Mr. Holloway and the oiled metallic smell of the delicate snowflake-interiored watches he repaired in his home shop. Or maybe he would bring Mr. Jacobs, the grocer, whose clothes were rich with lettuce, celery, tomatoes, and the secret tinned and hidden smell of the red demons stamped on cans of deviled ham. Mr. Jacobs and his unseen pink-meat devils waved often from the yard below. Or Dog brought Mr. Jackson, Mrs. Gillespie, Mr. Smith, Mrs. Holmes, *any* friend or near-friend, encountered, cornered, begged, worried, and at last shepherded home for lunch, or tea and biscuits.

Now, listening, Martin heard Dog below, with footsteps moving in a light rain behind him. The downstairs bell rang, Mom opened the door, light voices murmured. Martin sat forward, face shining. The stair treads creaked. A young woman's voice laughed quietly. Miss Haight, of course, his teacher from school!

The bedroom door sprang open.

Martin had company.

Morning, afternoon, evening, dawn and dusk, sun and moon circled with Dog, who faithfully reported temperatures of turf and air, color of earth and tree, consistency of mist or rain, but—most important of all—brought back again and again and again—Miss Haight.

On Saturday, Sunday, and Monday she baked Martin orange-iced cupcakes, brought him library books about dinosaurs and cavemen. On Tuesday, Wednesday, and Thursday somehow he beat her at dominoes, somehow she lost at checkers, and soon, she cried, he'd defeat her handsomely at chess. On Friday, Saturday, and Sunday they talked and never stopped talking, and she was so young and laughing and handsome and her hair was a soft, shining brown like the season outside the window, and she walked clear, clean, and quick, a heartbeat warm in the bitter afternoon when he heard it. Above all, she had the secret of signs, and could read and interpret Dog and the symbols she searched out and plucked forth from his coat with her miraculous fingers. Eyes shut, softly laughing, in a gypsy's voice, she divined the world from the treasures in her hands.

And on Monday afternoon, Miss Haight was dead.

Martin sat up in bed, slowly.

"Dead?" he whispered.

Dead, said his mother, yes, dead, killed in an auto accident a mile out of town. Dead, yes, dead, which meant cold to Martin, which meant silence and whiteness and winter come long before its time. Dead, silent, cold, white. The thoughts circled round, blew down, and settled in whispers.

Martin held Dog, thinking; turned to the wall. The lady with the autumn-colored hair. The lady with the laughter that was very gentle and never made fun and the eyes that watched your mouth to see everything you ever said. The-other-half-of-autumn-lady, who told what was left untold by Dog, about the world. The heartbeat at the still center of gray afternoon. The heartbeat fading . . .

"Mom? What do they do in the graveyard, Mom, under the ground? Just lay there?"

"*Lie* there."

"Lie there? Is that *all* they do? It doesn't sound like much fun."

"For goodness' sake, it's not made out to be fun."

"Why don't they jump up and run around once in a while if they get tired of lying there? God's pretty silly—"

"Martin!"

"Well, you'd think He'd treat people better than to tell them to lie still for keeps. That's impossible. Nobody can do it! I tried once. Dog tries. I tell him, 'Dead Dog!' He plays dead awhile, then gets sick and tired and wags his tail or opens one eye and looks at me, bored. Boy, I bet sometimes those graveyard people do the same, huh, Dog?"

Dog barked.

"Be still with that kind of talk!" said Mother.

Martin looked off into space.

"Bet that's exactly what they do," he said.

Autumn burned the trees bare and ran Dog still farther around, fording creek, prowling graveyard as was his custom, and back in the dusk to fire off volleys of barking that shook windows wherever he turned.

In the late last days of October, Dog began to act as if the wind had changed and blew from a strange country. He stood quivering on the porch below. He whined, his eyes fixed at the empty land beyond town. He brought no visitors for Martin. He stood for hours each day, as if leashed, trembling, then shot away straight, as if someone had called. Each night he returned later, with no one following. Each night, Martin sank deeper and deeper in his pillow.

"Well, people are busy," said Mother. "They haven't time to notice the tag Dog carries. Or they mean to come visit, but forget."

But there was more to it than that. There was the fevered shining in Dog's eyes, and his whimpering tic late at night, in some private dream. His shivering in the dark, under the bed. The way he sometimes stood half the night, looking at Martin as if some great and impossible secret was his and he knew no way to tell it save by savagely thumping his tail, or turning in endless circles, never to lie down, spinning and spinning again.

On October 30, Dog ran out and didn't come back at all, even when after supper Martin heard his parents call and call. The hour grew late, the streets and sidewalks stood empty, the air moved cold about the house, and there was nothing, nothing.

Long after midnight, Martin lay watching the world beyond the cool, clear glass windows. Now there was not even autumn, for there was no Dog to fetch it in. There would be no winter, for who could bring the snow to melt in your hands? Father, Mother? No, not the same. They couldn't play the game with its special secrets and rules, its sounds and pantomimes. No more seasons. No more time. The go-between, the emissary, was lost to the wild throngings of civilization, poisoned, stolen, hit by a car, left somewhere in a culvert. . . .

Sobbing, Martin turned his face to his pillow. The world was a picture under glass, untouchable. The world was dead.

Martin twisted in bed and in three days the last Halloween pumpkins were rotting in trash cans, papier-mâché skulls and witches were burnt on bonfires, and ghosts were stacked on shelves with other linens until next year.

To Martin, Halloween had been nothing more than one evening when tin horns cried off in the cold autumn stars, children blew like goblin leaves along the flinty walks, flinging their heads, or cabbages, at porches, soap-writing names or similar magic symbols on icy windows. All of it as distant, unfathomable, and nightmarish as a puppet show seen from so many miles away that there is no sound or meaning.

For three days in November, Martin watched alternate light and shadow sift across his ceiling. The fire pageant was over forever; autumn lay in cold ashes. Martin sank deeper, yet deeper in white marble layers of bed, motionless, listening, always listening. . . .

Friday evening, his parents kissed him good night and walked out of the house into the hushed cathedral weather toward a motion-picture show. Miss Tarkins from next door stayed on in the parlor below until Martin called down he was sleepy, then took her knitting off home.

In silence, Martin lay following the great move of stars down a clear and moonlit sky, remembering nights such as this when he'd spanned the town with Dog ahead, behind, around about, tracking the green-plush ravine, lapping slumbrous streams gone milky with the fullness of the moon, leaping cemetery tombstones while whispering the marble names; on, quickly on, through shaved meadows where the only motion was the off-on quivering of stars, to streets where shadows would not stand aside for you but crowded all the sidewalks for mile on mile. Run, now, run! Chasing, being chased by bitter smoke, fog, mist, wind, ghost of mind, fright of memory; home, safe, sound, snug-warm, asleep. . . .

Nine o'clock.

Chime. The drowsy clock in the deep stairwell below. Chime.

Dog, come home, and run the world with you. Dog, bring a thistle with frost on it, or bring nothing else but the wind. Dog, where *are* you? Oh, listen now, I'll call.

Martin held his breath.

Way off somewhere—a sound.

Martin rose up, trembling.

There, again—the sound.

So small a sound, like a sharp needle-point brushing the sky long miles and many miles away.

The dreamy echo of a dog—barking.

The sound of a dog crossing fields and farms, dirt roads and rabbit paths, running, running, letting out great barks of steam, cracking the night. The sound of a circling dog which came and went, lifted and faded, opened up, shut in, moved forward, went back, as if the animal were kept by someone on a fantastically long chain. As if the dog were running and someone whistled under the chestnut trees, in mold-shadow, tar-shadow, moon-shadow, walking, and the dog circled back and sprang out again toward home.

Dog! Martin thought, Oh, Dog, come home, boy! Listen, oh, listen, where you *been?* Come on, boy, make tracks!

Five, ten, fifteen minutes; near, very near, the bark, the sound. Martin cried out, thrust his feet from the bed, leaned to the window. Dog! Listen, boy! Dog! Dog! He said it over and over. Dog! Dog! Wicked Dog, run off and gone all these days! Bad Dog, good Dog, home, boy, hurry, and bring what you can!

Near now, near, up the street, barking, to knock clapboard housefronts with sound, whirl iron cocks on rooftops in the moon, firing of volleys—Dog! now at the door below. . . .

Martin shivered.

Should he run—let Dog in, or wait for Mom and Dad? Wait? Oh, God, wait? But what if Dog ran off again? No, he'd go down, snatch the door wide, yell, grab Dog in, and run upstairs so fast, laughing, crying, holding tight, that . . .

Dog stoped barking.

Hey! Martin almost broke the window, jerking to it.

Silence. As if someone had told Dog to hush now, hush, hush.

A full minute passed. Martin clenched his fists.

Below, a faint whimpering.

Then, slowly, the downstairs front door opened. Someone was kind enough to have opened the door for Dog. Of course! Dog had brought Mr. Jacobs or Mr. Gillespie or Miss Tarkins, or . . .

The downstairs door shut.

Dog raced upstairs, whining, flung himself on the bed.

"Dog, Dog, where've you *been,* what've you *done!* Dog, Dog!"

And he crushed Dog hard and long to himself, weeping. Dog, Dog. He laughed and shouted. Dog! But after a moment he stopped laughing and crying, suddenly.

He pulled back away. He held the animal and looked at him, eyes widening.

The odor coming from Dog was different.

It was a smell of strange earth. It was a smell of night within night, the smell of digging down deep in shadow through earth that had lain cheek by jowl with things that were long hidden and decayed. A stinking and rancid soil fell away in clods of dissolution from Dog's muzzle and paws. He had dug deep. He had dug very deep indeed. That *was* it, wasn't it? Wasn't it? *Wasn't* it!

What kind of message was this from Dog? What could such a message mean? The stench—the ripe and awful cemetery earth.

Dog was a bad dog, digging where he shouldn't. Dog was a good dog, always making friends. Dog loved people. Dog brought them home.

And now, moving up the dark hall stairs, at intervals, came the sound of feet, one foot dragged after the other, painfully, slowly, slowly, slowly.

Dog shivered. A rain of strange night earth fell seething on the bed.

Dog turned.

The bedroom door whispered in.

Martin had company.

*R. K. Narayan*

# THE BLIND DOG

It was not a very impressive or high-class dog; it was one of those commonplace dogs one sees everywhere—color of white and dust, tail mutilated at a young age by God knows whom, born in the street, and bred on the leavings and garbage of the marketplace. He had spotty eyes and undistinguished carriage and needless pugnacity. Before he was two years old he had earned the scars of a hundred fights on his body. When he needed rest on hot afternoons he lay curled up under the culvert at the eastern gate of the market. In the evenings he set out on his daily rounds, loafed in the surrounding streets and lanes, engaged himself in skirmishes, picked up edibles on the roadside, and was back at the Market Gate by nightfall.

This life went on for three years. And then a change in his life occurred. A beggar, blind in both eyes, appeared at the Market Gate. An old woman led him up there early in the morning, seated him at the gate, and came up again at midday with some food, gathered his coins and took him home at night.

The dog was sleeping nearby. He was stirred by the smell of food. He got up, came out of his shelter, and stood before the blind man, wagging his tail and gazing expectantly at the bowl, as he was eating his sparse meal. The blind man swept his arms about and asked, "Who is there?" at which the dog went up and licked his hand. The blind man stroked its coat gently tail to ear and said, "What a beauty you are. Come with me." He threw a handful of food, which the dog ate gratefully. It was perhaps an auspicious moment for starting a friendship. They met every day there, and the dog cut off much of its rambling to sit up beside the blind man and watch him receive alms morning to evening. In course of time, observing him, the dog understood that the passersby must give a coin, and whoever went away without dropping a coin was chased by the dog; he tugged the edge of their clothes by his teeth and pulled them back to the old man at the gate, and let go only after something was dropped in his bowl. Among those who frequented this place was a village urchin, who had the mischief of a devil in him. He liked to tease the blind man by calling him names and by trying to pick up the coins in his bowl. The blind man helplessly shouted and cried and whirled his staff. On Thursdays this boy appeared at the gate, carrying on his head a basket loaded with cucumber or plantain. Every Thursday afternoon it was a crisis in the blind man's life. A seller of bright-colored but doubtful perfumes with his wares mounted on a wheeled platform, a man who spread out cheap storybooks on a gunnysack, another man who carried colored ribbons on an elaborate frame—these were the people who usually gathered under the same arch. On a Thursday when the young man appeared at the eastern gate one of them remarked, "Blind fellow! Here comes your scourge."

"Oh, God, is this Thursday?" he wailed. He swept his arms about and called, "Dog, dog, come here, where are you?" He made the peculiar noise which brought the dog to his side. He stroked his head and muttered, "Don't let that little rascal—" At this very moment the boy came up with a leer on his face.

"Blind man! Still pretending you have no eyes. If you are really blind, you should not know this either—" He stopped, his hand moving toward the bowl. The dog sprang on him and snapped his jaws on the boy's wrist. The boy extricated his hand and ran for his life. The dog bounded up behind him and chased him out of the market.

"See the mongrel's affection for this old fellow," marveled the perfume vendor.

One evening at the usual time the old woman failed to turn up, and the blind man waited at the gate, worrying as the evening grew into night. As he sat fretting there, a neighbor came up and said, "Sami, don't wait for the old woman. She will not come again. She died this afternoon."

The blind man lost the only home he had, and the only person who cared for him in this world. The ribbon vendor suggested, "Here, take this white tape"—he held a length of the white cord which he had been selling—"I will give this to you free of cost. Tie it to the dog and let him lead you about if he is really so fond of you."

Life for the dog took a new turn now. He came to take the place of the old woman. He lost his freedom, completely. His world came to be circumscribed by the limits of the white cord which the ribbon vendor had spared. He had to forget wholesale all his old life—all his old haunts. He simply had to stay on forever at the end of that string. When he saw other dogs, friends or foes, instinctively he sprang up, tugging at the string, and this invariably earned him a kick from his master. "Rascal, want to tumble me down—have sense." In a few days the dog learned to discipline his instinct and impulse. He ceased to take notice of other dogs, even if they came up and growled at his side. He lost his own orbit of movement and contact with his fellow creatures.

To the extent of this loss his master gained. He moved about as he had never moved in his life. All day he was on his legs, led by the dog. With the staff in one hand and the dog lead in the other, he moved out of his home—a corner in a *choultry* veranda a few yards off the market; he had moved in there after the old woman's death. He started out early in the day. He found that he could treble his income by moving about instead of staying in one place. He moved down the *choultry* street, and wherever he heard people's voices he stopped and held out his hands for alms. Shops, schools, hospitals, hotels—he left nothing out. He gave a tug when he wanted the dog to stop, and shouted like a bullock driver when he wanted him to move on. The dog protected his feet from going into pits, or stumping against steps or stones, and took him up inch by inch on safe ground and steps. For this sight people gave coins and helped him. Children gathered round him and gave him things to eat. A dog is essentially an active creature who punctuates his hectic rounds with well-defined periods of rest. But now this dog (henceforth to be known as Tiger) had lost all rest. He had rest only when the old man sat down somewhere. At night the old man slept with the cord turned around his finger. "I can't take chances with you," he said. A great desire to earn more money than ever before seized his master, so that he felt any resting a waste of opportunity, and the dog had to be continuously on his feet. Sometimes his legs refused to move. But if he slowed down even slightly his master goaded him on fiercely with his staff. The dog whined and groaned under this thrust. "Don't whine, you rascal. Don't I give you your food? You want to loaf, do you?" swore the blind man. The dog lumbered up and down and round and round the marketplace with slow steps, tied down to the blind tyrant. Long after the traffic at the market ceased, you could hear the night stabbed by the faroff wail of the tired dog. It lost its original appearance. As months rolled on, bones stuck up at his haunches and ribs were reliefed through his fading coat.

The ribbon seller, the novel vendor, and the perfumer observed it one evening when business was slack, and held a conference among themselves. "It rends my heart to see that poor dog slaving. Can't we do something?" The ribbon seller remarked, "That rascal has started lending money for interest —I heard it from the fruit seller—he is earning more than he needs. He has become a very devil for money." At this point the perfumer's eyes caught the scissors dangling from the ribbon rack. "Give it here," he said and moved on with the scissors in hand.

The blind man was passing in front of the eastern gate. The dog was straining the lead. There was a piece of bone lying on the way and the dog was straining to pick it up. The lead became taut and hurt the blind man's hand, and he tugged the string and kicked till the dog howled. It howled, but could not pass the bone lightly; it tried to make another dash for it. The blind man was heaping curses on it. The perfumer stepped up, applied the scissors, and snipped the cord. The dog bounced off and picked up the bone. The blind man stopped dead where he stood, with the other half of the string dangling in his hand. "Tiger! Tiger! Where are you?" he cried. The perfumer moved away quietly, muttering, "You heartless devil! You will never get at him again! He has his freedom!" The dog went off at top speed. He nosed about the ditches happily, hurled himself on other dogs, and ran round and round the fountain in the Market Square barking, his eyes sparkling with joy. He returned to his favorite haunts and hung about the butcher's shop, the tea stall, and the bakery.

The ribbon vendor and his two friends stood at the Market Gate and enjoyed the sight immensely as the blind man struggled to find his way about. He stood rooted to the spot, waving his stick; he felt as if he were hanging in midair. He was wailing, "Oh, where is my dog? Where is my dog? Won't someone give him back to me? I will murder it when I get at it again!" He groped about, tried to cross the road, came near being run over by a dozen vehicles at different points, tumbled and struggled and gasped. "He'd deserve it if he was run over, this heartless blackguard," they said, observing him. However, the old man struggled through and with the help of someone found his way back to his corner in the *choultry* veranda and sank down on his gunnysack bed, half-faint with the strain of his journey.

He was not seen for ten days, fifteen days, and twenty days. Nor was the dog seen anywhere. They commented among themselves: "The dog must be loafing over the whole earth, free and happy. The beggar is perhaps gone forever." Hardly was this sentence uttered when they heard the familiar tap-tap of the blind man's staff. They saw him again coming up the pavement—led by the dog. "Look! Look!" they cried. "He has again got at it and tied it up." The ribbon seller could not contain himself. He ran up and said, "Where have you been all these days?"

"Know what happened!" cried the blind man. "This dog ran away. I should have died in a day or two, confined to my corner, no food, not an anna to earn—imprisoned in my corner. I should have perished if it continued for another day. But this thing returned."

"When? When?"

"Last night. At midnight as I slept in bed, he came and licked my face. I felt like murdering him. I gave him a blow which he will never forget again," said the blind man. "I forgave him, after all a dog! He loafed as long as he could pick up some rubbish to eat on the road, but real hunger has driven him back to me, but he will not leave me again. See! I have got this," and he shook the lead; it was a steel chain this time.

Once again there was the dead, despairing look in the dog's eyes. "Go on, you fool," cried the blind man, shouting like an ox driver. He tugged the chain, poked with the stick, and the dog moved away on slow steps. They stood listening to the tap-tap going away.

"Death alone can help that dog," cried the ribbon seller, looking after it with a sigh. "What can we do with a creature who returns to his doom with such a free heart?"

*R. K. Narayan*

# ATTILA

In a mood of optimism they named him Attila. What they wanted of a dog was strength, formidableness, and fight, and hence he was named after the "Scourge of Europe."

The puppy was only a couple of months old; he had square jaws, red eyes, a pug nose, and a massive head, and there was every reason to hope that he would do credit to his name. The immediate reason for buying him was a series of housebreakings and thefts in the neighborhood, and our householders decided to put more trust in a dog than in the police. They searched far and wide and met a dog fancier. He held up a month-old black-and-white puppy and said, "Come and fetch him a month hence. In six months he will be something to be feared and respected." He spread out before them a pedigree sheet which was stunning. The puppy had running in his veins the choicest and the most ferocious blood.

They were satisfied, paid an advance, returned a month later, put down seventy-five rupees and took the puppy home. The puppy, as I have already indicated, did not have a very prepossessing appearance and was none too playful, but this did not prevent his owners from sitting in a circle around him and admiring him. There was a prolonged debate as to what he should be named. The youngest suggested, "Why not call him Tiger?"

"Every other street mongrel is named Tiger," came the reply. "Why not Caesar?"

"Caesar! If a census was taken of dogs you would find at least fifteen thousand Caesars in South India alone. . . . Why not Fire?"

"It is fantastic."

"Why not Thunder?"

"It is too obvious."

"Grip?"

"Still obvious, and childish."

There was a deadlock. Someone suggested Attila, and a shout of joy went up to the skies. No more satisfying name was thought of for man or animal.

But as time passed our Attila exhibited a love of humanity which was sometimes disconcerting. The Scourge of Europe—could he ever have been like this? They put it down to his age. What child could help loving all creatures? In their zeal to establish this fact, they went to the extent of delving into ancient history to find out what the Scourge of Europe was like when he was a child. It was rumored that as a child he clung to his friends and to his parents' friends so fast that often he had to be beaten and separated from them. But when he was fourteen he showed the first sign of his future: he knocked down and plunged his knife into a fellow who tried to touch his marbles. Ah, this was encouraging. Let our dog reach the parallel of fourteen years and people would get to know his real nature.

But this was a vain promise. He stood up twenty inches high, had a large frame and a forbidding appearance on the whole—but that was all. A variety of people entered the gates of the house every day: mendicants, bill collectors, postmen, tradesmen, and family friends. All of them were warmly received by Attila. The moment the gate clicked he became alert and stood up looking toward the gate. By the time anyone entered the gate Attila went blindly charging forward. But that was all. The person had only to stop and smile, and Attila would melt. He would behave as if he apologized for even giving an impression of violence. He would lower his head, curve his body, tuck his tail between his legs, roll his eyes, and moan as if to say, "How sad that you should have mistaken my gesture! I only hurried down to greet you." Till he was patted on the head, stroked and told that he was forgiven, he would be in extreme misery.

Gradually he realized that his bouncing advances caused much unhappy misunderstanding. And so when he heard the gate click he hardly stirred. He merely looked in that direction and wagged his tail. The people at home did not like this attitude very much. They thought it rather a shame.

"Why not change his name to Blind Worm?" somebody asked.

"He eats like an elephant," said the mother of the family. "You can employ two watchmen for the price of the rice and meat he consumes. Somebody comes every morning and steals all the flowers in the garden and Attila won't do anything about it."

"He has better business to do than catch flower thieves," replied the youngest, always the defender of the dog.

"What is the better business?"

"Well, if somebody comes in at dawn and takes away the flowers, do you expect Attila to be looking out for him even at that hour?"

"Why not? It's what a well-fed dog ought to be doing instead of sleeping. You ought to be ashamed of your dog."

"He does not sleep all night, Mother. I have often seen him going round the house and watching all night."

"Really! Does he prowl about all night?"

"Of course he does," said the defender.

"I am quite alarmed to hear it," said the mother. "Please lock him up in a room at night, otherwise he may call in a burglar and show him round. Left alone, a burglar might after all be less successful. It wouldn't be so bad if he at least barked. He is the most noiseless dog I have ever seen in my life."

The young man was extremely irritated at this. He considered it to be the most uncharitable cynicism, but the dog justified it that very night.

Ranga lived in a hut three miles from the town. He was a "gang coolie"—often employed in road mending. Occasionally at nights he enjoyed the thrill and profit of breaking into houses. At one o'clock that night Ranga removed the bars of a window on the eastern side of the house and slipped in. He edged along the wall, searched all the trunks and *almirahs* in the house, and made a neat bundle of all the jewelry and other valuables he could pick up.

He was just starting to go out. He had just put one foot out of the gap he had made in the window when he saw Attila standing below, looking up expectantly. Ranga thought his end had come. He expected the dog to bark. But not Attila. He waited for a moment, grew tired of waiting, stood up, and put his forepaws on the lap of the burglar. He put back his ears, licked Ranga's hands, and rolled his eyes. Ranga whispered, "I hope you aren't going to bark. . . ."

"Don't you worry. I am not the sort," the dog tried to say.

"Just a moment. Let me get down from here," said the burglar.

The dog obligingly took away his paws and lowered himself.

"See there," said Ranga, pointing to the backyard, "there is a cat." Attila put up his ears at the mention of the cat and dashed in the direction indicated. One might easily have thought he was going to tear up a cat, but actually he didn't want to miss the pleasure of the company of a cat if there was one.

As soon as the dog left him Ranga made a dash for the gate. Given a second more he would have hopped over it. But the dog turned and saw what was about to happen and in one spring was at the gate. He looked hurt. "Is this proper?" he seemed to ask. "Do you want to shake me off?"

He hung his heavy tail down so loosely and looked so miserable that the burglar stroked his head, at which he revived. The burglar opened the gate and went out, and the dog followed him. Attila's greatest ambition in life was to wander in the streets freely. Now things seemed to be shaping up ideally.

Attila liked his new friend so much that he wouldn't leave him alone even for a moment. He lay before Ranga when he sat down to eat, sat on the edge of his mat when he slept in his hut, waited patiently on the edge of the pond when Ranga went there now and then for a wash, slept on the roadside when Ranga was at work.

This sort of companionship got on Ranga's nerves. He implored, "Oh, dog. Leave me alone for a moment, won't you?" Unmoved, Attila sat before him with his eyes glued on his friend.

Attila's disappearance created a sensation in the bungalow. "Didn't I tell you," the mother said, "to lock him up?

Now some burglar has gone away with him. What a shame! We can hardly mention it to anyone."

"You are mistaken," replied the defender. "It is just a coincidence. He must have gone off on his own account. If he had been here no thief would have dared to come in. . . ."

"Whatever it is, I don't know if we should after all thank the thief for taking away that dog. He may keep the jewels as a reward for taking him away. Shall we withdraw the police complaint?"

This facetiousness ceased a week later, and Attila rose to the ranks of a hero. The eldest son of the house was going toward the market one day. He saw Attila trotting behind someone on the road.

"Hey," shouted the young man; at which Ranga turned and broke into a run. Attila, who always suspected that his new friend was waiting for the slightest chance to desert him, galloped behind Ranga.

"Hey, Attila!" shouted the young man, and he also started running. Attila wanted to answer the call after making sure of his friend; and so he turned his head for a second and galloped faster. Ranga desperately doubled his pace. Attila determined to stick to him at any cost. As a result, he ran so fast that he overtook Ranga and clumsily blocked his way, and Ranga stumbled over him and fell. As he rolled on the ground a piece of jewelry (which he was taking to a receiver of stolen property) flew from his hand. The young man recognized it as belonging to his sister and sat down on Ranga. A crowd collected and the police appeared on the scene.

Attila was the hero of the day. Even the lady of the house softened toward him. She said, "Whatever one might say of Attila, one has to admit that he is a very cunning detective. He is too deep for words."

It was as well that Attila had no powers of speech. Otherwise he would have burst into a lamentation which would have shattered the pedestal under his feet.

*Arthur C. Clarke*

# DOG STAR

When I heard Laika's frantic barking, my first reaction was one of annoyance. I turned over in my bunk and murmured sleepily, "Shut up, you silly bitch." That dreamy interlude lasted only a fraction of a second; then consciousness returned—and with it fear. Fear of loneliness, and fear of madness.

For a moment I dared not open my eyes; I was afraid of what I might see. Reason told me that no dog had ever set foot upon this world, that Laika was separated from me by a quarter of a million miles of space—and, far more irrevocably, five years of time.

"You've been dreaming," I told myself angrily. "Stop being a fool—open your eyes! You won't see anything except the glow of the wall paint."

That was right, of course. The tiny cabin was empty, the door tightly closed. I was alone with my memories, overwhelmed by the transcendental sadness that often comes when some bright dream fades into drab reality. The sense of loss was so desolating that I longed to return to sleep. It was well that I failed to do so, for at that moment sleep would have been death. But I did not know this for another five seconds, and during that eternity I was back on Earth, seeking what comfort I could from the past.

No one ever discovered Laika's origin, though the Observatory staff made a few inquiries and I inserted several advertisements in the Pasadena newspapers. I found her, a lost and lonely ball of fluff, huddled by the roadside one summer evening when I was driving up to Palomar. Though I have never liked dogs, or indeed any animals, it was impossible to leave this helpless little creature to the mercy of the passing cars. With some qualms, wishing that I had a pair of gloves, I picked her up and dumped her in the baggage compartment. I was not going to hazard the upholstery of my new '92 Vik, and felt that she could do little damage there. In this, I was not altogether correct.

When I had parked the car at the Monastery—the astronomers' residential quarters, where I'd be living for the next week—I inspected my find without much enthusiasm. At that stage, I had intended to hand the puppy over to the janitor; but then it whimpered and opened its eyes. There was such an expression of helpless trust in them that—well, I changed my mind.

Sometimes I regretted that decision, though never for long. I had no idea how much trouble a growing dog could cause, deliberately and otherwise. My cleaning and repair bills soared; I could never be sure of finding an unravaged pair of socks or an unchewed copy of the *Astrophysical Journal.* But eventually Laika was both house-trained and observatory-trained: she must have been the only dog ever to be allowed inside the two-hundred-inch dome. She would lie there quietly in the shadows for hours, while I was up in the cage making adjustments, quite content if she could hear my voice from time to time. The other astronomers became equally fond of her (it was old Dr. Anderson who suggested her name), but from the beginning she was my dog, and would obey no one else. Not that she would always obey me.

She was a beautiful animal, about 95 percent Alsatian. It was that missing 5 percent, I imagine, that led to her being abandoned. (I still feel a surge of anger when I think of it, but since I shall never know the facts, I may be jumping to false conclusions.) Apart from two dark patches over the eyes, most of her body was a smoky gray, and her coat was soft as silk. When her ears were pricked up, she looked incredibly intelligent and alert; sometimes I would be discussing spectral types or stellar evolution with my colleagues, and it would be hard to believe that she was not following the conversation.

Even now, I cannot understand why she became so attached to me, for I have made very few friends among human beings. Yet when I returned to the observatory after an absence, she would go almost frantic with delight, bouncing around on her hind legs and putting her paws on my shoulders—which she could reach quite easily—all the while uttering small squeaks of joy which seemed highly inappropriate from so large a dog. I hated to leave her for more than a few days at a time, and though I could not take her with me on overseas trips, she accompanied me on most of my shorter journeys. She was with me when I drove north to attend that ill-fated seminar at Berkeley.

We were staying with university acquaintances; they had

been polite about it, but obviously did not look forward to having a monster in the house. However, I assured them that Laika never gave the slightest trouble, and rather reluctantly they let her sleep in the living room. "You needn't worry about burglars tonight," I said. "We don't have any in Berkeley," they answered, rather coldly.

In the middle of the night, it seemed that they were wrong. I was awakened by a hysterical, high-pitched barking from Laika which I had heard only once before—when she had first seen a cow, and did not know what on earth to make of it. Cursing, I threw off the sheets and stumbled out into the darkness of the unfamiliar house. My main thought was to silence Laika before she roused my hosts—assuming that this was not already far too late. If there had been an intruder, he would certainly have taken flight by now. Indeed, I rather hoped that he had.

For a moment I stood beside the switch at the top of the stairs, wondering whether to throw it. Then I growled, "Shut up, Laika!" and flooded the place with light.

She was scratching frantically at the door, pausing from time to time to give that hysterical yelp. "If you want out," I said angrily, "there's no need for all that fuss." I went down, shot the bolt, and she took off into the night like a rocket.

It was very calm and still, with a waning Moon struggling to pierce the San Francisco fog. I stood in the luminous haze, looking out across the water to the lights of the city, waiting for Laika to come back so that I could chastise her suitably. I was still waiting when, for the second time in the twentieth century, the San Andreas Fault woke from its sleep.

Oddly enough, I was not frightened—at first. I can remember that two thoughts passed through my mind, in the moment before I realized the danger. Surely, I told myself, the geophysicists could have given us *some* warning. And then I found myself thinking, with great surprise, "I'd no idea that earthquakes make so much noise!"

It was about then that I knew that this was no ordinary quake; what happened afterward, I would prefer to forget. The Red Cross did not take me away until quite late the next morning, because I refused to leave Laika. As I looked at the shattered house containing the bodies of my friends, I knew that I owed my life to her; but the helicopter pilots could not be expected to understand that, and I cannot blame them for thinking that I was crazy, like so many of the others they had found wandering among the fires and the debris.

After that, I do not suppose we were ever apart for more than a few hours. I have been told—and I can well believe it—that I became less and less interested in human company, without being actively unsocial or misanthropic. Between them, the stars and Laika filled all my needs. We used to go for long walks together over the mountains; it was the happiest time I have ever known. There was only one flaw; I knew, though Laika could not, how soon it must end.

We had been planning the move for more than a decade. As far back as the 1960s it was realized that Earth was no place for an astronomical observatory. Even the small pilot instruments on the Moon had far outperformed all the telescopes peering through the murk and haze of the terrestrial atmosphere. The story of Mount Wilson, Palomar, Greenwich, and the other great names was coming to an end; they would still be used for training purposes, but the research frontier must move out into space.

I had to move with it; indeed, I had already been offered the post of Deputy Director, Farside Observatory. In a few months, I could hope to solve problems I had been working on for years. Beyond the atmosphere, I would be like a blind man who had suddenly been given sight.

It was utterly impossible, of course, to take Laika with me. The only animals on the Moon were those needed for experimental purposes; it might be another generation before pets were allowed, and even then it would cost a fortune to carry them there—and to keep them alive. Providing Laika with her usual two pounds of meat a day would, I calculated, take several times my quite comfortable salary.

The choice was simple and straightforward. I could stay on Earth and abandon my career. Or I could go to the Moon—and abandon Laika.

After all, she was only a dog. In a dozen years, she would be dead, while I should be reaching the peak of my profession. No sane man would have hesitated over the matter; yet I did hesitate, and if by now you do not understand why, no further words of mine can help.

In the end, I let matters go by default. Up to the very week I was due to leave, I had still made no plans for Laika. When Dr. Anderson volunteered to look after her, I accepted numbly, with scarcely a word of thanks. The old physicist and his wife had always been fond of her, and I am afraid that they considered me indifferent and heartless—when the truth was just the opposite. We went for one more walk together over the hills; then I delivered her silently to the Andersons, and did not see her again.

Takeoff was delayed almost twenty-four hours, until a major flare storm had cleared the Earth's orbit; even so, the Van Allen belts were still so active that we had to make our exit through the North Polar Gap. It was a miserable flight; apart from the usual trouble with weightlessness, we were all groggy with antiradiation drugs. The ship was already over Farside before I took much interest in the proceedings, so I missed the sight of Earth dropping below the horizon. Nor was I really sorry; I wanted no reminders, and intended to think only of the future. Yet I could not shake off that feeling of guilt; I had deserted someone who loved and trusted me, and was no better than those who had abandoned Laika when she was a puppy, beside the dusty road to Palomar.

The news that she was dead reached me a month later. There was no reason that anyone knew; the Andersons had done their best, and were very upset. She had just lost interest in living, it seemed. For a while, I think I did the same; but work is a wonderful anodyne, and my program was just getting under way. Though I never forgot Laika, in a little while the memory ceased to hurt.

Then why had it come back to haunt me, five years later, on the far side of the Moon? I was searching my mind for the reason when the metal building around me quivered as if under the impact of a heavy blow. I reacted without thinking, and was already closing the helmet of my emergency suit when the foundations slipped and the wall tore open with a short-lived scream of escaping air. Because I had automatically pressed the General Alarm button, we lost only two men, despite the fact that the tremor—the worst ever recorded on Farside—cracked all three of the observatory's pressure domes.

It is hardly necessary for me to say that I do not believe in the supernatural; everything that happened has a perfectly rational explanation, obvious to any man with the slightest knowledge of psychology. In the second San Francisco earthquake, Laika was not the only dog to sense approaching disaster; many such cases were reported. And on Farside, my own memories must have given me that heightened awareness, when my never-sleeping subconscious detected the first faint vibrations from within the Moon.

The human mind has strange and labyrinthine ways of going about its business; it knew the signal that would most swiftly rouse me to the knowledge of danger. There is nothing more to it than that; though in a sense one could say that Laika woke me on both occasions, there is no mystery about it, no miraculous warning across the gulf that neither man nor dog can ever bridge.

Of that I am sure, if I am sure of anything. Yet sometimes I wake now, in the silence of the Moon, and wish that the dream could have lasted a few seconds longer—so that I could have looked just once more into those luminous brown eyes, brimming with an unselfish, undemanding love I have found nowhere else on this or on any other world.

*Françoise Sagan*

# A DOG'S NIGHT

In appearance, Monsieur Ximenestre closely resembled a drawing by Chaval: corpulent, with an air of amiable bewilderment. But now that the month of December had begun, he wore an expression so woebegone as to make every passerby with any heart at all want to stop and ask him what the matter was. The trouble lay in the approach of Christmas, which Monsieur Ximenestre, good Christian though he was, was this year contemplating with dismay, not having a sou with which to pamper the gift-hungry Madame Ximenestre, his good-for-nothing son, Charles, and his daughter, Augusta, an excellent calypso dancer. Not a sou; that was the exact state of his affairs. And there was no question of advances or loans. Both had already been obtained, without the knowledge of Madame Ximenestre and his children, in order to gratify the latest vice of this supposed breadwinner; in short, to gratify Monsieur Ximenestre's fatal passion: gambling.

Not just the ordinary kind of gambling where the gold trickles over the green baize, nor yet the kind where horses strain to the last gasp over another sort of green baize, but a game, yet unknown in France, which had, alas, become the craze in a café in the Seventeenth Arrondissement where Monsieur Ximenestre was in the habit of taking a glass of vermouth every evening before going home: a game of darts, but played with a peashooter and ten-franc notes. All the regulars were made about it, apart from one man, who had had to give it up owing to chronic shortage of breath. Imported by an Australian newly arrived in the district, this thrilling game had quickly become the object of an exclusive club, which met in the back room, where the proprietor, a fan himself, had sacrificed the billiard table.

To cut a long story short, Monsieur Ximenestre had ruined himself, despite a promising start. What was he to do? From whom could he borrow the money for the handbag, the motor scooter, and the record player that, from various pointed hints at mealtimes, he knew were expected of him? The days passed, eyes glowed with anticipation, and the snow began to fall with gay abandon. Monsieur Ximenestre's complexion took on a yellowish tinge and he hoped that he might fall ill. In vain.

On the morning of Christmas Eve, Monsieur Ximenestre left home followed by three expectant glances, Madame Ximenestre's daily search having failed to reveal the longed-for parcels. He's cutting it fine, she thought, rather sourly but without a trace of anxiety.

In the street, Monsieur Ximenestre wound his scarf three times around the lower half of his face, and in doing so, momentarily contemplated a holdup. An idea he quickly rejected, fortunately. He padded along in his bearlike fashion, shambling and good-natured, and ended up on a bench, where the falling snow soon threatened to turn him into an iceberg. The idea of the pipe, the briefcase, and the bright-red tie (incidentally unwearable) that he knew to be awaiting him at home only served to add to his misery.

There were a few passersby, with glowing cheeks, springy step, and parcels dangling from every finger—husbands and fathers worthy of the name. A limousine drew up in front of Monsieur Ximenestre, and a dream creature, followed by two lapdogs on a leash, got out. Monsieur Ximenestre, albeit an admirer of the fair sex, looked at her without the slightest interest. Then his eyes strayed to the two dogs and suddenly lit up with a bright gleam. Brushing off the pile of snow that had accumulated on his knees, he jumped to his feet and uttered an exclamation, which was smothered by the snow that came tumbling from his hat into his eyes and down his neck.

"The dogs' home!" he cried.

The dogs' home was a dismal place, and the inmates, either pathetic or frantic, rather alarmed Monsieur Ximenestre. He finally picked out a dog that was indefinable as to breed and color but had, as they say, nice eyes. And Monsieur Ximenestre was quite sure that it would take the nicest of eyes to make up for a handbag, a record player, and a scooter. He christened his find Rover without further ado, and leading him on a length of rope, ventured into the street.

Rover's joy found immediate expression in a frenzy that communicated itself willy-nilly to Monsieur Ximenestre, who was taken by surprise at such canine energy. He was dragged along for several hundred feet at a fast trot (the time when the word gallop could be applied to Monsieur Ximenestre was long past) and ended up by barging into a passerby, who grunted something about "Dirty brutes!" Like a water-skier, Monsieur Ximenestre thought that his best course might be to let go of the rope and return home. But Rover, barking, jumped up at him with delight, his dirty yellowish coat full of snow, and it crossed Monsieur Ximenestre's mind that it was a long time since anyone had made such a fuss over him. His heart melted. His blue eyes gazed deep into Rover's brown ones and they shared a moment of indescribable sweetness.

Rover was the first to recover. He took off again down the street, and the chase continued. Monsieur Ximenestre thought vaguely of the anemic basset hound that had been in the kennel next to Rover's, and that he hadn't even considered, being of the opinion that a dog should be robust. By now he was literally flying in the direction of home. They stopped in a café just long enough for Monsieur Ximenestre to gulp down three rums and Rover three lumps of sugar, which were presented to him by the sympathetic proprietress. "Poor dog, hasn't he got a little overcoat, then, in this nasty cold weather!" Monsieur Ximenestre, panting from his exertions, did not reply.

The sugar had an invigorating effect on Rover, but it was a pale shadow of a man who rang the doorbell of the Ximenestre apartment. Madame Ximenestre opened the door, Rover burst in, and Monsieur Ximenestre, sobbing with fatigue, fell into his wife's arms.

"Whatever's this?"

Madame Ximenestre's cry was wrung from her breast.

"It's Rover," gasped Monsieur Ximenestre, and with a desperate effort, he added: "Merry Christmas, my dear!"

"Merry Christmas? Merry Christmas?" spluttered Madame Ximenestre. "What on earth are you talking about?"

"It's Christmas Eve, isn't it?" cried Monsieur Ximenestre, himself again now that he was back in the warmth and safety of his own home. "Well, then, here's my Christmas present to you, to you all," he added, as his children emerged, wide-eyed, from the kitchen. "I'm giving you Rover. There!"

And he strode resolutely into the bedroom. Once there, however, he collapsed onto the bed and picked up his pipe, a pipe that dated from World War I and of which he was fond of saying, "It's seen a few things, I can tell you." With trembling hands he filled it and lit it, pulled the bedspread over his legs, and awaited the onslaught.

Madame Ximenestre, livid—horrifyingly livid, Monsieur Ximenestre thought privately—entered the room almost immediately. Monsieur Ximenestre's first reaction was that of a soldier in the trenches: He tried to bury himself completely beneath the bedspread. . . . All that could be seen of him was one of his few remaining tufts of hair and the smoke from his pipe. But this sufficed for Madame Ximenestre's wrath:

"Would you mind telling me what this dog is supposed to be?"

"It's a kind of sheepdog, I think," Monsieur Ximenestre's voice replied weakly.

"A kind of sheepdog?" Madame Ximenestre was beside herself with fury. "And what do you think your son expected for Christmas? And your daughter? As for me, I know I don't count. . . . But what about them? And you bring back this frightful animal!"

Rover entered on cue. He jumped up onto Monsieur Ximenestre's bed, curled up beside him, and laid his head on his. Tears of tenderness, luckily hidden by the bedspread, welled up in his friend's eyes.

"It's too much," said Madame Ximenestre. "How do you know that the creature isn't rabid?"

"That would make two of you," Monsieur Ximenestre said coldly.

This shocking retort had the effect of getting rid of Madame Ximenestre. Rover licked his master and went to sleep. At midnight, his wife and children went to Mass without telling him. Feeling slightly queasy, at a quarter to one he decided to take Rover for a short walk. He put on his big muffler and ambled off in the direction of the church, Rover sniffing in all the doorways.

The church was packed, and Monsieur Ximenestre tried in vain to push his way through the door. He had to wait outside in the snow, his muffler up to his eyes, while the carols of good Christmas echoed in his ears. Rover pulled so hard on his rope that in the end Monsieur Ximenestre sat down and attached it to his foot. Little by little, cold and emotion numbed his already distraught mind, until he no longer quite knew what he was doing there. So that when the flood of faithful suddenly poured out of the church he was taken by surprise. Before he had time to get to his feet and untie the rope, a young woman's voice cried:

"Oh, look at the lovely dog! Oh! The poor man! . . . Jean-Claude, wait."

And to Monsieur Ximenestre's bewilderment, a five-franc piece dropped into his lap. He stood up, stammering, and the man called Jean-Claude, moved to pity, gave him a second coin and wished him a Merry Christmas.

"But," stammered Monsieur Ximenestre, "but . . . look here . . ."

We all know how contagious charity can be. Nearly every member of the congregation who left by the north aisle of the church gave alms to Monsieur Ximenestre and Rover. Dazed, covered in snow, Monsieur Ximenestre tried in vain to dissuade them.

Having left by the south aisle, Madame Ximenestre and her children returned home. Monsieur Ximenestre arrived back shortly afterward, apologized for his little joke earlier in the day, and gave each of them a sum of money equivalent to the cost of their presents. The Christmas feast that night went off very well. Afterward, Monsieur Ximenestre and Rover went to bed gorged with turkey, and side by side they slept the sleep of the just.

*Translated by Joanna Kilmartin*